PELICAN BOOKS

THE PELICAN BOOK OF ENGLISH PROSE

VOLUME 2

Raymond Williams is a Fellow of Jesus College, Cambridge, where he is University Reader in drama. He was born in 1921 and educated at Abergavenny Grammar School and Trinity College, Cambridge. He is general editor of the New Thinker's Library, has published many essays in literary journals, and is well known as a book-reviewer for the *Guardian*. His other books published by Penguins are *Culture and Society, 1780–1950* (1958), *Border Country,* a novel (1960), *The Long Revolution* (1961), *Drama from Ibsen to Eliot* (revised edition 1964), and *Communications* (revised edition 1966). He has also edited the Penguin Special *May Day Manifesto 1968.* At the moment he is preparing *The English Novel from Dickens to Lawrence.*

D1347759

THE PELICAN BOOK OF

ENGLISH PROSE

VOLUME 2

From 1780 to the present day

EDITED BY
RAYMOND WILLIAMS

PENGUIN BOOKS

Penguin Books Ltd, Harmondsworth, Middlesex, England
Penguin Books Inc., 7110 Ambassador Road, Baltimore, Maryland 21207, U.S.A.
Penguin Books Australia Ltd, Ringwood, Victoria, Australia

—

First published in Pelican Books 1969
Reprinted 1973

—

Preface, Introduction and Notes copyright © Raymond Williams, 1969

—

Made and printed in Great Britain
by Hazell Watson & Viney Ltd
Aylesbury, Bucks
Set in Monotype Bembo

CONTENTS

CONTENTS

CONTENTS

CONTENTS

1895–Present

CONTENTS

PREFACE

THIS selection of English prose written between the 1780s and the 1960s is arranged in two simple ways. First, there is a division by period: 1780–1830; 1830–95; 1895 to the present. Most dates in literary development are arbitrary, but these periods offer a possible way of seeing some of the main stages in what is undoubtedly a continuous and complicated development. Too much significance should not be attached to the exact years, but somewhere in the early 1830s, and again somewhere in the 1890s, major social and cultural changes are evident. It would be possible to define other periods of change: in the 1860s, for example, and again after 1920. But, for simplicity, the initial threefold division has been adopted. Writers, of course, do not come in neat periods, and do not necessarily make their most important contributions at the same stages of their lives. Keats and Carlyle were exact contemporaries, but their important writing is a full twenty years apart. I have been forced, sometimes, to make decisions about periods which slightly overlap the fixed dates; I have done this, in each case, to give the arrangement what seems to me its true critical and historical significance. Then, second, there is a division by subject or method; the question of which of these two it is must always be controversial. I have named these divisions within each period 'Observation', 'Imagination' and 'Argument'. Again I would not insist on these as exact divisions. What appears under 'Imagination' is mainly from novels, but it is characteristic of the history of prose in this period that there is much detailed observation in this most imaginative of prose forms, and, in significant ways, a use of imaginative techniques in what is literally observation – records of things done and seen. I hope that the relations between observation and imagination will be considered as often as the formal distinctions. Argument, on the whole, is more distinct as a category, but even here there are real overlaps with the materials and methods of observation and imagination. As with the historical divisions, these categories are meant to be starting points: initial ways of seeing the plan of the book.

Any selection from the vast quantity of prose written since 1780 is of course what it offers to be: a particular selection. My own reading of the period as a whole is the basis of what I have chosen. I have included some writers whom I do not much like. Other writers, whom I often read, I have not found space to include. But in general I have chosen extracts which, taken as a whole, seem to me to give ways of understanding the period, in its major literary and social developments. At the centre of my selection is an interest in the development of the novel, which is the outstanding prose achievement of these years. I have been closely concerned, in relation to this, with the problem of written and spoken forms in a rapidly changing society, and with the changing relationships between writers and readers. I discuss these themes in my introduction, and the selection as a whole will, I think, be seen as a basis for this discussion. In the sections of 'Observation', I have again been mainly concerned with these questions, but the passages give also a first impression of the general character of the period, at the same time as they draw attention to ways of seeing and the positions from which things are seen. In the sections of 'Argument' I have again emphasized these questions – of how we observe and how we write – while trying also to give a first impression of some of the major movements of thought.

Books of prose are always available as occasional reading: this one no less than any other. But it should also be possible to use this selection for detailed and connected study and discussion. The chosen extracts are relatively long, so that there would be enough material, in each case, for a specific discussion and analysis. And then to the extent that teachers and students can share my interest in the themes discussed in the introduction, there is considerable material for comparison; I have been able to take up only some of the points which relate even to these themes.

R.W.

ACKNOWLEDGEMENTS

For permission to reprint the extracts specified we are indebted to Faber and Faber Ltd and Random House Inc. for an extract from *The Dyer's Hand* by W. H. Auden; Mrs Dorothy Cheston Bennett, Methuen & Co. Ltd and Doubleday & Company Inc. for an extract from *Clayhanger* by Arnold Bennett; Blackwell Scientific Publications Ltd for an extract from *Mind, Perception and Science* by Russell Brain; Michael Joseph Ltd and Harper and Row, Publishers (Copyright 1944 Joyce Cary) for an extract from *The Horse's Mouth* by Joyce Cary; J. M. Dent and Sons Ltd and the Trustees of the Joseph Conrad Estate for an extract from *Heart of Darkness* by Joseph Conrad; Faber and Faber Ltd and Harcourt, Brace and World Inc. (Copyright, 1932, 1936, 1950, by Harcourt Brace and World Inc.; © 1960, 1964 by T. S. Eliot) for an extract from *Tradition and the Individual Talent* from *Selected Essays of T. S. Eliot*: Chatto and Windus Ltd and New Directions Publishing Corporation, New York for an extract from *The Structure of Complex Words* by William Empson; Edward Arnold (Publishers) Ltd and Alfred A. Knopf Inc. (published 1921) for an extract from *Howard's End* by E. M. Forster; Hutchinson Publishing Group Ltd for an extract from *A Scots Quair* by Lewis Grassic Gibbon; William Heinemann Ltd and The Viking Press Inc. (Copyright © 1955 by Graham Greene) for an extract from *The Quiet American* by Graham Greene; Macmillan and Co Ltd, The Trustees of the Hardy Estate and The Macmillan Company of Canada Ltd for extracts from *The Woodlanders* and *Tess of the D'Urbervilles* by Thomas Hardy; Chatto and Windus Ltd and Oxford University Press Inc., 1957, for an extract from *The Uses of Literacy* by Richard Hoggart; Associated Book Publishers Ltd for an extract from *Flesh Wounds* by David Holbrook; Routledge and Kegan Paul Ltd and Charles Scribner's Sons (Copyright © 1966 John Holloway) for an extract from *A London Childhood* by John Holloway; Routledge and Kegan Paul Ltd and New York: Humanities Press Inc. for an extract from *Speculations* by T. E. Hulme; Chatto and Windus Ltd and Harper and Row, Publishers (Copyright 1962 by Aldous Huxley) for an extract from *Island* by Aldous Huxley; Faber and

ACKNOWLEDGEMENTS

Faber Ltd and Chilmark Press Inc. for an extract from *Anathemata* by David Jones; Mrs Katherine Jones, The Hogarth Press Ltd and Basic Books Inc., Publishers, New York (© by Ernest Jones) for an extract from Volume 3 of *The Life and Work of Sigmund Freud* by Ernest Jones; The Bodley Head and Random House Inc. (Copyright 1914, 1918 by Margaret Caroline Anderson and renewed 1942, 1946 by Nora Joseph Joyce) for an extract from *Ulysses* by James Joyce; The Society of Authors and The Viking Press Inc. (Copyright 1939, by James Joyce, and renewed 1967 by George Joyce and Lucia Joyce) for an extract from *Finnegans Wake* by James Joyce; Philip Larkin and Faber and Faber Ltd for an extract from *A Girl in Winter* by Philip Larkin; William Heinemann Ltd and The Viking Press Inc. (All rights reserved) for an extract from *Odour of Chrysanthemums* from *The Complete Short Stories of D. H. Lawrence, Volume II*; William Heinemann Ltd and The Viking Press Inc. (All rights reserved) for an extract from *We Need One Another* from *Phoenix: The Posthumous Papers of D. H. Lawrence*, edited by Edward D. McDonald; Methuen and Co. Ltd for an extract from *Childermass* by Wyndham Lewis; MacGibbon and Kee Ltd and Walker and Company for an extract from *At Swim-Two-Birds* by Flann O'Brien; Miss Sonia Brownell, Secker and Warburg Ltd and Harcourt, Brace and World Inc. for an extract from *The Road to Wigan Pier* by George Orwell; Cambridge University Press for an extract by H. Munro Fox from *The Cell and the Organism* edited by Ramsey and Wigglesworth; George Allen and Unwin Ltd for an extract from *In Praise of Idleness* by Bertrand Russell; The Society of Authors for an extract from the preface to *Back to Methuselah* by George Bernard Shaw; Alan Sillitoe, Alfred A. Knopf Inc. (© Copyright by Alan Sillitoe) for an extract from *Key to the Door* by Alan Sillitoe; Longmans Green and Co. Ltd and Crowell-Collier and the Macmillan Co., N.Y., © David Storey 1960 for an extract from *This Sporting Life* by David Storey; George Allen and Unwin Ltd for an extract from *Equality* by R. H. Tawney; John Wain and Macmillan and Co Ltd for an extract from *Nuncle* by John Wain; A. D. Peters and Co and Little, Brown and Co (Copyright 1930 by Evelyn Waugh) for an extract from *Vile Bodies* by Evelyn Waugh; The London School of Economics for an extract from *My Apprenticeship* by Beatrice Webb; The Executors of the Estate of H. G. Wells and Charles Scribner's

ACKNOWLEDGEMENTS

Sons (Copyright 1906 by Century Co; renewal copyright 1934 by H. G. Wells) for an extract from *In the Days of the Comet* by H. G. Wells; Secker and Warburg Ltd and The Viking Press Inc. (Copyright 1952 by Angus Wilson) for an extract from *Hemlock and After* by Angus Wilson; Leonard Woolf and The Hogarth Press Ltd for an extract from *Essays on Literature* by Leonard Woolf; Leonard Woolf; The Hogarth Press Ltd and Harcourt, Brace and World Inc. (Copyright, 1927 by Harcourt, Brace and World Inc.; renewed 1955 by Leonard Woolf) for an extract from *To the Lighthouse* by Virginia Woolf.

INTRODUCTION

SOME of the prose being written at the end of the eighteenth century is not very different from some of the prose being written today. We can usually notice words, phrases, sentences, constructions, which would not now normally be used, but in many other words and phrases and sentences we are aware mainly of continuity, within a relatively stable modern English. Most of the prose forms with which we are now familiar – the novel, the essay, the treatise, the journal – were then in regular use, and there are also some important continuities in ideas and feelings.

We shall see, on closer examination, how much has changed in our prose, but the stress on continuity is worth making at the beginning. It is now getting on for 200 years since the earliest passages in this book were written, but these two centuries are the making of modern Britain, and the connexions between some of the early and some of the later stages are significant. There are moments when we know Coleridge or Cobbett or Paine or Jane Austen as ancestors: as connected with us in a land and through a language, but across an evident gap of historical time. There are also moments when in a thing seen, a thing said, a thing written in a particular way, we feel not distance but closeness: a man or woman; a writer; a known experience or idea; a known country.

We can see, reading this book, how much has changed in these centuries, in the social and physical landscape of Britain. In this introduction I want to consider how the writer's landscape has changed: in connexion, undoubtedly, with the more general changes; but specifically, also, in his position as writer, and in his relations with readers. I find I have always to remind myself, as I read the prose of these centuries, how substantial these changes have been. In some simple ways, the signs are everywhere, but certain important kinds of prose, now as then, are written and read by a minority, in which there is less apparent change. To what extent can I feel, passing, say, from Coleridge to Empson, that in the years between them literacy has become a quite different kind of social fact? Each man is writing, in these instances, for readers with his own particular interests; the reader, in a critical way, seems in each case to include the writer. It can be different with their contemporaries: Cobbett writing in the *Political Register*; Lawrence in a popular magazine. Here the flow is all outward, and the writer is not – does not seem to be – speaking in any way to himself; he is writing (though speaking is a good way of putting it, as we listen to the sentences) *for* himself, *in front of* a public. There are strengths and weaknesses in each mode; I give the examples, at this stage, simply to indicate the complexity of the actual history.

On the British mainland, at the end of the eighteenth century, there were less than eleven million people. By the middle of the nineteenth century there were twice as many; by the early twentieth century twice as many again. In our own period, the 1960s, there are more than fifty-one millions. At the end of the eighteenth century, most people were living in country areas. By 1851, the urban population exceeded the rural, for the first time in any society in the history of the world. By the end of the nineteenth century three people lived in towns for every one in the country. In our own period the proportion is four to one. These extraordinary changes, in numbers and in kinds of community, were bound to affect, though in complicated ways, so important a means of communication as prose. When we feel this history not as figures but as people and places, we know that this must be so.

In the same history, more people were learning to read. We cannot tell exactly how many readers there were at the end of the eighteenth century. The nearest estimate I can make is some four or five million. But from just this time, standards of literacy were rising, and when we put these to the increasing number of people, the number of readers was increasing remarkably. By 1840 it was getting on for twelve million; by 1870, it was more than twenty million; by 1900, more than thirty million. In our own century, with nearly universal literacy, readers on the British mainland have grown to between forty and fifty million: about ten times as many as when the first passages in this book were written.

Much depends, then, not on the simple increase in numbers of readers, though this is in many ways a transforming social fact, but on the kinds of writing made available to them, and thus on the real relations between so many different readers and so many kinds of writer. If we look first at books, we see, as a matter of numbers, the kinds of change we would expect. At the end of the eighteenth century the number of titles published each year was rising sharply. It had been stuck at about 100 a year in the middle of the century, but in the 1790s it averaged 372, and was continuing to rise. Between 1802 and 1827, the annual number of titles (new books and reissues) averaged 580; an important part of this increase was in novels, as it had been since 1780. By the middle of the nineteenth century, the average annual figure was more than 2,600; by 1901, more than 6,000; by 1913, more than 12,000; by 1937, more than 17,000; by the 1960s, well over 20,000. Most of these books, throughout, were in prose, and this reminds us of the vastness of the period we are trying to represent and understand.

Yet although the increase in titles almost matched the increase in literacy, the book-reading public increased only slowly and unevenly. Tom Paine's *Rights of Man*, in the 1790s, sold 50,000 copies in a few weeks, and much more widely in a cheap edition. But the average size of an edition was about 1,250 for a novel, 750 for more general works. Walter Scott, the most popular novelist of the early nineteenth century, sold 10,000 copies of *Rob Roy* in a fortnight, but this was not a much higher figure than those of earlier popular successes, in the mid-eighteenth century. Twenty years later, the edition of the first number of Dickens's *Pickwick Papers* was 400; this had climbed, by the fifteenth number, to 40,000. This was in serial publication, of course. *Uncle Tom's Cabin*, in book form, sold 150,000 in its first six months, but George Eliot's popular success, *Adam Bede*, in the same decade (the 1850s) sold some 14,000–15,000. A main obstacle was cost. Books became markedly cheaper in the 1830s and 1840s, with new printing methods and cloth instead of leather binding. There had been many ventures, since the 1780s, in cheap reprint series. Yet in a wretched general standard of living, books were still, for most people, occasional luxuries; and for all the devices of libraries and other corporate buying, the book-reading public was largely defined by social and economic class, and continued to be so even as literacy was becoming universal. It is only in our own century, and still in incomplete ways, that books began to come with any convenience to the majority of people. If, today, we take all kinds of distribution into account (including the important and spectacular growth of public-library issues) we find some fifteen to twenty books read each year for every adult in the population; but this average figure conceals extremely unequal individual uses. I have estimated that it was only in the 1950s, when a majority of the population had been literate for well over a century, that a majority came to read books with any sort of regularity; and since this majority is a bare one, the development of the book-reading public has still a considerable way to go.

The increases in population and literacy were matched much earlier by other kinds of writing, in newspapers and magazines. Already in the 1820s people bought more than a million copies of the *Last Dying Speech and Confession* of the murderer of Maria Marten, but this was occasional reading; the regular reading of newspapers and magazines had to wait on lower costs and improved distribution. I have estimated that in 1820 about one person in a hundred read daily or Sunday newspapers; about ten in a hundred the occasional broadsheet. In 1860 about three in a hundred read a daily newspaper, twelve in a hundred a Sunday paper. These figures are of course very markedly lower than the actually literate population. Eventually, a majority read Sunday papers by about 1910, and daily papers by about 1920. Sunday papers reached nearly universal distribution between the wars, and daily papers during the Second World War. Here then, in newspapers, was the most widely distributed prose. The prose of books, in relation to it, was and is a minority matter.

This history has important implications in the tones and styles of prose, though they are not all on the surface, as we shall see. Yet it is still only part of the real history of the relations between writers and readers. When we consider those writers who are still read, we find that here, also, there is a social history. Just before the period of this book, in the mid-eighteenth century, the social and educational background of the most important writers was beginning to change, with many more from middle-class and professional families, and less, in proportion, who had passed through the universities of Oxford and Cambridge. More, too, were becoming professional writers, in the sense of having no independent income or other employment, though the really marked period for this change does not begin until the 1830s. In the late eighteenth and early nineteenth centuries, the relative importance of middle-class writers continued, but new social groups began to be better represented, with writers born in the families of tradesmen, farmers and craftsmen. This trend, together with the increasing importance of women writers, continued through the nineteenth century, but it was modified by the extensive reorganization of education in the period, especially in the universities and the new public schools. In some ways, English writers of the late nineteenth and early twentieth century are more homogeneous as a class than their early

Victorian predecessors; and it has remained a decisive element in the relation of writers to readers that even where social origins have become more varied, the educational pattern has been more uniform; this is particularly important in such kinds of writing as history, philosophy, social criticism and science. In the twentieth century, as a result of some improved access from elementary to higher education, writers have had more varied social origins than their immediate predecessors, but many of their ideas about writing have been mediated through a minority area of higher education, both directly and indirectly. It is still quite clear in Britain today that there is not only a marked inequality of representation in writers, as between different social groups, with the majority of writing still coming from a highly organized middle class; but also, in relation to this, a definition of interest which has to do with their quite common educational background, which only a few share with the majority of their potential readers. The results of this situation, in actual prose, are very difficult to analyse; we shall consider some important examples, from different periods and in very different men. But it is necessary to be aware of it from the beginning. In its most general sense, the writing of prose is a transaction between discoverable numbers of writers and readers, organized in certain changing social relations which include education, class habits, distribution and publishing costs. At the same time, in its most important sense, the writing of prose is a sharing of experience which, in its human qualities, is both affected by and can transcend the received social relations. It is always so, in the relation between literature and society: that the society determines, much more than we realize and at deeper levels than we ordinarily admit, the writing of literature; but also that the society is not complete, not fully and immediately present, until the literature has been written, and that this literature, in prose as often as in any other form, can come through to stand as if on its own, with an intrinsic and permanent importance, so that we see the rest of our living through it as well as it through the rest of our living.

2

The most important single development in English prose since 1780 is the emergence of the novel as the major literary form. Perhaps between 1730 and 1750 it was temporarily dominant, but it is from the 1830s that it is regularly the form in which most of the major writers of a period work. Before the 1830s, such important novelists as Jane Austen and Scott seem relatively isolated figures beside the two generations of Romantic poets. After the 1830s, it is the generations of novelists which are most marked, and it is in the novel, primarily, that the great creative discoveries are made. It is not only, as it is sometimes put, that the novel began to include kinds of experience which would have been previously written in verse. It is mainly that new kinds of experience, in an essentially different civilization, flowed into the novel and were the bases of its new and extraordinary growth and achievement. The effects on prose are then very marked. It becomes normal to look, in prose, for much of the finest writing of the age. But, further, this development of the novel transforms many received ideas of what literature is, and among these received ideas is the traditional assumption of the character of good prose. It is still remarkable, in a persistently narrow critical tradition, that the contrast between verse and prose can be made as if it were self-evidently a contrast between the 'imaginative' and the 'prosaic'. This is related to the still common habit of using 'poetry' as a normal and adequate synonym for 'literature', and to such symptoms, even in some of the best critical writing on the novel, as describing its organization as that of a 'dramatic poem'. What needs to be stressed is the originality of every kind, in form, language and subject, which can be found in the English novel from Dickens to Lawrence. This originality requires its own and specific critical recognitions, but it throws light, also, on kinds of writing outside itself. Before the novel was the major literary form, the best prose was normally looked for in essays and in similar kinds of general discourse. Such prose, of course, has continued to be important, but the notions of style derived from it have been damaging, not only to the novel, but to other kinds of writing. It is at this point, and especially as it refers to a polite and learned tradition, that the altered relations of writers and readers, which we have already discussed in a general way, become evident in new and particular ways.

One of the marks of a conservative society is that it regards style as an absolute. A style of writing or speaking is judged as a question of manners, and appreciation of this style as a question of breeding and taste. In important literary criticism, since Coleridge, this conventional assumption has been set aside. Style is known, not as an abstract quality, but as inseparable from the substance of the ideas and feelings expressed. In modern communication theory, a new dimension has been added: style is inseparable also from the precise relationship of which it is a form: commonly the relationship, whether explicit or implicit, between a writer or speaker and his expected reader or audience. This relationship is never mechanical. The ordinary formula in communication theory – 'who says what to whom with what effect?' – characteristically neglects the real sources of communication. In practice, in studying communication, we have to add the question 'why?'. The precise relationship, which is only rarely static, is then inseparable from the substantial ideas and feelings, which might otherwise be abstracted as a 'content' without form. In almost all writing the language, which is at once form and content, includes, though often unconsciously, the real relationships and the tension between these and the precise relationship of the writer and other men.

It is remarkable how often, in literary criticism but especially in ephemeral commentary, the mechanical version of style as an abstract quality, supported of course by the unnoticed tones and conventions of particular social groups, is taken for granted. We shall observe the effect of this on some of our greatest novelists: on Dickens, on George Eliot, on Hardy, on Lawrence, who have all been said to write badly, or often badly, and who have all also, significantly, been called (there is a world of social meaning in the term) 'autodidacts'. But before approaching this matter directly, we can examine, in a simpler case, the relation between writer and reader which the ordinary version of style is designed to suppress. In writing which is not primarily literary, style is regarded, in the tradition of the polite essay, as decoration, a merely tasteful or mannered addition to substance: even in political writing, where the kind of experience being drawn on and the version of other men indicated by a particular way of addressing them are not only substantial but are crucial to the precise nature of a political argument. It is especially significant in our own political world of public relations and managed political images. But it happens that we can illustrate it most readily from an earlier time: the first period of this book, when the struggle for and against democracy was taking place in a country being transformed both economically and socially. What was really being argued, throughout, was the question to whom political decisions should be referred: to whom, in the simple sense of what classes of men had the right to political opinions and influence; to whom, also, in a more complex sense, of what idea of humanity, what kind of living experience, was politically relevant? And then as a way of highlighting this question, we can ask why Edmund Burke's denunciation of the French Revolution – the famous *Reflections* – was published in the form of an open letter. The form was well known, of course; it had been successfully used in the Letters of Junius, where the whole point was the extension to a wider public of a particular kind of personal denunciation, which is written within the moral conventions of a ruling class but which then breaks just one of those conventions – the closed circle within which political argument is supposed to occur. This is still, however, a political challenge within existing terms: an out-group using publication against an in-group. None of this applies in the case of Burke's *Reflections*: it is a denunciation of a people, or at least of their revolution, in terms of high political principle but in the form of a letter to 'a very young gentleman at Paris'. But then what appears at first sight an uncertainty or confusion of form turns out, on examination, to be the substance of the political argument, as determined by a particular relation between writer and readers. For Burke's essential argument is at least as much about English as about French politics; what he fears is an English revolution. But then by writing as an Englishman to a Frenchman he can assume what he could not prove: a representative quality, describing the English constitution *as if* to a foreigner, and thus enlisting behind him the feelings of a united patriotism. Where Junius relied on the itch for scandal which could be directed into an indignation for liberty, Burke relied on a pretended unity of national feeling to which in fact he was trying to persuade his *English* readers. Thus the literary method becomes, if we are not careful, the political proof. The youth of the 'very young gentleman at Paris' is a comparable device. It permits the decisive tone of the reflections, from settled wisdom (English politics) to inexperience (French politics), and the more subtle tactic of engaging sympathy in the very act of denunciation: the conventional presence of the correspondent, used only when it suits this particular appeal, supports the necessary distinction, for Burke's purposes, between what the French are and what they have done; the spirit of the people and the actual revolution. Thus an argument against revolution is developed by the setting-up, in form and language, of would-be and hoped-for relations, which in fact serve to disguise the actual relations. We can then understand why Tom Paine, in his reply, cut through to direct public address, against what he called Burke's theatrical performance. Yet as we read *The Rights of Man* we find another uncertainty: the tone veers between open argument, in line with his appeal to government by reason, and what is really an anxious appeal to men of his own kind to understand the feelings of 'a large class of people of that description, which in England is called the "mob"'. Political prose then developed in two ways. It became open rational argument, to men as such, and in doing so was *addressed* to nobody and was necessarily, in substance and manner, abstract. The strengths of this kind of prose have been underestimated, in a common prejudice, but there is a real and inescapable weakness in that it assumes the political forms of open and rational discourse which in fact it is trying to create. Alternatively, it became direct address to an ever-widening public, having the strengths of contact, of the sounds of actual voices and experiences, as most notably in Cobbett, but in danger, always, of declining to opportunism – the devices of flattery, of any public, which could be easily learned – and to simplification, where the voice of plain man-to-man common sense could be used against connected reasoning and against real complexities. My point is that when we read passages of these very different kinds of prose we cannot refer the question of their value to any simple criterion of style. What each method discloses is not only the general substance of the argument, but also that other substance which is the real relation of writer and reader, and at times a desired but not yet existing relation. It is difficult to feel, reading late eighteenth-century and early nineteenth-century political prose, that any of these relations was adequate, though the genius of some of the writers is very clear. But then to say that is only to say, in another way, that the new political feelings had as yet no adequate social forms: what we can learn from looking at the institutions we can learn also from looking at the prose; just as we can see in the prose, as in the history of the time, certain new relationships struggling to be formed.

3

In the development of the novel, the evidence is even more interesting. In descriptive power, prose was already mature, as we can see in the vividness of many journals and memoirs. But now two other uses were remarkably developed. First, there is the power of sustained analysis of a situation or state of mind. We can find in this period, from Jane Austen through George Eliot and Henry James to E. M. Forster, an assured mastery in just this faculty, though we notice also the problem of combining such analysis, isolating and static as it must often be, with the essentially different rhythms of narrative continuity. This problem appears sometimes more acute in the later examples, as increasingly, from George Eliot's later novels onward, the form of fiction of this kind comes to be determined, overall, by analysis rather than by narrative. Then, related to this, there is the second development, which appears to work, at times, in quite other directions. This is the incorporation, in prose, of spoken as opposed to written rhythms and constructions. The most evident local example of this development is in the reported direct speech (what is still, in the critical power of the dramatic tradition, called the dialogue) of the novels. Here undoubtedly, in the period we are examining, there are important developments and discoveries. But this is only one aspect of a general movement, running through the nineteenth century and reaching a climax in our own, towards the restoration of speech rhythms as the normal basis for many different kinds of prose. When we set this fact beside the increasing precision and refinement of analysis, we find some elements of contradiction and tension, which are enough in themselves to remind us, as the straight reading of the novels of course reminds us, that there is no single tradition of fiction in the period, and not even a single major tradition. We have to relate these tensions, I believe, to one of the most important results of the altering relations between writers and readers.

It seems clear that the base from which fictional analysis was developed is the important eighteenth-century tradition of philosophical and critical analysis, itself often well evidenced in the essay. The strengths of this tradition are, in a special way, the strengths of literacy. It is easy to react against the formalities of diction and construction which of course occur in such prose, but these are only the surface marks of an essential stance between writer and reader, willingly and habitually accepted on both sides, in which rationality, precision and sustained argument become possible, in new ways, once the language has been learned. It is true that this method has been repeatedly imitated, as a kind of social manner: in sermons, correspondence columns, political speeches, we can hear the whirring sound of a merely polite mind putting pen to paper. But it is only in ignorance or prejudice that we would then disregard, for all the hated formality of the sound, the real reach of this prose: the composed page; the sense of time gained, time given; the mind working but also the mind prepared, in an exposition which assumes patience, reference, inspection, re-reading. Such prose, indeed, is a kind of climax of print, and especially of the printed book: a uniformity of tone and address; an impersonality, assuming no immediate relation between writer and reader but only possession, in a social way, of this language; a durability, as in the object itself, beyond any temporary impulse or occasion. As we read Coleridge, considering the marks of an educated mind, or Newman on liberalism, Mill on utility and calculation, or Tawney on equality, we must know what we have gained by this very special achievement: a seriousness capable of matching the real complexity of the issues. But it is when we go across from these intellectual reflections to Jane Austen on

Emma, George Eliot on Lydgate, Henry James on John Marcher, E. M. Forster on the Schlegels, that we can count wider gains: a seriousness, a sustained attention, not only to abstract questions, but to immediate human issues and emotions. We can feel the strain certainly, the increasing strain, but we are not likely, in any settled judgement, to want or expect its relaxation. If we put such prose down, as we may well at times do, it is still with the certainty that in its special achievement it continues to be there; that it is not dependent, in obvious ways, on mood or address, which seem to belong elsewhere while this intent and particular analysis is composed.

Yet such a feeling is, in part, an illusion. What seems, in abstraction, simply a quality of prose is also, in fact, a community of language and sensibility: a precise community, which can by no means be taken for granted. In the long development of this particular manner, the evolution of what can be called in the best sense an educated style, there were decisive social relationships, no less so when these became habitual. It is not only the increasing separation of written language from ordinary speech. This has been masked, at times, by the adoption of habits of speech, even on private occasions, which derive from the printed forms: an increasingly self-conscious formality, dependent for its success on arranged and self-conscious circles of social conversation, which indeed one still hears, but with a deep and eloquent release of breath and of tension as they break and disperse. Within a wholly written form, the distance between what can be written and what can normally be said is itself an accepted convention. It is what Jane Austen acknowledges when she writes: 'seldom, very seldom, does complete truth belong to any human disclosure': a recognition, certainly, of a general human fact, but one which impels the novelist to particular means of disclosure, beyond what can be represented in speech or even in behaviour: not only analysis, but a deliberate variation in levels of reported speech, from the simple representative ease of 'You are going in, I suppose?' to the anxious, qualifying formality, characteristically self-aware of the conventional danger of speechmaking, which is there in 'whatever the event of this hour's conversation' and its related, composed rhythms. This is in part a social problem, of polite speech. But it is more than that, in its best examples: we can see the same shift, from the representative to the composed, in the radically different sensibility of Emily Brontë; from the simplicity of '"Why?", she asked, gazing nervously round' to the full convention (acknowledged to the reader in 'this speech' or again in 'I was only going to say that . . .' or 'I cannot express it; but surely . . .') of the central, composed manner, in the sentences beginning 'What were the use of my creation, if I were entirely contained here?' The convention and the substance of the insight are then one, but since, in the general development, the literary and the social convention proved not to be identical, the real strains – not of attention but of anxiety – increased. George Eliot, in her brilliant chapter on Lydgate's vote, even exploits these strains: the language of necessary analysis precedes the inadequacy of full disclosure in the talk at the meeting, but also its rhythms, its formalities, need be only slightly displaced to represent the 'rich tanner of fluent speech', with the 'glittering spectacles and erect hair', whose public manner can be effectively broken in on, 'whip in hand', with a representative 'Oh, damn the divisions.' Henry James shifts his analysis towards the appearance of anxious, qualifying talk, and includes, to sustain this, what are then rather obvious colloquialisms – 'he had a screw loose for her but she liked him in spite of it'; but at the same time, moving in from the other direction, incorporates almost every word spoken – even the vaguest 'Oh' – in a related and anxiously qualifying analysis. Within this tradition – there are of course many other examples – the relations between the received written language and the unevenness of the spoken language and of conversation forced a technical complication which came radically to affect the total form.

This is not, however, the whole tradition of major nineteenth-century fiction. As we turn to Dickens, we find not only a different individual genius, but a different underlying relationship between writer and reader. This is connected, of course, in obvious ways, with the expansion of the reading public, which was at an important new stage just as Dickens was beginning to write. But an altered relation, of this profound kind, is not only a consequence of altering general relationships. It is also something brought to an emerging situation: a voice, a structure of feeling, an habitual social tone. It would be fair to say that Dickens both formed and was formed by a new public for literature; but as we look at his very individual yet characteristic genius, we have to stress something more than formation and reaction; we have to insist, indeed, on an element which we can best describe as release: the bringing of a particular energy, already present in speech, to the new problems and opportunities of an expanding prose. The genius of Dickens was of course crucial, but as we read Alexander Somerville's description of the bustle and conversation at the inn, or Henry Mayhew's recording of the scavenger's description of his life, we can recognize behind the distinctive energy of Dickens's new rhythms a common pressure: restless, crowded, vivid: a social world of a radically different kind from that which was still there, and still important, as a basis for the composed, quiet and connected prose of the formally educated tradition. Whenever such a change happens, it is easy for those who are used to the existing conventions to see only the rough edges, hear only the loudness and crudeness of this different manner. There is a kind of answer in Cobbett on the accusation of coarseness, which is in fact, in its essential claim, a truth to set beside Coleridge's classical emphasis on order and composure. But there is also another answer, of particular interest because it comes from a writer whose own settled manner is in the formal tradition. What George Eliot says about emphasis, in the passage from *The Mill on the Floss*, is important not only as a way of approaching the new prose of Dickens and his successors, but as the mark of a critical and increasingly important cultural change. It is not only the material life of 'good society', but, she argues, its associated tones of moderation and irony, which are a 'very expensive production'. It is not only luxury, but the leisure, the confidence, the assurance of continuity, which are in fact enjoyed at the expense of a 'wide national life ... based entirely on emphasis – the emphasis of want'. The complexity of this situation needs the most careful analysis. The strengths of that social prose, based on a small educated class, have already been acknowledged, and indeed they continue to be relevant, for certain definite purposes, in a society in which more and more people have been gaining education and an access to books. Yet for other purposes, and in particular for expressing the actual life of a hard-pressed, hard-driven, excluded majority, a different prose was absolutely required: a different language as expressing the altered relation of writer and reader. The new writers and the new readers, in such a moment of change, often appear together. Much is gained, of a permanent kind, as the achievement of Dickens continues to remind us. But we have also to notice that something is lost, or can be lost: not the older assurance and seriousness, which with only the normal modifications of time has continued to be available for certain precise purposes; but the common and intrinsic assumption of a natural equality, an effective continuity, between writer and reader, which of course at times is only a matter of polite address but which is capable also of limiting the opportunities for mere exploitation: exploitation of the reader; exploitation of the experience; exploitation, in the bad sense, of the resources of the language. Much restless and superficially vivid prose has been exploiting in just these ways; the examples are everywhere in routine popular journalism, and it is easy to trace a bad as well as a good inheritance from Cobbett – the fearless, radical-sounding oracle, exploiting his personality and his assumed relationship with his readers, has unfortunately been a good deal more common than that actual radical, closely and seriously engaged with the central issues of his time, and putting himself at risk, with a necessary and urgent defiance, in every sentence and every opinion.

To reach the right way of describing the change, we have to recognize that the relation between writer and reader is not abstract; indeed cannot be, without corruption, a matter of address alone; of presentation, as a technique separable from substance. The deadness we noticed earlier, when a merely polite mind puts pen to paper, and the formalities of diction and construction merely suggest a seriousness which is never in substance confirmed, is perhaps easier to spot than this other deadness, when a merely restless mind makes a vivid scrawl at experience, with the words and rhythms of a close, excited colloquialism, suggesting immediacy but never, past its weighed condiments of adjectives and its snatching, elbow-pulling rhythms, really engaging with anything. What is happening then is a writing not to the hard-pressed but to the jaded mind; it is this crucial distinction which the abstraction of presentation, the reification of style, simply blur and hide.

The most important thing to say about Dickens, then, is not that he is writing in a new way, but that he is experiencing in a new way, and that this is the substance of his language. The change in Staggs's Gardens, when the railway comes, is a change of a new kind, as we can recognize at once, in substance and language, if we compare it with Jane Austen's account of the improvement of Uppercross. And if we set beside both the measured, reminiscent account by Nasmyth (the inventor of the steam-hammer, but here a public figure, mediated by Samuel Smiles), when the phenomenon is Coal-brookdale, but the mind, for all its attention, still follows the polite allusions to Vulcan and Ceres, we can see more clearly what Dickens is doing: altering, transforming a whole way of writing, rather than putting an old style at a new experience. It is not the method of the more formal novelists, including the sounds of measured or occasional speech in a solid frame of analysis and settled exposition. Rather, it is a speaking, persuading, directing voice, of a new kind, which has taken over the narrative, the exposition, the analysis, in a single operation. Here, there, everywhere, as we read in the first paragraph; the restless production of a seemingly chaotic detail; the hurrying, pressing, miscellaneous clauses, with here a gap to push through, there a restless pushing at repeated obstacles, everywhere a crowding of objects, forcing attention; the prose, in fact, of a new order of experience; the prose of the city. And then not only the exposition but the analysis is of a new kind: 'railway patterns ... railway journals ... railway hotels ... railway plans ... railway ... railway ... railway ... railway ... even railway time'. And this is not now just the excited emphasis of objects, the miscellaneity, the chaos, the devastation; it is the reorganization, through a single and repeated emphasis, of a whole way of life around a decisive new element. The necessary generalization, that is to say, is of a different order; it is not outward, by allusion or reference, to a familiar world; it is from within, by the mounting emphasis of a new and radical and organizing principle. Seriousness, connexion, intelligent disclosure are not lost but transformed; a new prose has come to inhabit and to organize an essentially different world.

Or consider Dickens in a different manner, on the political system. His parade of nonentities from Boodle to Noodle is the sort of thing that by the standards of traditional formal argument, traditional formal prose, could be dismissed (it is still sometimes dismissed) as a ranting, jeering prejudice. It is nothing of the kind; it is a way of seeing a system. Not a new system, but an old system, seen from a new point of view.

Junius denouncing Grafton was person-to-person, through the extending device of the open letter. But what Dickens sees and seizes on, from Boodle to Noodle, is a class: with individual differences, no doubt, varying claims and prejudices, but as seen from outside the 'brilliant and distinguished circle', by those who are not the 'born first-actors, managers and leaders', differing by no more than a passing initial in a chiming community: what they have in common – the party from Boodle to Noodle and the party from Buffy to Puffy – being more important to those who have to watch and live under them than the distinctions they would make, in obviously different tones, among themselves. Then a way of seeing, a necessary way of seeing, has been learned and communicated, in an altered prose. 'Who have found out the perpetual stoppage. Who are to rejoice at nothing, and be sorry for nothing. Who are not to be disturbed by ideas.' The capital, general, dissected Who.

Just as clearly, however, in other parts of his writing, Dickens exploits the tension between the two kinds of language. This is a basic source of his comedy. Pecksniff's conversational style, to take only one example, is a demonstration of pompous emptiness in its mechanical reproduction of a familiar formal rhythm:

'When your mind requires to be refreshed, by change of occupation, Thomas Pinch will instruct you in the art of surveying the back garden, or in ascertaining the dead level of the road between this house and the finger-post, or in any other practical and pleasing pursuit.'

Whenever something is seen as ridiculous, in just this unconnected way, the decayed rhythm of a formal prose is likely to be used. On the origin of the name of Staggs's Gardens, for example:

Others, who had a natural taste for the country, held that it dated from those rural times when the antlered herd, under the familiar denomination of Staggses, had resorted to its shady precincts.

Or, making the contrast more explicit:

Bending over a steaming vessel of tea, and looking through the steam, and breathing forth the steam, like a malignant Chinese enchantress engaged in the performance of unholy rites, Mr F's Aunt put down her great teacup and exclaimed, 'Drat him, if he an't come back again!' It would seem from the foregoing exclamation that this uncompromising relative of the lamented Mr F, measuring time by the acuteness of her sensations and not by the clock, supposed Clennam to have lately gone away; whereas at least a quarter of a year had elapsed since he had had the temerity to present himself before her.

And this example reminds us that the comic effect is two-way. As in other periods of deep and uncomfortable cultural change, the habit of what is still felt as vulgar speech is as often the target as a decaying formality; indeed it is the cultural distance between them, when they are suddenly slapped together, that brings the uneasy but relieving laugh. Immediately after the sentences quoted, we are launched into the full stream of Flora's miscellaneous consciousness, in a passage which may technically anticipate the famous last chapter of *Ulysses* but which is radically different in feeling because it is not taken seriously; it is not yet the spontaneity, the feeling association, of a reflecting and private mind; it is rather the unorganized jumble of the nervous, the pretentious and the ignorant. In his observation on method as the mark of an educated mind, Coleridge had instanced, as a contrast, the processes of untrained speech, which can still often be heard:

The necessity of taking breath, the efforts of recollection, and the abrupt rectification of its failures, produce all his pauses; and with exception of the '*and then*', and '*and there*,' and the still less significant '*and so*', they constitute likewise all his connections.

It is a fair comment, but that it should come from Coleridge is especially significant evidence of the power of the formal tradition: a rational and public habit of mind is unquestion-ingly preferred to the essentially different organization of ordinary speech and thought. Eventually, in our prose, and especially in the novel, the resources of this spoken and think-ing dimension were to be brought to full use; but this is not Dickens's achievement; what happened there was the dis-covery of a new and more emphatic but still public mode.

It is in another kind of novel, feeling its way simultaneously towards the lives of ordinary people and towards a respecting naturalism of reported speech, that one element of the larger change can be seen to begin.

'Going– art thou going to work this time o' day?'
'No, stupid, to be sure not. Going to see the chap thou spoke on.'

Mrs Gaskell, in her change of subject, in her altered relation to it, begins to acknowledge directly the positive resources of spoken English. It is a considerable achievement, but it is still qualified by reservations: as in the anxious footnotes explaining the meaning of unfamiliar dialect words – as if in anthropologi-cal presentation to a standard reader; and in the often un-changed prose of the main narrative, which includes such distancing devices as 'our friends were not dainty, but even they picked their way', even when at times it has the nerve to confront the experience directly and in its own terms. Mrs Gaskell's alternation between successful direct description and an anxious voice-over commentary is in fact her alternation between direct response to a humanity in poverty and a separated, sympathizing production of evidence and argu-ment. It is an alternation towards which many novelists have been pressed, and which is a crucial phase in our social history. To the degree that there is still alienation between writers and most of the life around them, and uncertainty, then, in the relation of writer and reader, this problem in writing is still often unsolved. Yet we can look from Elizabeth Gaskell to D. H. Lawrence, in one of his early stories, and see that when these relations are (if only temporarily) right, a development in prose that is also a development in feeling is clearly achieved. It is not only that the reported speech is an actual flow, in the course of living: at once serious and adequate, yet recognizing the limits of what can be ordinarily said, by anyone, in the deepest human crises. It is also that there is now a continuity between this speech and the hitherto separated modes of analysis and narrative. This is more than integration, though even as such it is important. It is the discovery, in prose, of a response to death, rather than a reflection on it. The response is confused, painful; it is now deeply moved, now flatly cutting off. By traditional formal standards it has no method, no presentation at all; but it is not fragmentary, or inarticulate. It is the response as it comes, in words necessarily not far from words that might be spoken; in rhythms connecting and extending only so much as to carry the brief exclamations, questions, instructions, reassurances into a searching of heart and mind. It is written speech; a written searching. But it is controlled by, as it is based on, an ordinary voice.

In other situations, Lawrence experienced, and sometimes failed to overcome, the traditional difficulties. It is a problem of the most acute and continuing kind, if we see it, as I think we must, as a still unresolved social history. It would be very much simpler if we could merely discard one of the contrasted methods, and the whole structure that supports it. Any individual writer may of course do this, or think he has done it. If he never writes argument, or factual exposition, he can join in the reaction against the formal tradition; move his prose, deliberately, towards the words and rhythms of ordinary everyday speech. Or if he never writes of ordinary life processes, has never to describe men speaking and thinking but only the results, the products, of thought and behaviour, he can carry on with his own variant of what is still an educated prose: insisting on formal arrangement; on certain complicated constructions which correspond to his material; on words which although unfamiliar carry a precise, identifying, discriminating meaning. One solution or the other may be possible to the individual writer, but neither, evidently, is possible to a culture or a language as a whole. For some writers now, since the separated categories can and must overlap, in particular histories and circumstances, it is a matter of conscious choice, in this or that piece of writing. In which dimension, by what experience, is he now, in this writing, related? We can perhaps see this more clearly if we take it historically, for since George Eliot and Hardy this has been a general problem.

When a critic described George Eliot, Hardy and Lawrence as 'our three great autodidacts', he knew what he was doing, and it was just his bad luck that his audience included someone in the same separate and therefore critical position. For what his description depends on is an unstated and common assumption of what it is to have been properly taught. George Eliot, Hardy and Lawrence were all formally educated, to a standard still higher than that of three quarters of our children. All three, moreover, were in the most general sense intellectuals; they continued, after their formal education, to read, study, think and write for themselves. What they did not have – and it is all that they did not have, in this sense – was a standard upper-class English education, as this was coming to be in just their period: preparatory school; 'public' school; Oxford or Cambridge University. And yet there they are: add Dickens, another 'autodidact'; add Elizabeth Gaskell, Emily and Charlotte Brontë, all three in the same state; add Henry James and Joseph Conrad, educated quite elsewhere; add Wells and Gissing; and what you have is a list, with very few exceptions, of the major English novelists from 1840 to 1914. Only Mr Forster, perhaps, among considerable figures, can be said *not* to have been an 'autodidact'.

I am considering this now as a question of prose. I think there is an important point about George Eliot, if we set what she had to say in *Mill on the Floss* about emphasis and irony beside parts of *Felix Holt* or against the detached, critically inspecting construction of *Middlemarch*. But the question is most immediately accessible in Hardy, who so often, we are told, 'wrote badly'. The extract from *Tess of the D'Urbervilles* is especially relevant here. It sets out, in an explicit way, what is often present as a deeper awareness in the whole substance of the novels: in the relationship of Tess and Angel, for example; in the whole of *Return of the Native*; in Jude and Arabella and Sue. Tess, we remember, had 'two languages':

Mrs Durbeyfield habitually spoke the dialect; her daughter, who had passed the Sixth Standard in the National School under a London-trained mistress, spoke two languages; the dialect at home, more or less; ordinary English abroad and to persons of quality.

But this situation, which has since become so familiar, is already seen from a particular viewpoint: the easy contrast between the 'dialect' and 'ordinary English', which, left like that, raises none of the real questions. We have to consider, for example, the confidence of that 'ordinary English', and ask how ordinary it was, and where, ultimately, the standard was set. It is here that Angel's reflections on his brothers can help us. It is not a question, now, of what is said about fashion, though in the real history of English that too is important. It is a question of the connexion made between experience and expression:

perhaps, as with many men, their opportunities of observation were not so good as their opportunities of expression.

It is interesting that Hardy, tracing the roots of this lack, adopts so perfectly the smooth irony which was the opportunity of expression most frequently taken:

each brother candidly recognised that there were a few unimportant scores of millions of outsiders in civilised society, persons who were neither University men nor churchmen.

But the connexion he is trying to trace, between observation and expression, is complicated. It is a matter, ultimately, of how he himself is to write. We know that he was worried about his prose, and that he was reduced by the ordinary educated assumptions of his period to studying Defoe, Fielding, Addison, Scott and *The Times*, as if they could have helped him. The real difficulty came from the complexity of his own position as an observer: a complexity that can be seen now as representative. His problem of style is not quite that of the two languages of Tess: the consciously educated and the unconsciously customary. This situation, however embarrassing, can often be lived with: in distinct social groups, one or other language is evident and available. But Hardy as a writer was mainly concerned with the interaction between the two conditions – the educated and the customary: not just as the characteristics of social groups, but as ways of seeing and feeling, within a single mind. And then neither established language would serve, to express this tension and disturbance. Neither in fact was sufficiently articulate. An educated style, as it had developed in a particular and exclusive group, was dumb in intensity and limited in humanity. A customary style, while carrying the voice of feeling, was still thwarted by ignorance and complacent in repetition and habit. Hardy veered between them, and the idiosyncrasy of his writing is related to this: the unusual combination of formal and colloquial words; of simple and elaborate rhythms. For example:

The season developed and matured. Another year's instalment of flowers, leaves, nightingales, thrushes, finches and such ephemeral creatures, took up their positions where only a year ago others had stood in their place when these were nothing more than germs and inorganic particles. Rays from the sunshine drew forth the buds and stretched them into long stalks, lifted up sap in noiseless streams, opened petals, and sucked out scents in invisible jets and breathings.

Dairyman Crick's household of maids and men lived on comfortably, placidly, even merrily. Their position was perhaps the happiest of all positions in the social scale, being above the line at which neediness ends, and below the line at which the *convenances* begin to cramp natural feeling, and the stress of threadbare modishness makes too little of enough.

Thus passed the leafy time when arborescence seems to be the one thing aimed at out of doors. Tess and Clare unconsciously studied each other, ever balanced on the edge of a passion, yet apparently keeping out of it. All the while they were converging, under an irresistible law, as surely as two streams in one vale.

This passage is neither the best nor the worst of Hardy. Rather, it shows the many complicated pressures working within what had to seem a single intention. 'The leafy time when arborescence', for example, is mere inflation to an educated style; but *'convenances'*, which might appear merely fashionable (it was in just this period that the inclusion of French words in English prose, and drawing attention to them, became a common gesture of elegance), carries a precise feeling, in just its awkward suddenness. 'The stress of threadbare modishness' is cold and precise; from a distance, this manner was always easily available. The more interesting uses of formal words and phrases are within a natural and involving description. In the second sentence, 'instalment' and 'ephemeral' are at once disturbing and active: an abstract consciousness of what the whole natural process is, in 'germs and inorganic particles', is a necessary accompaniment, in Hardy, of the more direct and more enjoyed sights and scents of spring: 'nightingales, thrushes, finches . . . sunrise . . . buds . . . stalks . . . sap . . . streams . . . petals . . . sucked'. The two ways of seeing, awkwardly but actively, are being brought together. Indeed when we come to the next simple sentence, it is loss not gain as Hardy reverts to the simpler and cruder abstraction of 'Dairyman Crick's household of maids and men', which might be supposed, in its traditional sound, to be the countryman speaking, but is actually the voice of the detached observer, at a low level of interest. The more fully

Hardy uses the resources of the whole language, the more adequate the writing is. There is more strength in 'unconsciously studied each other', which is at once formal and engaged, than in the 'two streams in one vale' which is the traditional gesture. What Hardy is reaching for, always, is unambiguously an educated style, in which the extension of vocabulary and the complication of construction are necessary to the intensity and precision of the observation:

The gray tones of daybreak are not the gray half-tones of the day's close, though the degree of their shade may be the same. In the twilight of the morning, light seems active, darkness passive; in the twilight of evening, it is the darkness which is active and crescent, and the light which is the drowsy reverse.

This successful observation and description is in a manner characteristic of some of the best nineteenth-century prose: compare Ruskin's observations of clouds, and Richard Jefferies's description of the early morning to which the reaper goes out. But what we notice in Jefferies, as in Hardy, is the human problem: that this is a kind of observation which seems to depend on detachment. And then if this is a detachment from human beings, or from a whole class of human beings, the manner itself can wither. Jefferies tells us that the reaper, with his day's work in front of him, does not see what the observer is seeing. What is also relevant, as Jefferies in his later work recognized, is that the educated observer, seeing nature, does not see the human being who is the reaper; or, if he sees him, sees him as only a figure in a landscape. Hardy, in more extended and complicated ways, works through this complexity of choice. Without the insights of consciously learned history, and of the educated understanding of nature and behaviour, he cannot really observe at all, either with adequate precision or with an adequately extending human respect. But then the ordinary social model, the learned language, which includes these capacities, is, very clearly, in a divided culture, a form which includes an alienation – 'a few unimportant scores of millions of outsiders', and a nullity – 'to be tolerated rather than reckoned with and respected'. The tension which then follows, when the observer holds to educated procedures but is unable to feel with the existing educated class, is severe. It is not the countryman awkward in his town clothes, or the 'autodidact' awkward among people of settled learning. It is the more significant tension, of course with its awkwardnesses, its frequent uncertainties of tone, its spurts of bitterness and nostalgia, of the man caught by his personal history in the general crisis of the relation between education and class. What that crisis comes out as, in real terms, is the relation between intelligence and fellow-feeling, but this relation in the nineteenth and twentieth centuries had to be worked out at a time when education was consciously used to train members of a class and to divide them from their own passions as surely as from other men: the two processes, inevitably, are deeply connected. The writer moving through this history had to explore, as if on his own, the resources of what seemed to be but was not yet in fact a common language. In the novel, especially, this is the significant line of development.

4

Though the novel is the greatest achievement, in prose, of the period with which we are concerned, it is a more disturbed form than other kinds of writing. Some of the difficulties we have noticed in the novel were also present in social criticism: in Carlyle, for example, where the use of the persuading, presenting voice is very like that of Dickens, but is now often more difficult to read because of its formal quality, with certain formal expectations, as argument. Wherever really new ways of seeing and feeling are in question, Victorian prose is disturbed. Yet the bulk of Victorian prose is remarkably settled and solid: an achieved, confident and still powerful manner. Where a novelist shared this essential outlook, he could write so simply that he hardly seems to be writing: Trollope is an obvious example, and he has had many successors. It is often said that this manner is heavy, but look at the passage from Macaulay and then at Bagehot. It is just Macaulay's silvery confidence that now divides us. He shares so much with his readers, in ways of seeing and dealing with the world, that he becomes a kind of model: an admirable style. While the ways of seeing and dealing last, that is English, and schoolboys can be set to learn it: the attitudes and the style in a single operation:

Let the Government do this: the people will assuredly do the rest.

Or, as we might say, see Hansard, *passim*.

This division between the confident and the disturbed, in the long crisis of an industrial civilization, can hardly be over-stressed. It is in effect a division between a prose with many strengths of clarity and fluency, and a prose often tortured, uncertain, obscure – its lucidities dependent on new ways of seeing and feeling being learned; its strengths on unexpected connexions; its flow on inarticulate and still struggling emotions. The confident prose is not just a matter of optimism, of a belief in progress. Bagehot is very remarkable as a pioneer of a style now very common but still difficult to describe: a complacency and a cynicism, which might appear opposite qualities, are brilliantly fused, into a sort of brittle durability, a penetrating reassurance. It is a style admirably suited to expose illusions as a way of maintaining them: the accent, the new poise, of a ruling class under pressure and using a style as a control. Bagehot is full of insights and illuminations, and among them, as we consider the subsequent history of this manner, we must insist on including, as an observation of the effect on others:

Their imagination is bowed down; they feel they are not equal to the life which is revealed to them.

We must then add that this result – a bowing down of the imagination – is often evident, also, in those who are using such a style to impress others. The poise can replace and annihilate the man.

Much depends, here, on the immediate subject. Parts of Leslie Stephen's 'agnostic's apology' are straightforward and serious: an obstinate, solid Victorian questioning. But as he approaches a climax of his argument, in the last sentence of the present extract, he begins to use 'utter' as a repetitive adjective: 'utter want', 'utter ignorance', 'utter incapacity'; and we catch in this a kind of domineering scepticism, which has since been widely prevalent: in some serious argument, but more generally in a persistent type of conservative journalism. 'Anything but the laughter of sceptics and the contempt of the healthy human intellect' has behind it the admirable rationality of much earlier prose; but a long way behind it, for what has entered and weakened it is a confident social tone which depends, and knows it can depend, on a certain kind of reader doing most of the work of the apparent proof. Matthew Arnold, similarly, is at a point of transition. We can see in his prose a genuinely questioning, flexible mind: an actual openness, which gets beyond 'stock notions' and 'mechanical pursuits'. But Arnold also relies, at certain crucial points, on a kind of complacent raillery; an overbearing by style: not the heavy or the pompous, certainly, but the engaging compact with the reader that he and the author share the only relevant kind of intelligence, so that certain positions do not have to be really weighed, but can be smiled or shrugged off into a pathetic inadequacy. There is a relation between this and the fully controlled irony of Samuel Butler in *Erewhon*, where the total convention of an ironically conceived world allows a singular purity: from which, all the same, a disturbing imagination, a disturbing engagement, are deliberately excluded. Or we can see what is in a way the triumph of this manner in Shaw, where the confident lucidity is genuinely remarkable, the prose in its own terms so excellent an instrument, and yet where the selected occasions for the use of intelligence come to seem, after a while, so narrow a world. The bright, entertaining and useful challenge, as in the extract, comes not only to harden into a party trick, but takes over as a whole way of experiencing others and the world, in which people and objects shrink to fixed appearances, and nothing is left but, playing entertainingly over them, a single confident voice.

The development of this kind of prose is closely connected with social and political attitudes: in the nineteenth century, mainly liberal; in the twentieth century, mainly conservative. Its cutting edge can still be felt in Bertrand Russell, though here the return of indignation begins to introduce a different tone. It is present sometimes, also, in Tawney, but in the extract what we mainly notice is another tradition: a connected seriousness. For the purposes of genuinely serious argument, an important continuity can be observed, from Victorian to twentieth-century prose. There is some lightening of vocabulary, some simplification of construction, but the tone holds, in many thousands of cases: the example from Russell Brain is simply the nearest to hand. A different kind of irony – on the whole self-deprecating rather than self-regarding – is also evident and successful, as in the paragraphs by Empson: the edge is sharp, but there is less monotony, as we can never be certain which way it will turn. But perhaps the most interesting development is that represented by Hulme: a new style of argument, as if in a new typography (the same sense of a style related to an arrangement on the page can be seen in the extract from Auden). It is a probing relativism; an irregular thinking-aloud which is yet quite formal and even abstract; a combination of technical and colloquial words and rhythms: now a strained, straining definition; now flat assertion; an open undogmatic inquiry both capped by and capping a suddenly consciously stylish and overbearing epigram. Eliot, always, has more continuity of rhythm and tone, but his most interesting prose, as in the present extract, represents just this mixed and contemporary sensibility. It is of course a written and lonely style: an address to the page, it would seem, quite as often as to the reader. As such it can be contrasted with what is essentially a speaking prose: the strong rhetoric of the voice, as in Morris, where a good deal depends on the sense of a public meeting – not just the raised platform but the interested, collected audience; or the private persuasive intensity, as across the table, or the face leaning forward from the dimly-lit chair, as in Lawrence – in fact the style of the private letter, as if speaking to someone, yet not quite personally; the private letter that will eventually be collected and published, and that stands as a model for a very personal, connecting article. Perhaps the main fact, about twentieth-century discursive prose, is the coexistence, the public recognition, of so great a range of possible styles. The real diversity of occasion and relationship, in an expanded, multifarious and yet still divided society, could be matched only by this, and no single public style could serve.

5

Already in Victorian England the novel had ceased to be, in any simple sense, a form, and had become, in effect, a whole literature. It is hardly necessary to stress the advantages of this development; we have only to instance such radically different works as *Wuthering Heights* and *Dombey and Son* and *Mary Barton* appearing within months of each other: deep variations of experience and convention, finding their own forms. The strength of this diversity has never since been absent: Joyce and Lawrence and Forster, to take only three very obvious examples, could differ radically, in a single generation, and yet find novels a natural medium: *Ulysses*, *Women in Love*, *A Passage to India*: radically different works, but with a unity, in each, of a particular experience and a particular form. Just as we saw a necessary range in discursive prose, so we can see this imaginative range as a vitality and a strength. But of course it is always possible to see the range as a miscellaneity; to deplore the absence of a central and dominating tradition; to conclude that since this or that creative generation, the form, the prose, has disintegrated.

There are problems now, certainly. For some considerable time the journal or memoir has been overlapping with the novel, and there has been a further overlap between fiction and argument, fiction and organized observation. It is easy, for example, to see the influence of the novel behind Beatrice Webb's account of her family, her father and her acquisition of a voice that could give orders. Then there is a clear relation between Thomas Dry's letter from Gallipoli and David Holbrook's scene of the Normandy fighting in his novel *Flesh Wounds*. Parts of Richard Hoggart's and John Holloway's accounts are close to a recognizable kind of fiction, as is Alan Sillitoe's description of the tip. It is sometimes difficult to tell, in a paragraph by Orwell, which is reporting and which is fiction. Wells's account of the burning of an old world is technically science fiction, but is close in feeling and method to many of his explicit arguments.

It would then be possible to separate a particular class of imaginative writing: that of Virginia Woolf, say. We could argue that here the facts of an observable world and of common experience have been properly subordinated to an imaginative flow and recreation. But though the subordination will not be doubted, the problem of value cannot be settled *a priori*. What is quite evident in Virginia Woolf's prose is a particular relation to objects and people (the people, below a certain class line, not really very different from objects) which makes any simple abstraction of 'imagination' impossible. This is a way of seeing the world from a precise social position: the rhythms and the language follow from what is really an uncertainty, a wonder, that depends on quite other certainties, and in particular on the writer's isolation from the very general natural and human processes, which must then be not so much described as evoked. I do not say this is an unfruitful situation. We can see how a very similar isolation, in Joyce, leads, first, to a use of language to describe, in almost tactile ways, a confusion which is a convincing consciousness, as in the passage from *Ulysses*; and, second, to what is in effect a remaking of language to dissolve all reference points (those obstinate, isolated sights, sounds and smells in Bloom's mind) into a flow of lament for what is literally a dissolving world, as in the passage from *Finnegans Wake*. But what we cannot then say is that this is uniquely the modern literary imagination; it is the necessary and convincing prose of a particular phase of consciousness, in which the temporary relation of a writer and his world is the principle of organization, to be confirmed by the paradoxical community (the remaining relation between a writer and his readers) of a shared isolation. A critic who belongs to this community will claim, understandably, a total significance for literature of this kind. The novel as a whole, under the suggestively ratifying label of 'modern', will be re-defined in its terms. But what we have really to see is a representative significance, in altering real relations.

The tension of such a position is in fact exploited, successfully, in the self-consciousness and comedy of Joyce Cary and Angus Wilson. We can feel *Ulysses* behind *The Horse's Mouth*, but with a diminution of confidence, and thence of power, that is also a recognition of the instability of what has seemed the 'imaginative' relation. Much of the overtly comic writing of recent fiction is directly related to just this uneasiness. The extreme self-consciousness of the Angus Wilson passage is an awareness of much the same problem: the 'placing' has behind it George Eliot and Forster, but though its mode is inevitable, its certainty has still further diminished, and the tone reflects just this quick, anxious strain.

When we have seen this, we can look again at those different writers who are attempting, in what is really a connected process of observation and imagination, to find a prose which is capable of including a more common experience: in which the writer is still certainly the imaginative recorder, the observing creator, but where there is no *necessary* separation between his prose and his world. The altering relations, in the history of the novel, between reporting, analysis and imaginative shaping, are of course still altering. The emergence of a number of writers from social groups with no immediate literary tradition has been very complicated, in practice. They have been affected, inevitably, by the major prose of an immediately preceding generation, but in what they are writing about, in new physical and social landscapes, they draw just as evidently on a nineteenth-century tradition in which a certain confidence of description – indeed a confidence of a knowable world – was based on an actual community between writer and subject, and thence an attainable public relation between writer and reader: a prose directly related to the ordinary language of the world.

It is as yet too early to know how these relations will develop. But we can say with some confidence that the particular achievements of Joyce and Virginia Woolf are as historical, in every real sense, as the achievements of Dickens and George Eliot. 'Modern', as what seems an endlessly persistent adjective, gives quite the wrong lead. The development we traced through Hardy and Lawrence, in which the whole problem was the relation between a received method and a changing society, is of course still active. It seems at times so difficult that it is merely exploited: in an edgy comedy or in a noisy opportunism. But here and there it is being faced, in its real significance, and new prose, new ideas, new feelings, are coming steadily through.

The point of this argument is not a sudden climax. Real development is only rarely of that kind. But we set out to consider whether the question of good prose, of what is called style, can be abstracted from the whole experience of those years in which a land and a people have been transformed. My point was to suggest, with some examples, that good prose and style are not things but relationships; that questions of method, subject and quality cannot be separated from the changing relations of men which are evident elsewhere in changing institutions and in a changing language; that to see English prose since 1780 as this real history is to make new emphases, ask different questions, and see the present as well as the past in new ways. I have only begun this discussion. It will continue elsewhere, but also, I hope, in the rest of this book: in reading and response. I shall be glad to hear what people think.

Cambridge, 1967   RAYMOND WILLIAMS

1780–1830

––––––––––⊰•⊱––––––––––

Observation

◄◄◄►►►

ON THE COMMON
(c. 1780)

ANTHONY LIDDELL was a man of very singular character,
and was noticed as such by the whole neighbourhood; but a
full account of him would far exceed the bounds I wish to set
to my narrative. He might, indeed, be called the 'village
Hampden'. The whole cast of his character was formed by the
Bible, which he had read with attention, through and through.
Acts of Parliament which appeared to him to clash with the
laws laid down in it, as the Word of God, he treated with contempt. He maintained that the fowls of the air and the fish of the
sea were free for all men; consequently, game laws, or laws to
protect the fisheries, had no weight with him. He would not,
indeed, take a salmon out of the locks on any account, but
what he could catch with his 'click-hook', in the river, he
deemed his own. As to what he could do in shooting game, he
was so inexpert, that he afforded to sportsmen many a hearty
laugh at his awkwardness; for he could shoot none till he fixed
a hay-fork in the ground to rest his piece upon. Indeed, the
very birds themselves might, by a stretch of imagination, be
supposed also to laugh at him; but his deficiencies did not
deter him from traversing over the countryside as eagerly as
other sportsmen, notwithstanding his want of success. Whatever he did was always done in open day; for, as he feared no
man, he scorned to skulk or to do anything by stealth. The
gaol had no terrors for him, for he lived better there than he
did at home; and on one occasion of his being confined when
he returned home he expressed his surprise to his neighbours,
that all the time 'he had not had a single hand's turn to do',

and exulted not a little that the opportunity had thus been given him of again reading the Bible through. He was a great reader of history, especially those parts where wars and battles were described; and, in any meetings with his neighbours, he took the lead in discourses founded on knowledge of that kind. After the Bible, 'Josephus' was his favourite author, next the 'Holy Wars' – these and 'Bishop Taylor's Sermons' composed his whole library; and his memory enabled him nearly to repeat whatever he had read. His deportment and behaviour were generally the reverse of anything like sauciness; but, except in ability and acquirements – which, indeed, commanded his respect – he treated all men as equals. When full-dressed, he wore a rusty black coat. In other respects he was like no other person. In what king's reign his hat had been made was only to be guessed at, but the flipes of it were very large. His wig was of the large curled kind, such as was worn about the period of the revolution. His waistcoat, or doublet, was made of the skin of some animal. His buckskin breeches were black and glossy with long wear, and of the same anti-quated fashion as the rest of his apparel. Thus equipt, and with his fierce look, he made a curious figure when taken before the justices of the peace; and this, together with his always – when summoned before them – undauntedly pleading his own cause, often afforded them so much amusement that it was difficult for them to keep their gravity. Others of them of a more grave deportment made use of threats to make him behave more respectfully. These he never failed to show that he despised, and on one occasion of this kind, he told the Justice that 'he was not a bit flaid of him' – that there was 'nobbit yen place that he was flaid of and that was Hell, and he could not send him there'. After this quarrel he was ordered out of court. He waited below in expectation of the Justice's following him to have the matter settled by a fight, and desired a gentleman to tell the Justice that he waited for him for that purpose. When he was told he had behaved insolently to him – 'Oh sir,' said he (spitting into his hands) 'tell him to come here – he does not know what a fellow aw is (I am).'

THOMAS BEWICK, *Memoir of Thomas Bewick by Himself* (1862).

THE DOCTRINE OF AIR
(1795)

BUT nothing of a nature foreign to the duties of my profession enagaged my attention while I was at Leeds so much as the prosecution of my experiments relating to electricity, and especially the doctrine of air. The last I was led into in consequence of inhabiting a house adjoining to a public brewery, where I at first amused myself with making experiments on the fixed air which I found ready-made in the process of fermentation. When I removed from that house I was under the necessity of making the fixed air for myself; and one experiment leading to another, as I have distinctly and faithfully noted in my various publications on the subject, I by degrees contrived a convenient apparatus for the purpose, but of the cheapest kind.

When I began these experiments, I knew very little of chemistry, and had in a manner no idea on the subject before I attended a course of chemical lectures, delivered in the academy at Warrington, by Dr Turner, of Liverpool. But I have often thought that upon the whole this circumstance was no disadvantage to me; as in this situation I was led to devise an apparatus, and processes of my own, adapted to my peculiar views. Whereas, if I had been previously accustomed to the usual chemical processes, I should not have so easily thought of any other; and without new modes of operation I should hardly have discovered anything materially new.

My first publication on the subject of air was in 1772. It was a small pamphlet on the method of impregnating water with fixed air; which being immediately translated into French, excited a great degree of attention to the subject, and this was much increased by the publication of my first paper of experiments, in a large article of the *Philosophical Transactions*, the year following, for which I received the gold medal of the Society. My method of impregnating water with fixed air was considered at a meeting of the College of Physicians, before whom I made the experiments, and by them it was recommended to the Lords of the Admiralty (by whom they had been summoned for the purpose) as likely to be of use in the sea scurvy.

The only person in Leeds who gave much attention to my experiments was Mr Hey, a surgeon. He was a zealous Methodist, and wrote answers to some of my theological tracts; but we always conversed with the greatest freedom on philosophical subjects, without mentioning anything relating to theology. When I left Leeds, he begged of me the earthen trough in which I had made all my experiments on air while I was there. It was such a one as is there commonly used for washing linen.

Having succeeded so well in the *History of Electricity*, I was induced to undertake the history of all the branches of experimental philosophy; and at Leeds I gave out proposals for that purpose, and published the *History of Discoveries Relating to Vision, Light, and Colors*. This work, also, I believe I executed to general satisfaction, and being an undertaking of great expense, I was under the necessity of publishing it by subscription. The sale, however, was not such as to encourage me to proceed with a work of so much labor and expense; so that after purchasing a great number of books, to enable me to finish my undertaking, I was obliged to abandon it, and to apply wholly to original experiments.

In writing the *History of Discoveries Relating to Vision*, I was much assisted by Mr Michell, the discoverer of the method of making artificial magnets. Living at Thornhill, not very far from Leeds, I frequently visited him, and was very happy in his society, as I also was in that of Mr Smeaton, who lived still nearer to me. He made me a present of his excellent air pump, which I constantly use to this day. Having strongly recommended his construction of this instrument, it is now generally used; whereas before that, hardly any had been made during the twenty years which had elapsed after the account that he had given of it in the *Philosophical Transactions*.

I was also instrumental in reviving the use of large electrical machines and batteries in electricity, the generality of electrical machines being little more than playthings at the time that I began my experiments. The first very large electrical machine was made by Mr Nairne, in consequence of a request made to me by the Grand Duke of Tuscany, to get him the best machine that we could make in England. This, and another that he made for Mr Vaughan, were constituted on a plan of my own. But afterwards Mr Nairne made large machines on a more simple and improved construction; and in consideration of the service which I had rendered him, he made me a present of a pretty large machine of the same kind.

The review of my *History of Electricity* by Mr Bewley, who was acquainted with Mr Michell, was the means of opening a correspondence between us, which was the source of much satisfaction to me as long as he lived. I instantly communicated to him an account of every new experiment that I made, and in return was favored with his remarks upon them. All that he published of his own were articles in the 'Appendices' to my volumes on air, all of which are ingenious and valuable. Always publishing in this manner, he used to call himself my 'satellite'. There was a vein of pleasant wit and humor in all his correspondence, which added greatly to the value of it. His letters to me would have made several volumes, and mine to him still more. When he found himself dangerously ill, he made a point of paying me a visit before he died; and he made a journey from Norfolk to Birmingham, accompanied by

Mrs Bewley, for that purpose; and after spending about a week with me, he went to his friend Dr Burney, and at his house he died.

While I was at Leeds, a proposal was made to me to accompany Captain Cook in his second voyage to the South Seas. As the terms were very advantageous, I consented to it, and the heads of my congregation had agreed to keep an assistant to supply my place during my absence. But Mr Banks informed me that I was objected to by some clergymen in the Board of Longitude, who had the direction of this business, on account of my religious principles; and presently after I heard that Dr Forster, a person far better qualified for the purpose, had got the appointment. As I had barely acquiesced in the proposal, this was no disappointment to me, and I was much better employed at home, even with respect to my philosophical pursuits. My knowledge of natural history was not sufficient for the undertaking; but at that time I should, by application, have been able to supply my deficiency, though now I am sensible I could not do it.

JOSEPH PRIESTLEY, *Memoirs of the Rev. Dr. Joseph Priestley to the year 1795. Written by Himself.*

ARTIFICIAL CAMPHOR
(1820)

ARTIFICIAL CAMPHOR. Rather heavier than water when fused – requires a higher heat than $212°$ for its volatilisation – readily fuses and is not so volatile as the new substance – burns with bright flame. It will bear fusion with potash for some minutes without decomposition. Heated with oxide of Zinc it is immediately decomposed giving mur. zinc and oil turpentine. Heated with Zinc it acts on it evolving much Mur. Acid gas, probably also hydrogen and forming Mur. Zinc and oil of turpentine which remain fluid.

Artificial camphor in chlorine – heated, partly sublimed and fused – much M. A. Gas formed, but bulk of gas not changed – hence chlorine absorbed, hydrogen evolved. Substance now seems purer than before, the first kind being probably a mixture of this with oil of turpentine. It was now not acid – volatile – crystallisable – not by any means so combustible as before, but when burning giving off very much smoke and M. A. Gas – soluble in Alcohol, etc. Acting violently on oxide of zinc making it of a very dark red or crimson colour and forming chloride of zinc – water – a little bituminous looking substance and a volatile combustible fluid matter exactly resembling in appearance and *smell* the volatile oil produced by distilling fixed oil 3 or 4 times.

Put a larger portion of the camphor into a retort and acted on it by chlorine, melting the substance in it. Nearly the whole of the gas became M. A. Gas – blew this out and put a second atmosphere in – whilst heating the substance in the retort it took fire within, the hydrogen burning and the charcoal depositing. It was only the vapour which burn[t], the portion below remaining unchanged except by a little dirt.

Put in fresh chlorine and it again burnt on heating – did so a third time – the fourth time it did not, the heat being very gently applied. The substance taken out – dissolved in alcohol – crystallised, etc. and examined proved still to be the same substance as before.

MICHAEL FARADAY, *Diary* (1820–62).

A SEA TRIP

(1801)

WE took places accordingly in the first hoy that was about to sail, and speedily found ourselves seated and moving. We thought the passengers a singularly staid set of people for holiday-makers, and could not account for it. The impression by degrees grew so strong, that we resolved to inquire into the reason; and it was with no very agreeable feelings, that we found ourselves fixed for the day on board what was called the 'Methodist hoy'. The vessel, it seems, was under the particular patronage of the sect of that denomination; and it professed to sail 'by Divine Providence'.

Dinner brought a little more hilarity into the faces of these children of heaven. One innocently proposed a game at riddles; another entertained a circle of hearers by a question in arithmetic; a third (or the same person, if I remember – a very dreary gentleman) raised his voice into some remarks on 'atheists and deists', glancing, while he did it, at the small knot of the uninitiated who had got together in self-defence; on which a fourth gave out a hymn of Dr Watts's, which says that:

> Religion never was designed
> To make our pleasure less.

It was sung, I must say, in a tone of the most impartial misery, as if on purpose to contradict the opinion.

Thus passed the hours, between formality, and eating and drinking, and psalm singing, and melancholy attempts at a little mirth, till night came on; when our godly friends vanished below into their berths. The wind was against us: we beat out to sea, and had a taste of some cold autumnal weather. Such of us as were not prepared for this, adjusted ourselves as well as we could to the occasion, or paced about the deck to warm ourselves, not a little amused with the small crew of sailors belonging to the vessel, who sat together singing songs in a low tone of voice, in order that the psalm singers below might not hear them.

During one of these pacings about the deck, my foot came in contact with a large bundle which lay as much out of the way as possible, but which I had approached unawares. On stooping to see what it was, I found it was a woman. She was sleeping, and her clothes were cold and damp. As the captain could do nothing for her, except refer me to the 'gentlefolks' below, in case any room could be made for her in their dormitory, I repaired below accordingly; and with something of a malicious benevolence, persisted in waking every sleeper in succession, and stating the woman's case. Not a soul would stir. They had paid for their places: the woman should have done the same; and so they left her to the care of the 'Providence' under which they sailed. I do not wish to insinuate by this story that many excellent people have not been Methodists. All I mean to say is, that here was a whole Margate hoy full of them; that they had feathered their nests well below; that the night was trying; that to a female it might be dangerous; and that not one of them, nevertheless, would stir to make room for her.

As Methodism is a fact of the past and of the present, I trust it may have had its uses. The degrees of it are various, from the blackest hue of what is called Calvinistic Methodism to colours little distinguishable from the mildest and pleasantest of conventional orthodoxy. Accidents of birth, breeding, brain, heart, and temperament make worlds of difference in this respect, as in all others. But where the paramount doctrine of a sect, whatever it may profess to include, is self-preservation, and where this paramount doctrine, as it needs must when actually paramount, blunts in very self-defence the greatest final sympathies with one's fellow-creatures, the transition of ideas is easy from unfeelingness in a future state to unfeelingness in the present; and it becomes a very little thing indeed to let a woman lie out in the cold all night, while saints are snoozing away in comfort.

My companion and I, much amused, and not a little indignant, took our way from Ramsgate along the coast, turning cottages into inns as our hunger compelled us, and sleeping at night the moment we laid our heads on our pillows.

LEIGH HUNT, *Autobiography* (1859).

COBBETT'S RIDE

(1821)

Marlborough, *Tuesday noon*, *Nov. 6.*

I LEFT Uphusband this morning at 9, and came across to this place (20 miles) in a post-chaise. Came up the valley of Uphusband, which ends at about 6 miles from the village, and puts one out upon the Wiltshire downs, which stretch away towards the west and south-west, towards Devizes and towards Salisbury. After about half a mile of down we came down into a level country; the flints cease, and the chalk comes nearer the top of the ground. The labourers along here seem very poor indeed. Farm houses with twenty ricks round each, besides those standing in the fields; pieces of wheat, 50, 60, or 100 acres in a piece; but a group of women labourers, who were attending the measurers to measure their reaping work, presented such an assemblage of rags as I never before saw even amongst the hoppers at Farnham, many of whom are common beggars. I never before saw *country* people, and reapers too, observe, so miserable in appearance as these. There were some very pretty girls, but ragged as colts and as pale as ashes. The day was cold too, and frost hardly off the ground; and their blue arms and lips would have made any heart ache but that of a seat-seller or a loan-jobber. A little after passing by these poor things, whom I left, cursing, as I went, those who had brought them to this state, I came to a group of shabby houses upon a hill. While a boy was watering his horses, I asked the ostler the *name* of the place; and, as the old women say, 'you might have knocked me down with a feather,' when he said, '*Great Bedwin.*' The whole of the houses are not intrinsically worth a thousand pounds. There stood a thing out in the middle of the place, about 25 feet long and 15 wide, being a room stuck up on unhewed stone pillars about 10 feet high. It was the Town Hall, where the ceremony of choosing the *two members* is performed. 'This place sends members to parliament, don't it?' said I to the ostler. 'Yes, sir.' 'Who are members *now*?' 'I *don't know*, indeed, sir.' – I have not read the *Henriade* of Voltaire for these 30 years; but in ruminating upon the ostler's answer; and in thinking how the world, yes, *the whole world*, has been deceived as to this matter, two lines of that poem came across my memory:

> Représentans du peuple, les Grands et le Roi:
> Spectacle magnifique! Source sacrée des lois!

The Frenchman, for want of understanding the THING as well as I do, left the eulogium incomplete. I therefore here add four lines, which I request those who publish future editions of the *Henriade* to insert in continuation of the above eulogium of Voltaire.

> Représentans du peuple, que celui-ci ignore,
> Sont fait à miracle pour garder son Or!
> Peuple trop heureux, que le bonheur inonde!
> L'envie de vos voisins, admiré du monde!

The first line was suggested by the ostler; the last by the words which we so very often hear from the bar, the bench, the *seats*, the pulpit, and the throne. Doubtless my poetry is not equal to that of Voltaire; but my rhyme is as good as his, and my *reason* is a great deal better. – In quitting this villainous place we see the extensive and uncommonly ugly park and domain of Lord Aylesbury, who seems to have tacked park on to park, like so many outworks of a fortified city. I suppose here are 50 or 100 farms of former days swallowed up. They have been bought, I dare say, from time to time; and it would be a labour very well worthy of reward by the public, to trace to its source, the money by which these immense domains, in different parts of the country, have been formed! – Marlborough, which is an ill-looking place enough, is succeeded, on my road to Swindon, by an extensive and very beautiful down about 4 miles over. Here nature has flung the earth about in a great variety of shapes. The fine short smooth grass has about 9 inches of mould under it, and then comes the chalk. The water that runs down the narrow side-hill valleys is caught, in different parts of the down, in basins made on purpose, and lined with clay apparently. This is for watering the sheep in summer; sure sign of a really dry soil; and yet the grass never *parches* upon these downs. The chalk holds the moisture, and the grass is fed by the dews in hot and dry weather. – At the end of this down the high-country ends. The hill is high and steep, and from it you look immediately down into a level farming country; a little further on into the dairy-country, whence the North-Wilts cheese comes; and, beyond that, into the vale of Berkshire, and even to Oxford, which lies away to the north-east from this hill. – The land continues good, flat and rather wet to Swindon, which is a plain country town, built of the stone which is found at about 6 feet under ground about here. – I come on now towards Cirencester, through the dairy country of North Wilts.

WILLIAM COBBETT, *Rural Rides* (1821).

A LETTER FROM KEATS
(1817)

MY DEAR BAILEY,

I will get over the first part of this (*unsaid*) Letter as soon as possible for it relates to the affair of poor Crips – To a Man of your nature such a Letter as Haydon's must have been extremely cutting – What occasions the greater part of the World's Quarrels? simply this, two Minds meet and do not understand each other time enough to prevent any shock or surprise at the conduct of either party – As soon as I had known Haydon three days I had got enough of his character not to have been surprised at such a Letter as he has hurt you

with. Nor when I knew it was it a principle with me to drop
his acquaintance although with you it would have been an
imperious feeling. I wish you knew all that I think about
Genius and the Heart – and yet I think you are thoroughly
acquainted with my innermost breast in that respect, or you
could not have known me even thus long and still hold me
worthy to be your dear friend. In passing however I must say
of one thing that has pressed upon me lately and encreased my
Humility and capability of submission and that is this truth –
Men of Genius are great as certain ethereal Chemicals operating on the Mass of neutral intellect – by [*for* but] they have not
any individuality, any determined Character – I would call the
top and head of those who have a proper self Men of Power –

But I am running my head into a Subject which I am
certain I could not do justice to under five years S[t]udy and
3 vols octavo – and moreover long to be talking about the
Imagination – so my dear Bailey do not think of this unpleasant
affair if possible – do not – I defy any harm to come of it – I
defy. I'll shall write to Crips this Week and request him to tell
me all his goings on from time to time by Letter whererever
I may be – it will all go on well so don't because you have
suddenly discover'd a Coldness in Haydon suffer yourself to
be teased. Do not my dear fellow. O I wish I was as certain of
the end of all your troubles as that of your momentary start
about the authenticity of the Imagination. I am certain of
nothing but of the holiness of the Heart's affections and the
truth of Imagination – What the imagination seizes as Beauty
must be truth – whether it existed before or not – for I have
the same Idea of all our Passions as of Love they are all in
their sublime, creative of essential Beauty. In a Word, you
may know my favorite Speculation by my first Book and the
little song I sent in my last – which is a representation from
the fancy of the probable mode of operating in these Matters.
The Imagination may be compared to Adam's dream – he
awoke and found it truth. I am the more zealous in this affair,

because I have never yet been able to perceive how any thing can be known for truth by consequitive reasoning – and yet it must be. Can it be that even the greatest Philosopher ever arrived at his goal without putting aside numerous objections. However it may be, O for a Life of Sensations rather than of Thoughts! It is 'a Vision in the form of Youth' a Shadow of reality to come – and this consideration has further convinced me for it has come as auxiliary to another favorite Speculation of mine, that we shall enjoy ourselves here after by having what we called happiness on Earth repeated in a finer tone and so repeated. And yet such a fate can only befall those who delight in Sensation rather than hunger as you do after Truth. Adam's dream will do here and seems to be a conviction that Imagination and its empyreal reflection is the same as human Life and its Spiritual repetition. But as I was saying – the simple imaginative Mind may have its rewards in the repeti-[ti]on of its own silent Working coming continually on the Spirit with a fine Suddenness – to compare great things with small – have you never by being Surprised with an old Melody – in a delicious place – by a delicious voice, fe[l]t over again your very Speculations and Surmises at the time it first operated on your Soul – do you not remember forming to yourself the singer's face more beautiful that [*for* than] it was possible and yet with the elevation of the Moment you did not think so – even then you were mounted on the Wings of Imagination so high – that the Prototype must be here after – that delicious face you will see. What a time! I am continually running away from the subject – sure this cannot be exactly the case with a complex Mind – one that is imaginative and at the same time careful of its fruits – who would exist partly on Sensation partly on thought – to whom it is necessary that years should bring the philosophic Mind – such an one I consider your's and therefore it is necessary to your eternal Happiness that you not only drink this old Wine of Heaven, which I shall call the redigestion of our most ethereal

Musings on Earth; but also increase in knowledge and know all things. I am glad to hear you are in a fair way for Easter – you will soon get through your unpleasant reading and then! – but the world is full of troubles and I have not much reason to think myself pesterd with many – I think Jane or Marianne has a better opinion of me than I deserve – for really and truly I do not think my Brothers illness connected with mine – you know more of the real Cause than they do nor have I any chance of being rack'd as you have been – You perhaps at one time thought there was such a thing as Worldly Happiness to be arrived at, at certain periods of time marked out – you have of necessity from your disposition been thus led away – I scarcely remember counting upon any Happiness – I look not for it if it be not in the present hour – nothing startles me beyond the Moment. The setting Sun will always set me to rights – or if a Sparrow come before my Window I take part in its existence and pick about the Gravel. The first thing that strikes me on hearing a Misfortune having befalled another is this. 'Well it cannot be helped – he will have the pleasure of trying the resources of his spirit' – and I beg now my dear Bailey that hereafter should you observe any thing cold in me not to but [*for* put] it to the account of heartlessness but abstraction – for I assure you I sometimes feel not the influence of a Passion or affection during a whole week – and so long this sometimes continues I begin to suspect myself and the genui[ne]ness of my feelings at other times – thinking them a few barren Tragedy-tears – My Brother Tom is much improved – he is going to Devonshire – whither I shall follow him – at present I am just arrived at Dorking to change the Scene – change the Air and give me a spur to wind up my Poem, of which there are wanting 500 Lines. I should have been here a day sooner but the Reynoldses persuaded me to stop in Town to meet your friend Christie. There were Rice and Martin – we talked about Ghosts. I will have some talk with Taylor and let you know – when please God I come down

at Christmas. I will find that Examiner if possible. My best
regards to Gleig. My Brothers to you and Mrs Bentley's
Your affectionate friend
John Keats –

I want to say much more to you – a few hints will set me
going.

A LONDON APARTMENT
(1820)

TOWARDS nightfall I went down to Greek Street; and found,
on taking possession of my new quarters, that the house
already contained one single inmate, a poor, friendless child,
apparently ten years old; but she seemed hunger-bitten; and
sufferings of that sort often make children look older than
they are. From this forlorn child I learned that she had slept
and lived there alone for some time before I came; and great
joy the poor creature expressed, when she found that I was in
future to be her companion through the hours of darkness.
The house could hardly be called large – that is, it was not
large on each separate storey; but, having four storeys in all,
it was large enough to impress vividly the sense of its echoing
loneliness; and, from the want of furniture, the noise of the
rats made a prodigious uproar on the staircase and hall; so
that, amidst the real fleshly ills of cold and hunger, the forsaken child had found leisure to suffer still more from the self-
created one of ghosts. Against these enemies I could promise
her protection; human companionship was in itself protection;
but of other and more needful aid I had, alas! little to offer.
We lay upon the floor, with a bundle of law-papers for a
pillow, but with no other covering than a large horseman's
cloak; afterwards, however, we discovered in a garret an
old sofa-cover, a small piece of rug, and some fragments of

other articles, which added a little to our comfort. The poor child crept close to me for warmth, and for security against her ghostly enemies. When I was not more than usually ill, I took her into my arms, so that, in general, she was tolerably warm, and often slept when I could not; for, during the last two months of my sufferings, I slept much in the daytime, and was apt to fall into transient dozings at all hours. But my sleep distressed me more than my watching; for, besides the tumultuousness of my dreams (which were only not so awful as those which I shall have hereafter to describe as produced by opium), my sleep was never more than what is called *dog-sleep*; so that I could hear myself moaning; and very often I was awakened suddenly by my own voice. About this time, a hideous sensation began to haunt me as soon as I fell into a slumber, which has since returned upon me, at different periods of my life – viz., a sort of twitching (I knew not where, but apparently about the region of the stomach), which compelled me violently to throw out my feet for the sake of relieving it. This sensation coming on as soon as I began to sleep, and the effort to relieve it constantly awaking me, at length I slept only from exhaustion; and through increasing weakness (as I said before), I was constantly falling asleep, and constantly awaking. Too generally the very attainment of any deep repose seemed as if mechanically linked to some fatal necessity of self-interruption. It was as though a cup were gradually filled by the sleepy overflow of some natural fountain, the fulness of the cup expressing symbolically the completeness of the rest: but then, in the next stage of the process, it seemed as though the rush and torrent-like babbling of the redundant waters, when running over from every part of the cup, interrupted the slumber which in their earlier stage of silent gathering they had so naturally produced. Such and so regular in its swell and its collapse – in its tardy growth and its violent dispersion – did this endless alternation of stealthy sleep and stormy awaking travel through stages as natural as the increments of twilight, or the kindlings of the dawn: no rest that was not a prologue to terror; no sweet tremulous pulses of restoration that did not suddenly explode through rolling clamours of fiery disruption. Meantime, the master of the house sometimes came in upon us suddenly, and very early; sometimes not till ten o'clock; sometimes not at all. He was in constant fear of arrest. Improving on the plan of Cromwell, every night he slept in a different quarter of London; and I observed that he never failed to examine, through a private window, the appearance of those who knocked at the door, before he would allow it to be opened. He breakfasted alone; indeed, his tea equipage would hardly have admitted of his hazarding an invitation to a second person, any more than the quantity of esculent *material*, which, for the most part, was little more than a roll, or a few biscuits, purchased on his road from the place where he had slept. Or, if he *had* asked a party, as I once learnedly observed to him, the several members of it must have *stood* in the relation to each other (not *sat* in any relation whatever) of succession, and not of co-existence; in the relation of parts of time, and not of the parts of space. During his breakfast, I generally contrived a reason for lounging in; and, with an air of as much indifference as I could assume, took up such fragments as might chance to remain; sometimes, indeed, none at all remained. In doing this, I committed no robbery, except upon Mr Brunell himself, who was thus obliged, now and then, to send out at noon for an extra biscuit; but he, through channels subsequently explained, was repaid a thousandfold; and, as to the poor child, *she* was never admitted into his study (if I may give that name to his chief depository of parchments, law-writings, etc.); that room was to her the Bluebeard room of the house, being regularly locked on his departure to dinner, about six o'clock, which usually was his final departure for the day. Whether this child were an illegitimate daughter of Mr Brunell, or only a servant, I could not ascertain; she did not herself know; but certainly she was treated altogether as a menial servant. No sooner did Mr Brunell make his appearance than she went below-stairs, brushed his shoes, coat, etc.; and, except when she was summoned to run upon some errand, she never emerged from the dismal Tartarus of the kitchens to the upper air, until my welcome knock towards nightfall called up her little trembling footsteps to the front-door. Of her life during the daytime, however, I knew little but what I gathered from her own account at night; for, as soon as the hours of business commenced, I saw that my absence would be acceptable; and, in general, therefore, I went off and sat in the parks or elsewhere until the approach of twilight.

DE QUINCEY, *The Confessions of an English Opium-Eater* (1821).

PETERLOO
(1819)

THE place appointed for the meeting was a large vacant piece of ground on the north side of St Peter's Church, which is well known in Manchester by the name of St Peter's-place. At half past 10 o'clock about 250 idle individuals might be collected within it. About half-past 11 the first body of Reformers arrived on the ground, bearing two banners, each of which was surmounted by a cap of liberty. The first bore upon a white ground the inscription of 'Annual Parliaments, and Universal Suffrage;' on the reverse side, 'No Corn Laws.' The other bore upon a blue ground the same inscription, with the addition of 'Vote by Ballot.' After these flags had been paraded over the field for some time, it was thought fit by the leaders of the party which had brought them, that they should remain stationary. A post was accordingly assigned to the bearers of them, to which shortly afterwards, a dung-cart was brought, into which the standard bearers were ordered to mount, and from which all the standards arriving afterwards were most appropriately displayed. Numerous large bodies of Reformers continued to arrive from this time to 1 o'clock, from the different towns in the neighbourhood of Manchester, all with flags, and many of them drawn up five deep, and in regular marching order. A club of female Reformers, amounting in number, according to our calculation, to 156, came from Oldham; and another, not quite so numerous, from Royton. The first bore a white silk banner, by far the most elegant displayed during the day, inscribed *Major Cartwright's Bill, Annual Parliaments, Universal Suffrage, and Vote by Ballot.* In one compartment of it was Justice, holding the scales in one hand, and a sword in the other; in another, a large eye, which we suppose was impiously intended to represent the eye of Providence. On the reverse of this flag was another inscription; but in the hurry of the day we found it impossible to decipher what it was, and can only say that there were upon it two hands, both decorated in *shirt ruffles,* clasped in each other, and underneath them an inscription, *'Oldham Union.'* The latter (i.e. the females of Royton) bore two red flags, the one inscribed, *'Let us* (i.e. women) *die like men, and not be sold like slaves'*; the other, *'Annual Parliaments and Universal Suffrage.'* The Radicals of Saddleworth brought with them a black flag to the field, on one side of which was inscribed, *'Taxation without representation is unjust and tyrannical; equal representation or death;'* on the other side, *'Union is strength. – Unite and be free. Saddleworth and Mosley Union.'* The Reformers from Rochdale and Middleton marched to the sound of the bugle, and in very regular time, closing and expanding their ranks, and marching in ordinary and double quick time, according as it pleased the fancy of their leaders to direct them. They had two green banners, between which they had hoisted on a red pole a cap of liberty, crowned with leaves of laurel, and bearing the inscription, *'Hunt and Liberty.'* Another band bore a banner, in which Britannia was represented with her trident, leaning on a shield, upon which was inscribed the motto borne by Sir William Wallace, 'God armeth the Patriot.'

In this manner the business of the day proceeded till 1 o'clock, by which time we should suppose that 80,000 people were assembled on the ground. During this period we found it impossible to approach the waggon, though very desirous to do so, as a young lad, not more than 17 or 18, was addressing the meeting with great vehemence of action and gesture, and with great effect, if we may judge from the cheers which he every now and then extracted from his audience, who were now beginning to be impatient for the arrival of Hunt, and the other orators who were to follow in his train, like the satellites which attend on some mighty planet.

The Reformers who had up to this time arrived in the field demeaned themselves becomingly, though a posse of 300 or 400 constables, with the Boroughreeve at their head, had marched in a body into the field about 12 o'clock, unsupported by any military body to all outward appearance. Not the slightest insult was offered to them. The people did indeed rush to behold them; but this was probably occasioned by an idea that they were another body of Reformers. As soon as they saw who they were, they turned away from them with a smile; and, attracted by a crowd which was advancing from another corner of the area, went to meet it, crying, 'Let us keep peace and order, and go and welcome this body, which is one of ours.'

As we stood counting the members of the Oldham Female Reform Club in their procession by us, and whilst we were internally pitying the delusion which had led them to a scene so ill-suited to their usual habits, a group of the women of Manchester, attracted by the crowd, came to the corner of the street where we had taken our post. They viewed these Female Reformers for some time with a look in which compassion and disgust were equally blended; and at last burst out into an indignant exclamation – 'Go home to your families, and leave *sike-like matters as these* to your husbands and sons, who better understand them.' The women who thus addressed them were of the lower order in life.

We had waited up to one o'clock on the field of action for the arrival of Mr Hunt; but as he had not then made his appearance, we determined to go and meet the procession, which it was said was to attend the orator. We met it just by the Exchange, where the people were cheering most loudly, and Hunt and Johnson joining in the cheers. They were seated in an open landau, along with Carlisle, Knight, and others, and had moved in grand procession from Smedley-cottage, past New-cross, and Shude-hill, preceded by a large body of male, and followed by a scarcely less numerous body of female Manchester Reformers. Before them were carried two boards, on which were inscribed, 'Order, order;' these were followed by two flags for annual Parliaments and universal suffrage, and also by Hunt's old flag and cap of liberty, of Westminster notoriety, 'Hunt, and universal suffrage.' This latter was held by a female Reformer, seated on the *dicky* of the landau, which had the honour of carrying the illustrious band of patriots whose name we have just mentioned. It was now to be exhibited in the last of its fields.

The enthusiasm excited among the crowd by the presence of the Orator was certainly beyond any thing which we ever before witnessed; and the cheers with which he was hailed were loud and lasting. When he had taken his stand upon the hustings, which were formed of two carts lashed together, and boards spread over them, he expressed considerable disapprobation of the manner in which they were formed, and of the place in which they were situated. This will not excite surprise, when we state, that it was so arranged that the speaker had to talk against the wind; and also, that on Mr Hunt's last appearance at Manchester, the hustings were so slightly built as to yield to the pressure of the superincumbent crowd, though fortunately no accident happened from their giving way. After the different persons who intended to address the multitude had taken their position upon them, and silence had been obtained, Johnson came forward, and proposed that Henry Hunt be appointed their Chairman. Here a short pause ensued, as if Johnson had expected that some person would have come forward to second his proposition. No person, however, doing so, Johnson proceeded to call upon them to carry the question by acclamation. The meeting did so, and Henry Hunt was declared Chairman, amid cheers of 3 times 3. The noise continuing longer than usual, Hunt found it requisite to entreat his friends to preserve tranquillity. He commenced his address by calling the assembly 'gentlemen,' but afterwards changed the term to 'fellow countrymen.' He had occasion, he said, to entreat their indulgence. (*Noise continued.*) Every man wishing to hear, must himself keep silence. (*Laughter, but no silence.*) 'Will you,' said he, addressing himself to the mob, 'be so obliging as not to call silence while the business of the day is proceeding?' (*Silence was then obtained.*) He hoped that they would now exercise the all-powerful right of the people; and if any person would not be quiet, that they would put him down and keep him quiet. (*We will.*) For the honour which they had just conferred upon him, he returned them his most sincere thanks: and for any services which he either had or might render them, all that he asked was, that they would indulge him with a calm and patient attention. It was impossible for him to think that with the utmost silence he could make himself heard by every member of the numerous and tremendous meeting which he saw assembled before him. If those, however, who were near him were not silent, how could it be expected that those who were at a distance could hear what he should say? [*A dead silence now pervaded the multitude.*] It was useless for him to recall to their recollection the proceedings of the last 10 days in their town; they were all of them acquainted with the cause of the late meeting being postponed; and it would be therefore superfluous in him to say any thing about it, except, indeed, it were this – that those who had attempted to put them down by the most malignant exertions had occasioned them to meet that day in more than twofold numbers. (*Hear.*) (Knight here whispered something into Mr Hunt's ear, which caused him to turn round with some degree of asperity to Knight, and to say, 'Sir, I will not be interrupted: when you speak yourself, you will not like to experience such interruption.') They would have perceived, that since the old meeting had been put off, and the present one had been called – though their enemies flattered themselves with having obtained a victory, they showed by this that they had sustained a defeat. (*Long and loud applause.*) In the interval between the two meetings, two placards had been circulated, to which the names of two obscure individuals were attached: the first was signed by Tom Long or Jack Short, a printer in the town whom nobody knew.

At this stage of the business the Yeomanry Cavalry were seen advancing in a rapid trot to the area: their ranks were in disorder, and on arriving within it, they halted to breathe their horses, and to recover their ranks. A panic seemed to strike the persons at the outskirts of the meeting, who immediately began to scamper in every direction. After a moment's pause, the cavalry drew their swords, and brandished them fiercely in the air: upon which Hunt and Johnson desired the multitude to give three cheers, to show the military that they were not to be daunted in the discharge of their duty by their unwelcome presence. This they did upon which Mr Hunt again proceeded. This was a mere trick to interrupt the proceedings of the meeting: but he trusted that they would all stand firm. He had scarcely said these words, before the Manchester Yeomanry Cavalry rode into the mob which gave way before them, and directed their course to the cart from which Hunt was speaking. Not a brickbat was thrown at them – not a pistol was fired during this period: all was quiet and orderly, as if the cavalry had been the friends of the multitude, and had marched as such into the midst of them. A bugle-man went at their head, then an officer, and then came the whole troop. They wheeled round the waggons till they came in front of them, the people drawing back in every direction on their approach. After they had surrounded them in such a manner as to prevent all escape, the *officer* who commanded the detachment went up to Mr Hunt, and said, brandishing his sword, 'Sir, I have a warrant against you, and arrest you as my prisoner.' Hunt, after exhorting the people to tranquillity in a few words, turned round to the officer, and said, 'I willingly surrender myself to any civil officer who will show me his warrant.' Mr Nadin, the chief police officer at Manchester, then came forward and said, 'I will arrest you; I have got informations upon oath against you,' or something to that effect. The military officer then proceeded to say, that he had a warrant against Johnson. Johnson also asked for a civil-officer, upon which a Mr Andrew came forward, and Hunt and Johnson then leaped from off the waggon, and surrendered themselves to the civil power. Search was then made for Moorhouse and Knight, against whom warrants had also been issued. In the hurry of this transaction, they had by some means or other contrived to make their escape. As soon as Hunt and Johnson had jumped from the waggon, a cry was made by the cavalry, 'Have at their flags.' In consequence, they immediately dashed not only at the flags which were in the waggon, but those which were posted among the crowd, cutting most indiscriminately to the right and to the left in order to get at them. This set the people running in all directions, and it was not till this act had been committed that any brick-bats were hurled at the military. From that moment the Manchester Yeomanry Cavalry lost all command of temper. A person of the name of Saxton, who is, we believe, the editor of the *Manchester Observer*, was standing in the cart. Two privates rode up to him. 'There,' said one of them, 'is that villain, Saxton; do you run him through the body.' 'No,' replied the other, 'I had rather not – I leave it to you.' The man immediately made a lunge at Saxton, and it was only by slipping aside that the blow missed his life. As it was, it cut his coat and waistcoat, but fortunately did him no other injury. A man within five yards of us in another direction had his nose completely taken off by a blow of a sabre; whilst another was laid prostrate, but whether he was dead or had merely thrown himself down to obtain protection we cannot say. Seeing all this hideous work going on, we felt an alarm which any man may be forgiven for feeling in a similar situation: looking around us, we saw a constable at no great distance, and thinking that our only chance of safety rested in placing ourselves under his protection, we appealed to him for assistance. He immediately took us into custody, and on our saying that we merely attended to report the proceedings of the day, he replied, 'Oh, oh! You then are one of their writers – you must go before the Magistrates.' To this we made no objection; in consequence he took us to the house where they were sitting, and in our road thither, we saw a woman on the ground, insensible, to all outward appearance, and with two large gouts of blood on her left breast. Just as we came to the house, the constables were conducting Hunt into it, and were treating him in a manner in which they were neither justified by law nor humanity, striking him with their staves on the head. After he had been taken into the house, we were admitted also; and it is only justice to the man who apprehended us to state, that he did every thing in his power to protect us from all ill-usage, and showed us every civility consistent with his duty. In the room into which we were put, we found the Orator, Johnson, Saxton, and some other individuals of minor note, among whom was another woman in a fainting condition. Nadin the constable was also there. Hunt and Johnson both asked him to show them the warrants on which they had been apprehended. This he refused to do, saying that he had information upon oath against them, which was quite sufficient for him. Hunt then called upon the persons present to mark Nadin's refusal. Shortly after this transaction, Mr Hay, the chairman of the magistrates, came into the apartment, and asked Hunt if he was afraid to go down to the New Bailey; if he was, he himself would accompany him, and look after his safety. Hunt, who we forgot to mention had received a slight sabre wound on one of his hands, said, that he should have no objection to the Magistrate's company; he certainly did not like either a cut from a sabre or a blow from a staff, both of which had been dealt out to him in no small quantity. Mr Hay shortly afterwards went out, having first made a reply to Mr Hunt, which some riot out of doors prevented us from hearing. On casting our eyes at the place where the immense multitude had lately been assembled, we were surprised in the short space of ten minutes to see it cleared of all its former occupiers, and filled by various troops of military, both horse and foot. Shortly after this had occurred, a Magistrate came into the room, and bade the prisoners prepare to march off to the New Bailey. Hunt was consigned to the custody of Col. l'Estrange, of the 31st foot, and a detachment of the 15th Hussars; and under his care, he and all the other prisoners, who were each placed between two constables, reached the New Bailey in perfect safety. The staffs of two of Hunt's banners were carried in mock procession before him.

JOHN WILLIAM TYAS, *The Times* (19 August 1819).

RADICALS BEFORE THE
PRIVY COUNCIL
(1817)

ABOUT four o'clock in the afternoon we were conveyed in four coaches to the Secretary of State's office at Whitehall. On our arrival we were divided into two parties of four and four, and each party was placed in a separate room. A gentleman now appeared, who asked severally our names and occupations, which he wrote in a book, and then retired. In a short time another person came and called my name, and I rose and followed him along a darkish passage. I must confess that this part of the proceedings gave rise to some feelings of incertitude and curiosity, and brought to my recollection some matters which I had read when a boy about the Inquisition in Spain. My conductor knocked at a door and was told to go in, which he did, and delivered me to an elderly gentleman, whom I recognised as Sir Nathaniel Conant. He asked my christian and surname, which were given: he then advanced to another door, and desiring me to follow him, he opened it, and, bowing to a number of gentlemen seated at a long table covered with green cloth, he repeated my name and took his place near my left hand. The room was a large one, and grandly furnished, according to my notions of such matters. Two large windows, with green blinds and rich curtains, opened upon a richer curtain of nature – some trees, which were in beautiful leaf. The chimney-piece was of carved marble, and on the table were many books; and several persons sat there assiduously writing, whilst others fixed attentive looks upon me. I was motioned to advance to the bottom of the table, and did so: and the gentleman who sat at the head of the table said I was brought there by virtue of a warrant issued by him in consequence of my being suspected of high treason; that I should not be examined at that time, but must be committed to close confinement until that day se'nnight, when I should again be brought up for examination. Meantime, if I had anything to say on my own behalf, or any request to make, I was at liberty to do so; but I must observe they did not require me to say anything.

The person who addressed me was a tall, square, and bony figure, upwards of fifty years of age, I should suppose, and with thin and rather grey hair; his forehead was broad and prominent, and from their cavernous orbits looked mild and intelligent eyes. His manner was affable, and much more encouraging to freedom of speech than I had expected. On his left sat a gentleman whom I never made out; and next him again was Sir Samuel Shepherd, the Attorney-General, I think, for the time, who frequently made use of an ear trumpet. On Lord Sidmouth's right, for such was the gentleman who had been speaking to me, sat a good-looking person in a plum-coloured coat, with a gold ring on the small finger of his left hand, on which he sometimes leaned his head as he eyed me over – this was Lord Castlereagh.

'My lord,' I said, addressing the president, 'having been brought from home without a change of linen, I wish to be informed how I shall be provided for in that respect until I can be supplied from home?' The Council conferred a short time, and Lord Sidmouth said I should be supplied with whatever was necessary. I next asked, should I be allowed freely to correspond with my wife and child, inform them of my situation, and to receive their letters, provided such letters did not contain political information?

'You will be allowed to communicate with your family,' said his lordship; 'but I trust you will see the necessity of confining yourself to matters of a domestic nature. You will always write in the presence of a person who will examine your letters; you will, therefore, do well to be guarded in your correspondence, as nothing of an improper tendency will be suffered to pass. I speak this for your own good.'

'Could I be permitted to have pen, ink, and paper in prison?' I asked; 'and could I be allowed to keep a small day-book, or journal, for my amusement?'

'It is an indulgence,' was the reply, 'which has never been granted to any State prisoner; and as I do not see any reason for departing from the established rule, I should feel it my painful duty to refuse it.'

I said I had heard that the Suspension Act contained a clause securing to State prisoners the right of sending petitions to

Parliament; and I wished to be informed if there were such a clause.

His lordship said the Suspension Act did not contain any such clause, but the power to petition would be allowed by his Majesty's ministers, and I should have that liberty whenever I thought proper to use it. I bowed and retired.

The other prisoners were then severally called in and informed of the cause of their arrest, in the same terms that I had been; and that they would be again examined on that day se'nnight. All of them afterwards declared they had not made any statement or disclosure of any description; but that, according to the agreement mentioned, they had remained silent as to the purpose of their meetings. One characteristic incident was, however, said to have occurred before the Privy Council. On the doctor being asked how he spelled his surname, he answered in broad Lancashire, 'Haitch, hay, haa, I, hay, y' (H, e, a, l, e, y), but the pronunciation of the e and a being different in London, there was some boggling about reducing the name to writing, and a pen and paper were handed to him. The doctor knew that his *forte* lay not in feats of penmanship any more than in spelling; and to obviate any small embarrassment on that account, he pulled out an old pocket-book, and took from it one of his prescription labels, on which the figures of a pestle and mortar were imposed from a rudely engraved plate, and these words, 'Joseph Healey, Surgeon, Middleton. Plase take — tablespoonfuls of this mixture each — hours.' This he handed to Lord Sidmouth, who, as may be supposed, received it graciously, looked it carefully over, smiled, and read it again, and passed it round the Council table. Presently they were all tittering, and the doctor stood quite delighted at finding them such a set of merry gentlemen. The fact was, the first blank had been originally filled with a figure of two, 'Plase take 2 tablespoonfuls,' &c., but some mischievous wag had inserted two ciphers after the figure, and made it read '200 tablespoonfuls of this mixture each two hours.' However it was, the doctor certainly imbibed a favourable opinion of the Council. The circumstance was supposed to have transpired from his own lips; and I certainly had seen such a card in his possession before he went to London, but I never saw it afterwards.

In the same vehicle which brought us to the Home Office, we were next taken to the prison at Coldbath Fields, and placed in the inner lodge until a ward could be got ready for our occupation. O'Connor, who was unwell, and whose legs were swollen and painful from the gout and his chains, was taken from us and put into a sick ward, as was also Robert Ridings, who was likewise in delicate health, and who, being already incipiently consumptive, died soon after his return, from colds, as he thought, taken during his journey homewards.

Whilst we were in the lodge, Evans the younger, one of the London reformers – who, as well as his father, was confined in this prison under the Suspension Act – came to the gate to speak with a friend. Samuel Drummond also, who has been mentioned as being apprehended at the Blanket meeting, was walking in a courtyard, seemingly in good health and spirits.

When our place was ready a turnkey conducted the six of us who remained together through a number of winding passages to a flagged yard, into which opened a good room, or cell, about ten yards in length and three in width. On each side of the room were three beds, placed in what might be termed wooden troughs; at the head of the room a good fire was burning, and we found a stock of coal and wood to recruit it at our pleasure. There were also a number of chairs, a table, candles, and other requisites; so that, had it not been for the grating at the window above the door, and the arched roof, bound by strong bars of iron, we might have fancied ourselves to be in a comfortable barrack. After surveying the place thoroughly, and striking the walls to ascertain if they were hollow, we stirred up the fire, drew our seats to the hearth, and spent the evening in conversing about our families and friends until the hour of rest, when we concluded by singing 'The Union Hymn,' which I led for that purpose.

SAMUEL BAMFORD, *Passages in the Life of a Radical* (1840-44).

BRIGHTON
(1824)

'BRIGHTON, May 29th. The dignitary of the Church seems to have forgotten the dignitary of the easel. . . . I am busy here, but I dislike the place, and miss any letter from you. I am, however, getting on with my French affairs; one of the largest is quite complete, and is my best in sparkle with repose, which is my struggle just now. Brighton is the receptacle of the fashion and off-scouring of London. The magnificence of the sea, and its, to use your own beautiful expression, "everlasting voice", is drowned in the din and tumult of stage coaches, gigs, flys, etc., and the beach is only Piccadilly or worse by the seaside. Ladies dressed and undressed; gentlemen in morning-gowns and slippers, or without them or anything else, about knee deep in the breakers; footmen, children, nursery-maids, dogs, boys, fishermen, and Preventive Service men with hangers and pistols; rotten fish, and those hideous amphibious animals, the old bathing-women, whose language, both in oaths and voice, resembles men, all mixed together in endless and indecent confusion. The genteeler part, or Marine Parade, is still more unnatural, with its trimmed and neat appearance, and the dandy jetty or Chain Pier, with its long and elegant strides into the sea a full quarter of a mile.' (*Here the writing is interrupted by a sketch.*) 'In short, there is nothing here for a painter but the breakers and the sky, which have been lovely indeed, and always varying. The fishing-boats here are not so picturesque as the Hastings boats; the difference is this.' (*Here a sketch.*) 'But these subjects are so hacknied in the Exhibition, and are indeed so little capable of the beautiful sentiment that belongs to landscape, that they have done a great deal of harm. They form a class of art much easier than landscape, and have, in consequence, almost supplanted it. While in the fields, for I am at the west of this city, and quite out of it, I met with a most intelligent and elegant-minded man, Mr Phillips. We became intimate, and he contributes much to our pleasure here. He is a botanist, and all his works on Natural History are instructive and entertaining, calculated for children of all ages; his *History of Trees* is delightful. We are at No. 9, Mrs Sober's Gardens, so called from Mrs Sober, the lady of the manor; she has built a chapel; and a man who was taken before the magistrates quite drunk, when asked what he was, said he was "one of Mrs Sober's congregation". Last Tuesday, the finest day that ever was, we went to the Dyke, which is, in fact, the remains of a Roman encampment, overlooking one of the grandest natural landscapes in the world, and consequently a scene the most unfit for a picture. It is the business of a painter not to contend with nature, and put such a scene, a valley filled with imagery fifty miles long, on a canvas of a few inches; but to make something out of nothing, in attempting which, he must almost of necessity become poetical; but you understand all this better than I. My wife and children are delightfully well.'

JOHN CONSTABLE, Letter in *Memoirs of Constable*, C. R. Leslie (1845).

Imagination

◄◄─►►

ON THE RUN
(1794)

I HAD not stood up in this manner two minutes, before I heard the sound of feet, and presently saw the ordinary turnkey and another pass the place of my retreat. They were so close to me that, if I had stretched out my hand, I believe I could have caught hold of their clothes without so much as changing my posture. As no part of the overhanging earth intervened between me and them, I could see them entire, though the deepness of the shade rendered me almost completely invisible. I heard them say to each other, in tones of vehement asperity, 'Curse the rascal! Which way can he be gone?' The reply was, 'Damn him! I wish we had him but safe once again!' – 'Never fear!' rejoined the first, 'he cannot have above half a mile the start of us.' They were presently out of hearing; for, as to sight, I dared not advance my body, so much as an inch, to look after them, lest I should be discovered by my pursuers in some other direction. From the very short time that elapsed, between my escape and the appearance of these men, I concluded that they had made their way through the same outlet as I had done, it being impossible that they could have had time to come from the gate of the prison, and so round a considerable part of the town, as they must otherwise have done.

I was so alarmed at this instance of diligence on the part of the enemy, that, for some time, I scarcely ventured to proceed an inch from my place of concealment, or almost to change my posture. The morning, which had been bleak and drizzly, was succeeded by a day of heavy and incessant rain; and the gloomy state of the air and surrounding objects, together with the extreme nearness of my prison, and a total want of food, caused me to pass the hours in no very agreeable sensations. This inclemency of the weather however, which generated a feeling of stillness and solitude, encouraged me by degrees to change my retreat, for another of the same nature, but of somewhat greater security. I hovered with little variation about a single spot, as long as the sun continued above the horizon.

Towards evening, the clouds began to disperse, and the moon shone, as on the preceding night, in full brightness. I had perceived no human being during the whole day, except in the instance already mentioned. This had perhaps been owing to the nature of the day; at all events I considered it as too hazardous an experiment, to venture from my hiding-place in so clear and fine a night. I was therefore obliged to wait for the setting of this luminary, which was not till near five o'clock in the morning. My only relief during this interval was to allow myself to sink to the bottom of my cavern, it being scarcely possible for me to continue any longer on my feet. Here I fell into an interrupted and unrefreshing doze, the consequence of a laborious night, and a tedious, melancholy day; though I rather sought to avoid sleep, which, cooperating with the coldness of the season, would tend more to injury than advantage.

The period of darkness, which I had determined to use for the purpose of removing to a greater distance from my prison, was, in its whole duration, something less than three hours. When I rose from my seat, I was weak with hunger and fatigue, and, which was worse, I seemed, between the dampness of the preceding day, and the sharp, clear frost of the night, to have lost the command of my limbs. I stood up and shook myself; I leaned against the side of the hill, impelling in different directions the muscles of the extremities; and at length recovered in some degree the sense of feeling. This operation was attended with an incredible aching pain, and required no common share of resolution to encounter and prosecute it. Having quitted my retreat, I at first advanced with weak and tottering steps; but, as I proceeded, increased my pace. The barren heath, which reached to the edge of the town, was, at least on this side, without a path; but the stars shone, and guiding myself by them, I determined to steer as far as possible from the hateful scene where I had been so long confined. The line I pursued was of irregular surface, sometimes obliging me to climb a steep ascent, and at others to go down into a dark and impenetrable dell. I was often compelled, by the dangerousness of the way, to deviate considerably from the direction I wished to pursue. In the mean time I advanced with as much rapidity, as these and similar obstacles would permit me to do. The swiftness of the motion, and the thinness of the air, restored to me my alacrity. I forgot the inconveniences under which I laboured, and my mind became lively, spirited, and enthusiastic.

I had now reached the border of the heath, and entered upon what is usually termed the forest. Strange as it may seem, it is nevertheless true, that, in this conjuncture, exhausted with hunger, destitute of all provision for the future, and surrounded with the most alarming dangers, my mind suddenly became glowing, animated, and cheerful. I thought that, by this time, the most formidable difficulties of my undertaking were surmounted; and I could not believe that, after having effected so much, I should find any thing invincible in what remained to be done. I recollected the confinement I had undergone, and the fate that had impended over me, with horror. Never did man feel more vividly, than I felt at that moment, the sweets of liberty. Never did man more strenuously prefer poverty with independence, to the artificial allurements of a life of slavery. I stretched forth my arms with rapture; I clapped my hands one upon the other, and exclaimed, 'Ah, this is indeed to be a man! These wrists were lately galled with fetters; all my motions, whether I rose up or sat down, were echoed to with the clanking of chains; I was tied down like a wild beast, and could not move but in a circle of a few feet in circumference. Now I can run fleet as a grey-hound, and leap like a young roe upon the mountains. Oh, God! (if God there be that condescends to record the lonely beatings of an anxious heart) thou only canst tell with what delight a prisoner, just broke forth from his dungeon, hugs the blessings of new-found liberty! Sacred and indescribable moment, when man regains his rights! But lately I held my life in jeopardy, because one man was unprincipled enough to assert what he knew to be false; I was destined to suffer an early and inexorable death from the hands of others, because none of them had penetration enough to distinguish from falsehood, what I uttered with the entire conviction of a full-fraught heart! Strange, that men from age to age should con-sent to hold their lives at the breath of another, merely that each in his turn may have a power of acting the tyrant accord-ing to law! Oh, God! give me poverty! shower upon me all the imaginary hardships of human life! I will receive them all with thankfulness. Turn me a prey to the wild beasts of the desert, so I be never again the victim of man dressed in the gore-dripping robes of authority! Suffer me at least to call life and the pursuits of life my own! Let me hold it at the mercy of the elements, of the hunger of beasts or the revenge of barbarians, but not of the cold-blooded prudence of monopolists and kings!' – How enviable was the enthusiasm, which could thus furnish me with energy, in the midst of hunger, poverty and universal desertion!

WILLIAM GODWIN, *The Adventures of Caleb Williams or Things as They are* (1794).

WAVERLEY HONOUR
(1814)

THESE letters, as might have been expected, highly excited Waverley's indignation. From the desultory style of his studies, he had not any fixed political opinion to place in opposition to the movements of indignation which he felt at his father's supposed wrongs. Of the real cause of his disgrace, Edward was totally ignorant; nor had his habits at all led him to investigate the politics of the period in which he lived, or remark the intrigues in which his father had been so actively engaged. Indeed, any impressions which he had accidentally adopted concerning the parties of the times, were (owing to the society in which he had lived at Waverley Honour) of a nature rather unfavourable to the existing government and dynasty. He entered, therefore, without hesitation, into the resentful feeling of the relations who had the best title to dictate his conduct; and not perhaps the less willingly, when he remembered the tædium of his quarters, and the inferior figure which he had made among the officers of his regiment. If he could have had any doubt upon the subject, it would have been decided by the following letter from his commanding officer, which, as it is very short, shall be inserted verbatim:

SIR,

Having carried somewhat beyond the line of my duty, an indulgence which even the lights of nature, and much more those of Christianity, direct towards errors which may arise from youth and inexperience, and that, altogether without effect, I am reluctantly compelled, at the present crisis, to use the only remaining remedy which is in my power. You are, therefore, hereby commanded to repair to —, the headquarters of the regiment, within three days after the date of this letter. If you shall fail to do so, I must report you to the

War Office as absent without leave, and also take other steps, which
will be disagreeable to you, as well as to,

> Sir,
>
> Your obedient Servant,
> J. GARDINER, Lieut.-Col.
> Commanding the — Regt. Dragoons.

Edward's blood boiled within him as he read this letter.
He had been accustomed from his very infancy to possess, in
a great measure, the disposal of his own time, and thus
acquired habits which rendered the rules of military discipline as unpleasing to him in this as they were in some other
respects. An idea that in his own case they would not be
enforced in a very rigid manner, had also obtained full possession of his mind, and had hitherto been sanctioned by the
indulgent conduct of his lieutenant-colonel. Neither had anything occurred, to his knowledge, that should have induced
his commanding officer, without any other warning than the
hints we noticed at the end of the fourteenth chapter, so
suddenly to assume a harsh, and, as Edward deemed it, so
insolent a tone of dictatorial authority. Connecting it with
the letters he had just received from his family, he could not
but suppose, that it was designed to make him feel, in his
present situation, the same pressure of authority which had
been exercised in his father's case, and that the whole was a
concerted scheme to depress and degrade every member of
the Waverley family.

Without a pause, therefore, Edward wrote a few cold lines,
thanking his lieutenant-colonel for past civilities, and expressing regret that he should have chosen to efface the remembrance of them, by assuming a different tone towards him.
The strain of his letter, as well as what he (Edward) conceived
to be his duty, in the present crisis, called upon him to lay
down his commission; and he therefore enclosed the formal
resignation of a situation which subjected him to so unpleasant

a correspondence, and requested Colonel Gardiner would have the goodness to forward it to the proper authorities.

Having finished this magnanimous epistle, he felt somewhat uncertain concerning the terms in which his resignation ought to be expressed, upon which subject he resolved to consult Fergus Mac-Ivor. It may be observed in passing, that the bold and prompt habits of thinking, acting, and speaking, which distinguished this young Chieftain, had given him a considerable ascendency over the mind of Waverley. Endowed with at least equal powers of understanding, and with much finer genius, Edward yet stooped to the bold and decisive activity of an intellect which was sharpened by the habit of acting on a preconceived and regular system, as well as by extensive knowledge of the world.

When Edward found his friend, the latter had still in his hand the newspaper which he had perused, and advanced to meet him with the embarrassment of one who has unpleasing news to communicate. 'Do your letters, Captain Waverley, confirm the unpleasing information which I find in this paper?'

He put the paper into his hand, where his father's disgrace was registered in the most bitter terms, transferred probably from some London journal. At the end of the paragraph was this remarkable innuendo:

'We understand that "this same *Richard* who hath done all this," is not the only example of the *Wavering Honour* of W-v-r-l-y H-n-r. See the Gazette of this day.'

With hurried and feverish apprehension our hero turned to the place referred to, and found therein recorded, 'Edward Waverley, captain in — regiment dragoons, superseded for absence without leave'; and in the list of military promotions, referring to the same regiment, he discovered this further article, 'Lieut. Julius Butler, to be captain, *vice* Edward Waverley superseded.'

Our hero's bosom glowed with the resentment which

undeserved and apparently premeditated insult was calculated to excite in the bosom of one who had aspired after honour, and was thus wantonly held up to public scorn and disgrace. Upon comparing the date of his colonel's letter with that of the article in the Gazette, he perceived that his threat of making a report upon his absence had been literally fulfilled, and without inquiry, as it seemed, whether Edward had either received his summons, or was disposed to comply with it. The whole, therefore, appeared a formed plan to degrade him in the eyes of the public; and the idea of its having succeeded filled him with such bitter emotions, that, after various attempts to conceal them, he at length threw himself into Mac-Ivor's arms, and gave vent to tears of shame and indignation.

It was none of this Chieftain's faults to be indifferent to the wrongs of his friends; and for Edward, independent of certain plans with which he was connected, he felt a deep and sincere interest. The proceeding appeared as extraordinary to him as it had done to Edward. He indeed knew of more motives than Waverley was privy to for the peremptory order that he should join his regiment. But that, without further inquiry into the circumstances of a necessary delay, the commanding officer, in contradiction to his known and established character, should have proceeded in so harsh and unusual a manner, was a mystery which he could not penetrate. He soothed our hero, however, to the best of his power, and began to turn his thoughts on revenge for his insulted honour.

Edward eagerly grasped at the idea. 'Will you carry a message for me to Colonel Gardiner, my dear Fergus, and oblige me for ever?'

Fergus paused: 'It is an act of friendship which you should command, could it be useful, or lead to the righting your honour; but in the present case, I doubt if your commanding officer would give you the meeting on account of his having taken measures, which, however harsh and exasperating, were still within the strict bounds of his duty. Besides, Gardiner is a precise Huguenot, and has adopted certain ideas about the sinfulness of such rencontres, from which it would be impossible to make him depart, especially as his courage is beyond all suspicion. And besides, I – I, to say the truth – I dare not at this moment, for some very weighty reasons, go near any of the military quarters or garrisons belonging to this government.'

'And am I,' said Waverley, 'to sit down quiet and contented under the injury I have received?'

'That will I never advise my friend,' replied Mac-Ivor. 'But I would have vengeance to fall on the head, not on the hand; on the tyrannical and oppressive government which designed and directed these premeditated and reiterated insults, not on the tools of office which they employed in the execution of the injuries they aimed at you.'

'On the government?' said Waverley.

'Yes,' replied the impetuous Highlander, 'on the usurping House of Hanover, whom your grandfather would no more have served than he would have taken wages of redhot gold from the great fiend of hell!'

'But since the time of my grandfather two generations of this dynasty have possessed the throne,' said Edward coolly.

'True,' replied the Chieftain; 'and because we have passively given them so long the means of showing their native character, – because both you and I myself have lived in quiet submission, have even truckled to the times so far as to accept commissions under them, and thus have given them an opportunity of disgracing us publicly by resuming them, are we not on that account to resent injuries which our fathers only apprehended, but which we have actually sustained? Or is the cause of the unfortunate Stewart family become less just, because their title has devolved upon an heir who is innocent of the charges of misgovernment brought against his father? – Do you remember the lines of your favourite poet? –

> Had Richard unconstrain'd resign'd the throne,
> A king can give no more than is his own;
> The title stood entail'd had Richard had a son.

You see, my dear Waverley, I can quote poetry as well as Flora and you. But come, clear your moody brow, and trust to me to show you an honourable road to a speedy and glorious revenge. Let us seek Flora, who perhaps has more news to tell us of what has occurred during our absence. She will rejoice to hear that you are relieved of your servitude. But first add a postscript to your letter, marking the time when you received this calvinistical Colonel's first summons, and express your regret that the hastiness of his proceedings prevented your anticipating them by sending your resignation. Then let him blush for his injustice.'

The letter was sealed accordingly, covering a formal resignation of the commission, and Mac-Ivor despatched it with some letters of his own by a special messenger, with charge to put them into the nearest post-office in the Lowlands.

WALTER SCOTT, *Waverley* (1814).

CASTLE RACKRENT
(1800)

As to affording it, God knows it was little they knew of the matter; my lady's few thousands could not last for ever, especially the way she went on with them, and letters from tradesfolk came every post thick and threefold, with bills as long as my arm of years and years standing; my son Jason had 'em all handed over to him, and the pressing letters were all unread by Sir Condy, who hated trouble and could never be brought to hear talk of business, but still put it off and put it off, saying – settle it any how, or bid 'em call again tomorrow, or speak to me about it some other time. – Now it was hard to find the right time to speak, for in the mornings he was a-bed and in the evenings over his bottle, where no gentleman chuses to be disturbed. – Things in a twelve-month or so came to such a pass, there was no making a shift to go on any longer, though we were all of us well enough used to live from hand to mouth at Castle Rackrent. One day, I remember, when there was a power of company, all sitting after dinner in the dusk, not to say dark, in the drawing-room, my lady having rung five times for candles and none to go up, the housekeeper sent up the footman, who went to my mistress and whispered behind her chair how it was. – 'My lady (says he) there are no candles in the house.' – 'Bless me, (says she) then take a horse, and gallop off as fast as you can to Carrick O'Fungus and get some.' – 'And in the mean time tell them to step into the play-house, and try if there are not some bits left,' added Sir Condy, who happened to be within hearing. The man was sent up again to my lady, to let her know there was no horse to go but one that wanted a shoe. – 'Go to Sir Condy, then, I know nothing at all about the horses, (said my lady) why do you plague me with these things?' – How it was settled I really forget, but to the best of my remembrance, the boy was sent down to my son Jason's to borrow candles for the night. Another time in the winter, and on a desperate cold day, there was no turf in for the parlour and above stairs, and scarce enough for the cook in the kitchen, the little *gossoon* was sent off to the neighbours to see and beg or borrow some, but none could he bring back with him for love or money; so as needs must we were forced to trouble Sir Condy – 'Well, and if there's no turf to be had in the town or country, why what signifies talking any more about it, can't ye go and cut down a tree?' – 'Which tree, please your honour?' I made bold to say. – 'Any tree at all that's good to burn, (said Sir Condy); send offsmart, and get one down and the fires lighted before my lady gets up to breakfast, or the house will be too hot to hold us.' – He was always very considerate in all things about my lady, and she wanted for nothing whilst he had it to give. – Well, when things were tight with them about this time, my son Jason put in a word again about the lodge, and made a genteel offer to lay down the purchase money to relieve Sir Condy's distresses. – Now Sir Condy had it from the best authority, that there were two writs come down to the Sheriff against his person, and the Sheriff, as ill luck would have it, was no friend of his, and talked how he must do his duty, and how he would do it, if it was against the first man in the county, or even his own brother, let alone one who had voted against him at the last election, as Sir Condy had done. – So Sir Condy was fain to take the purchase money of the lodge from my son Jason to settle matters; and sure enough it was a good bargain for both parties, for my son bought the fee simple of a good house for him and his heirs for ever for little or nothing, and by selling of it for that same my master saved himself from a gaol. Every way it turned out fortunate for Sir Condy; for before the money was all gone there came a general election, and he being so well beloved in the county, and one of the oldest families, no one had a better right to stand candidate for the vacancy; and he was called upon by all his friends, and the whole county I may say, to declare himself against the old member, who had little thought of a contest. My master did not relish the thoughts of a troublesome canvas, and all the ill will he might bring upon himself by disturbing the peace of the country, besides the expence, which was no trifle; but all his friends called upon one another to subscribe, and formed themselves into a committee, and wrote all his circular letters for him, and engaged all his agents, and did all the business unknown to him, and he was well pleased that it should be so at last, and my lady herself was very sanguine about the election, and there was open house kept night and day at Castle Rackrent, and I thought I never saw my lady look so well in her life as she did at that time; there were grand dinners, and all the gentlemen drinking success to Sir Condy till they were carried off; and then dances and balls, and the ladies all finishing with a raking pot of tea in the morning. Indeed it was well the company made it their choice to sit up all nights, for there was not half beds enough for the sights of people that were in it, though there were shake downs in the drawing-room always made up before sun-rise, for those that liked it. For my part, when I saw the doings that were going on, and the loads of claret that went down the throats of them that had no right to be asking for it, and the sights of meat that went up to table and never came down, besides what was carried off to one or t'other below stairs, I couldn't but pity my poor master who was to pay for all, but I said nothing for fear of gaining myself ill will. The day of election will come some time or other, says I to myself, and all will be over – and so it did, and a glorious day it was as any I ever had the happiness to see; huzza! huzza! Sir Condy Rackrent for ever, was the first thing I hears in the morning, and the same and nothing else all day, and not a soul sober only just when polling, enough to give their votes as became 'em, and to stand the brow-beating of the lawyers who came tight enough upon us; and many of our freeholders were knocked off, having never a freehold that they could safely swear to, and Sir Condy was not willing to have any man perjure himself for his sake, as was done on the other side, God knows, but no matter for that. – Some of our friends were dumb-founded, by the lawyers asking them – had they ever been upon the ground where their freeholds lay? – Now Sir Condy being tender of the consciences of them that had not been on the ground, and so could not swear to a freehold when cross-examined by them lawyers, sent out for a couple of cleaves-full of the sods of his farm of Gulteeshinnagh: and as soon as the sods came into town he set each man upon his sod, and so then ever after, you know, they could fairly swear they had been upon the ground. – We gained the day by this piece of honesty. I thought I should have died in the streets for joy when I seed my poor master chaired, and he bare-headed and it raining as hard as it could pour; but all the crowds following him up and down, and he bowing and shaking hands with the whole town. – 'Is that Sir Condy Rackrent in the chair?' says a stranger man in the crowd – 'The same,' says I – 'who else should it be? God bless him!' – 'And I take it then you belong to him,' says he. – 'Not at all,' (says I) 'but I live under him, and have done so these two hundred years and upwards, me and mine.' – 'It's luck for you, then,' rejoins he, 'that he is where he is, for was he any where else but in the chair this minute he'd be in a worse place, for I was sent down on purpose to put him up, and here's my order for so doing in my pocket.' – It was a writ that villain the wine merchant had marked against my poor master, for some hundreds of an old debt which it was a shame to be talking of at such a time as this. – 'Put it in your pocket again, and think no more of it any ways for seven years to come, my honest friend, (says I), he's a member a Parliament now, praised be God, and such as you can't touch him; and if you'll take a fool's advice, I'd have ye keep out of the way this day, or you'll run a good chance of getting your deserts amongst my master's friends, unless you chuse to drink his health like every body else.' – 'I've no objection to that in life,' said he; so we went into one of the public houses kept open for my master, and we had a great deal of talk about this thing and that.

MARIA EDGEWORTH, *Castle Rackrent* (1800).

A COTTON MILL IS BUILT
(1821)

IT had been often remarked by ingenious men, that the Brawl burn, which ran through the parish, though a small, was yet a rapid stream, and had a wonderful capability for damming, and to turn mills. From the time that the Irville water deserted its channel this brook grew into repute, and several mills and dams had been erected on its course. In this year a proposal came from Glasgow to build a cottonmill on its banks, beneath the Witch-linn, which being on a corner of the Wheatrig, the property of Mr Cayenne, he not only consented thereto, but took a part in the profit or loss therein; and, being a man of great activity, though we thought him, for many a day, a serpent-plague sent upon the parish, he proved thereby one of our greatest benefactors. The cottonmill was built, and a spacious fabric it was – nothing like it had been seen before in our day and generation – and, for the people that were brought to work in it, a new town was built in the vicinity, which Mr Cayenne, the same being founded on his land, called Cayenneville, the name of the plantation in Virginia that had been taken from him by the rebellious Americans. From that day Fortune was lavish of her favours upon him; his property swelled, and grew in the most extraordinary manner, and the whole country side was stirring with a new life. For, when the mill was set a-going, he got weavers of muslin established in Cayenneville; and shortly after, but that did not take place till the year following, he brought women all the way from the neighbourhood of Manchester, in England, to teach the lassie bairns in our old clachan tambouring.

Some of the ancient families, in their turreted houses, were not pleased with this innovation, especially when they saw the handsome dwellings that were built for the weavers of the mills, and the unstinted hand that supplied the wealth required for the carrying on of the business. It sank their pride into insignificance, and many of them would almost rather have wanted the rise that took place in the value of their lands, than have seen this incoming of what they called o'er-sea speculation. But, saving the building of the cottonmill, and the beginning of Cayenneville, nothing more memorable happened in this year, still it was nevertheless a year of a great activity. The minds of men were excited to new enterprises; a new genius, as it were, had descended upon the earth, and there was an erect and outlooking spirit abroad that was not to be satisfied with the taciturn regularity of ancient affairs. Even Miss Sabrina Hooky, the schoolmistress, though now waned from her meridian, was touched with the enlivening rod, and set herself to learn and to teach tambouring, in such a manner as to supersede by precept and example that old time-honoured functionary, as she herself called it, the spinning-wheel, proving, as she did one night to Mr Kibbock and me, that, if more money could be made by a woman tambouring than by spinning, it was better for her to tambour than to spin.

But, in the midst of all this commercing and manufacturing, I began to discover signs of decay in the wonted simplicity of our country ways. Among the cotton-spinners and muslin weavers of Cayenneville were several unsatisfied and ambitious spirits, who clubbed together, and got a London newspaper to the Cross-Keys, where they were nightly in the habit of meeting and debating about the affairs of the French, which were then gathering towards a head. They were represented to me as lads by common in capacity, but with unsettled notions of religion. They were, however, quiet and orderly; and some of them since, at Glasgow, Paisley, and Manchester, even, I am told, in London, have grown into a topping way.

It seems they did not like my manner of preaching, and on that account absented themselves from public worship; which, when I heard, I sent for some of them, to convince them of their error with regard to the truth of divers points of doctrine; but they confounded me with their objections, and used my arguments, which were the old and orthodox proven opinions of the Divinity Hall, as if they had been the light sayings of a vain man. So that I was troubled, fearing that some change would ensue to my people, who had hitherto lived amidst the boughs and branches of the gospel un-molested by the fowler's snare, and I set myself to watch narrowly, and with a vigilant eye, what would come to pass.

There was a visible increase among us of worldly prosperity in the course of this year; insomuch that some of the farmers, who were in the custom of taking their vendibles to the neighbouring towns on the Tuesdays, the Wednesdays, and Fridays, were led to open a market on the Saturdays in our own clachan, the which proved a great convenience. But I cannot take it upon me to say, whether this can be said to have well begun in the present Ann. Dom., although I know that in the summer of the ensuing year it was grown into a settled custom; which I well recollect by the Macadams coming with their bairns to see Mrs Malcolm, their mother, suddenly on a Saturday afternoon; on which occasion me and Mrs Bal-whidder were invited to dine with them, and Mrs Malcolm bought in the market for the dinner that day, both mutton and fowls, such as twenty years before could not have been got for love or money on such a pinch. Besides, she had two bottles of red and white wine from the Cross-Keys, luxuries which, saving in the Breadland House in its best days, could not have been had in the whole parish, but must have been brought from a borough town; for Eaglesham Castle is not within the bounds of Dalmailing, and my observe does not apply to the stock and stores of that honourable mansion, but only to the dwellings of our own heritors, who were in general straitened in their circumstances, partly with upsetting, and partly by the eating rust of family pride, which hurt the edge of many a clever fellow among them, that would have done well in the way of trade, but sunk into divors for the sake of their genteelity.

JOHN GALT, *Annals of the Parish* (1821).

IMPROVEMENT AT UPPERCROSS

(1818)

UPPERCROSS was a moderate-sized village, which a few years back had been completely in the old English style, containing only two houses superior in appearance to those of the yeomen and labourers; the mansion of the squire, with its high walls, great gates, and old trees, substantial and unmodernized, and the compact, tight parsonage, enclosed in its own neat garden, with a vine and a pear-tree trained round its casements; but upon the marriage of the young squire, it had received the improvement of a farm-house, elevated into a cottage, for his residence, and Uppercross Cottage, with its veranda, French windows, and other prettinesses, was quite as likely to catch the traveller's eye as the more consistent and considerable aspect and premises of the Great House, about a quarter of a mile farther on.

Here Anne had often been staying. She knew the ways of Uppercross as well as those of Kellynch. The two families were so continually meeting, so much in the habit of running in and out of each other's house at all hours, that it was rather a surprise to her to find Mary alone; but being alone, her being unwell and out of spirits was almost a matter of course. Though better endowed than the elder sister, Mary had not Anne's understanding nor temper. While well, and happy, and properly attended to, she had great good humour and excellent spirits; but any indisposition sunk her completely. She had no resources for solitude; and, inheriting a considerable share of the Eliot self-importance, was very prone to add to every other distress that of fancying herself neglected and ill-used. In person, she was inferior to both sisters, and had, even in her bloom, only reached the dignity of being 'a fine girl'. She was now lying on the faded sofa of the pretty little drawing-room,

the once elegant furniture of which had been gradually growing shabby under the influence of four summers and two
children; and, on Anne's appearing, greeted her with –

'So you are come at last! I began to think I should never see
you. I am so ill I can hardly speak. I have not seen a creature
the whole morning!'

'I am sorry to find you unwell,' replied Anne. 'You sent
me such a good account of yourself on Thursday.'

'Yes, I made the best of it; I always do: but I was very far
from well at the time; and I do not think I ever was so ill in
my life as I have been all this morning: very unfit to be left
alone, I am sure. Suppose I were to be seized of a sudden in
some dreadful way, and not able to ring the bell! So Lady
Russell would not get out. I do not think she has been in this
house three times this summer.'

Anne said what was proper, and inquired after her husband.
'Oh! Charles is out shooting. I have not seen him since seven
o'clock. He would go, though I told him how ill I was. He
said he should not stay out long; but he has never come back,
and now it is almost one. I assure you I have not seen a soul
this whole long morning.'

'You have had your little boys with you?'

'Yes, as long as I could bear their noise; but they are so
unmanageable that they do me more harm than good. Little
Charles does not mind a word I say, and Walter is growing
quite as bad.'

'Well, you will soon be better now,' replied Anne, cheer-
fully. 'You know I always cure you when I come. How are
your neighbours at the Great House?'

'I can give you no account of them. I have not seen one of
them today, except Mr Musgrove, who just stopped and
spoke through the window, but without getting off his horse;
and though I told him how ill I was, not one of them have
been near me. It did not happen to suit the Miss Musgroves,
I suppose, and they never put themselves out of their way.'

'You will see them yet, perhaps, before the morning is gone. It is early.'

'I never want them, I assure you. They talk and laugh a great deal too much for me. Oh! Anne, I am so very unwell! It was quite unkind of you not to come on Thursday.'

'My dear Mary, recollect what a comfortable account you sent me of yourself! You wrote in the cheerfulest manner, and said you were perfectly well, and in no hurry for me; and that being the case, you must be aware that my wish would be to remain with Lady Russell to the last: and besides what I felt on her account, I have really been so busy, have had so much to do, that I could not very conveniently have left Kellynch sooner.'

'Dear me! what can *you* possibly have had to do?'

'A great many things, I assure you. More than I can recollect in a moment; but I can tell you some. I have been making a duplicate of the catalogue of my father's books and pictures. I have been several times in the garden with Mackenzie, trying to understand, and make him understand, which of Elizabeth's plants are for Lady Russell. I have had all my own little concerns to arrange, books and music to divide, and all my trunks to repack, from not having understood in time what was intended as to the waggons: and one thing I have had to do, Mary, of a more trying nature – going to almost every house in the parish, as a sort of take-leave. I was told that they wished it; but all these things took up a great deal of time.'

'Oh, well!' and after a moment's pause, 'but you have never asked me one word about our dinner at the Pooles yesterday.'

'Did you go, then? I have made no inquiries, because I concluded you must have been obliged to give up the party.'

'Oh yes! I went. I was very well yesterday; nothing at all the matter with me till this morning. It would have been strange if I had not gone.'

'I am very glad you were well enough, and I hope you had a pleasant party.'

'Nothing remarkable. One always knows beforehand what the dinner will be, and who will be there; and it is so very uncomfortable not having a carriage of one's own. Mr and Mrs Musgrove took me, and we were so crowded! They are both so very large, and take up so much room; and Mr Musgrove always sits forward. So there was I crowded into the back seat with Henrietta and Louisa; and I think it very likely that my illness today may be owing to it.'

A little farther perseverance in patience and forced cheerfulness on Anne's side produced nearly a cure on Mary's. She could soon sit upright on the sofa, and began to hope she might be able to leave it by dinner-time. Then, forgetting to think of it, she was at the other end of the room, beautifying a nosegay; then she ate her cold meat; and then she was well enough to propose a little walk.

'Where shall we go?' said she, when they were ready. 'I suppose you will not like to call at the Great House before they have been to see you?'

'I have not the smallest objection on that account,' replied Anne. 'I should never think of standing on such ceremony with people I know so well as Mrs and the Miss Musgroves.'

'Oh! but they ought to call upon you as soon as possible. They ought to feel what is due to you as *my* sister. However, we may as well go and sit with them a little while, and when we have got that over, we can enjoy our walk.'

Anne had always thought such a style of intercourse highly imprudent; but she had ceased to endeavour to check it, from believing that, though there were on each side continual subjects of offence, neither family could now do without it. To the Great House accordingly they went, to sit the full half-hour in the old-fashioned square parlour, with a small carpet and shining floor, to which the present daughters of the house were gradually giving the proper air of confusion by a grand pianoforte and a harp, flower-stands, and little tables placed in every direction. Oh! could the originals of the portraits against the wainscot, could the gentlemen in brown velvet and the ladies in blue satin have seen what was going on, have been conscious of such an overthrow of all order and neatness! The portraits themselves seemed to be staring in astonishment.

The Musgroves, like their houses, were in a state of alteration, perhaps of improvement. The father and mother were in the old English style, and the young people in the new. Mr and Mrs Musgrove were a very good sort of people; friendly and hospitable, not much educated, and not at all elegant. Their children had more modern minds and manners. There was a numerous family; but the only two grown up, excepting Charles, were Henrietta and Louisa, young ladies of nineteen and twenty, who had brought from a school at Exeter all the usual stock of accomplishments, and were now, like thousands of other young ladies, living to be fashionable, happy, and merry. Their dress had every advantage, their faces were rather pretty, their spirits extremely good, their manners unembarrassed and pleasant; they were of consequence at home, and favourites abroad. Anne always contemplated them as some of the happiest creatures of her acquaintance: but still, saved, as we all are, by some comfortable feeling of superiority from wishing for the possibility of exchange, she would not have given up her own more elegant and cultivated mind for all their enjoyments; and envied them nothing but that seemingly perfect good understanding and agreement together, that good-humoured, mutual affection, of which she had known so little herself with either of her sisters.

JANE AUSTEN, *Persuasion* (1818).

A PROPOSAL
(1816)

EMMA could not bear to give him pain. He was wishing to confide in her – perhaps to consult her; cost her what it would, she would listen. She might assist his resolution, or reconcile him to it; she might give just praise to Harriet, or, by representing to him his own independence, relieve him from that state of indecision which must be more intolerable than any alternative to such a mind as his. They had reached the house.

'You are going in, I suppose?' said he.

'No,' replied Emma, quite confirmed by the depressed manner in which he still spoke, 'I should like to take another turn. Mr Perry is not gone.' And, after proceeding a few steps, she added – 'I stopped you ungraciously, just now, Mr Knightley, and, I am afraid, gave you pain. But if you have any wish to speak openly to me as a friend, or to ask my opinion of anything that you may have in contemplation – as a friend, indeed, you may command me. I will hear whatever you like. I will tell you exactly what I think.'

'As a friend!' repeated Mr Knightly. 'Emma, that, I fear, is a word – no, I have no wish. Stay, yes, why should I hesitate? I have gone too far already for concealment. Emma, I accept your offer, extraordinary as it may seem, I accept it, and refer myself to you as a friend. Tell me, then, have I no chance of ever succeeding?'

He stopped in his earnestness to look the question, and the expression of his eyes overpowered her.

'My dearest Emma,' said he, 'for dearest you will always be, whatever the event of this hour's conversation, my dearest, most beloved Emma – tell me at once. Say "No," if it is to be said.' She could really say nothing. 'You are silent,' he cried, with great animation; 'absolutely silent! at present I ask no more.'

Emma was almost ready to sink under the agitation of this moment. The dread of being awakened from the happiest dream was perhaps the most prominent feeling.

'I cannot make speeches, Emma,' he soon resumed, and in a tone of such sincere, decided, intelligible tenderness as was tolerably convincing. 'If I loved you less, I might be able to talk about it more. But you know what I am. You hear nothing but truth from me. I have blamed you, and lectured you, and you have borne it as no other woman in England would have borne it. Bear with the truths I would tell you now, dearest Emma, as well as you have borne with them. The manner, perhaps, may have as little to recommend them. God knows, I have been a very indifferent lover. But you understand me. Yes, you see, you understand my feelings – and will return them if you can. At present, I ask only to hear – once to hear your voice.'

While he spoke, Emma's mind was most busy, and, with all the wonderful velocity of thought, had been able – and yet without losing a word – to catch and comprehend the exact truth of the whole; to see that Harriet's hopes had been entirely groundless, a mistake, a delusion, as complete a delusion as any of her own – that Harriet was nothing; that she was everything herself; that what she had been saying relative to Harriet had been all taken as the language of her own feelings; and that her agitation, her doubts, her reluctance, her discouragement, had been all received as discouragement from herself. And not only was there time for these convictions, with all their glow of attendant happiness, there was time also to rejoice that Harriet's secret had not escaped her, and to resolve that it need not, and should not. It was all the service she could now render her poor friend; for as to any of that heroism of sentiment which might have prompted her to entreat him to transfer his affection from herself to Harriet, as infinitely the most worthy of the two – or even the more simple sublimity of resolving to refuse him at once and for ever, without vouchsafing any motive because he could not marry them both, Emma had it not. She felt for Harriet, with pain and contrition; but no flight of generosity run mad, opposing all that could be probable or reasonable, entered her brain. She had led her friend astray, and it would be a reproach to her for ever; but her judgment was as strong as her feelings, and as strong as it had ever been before, in reprobating any such alliance for him, as most unequal and degrading. Her way was clear, though not quite smooth. She spoke then, on being so entreated. What did she say? Just what she ought, of course. A lady always does. She said enough to show there need not be despair – and to invite him to say more himself. He *had* despaired at one period; he had received such an injunction to caution and silence, as for the time crushed every hope – she had begun by refusing to hear him. The change had perhaps been somewhat sudden – her proposal of taking another turn, her renewing the conversation which she had just put an end to, might be a little extraordinary. She felt its inconsistency; but Mr Knightley was so obliging as to put up with it, and seek no further explanation.

Seldom, very seldom, does complete truth belong to any human disclosure; seldom can it happen that something is not a little disguised, or a little mistaken; but where, as in this case, though the conduct is mistaken, the feelings are not, it may not be very material. Mr Knightley could not impute to Emma a more relenting heart than she possessed, or a heart more disposed to accept of his.

He had, in fact, been wholly unsuspicious of his own in-fluence. He had followed her into the shrubbery with no idea of trying it. He had come, in his anxiety to see how she bore Frank Churchill's engagement, with no selfish view, no view at all, but of endeavouring, if she allowed him an opening, to soothe or to counsel her. The rest had been the work of the moment, the immediate effect of what he heard, on his feelings.

The delightful assurance of her total indifference towards Frank Churchill, of her having a heart completely disengaged from him, had given birth to the hope that, in time, he might gain her affection himself; but it had been no present hope; he had only, in the momentary conquest of eagerness over judgment, aspired to be told that she did not forbid his attempt to attach her. The superior hopes which gradually opened were so much the more enchanting. The affection which he had been asking to be allowed to create, if he could, was already his. Within half an hour he had passed from a thoroughly distressed state of mind, to something so like perfect happiness, that it could bear no other name.

Her change was equal. This one half-hour had given to each the same precious certainty of being beloved, had cleared from each the same degree of ignorance, jealousy, or distrust. On his side, there had been a long-standing jealousy, old as the arrival or even the expectation of Frank Churchill. He had been in love with Emma, and jealous of Frank Churchill, from about the same period, one sentiment having probably enlightened him as to the other. It was his jealousy of Frank Churchill that had taken him from the country. The Box Hill party had decided him on going away. He would save himself from witnessing again such permitted, encouraged attentions. He had gone to learn to be indifferent. But he had gone to a wrong place. There was too much domestic happiness in his brother's house; woman wore too amiable a form in it; Isabella was too much like Emma – differing only in those striking inferiorities which always brought the other in brilliancy before him, for much to have been done even had his time been longer. He had stayed on, however, vigorously, day after day – till this very morning's post had conveyed the history of Jane Fairfax. Then, with the gladness which must be felt, nay, which he did not scruple to feel, having never believed Frank Churchill to be at all deserving Emma, was there so much fond solicitude, so much keen anxiety for her, that he could stay no longer. He had ridden home through the rain; and walked up directly after dinner, to see how this sweetest and best of all creatures, faultless in spite of all her faults, bore the discovery.

He had found her agitated and low. Frank Churchill was a villain. He heard her declare that she had never loved him. Frank Churchill's character was not desperate. She was his own Emma, by hand, and word, when they returned into the house; and if he could have thought of Frank Churchill then, he might have deemed him a very good sort of fellow.

JANE AUSTEN, *Emma* (1816).

A ROMANTIC PERSONALITY
(1818)

SHORTLY after the disastrous termination of Scythrop's passion for Miss Emily Girouette, Mr Glowry found himself, much against his will, involved in a lawsuit, which compelled him to dance attendance on the High Court of Chancery. Scythrop was left alone at Nightmare Abbey. He was a burnt child, and dreaded the fire of female eyes. He wandered about the ample pile, or along the garden-terrace, with 'his cogitative faculties immersed in cogibundity of cogitation'. The terrace terminated at the south-western tower, which, as we have said, was ruinous and full of owls. Here would Scythrop take his evening seat, on a fallen fragment of mossy stone, with his back resting against the ruined wall, – a thick canopy of ivy, with an owl in it, over his head, – and the Sorrows of Werther in his hand. He had some taste for romance reading before he went to the university, where, we must confess, in justice to his college, he was cured of the love of reading in all its shapes; and the cure would have been radical, if disappointment in love, and total solitude, had not conspired to bring on a relapse. He began to devour romances and German tragedies, and, by the recommendation of Mr Flosky, to pore over ponderous tomes of transcendental philosophy, which reconciled him to the labour of studying them by their mystical jargon and necromantic imagery. In the congenial solitude of Nightmare Abbey, the distempered ideas of metaphysical romance and romantic metaphysics had ample time and space to germinate into a fertile crop of chimeras, which rapidly shot up into vigorous and abundant vegetation.

He now became troubled with the *passion for reforming the world.* He built many castles in the air, and peopled them with secret tribunals, and bands of illuminati, who were always the imaginary instruments of his projected regeneration of the human species. As he intended to institute a perfect republic, he invested himself with absolute sovereignty over these mystical dispensers of liberty. He slept with Horrid Mysteries under his pillow, and dreamed of venerable eleutherarchs and ghastly confederates holding midnight conventions in subterranean caves. He passed whole mornings in his study, immersed in gloomy reverie, stalking about the room in his nightcap, which he pulled over his eyes like a cowl, and folding his striped calico dressing-gown about him like the mantle of a conspirator.

'Action,' thus he soliloquised, 'is the result of opinion, and to new-model opinion would be to new-model society. Knowledge is power; it is in the hands of a few, who employ it to mislead the many, for their own selfish purposes of aggrandisement and appropriation. What if it were in the hands of a few who should employ it to lead the many? What if it were universal, and the multitude were enlightened? No. The many must be always in leading-strings; but let them have wise and honest conductors. A few to think, and many to act; that is the only basis of perfect society. So thought the ancient philosophers: they had their esoterical and exoterical doctrines. So thinks the sublime Kant, who delivers his oracles in language which none but the initiated can comprehend. Such were the views of those secret associations of illuminati, which were the terror of superstition and tyranny, and which, carefully selecting wisdom and genius from the great wilderness of society, as the bee selects honey from the flowers of the thorn and the nettle, bound all human excellence in a chain, which, if it had not been prematurely broken, would have commanded opinion, and regenerated the world.'

Scythrop proceeded to meditate on the practicability of reviving a confederation of regenerators. To get a clear view of his own ideas, and to feel the pulse of the wisdom and genius of the age, he wrote and published a treatise, in which his meanings were carefully wrapt up in the monk's hood of transcendental technology, but filled with hints of matter deep and dangerous, which he thought would set the whole nation in a ferment; and he awaited the result in awful expectation, as a miner who has fired a train awaits the explosion of a rock. However, he listened and heard nothing; for the explosion, if any ensued, was not sufficiently loud to shake a single leaf of the ivy on the towers of Nightmare Abbey; and some months afterwards he received a letter from his bookseller, informing him that only seven copies had been sold, and concluding with a polite request for the balance.

Scythrop did not despair. 'Seven copies,' he thought, 'have been sold. Seven is a mystical number, and the omen is good. Let me find the seven purchasers of my seven copies, and they shall be the seven golden candle-sticks with which I will illuminate the world.'

Scythrop had a certain portion of mechanical genius, which his romantic projects tended to develop. He constructed models of cells and recesses, sliding panels and secret passages, that would have baffled the skill of the Parisian police. He took the opportunity of his father's absence to smuggle a dumb carpenter into the Abbey, and between them they gave reality to one of these models in Scythrop's tower. Scythrop foresaw that a great leader of human regeneration would be involved in fearful dilemmas, and determined, for the benefit of mankind in general, to adopt all possible precautions for the preservation of himself.

The servants, even the women, had been tutored into silence. Profound stillness reigned throughout and around the Abbey, except when the occasional shutting of a door would peal in long reverberations through the galleries, or the heavy tread of the pensive butler would wake the hollow echoes of the hall. Scythrop stalked about like the grand inquisitor, and the servants flitted past him like familiars. In his evening meditations on the terrace, under the ivy of the ruined tower, the only sounds that came to his ear were the rustling of the wind in the ivy, the plaintive voices of the feathered choristers, the owls, the occasional striking of the Abbey clock, and the monotonous dash of the sea on its low and level shore. In the mean time, he drank Madeira, and laid deep schemes for a thorough repair of the crazy fabric of human nature.

THOMAS LOVE PEACOCK, *Nightmare Abbey* (1818).

Argument

◄┤◄►┤►

THE CONTRACT OF SOCIETY
(1790)

SOCIETY is indeed a contract. Subordinate contracts for objects of mere occasional interest may be dissolved at pleasure – but the state ought not to be considered nothing better than a partnership agreement in a trade of pepper and coffee, calico or tobacco, or some other such low concern, to be taken up for a little temporary interest, and to be dissolved by the fancy of the parties. It is to be looked on with other reverence; because it is not a partnership in things subservient only to the gross animal existence of a temporary and perishable nature. It is a partnership in all science; a partnership in all art; a partnership in every virtue, and in all perfection. As the ends of such a partnership cannot be obtained in many generations, it becomes a partnership not only between those who are living, but between those who are living, those who are dead, and those who are to be born. Each contract of each particular state is but a clause in the great primeval contract of eternal society, linking the lower with the higher natures, connecting the visible and invisible world, according to a fixed compact sanctioned by the inviolable oath which holds all physical and all moral natures, each in their appointed place. This law is not subject to the will of those, who by an obligation above them, and infinitely superior, are bound to submit their will to that law. The municipal corporations of that universal kingdom are not morally at liberty at their pleasure, and on their speculations of a contingent improvement wholly to separate and tear asunder the bands of their subordinate community, and to dissolve it into an unsocial, uncivil, unconnected chaos of elementary principles. It is the first and supreme necessity only, a necessity that is not chosen, but chooses, a necessity paramount to deliberation, that admits no discussion, and demands no evidence, which alone can justify a resort to anarchy. This necessity is no exception to the rule; because this necessity itself is a part too of that moral and physical disposition of things, to which man must be obedient by consent of force: but if that which is only submission to necessity should be made the object of choice, the law is broken, nature is disobeyed, and the rebellious are outlawed, cast forth, and exiled, from this world of reason, and order, and peace, and virtue, and fruitful penitence, into the antagonist world of madness, discord, vice, confusion, and unavailing sorrow.

EDMUND BURKE, *Reflections on the Revolution in France* (1790).

PREJUDICE AND DOCTRINE
(1790)

YOU see, sir, that in this enlightened age I am bold enough to confess, that we are generally men of untaught feelings; that, instead of casting away all our old prejudices, we cherish them to a very considerable degree, and, to take more shame to ourselves, we cherish them because they are prejudices; and the longer they have lasted and the more generally they have prevailed, the more we cherish them. We are afraid to put men to live and trade each on his own private stock of reason; because we suspect that the stock in each man is small, and that the individuals would do better to avail themselves of the general bank and capital of nations and of ages. Many of our men of speculation, instead of exploding general prejudices, employ their sagacity to discover the latent wisdom which prevails in them. If they find what they seek, and they seldom fail, they think it more wise to continue the prejudice, with the reason involved, than to cast away the coat of prejudice, and to leave nothing but the naked reason; because prejudice, with its reason, has a motive to give action to that reason, and an affection which will give it permanence. Prejudice is of ready application in the emergency; it previously engages the mind in a steady course of wisdom and virtue, and does not leave the man hesitating in the moment of decision, sceptical, puzzled, and unresolved. Prejudice renders a man's virtue his habit: and not a series of unconnected acts. Through just prejudice, his duty becomes a part of his nature.

Your literary men, and your politicians, and so do the whole clan of the enlightened among us, essentially differ in these points. They have no respect for the wisdom of others; but they pay it off by a very full measure of confidence in their own. With them it is a sufficient motive to destroy an old scheme of things, because it is an old one. As to the new, they are in no sort of fear with regard to the duration of a building run up in haste; because duration is no object to those who think little or nothing has been done before their time, and who place all their hopes in discovery. They conceive, very systematically, that all things which give perpetuity are mischievous, and therefore they are at inexpiable war with all establishments. They think that government may vary like modes of dress, and with as little ill effect; that there needs no principle of attachment, except a sense of present conveniency, to any constitution of the state. They always speak as if they were of opinion that there is a singular species of compact between them and their magistrates, which binds the magistrate, but which has nothing reciprocal in it, but that the majesty of the people has a right to dissolve it without any reason but its will. Their attachment to their country itself is only so far as it agrees with some of their fleeting projects; it begins and ends with that scheme of polity which falls in with their momentary opinion.

These doctrines, or rather sentiments, seem prevalent with

your new statesmen. But they are wholly different from those on which we have always acted in this country.

I hear it is sometimes given out in France, that what is doing among you is after the example of England. I beg leave to affirm that scarcely anything done with you has originated from the practice or the prevalent opinions of this people, either in the act or in the spirit of the proceeding. Let me add that we are as unwilling to learn these lessons from France, as we are sure that we never taught them to that nation. The cabals here, who take a sort of share in your transactions as yet consist of but a handful of people. If unfortunately by their intrigues, their sermons, their publications, and by a confidence derived from an expected union with the counsels and forces of the French nation, they should draw considerable numbers into their faction, and in consequence should seriously attempt anything here in imitation of what has been done with you, the event, I dare venture to prophesy, will be that, with some trouble to their country, they will soon accomplish their own destruction. This people refused to change their law in remote ages from respect to the infallibility of popes; and they will not now alter it from a pious implicit faith in the dogmatism of philosophers; though the former was armed with the anathema and crusade, and though the latter should act with the libel and the lamp-iron.

Formerly your affairs were your own concern only. We felt for them as men; but we kept aloof from them, because we were not citizens of France. But when we see the model held up to ourselves, we must feel as Englishmen, and feeling, we must provide as Englishmen. Your affairs, in spite of us, are made a part of our interest; so far at least as to keep at a distance your panacea, or your plague. If it be a panacea, we do not want it. We know the consequences of unnecessary physic. If it be a plague; it is such a plague that the precautions of the most severe quarantine ought to be established against it.

EDMUND BURKE, *Reflections on the Revolution in France* (1790).

REVOLUTION AND OUTRAGE
(1791)

IN the tremendous breaking forth of a whole people, in which all degrees, tempers, and characters are confounded, delivering themselves by a miracle of exertion from the destruction meditated against them, is it to be expected that nothing will happen? When men are sore with the sense of oppressions, and menaced with the prospect of new ones, is the calmness of philosophy or the palsy of insensibility to be looked for? Mr Burke exclaims against outrage; yet the greatest is that which himself has committed. His book is a volume of outrage, not apologized for by the impulse of a moment, but cherished through a space of ten months; yet Mr Burke had no provocation, no life, no interest at stake.

More of the citizens fell in this struggle than of their opponents; but four or five persons were seized by the populace and instantly put to death; the Governor of the Bastille, and the Mayor of Paris, who was detected in the act of betraying them; and afterwards Foulon, one of the new ministry, and Berthier, his son-in-law, who had accepted the office of intendant of Paris. Their heads were stuck upon spikes, and carried about the city; and it is upon this mode of punishment that Mr Burke builds a great part of his tragic scenes. Let us therefore examine how men came by the idea of punishing in this manner.

They learn it from the governments they live under, and retaliate the punishments they have been accustomed to behold. The heads stuck upon spikes, which remained for years upon Temple Bar, differed nothing in the horror of the scene from those carried about upon spikes at Paris; yet this was done by the English government. It may perhaps be said that it signifies nothing to a man what is done to him after he is dead; but it signifies much to the living; it either tortures their feelings or hardens their hearts, and in either case it instructs them how to punish when power falls into their hands.

Lay then the axe to the root, and teach governments humanity. It is their sanguinary punishments which corrupt mankind. In England the punishment in certain cases is by *hanging, drawing,* and *quartering*: the heart of the sufferer is cut out and held up to the view of the populace. In France, under the former government, the punishments were not less barbarous. Who does not remember the execution of Damien, torn to pieces by horses? The effect of those cruel spectacles exhibited to the populace is to destroy tenderness or excite revenge; and by the base and false idea of governing men by terror, instead of reason, they become precedents. It is over the lowest class of mankind that government by terror is intended to operate, and it is on them that it operates to the worst effect. They have sense enough to feel they are the objects aimed at; and they inflict in their turn the examples of terror they have been instructed to practise.

There is in all European countries a large class of people of that description, which in England is called the '*mob*'. Of this class were those who committed the burnings and devastations in London in 1780, and of this class were those who carried the heads upon spikes in Paris. Foulon and Berthier were taken up in the country, and sent to Paris, to undergo their examination at the Hotel de Ville; for the National Assembly, immediately on the new ministry coming into office, passed a decree, which they communicated to the King and Cabinet, that they (the National Assembly) would hold the ministry, of which Foulon was one, responsible for the measures they were advising and pursuing; but the mob, incensed at the appearance of Foulon and Berthier, tore them from their conductors before they were carried to the Hotel de Ville, and executed them on the spot. Why then does Mr Burke charge outrages of this kind on a whole people? As well may he charge the riots and outrages of 1780 on all the people of London, or those in Ireland on all his countrymen.

But everything we see or hear offensive to our feelings and derogatory to the human character should lead to other reflections than those of reproach. Even the beings who commit them have some claim to our consideration. How then is it that such vast classes of mankind as are distinguished by the appellation of the vulgar, or the ignorant mob, are so numerous in all old countries? The instant we ask ourselves this question, reflection feels an answer. They arise, as an unavoidable consequence, out of the ill construction of all old governments in Europe, England included with the rest. It is by distortedly exalting some men, that others are distortedly debased, till the whole is out of nature. A vast mass of mankind are degradedly thrown into the background of the human picture, to bring forward, with greater glare, the puppet-show of state and aristocracy. In the commencement of a revolution, those men are rather the followers of the *camp* than of the *standard* of liberty, and have yet to be instructed how to reverence it.

I give to Mr Burke all his theatrical exaggerations for facts, and I then ask him if they do not establish the certainty of what I here lay down? Admitting them to be true, they show the necessity of the French revolution, as much as any one thing he could have asserted. These outrages were not the effect of the principles of the revolution, but of the degraded mind that existed before the revolution, and which the revolution is calculated to reform. Place them then to their proper cause, and take the reproach of them to your own side.

THOMAS PAINE, *Rights of Man* (1791).

COBBETT'S COARSENESS
(1828)

'*Coarse!*' the sons and daughters of Corruption will exclaim. '*Coarse!*' will echo back the scoundrel *seat-sellers*, each of whom ought to swing on one of the trees that he has acquired by the wages of Corruption. 'Coarse, coarse!' will cry the reptiles who are the seat-seller's understrappers, and who ought to swing from their heels. 'Vary coarse, ma'awm!' will some grinning Scotch sycophant observe to some she sinecurist or pensioner. '*Coarse as neck beef!*' will growl out some Englishman, who has filled his bags by oppressions of the poor; or, some other one, who, feeling in his very bones and marrow an instinctive horror *of work*, is desperately bent on getting *a share of the taxes*.

Yes, it is *coarse* indeed, and coarse it ought to be in a case like this. SWIFT has told us not to chop *blocks* with *razors*. Any *edge*-tool is too fine for work like this: a pick-axe, that perforates with one end and drags about with the other, is the tool for this sort of business. It is, perhaps, seldom that men profit from reading poetry; but I have. When I was about 21 years of age, an old volume of the then 'EUROPEAN MAGAZINE' fell into my hands, at Fredericton in New Brunswick; and in it I stumbled upon the following lines, which I have several times repeated in the Register, and which, for the benefit of the young men of the present day, I will now repeat once more.

> Tender-handed press a nettle,
>   And it stings you for your pains;
> Press it like a man of mettle,
>   And it soft as silk remains.
>
> 'Tis the same with vulgar natures;
>   Treat them kindly, they rebel;
> But, be rough as nutmeg-graters,
>   And the rogues obey you well.

These lines took my fancy; they confirmed me in the conclusions which, young as I was, observation had caused me to draw; they have been fresh in my memory from that day to this; the precept they convey has been to me a rule of conduct; I have found success attend an observance of the rule; and I recommend it to the use of every young man of talent, who is too virtuous to be a slave of those who *call one another* 'Noble Lords' and 'Honourable Gentlemen', and who are aped in this respect, by that 'Honourable' Body, the Common Council of London, one of whose 'Honourable' committees spent, in one year, at the public expense, seven hundred pounds in eating and drinking and the like, and took, from the same source, a hundred and fifty pounds for 'a *summer excursion!*'

Coarse! aye, to be sure, towards one, who has the audacity to put himself before the people as an '*author*', and as an author, too, fit to instruct merchants and traders in the principles of their calling, and fit to point out to the nation the way to supersede the use of the king's coin! I shall, next week, show how fit you are to meddle with such matters, and shall make you, if you have one grain of prudence left, take care, for the future, how you venture, '*out of doors*', into *print*. '*In doors*', you are, doubtless, fit to put our finances to rights, and to do all other things; at any rate, *there* you are *safely* sheltered by that law, which *banishes us for life*, if we utter any thing '*coarse*' against you.

WILLIAM COBBETT, *Political Register* (May 1808).

THE EDUCATED MIND
(1818)

WHAT is that which first strikes us, and strikes us at once, in a man of education; and which among educated men so instantly distinguishes the man of superior mind, that (as was observed with eminent propriety of the late Edmund Burke) 'we cannot stand under the same archway during a shower of rain, without finding him out'? Not the weight or novelty of his remarks; not any unusual interest of facts communicated by him; for we may suppose both the one and the other precluded by the shortness of our intercourse and the triviality of the subjects. The difference will be impressed and felt, though the conversation should be confined to the state of the weather or the pavement. Still less will it arise from any peculiarity in his words and phrases. For if he be, as we now assume, a well-educated man as well as a man of superior powers, he will not fail to follow the golden rule of Julius Caesar, *Insolens verbum, tanquam scopulum, evitare*. Unless where new things necessitate new terms, he will avoid an unusual word as a rock. It must have been among the earliest lessons of his youth that the breach of this precept – at all times hazardous – becomes ridiculous in the topics of ordinary conversation. There remains but one other point of distinction possible, and this must be, and in fact is, the true cause of the impression made on us. It is the unpremeditated and evidently habitual *arrangement* of his words, grounded on the habit of foreseeing in each integral part, or (more plainly) in every sentence, the whole that he then intends to communicate. However irregular and desultory his talk, there is *method* in the fragments.

Listen, on the other hand, to an ignorant man, though perhaps shrewd and able in his particular calling, whether he be describing or relating. We immediately perceive, that his memory alone is called into action; and that the objects and events recur in the narration in the same order, and with the same accompaniments, however accidental or impertinent, as they had first occurred to the narrator. The necessity of taking breath, the efforts of recollection, and the abrupt rectification of its failures, produce all his pauses; and with exception of the '*and then*', the '*and there*', and the still less significant '*and so*', they constitute likewise all his connections.

Our discussion, however, is confined to method as employed in the formation of the understanding, and in the constructions of science and literature. It would indeed be superfluous to attempt a proof of its importance in the business and economy of active or domestic life. From the cotter's hearth or the workshop of the artisan to the palace or the arsenal, the first merit, that which admits neither substitute nor equivalent, is, that *every thing is in its place*. Where this charm is wanting, every other merit either loses its name, or becomes an additional ground of accusation and regret. Of one by whom it is eminently possessed, we say, proverbially, he is like clockwork. The resemblance extends beyond the point of regularity, and yet falls short of the truth. Both do, indeed, at once divide and announce the silent and otherwise indistinguishable lapse of time. But the man of methodical industry and honourable pursuits does more; he realizes its ideal divisions, and gives a character and individuality to its moments. If the idle are described as killing time, he may be justly said to call it into life and moral being, while he makes it the distinct object not only of the consciousness but of the conscience. He organizes the hours and gives them a soul; and that, the very essence of which is to fleet away, and evermore *to have been*, he takes up into his own permanence, and communicates to it the imperishableness of a spiritual nature. Of the good and faithful servant, whose energies, thus directed, are thus methodized, it is less truly affirmed that he lives in time, than that time lives in him. His days, months, and years, as the stops and punctual marks in the records of duties performed, will survive the wreck of worlds, and remain extant when time itself shall be no more.

SAMUEL TAYLOR COLERIDGE, in *The Friend* (1818).

THE LANGUAGE OF POETRY

(1802)

THE earliest Poets of all nations generally wrote from passion excited by real events; they wrote naturally, and as men: feeling powerfully as they did, their language was daring, and figurative. In succeeding times, Poets, and men ambitious of the fame of Poets, perceiving the influence of such language, and desirous of producing the same effect, without having the same animating passion, set themselves to a mechanical adoption of those figures of speech, and made use of them, sometimes with propriety, but much more frequently applied them to feelings and ideas with which they had no natural connection whatsoever. A language was thus insensibly produced, differing materially from the real language of men in *any situation*. The Reader or Hearer of this distorted language found himself in a perturbed and unusual state of mind: when affected by the genuine language of passion he had been in a perturbed and unusual state of mind also: in both cases he was willing that his common judgment and understanding should be laid asleep, and he had no instinctive and infallible perception of the true to make him reject the false; the one served as a passport for the other. The agitation and confusion of mind were in both cases delightful, and no wonder if he confounded the one with the other, and believed them both to be produced by the same, or similar causes. Besides, the Poet spake to him in the character of a man to be looked up to, a man of genius and authority. Thus, and from a variety of other causes, this distorted language was received with admiration; and Poets, it is probable, who had before contented themselves for the most part with misapplying only expressions which at first had been dictated by real passion, carried the abuse still further, and introduced phrases composed apparently in the spirit of the original figurative language by passion, yet altogether of their own invention, and distinguished by various degrees of wanton deviation from good sense and nature.

It is indeed true that the language of the earliest Poets was felt to differ materially from ordinary language, because it was the language of extraordinary occasions; but it was really spoken by men, language which the Poet himself had uttered when he had been affected by the events which he described, or which he had heard uttered by those around him. To this language it is probable that metre of some sort or other was early superadded. This separated the genuine language of Poetry still further from common life, so that whoever read or heard the poems of these earliest Poets felt himself moved in a way in which he had not been accustomed to be moved in real life, and by causes manifestly different from those which acted upon him in real life. This was the great temptation to all the corruptions which have followed: under the protection of this feeling succeeding Poets constructed a phraseology which had one thing, it is true, in common with the genuine language of poetry, namely, that it was not heard in ordinary conversation; that it was unusual. But the first Poets, as I have said, spake a language which, though unusual, was still the language of men. This circumstance, however, was disregarded by their successors; they found that they could please by easier means: they became proud of a language which they themselves had invented, and which was uttered only by themselves; and, with the spirit of a fraternity, they arrogated it to themselves as their own. In process of time metre became a symbol or promise of this unusual language, and whoever took upon him to write in metre, according as he possessed more or less of true poetic genius, introduced less or more of this adulterated phraseology into his compositions, and the true and the false became so inseparably interwoven that the taste of men was gradually perverted; and this language was received as a natural language; and, at length, by the influence of books upon men, did to a certain degree really become so. Abuses of this kind were imported from one nation to another, and with the progress of refinement this diction became daily more and more corrupt, thrusting out of sight the plain humanities of nature by a motley masquerade of tricks, quaintnesses, hieroglyphics, and enigmas.

WILLIAM WORDSWORTH, Appendix to *Lyrical Ballads* (1802).

THE ORIGINS OF POETRY
(1821)

IN the youth of the world, men dance and sing and imitate natural objects, observing in these actions, as in all others, a certain rhythm or order. And, although all men observe a similar, they observe not the same order, in the motions of the dance, in the melody of the song, in the combinations of language, in the series of their imitations of natural objects. For there is a certain order or rhythm belonging to each of these classes of mimetic representation, from which the hearer and the spectator receive an intenser and purer pleasure than from any other: the sense of an approximation to this order has been called taste by modern writers. Every man in the infancy of art, observes an order which approximates more or less closely to that from which this highest delight results: but the diversity is not sufficiently marked, as that its gradations should be sensible, except in those instances where the predominance of this faculty of approximation to the beautiful (for so we may be permitted to name the relation between this highest pleasure and its cause) is very great. Those in whom it exists to excess are poets, in the most universal sense of the word; and the pleasure resulting from the manner in which they express the influence of society or nature upon their own minds, communicates itself to others, and gathers a sort of reduplication from the community. Their language is vitally metaphorical; that is, it marks the before unapprehended relations of things and perpetuates their apprehension, until words, which represent them, become, through time, signs for portions or classes of thought, instead of pictures of integral thoughts; and then, if no new poets should arise to create afresh the associations which have been thus disorganised, language will be dead to all the nobler purposes of human intercourse. These similitudes or relations are finely said by Bacon to be 'the same footsteps of nature impressed upon the various subjects of the world'; – and he considers the faculty which perceives them as the storehouse of axioms common to all knowledge. In the infancy of society every author is necessarily a poet, because language itself is poetry; and to be a poet is to apprehend the true and the beautiful, in a word, the good which exists in the relation subsisting, first between existence and perception, and secondly between perception and expression. Every original language near to its source is in itself the chaos of a cyclic poem: the copiousness of lexicography and the distinctions of grammar are the works of a later age, and are merely the catalogue and the form of the creations of poetry.

But poets, or those who imagine and express this indestructible order, are not only the authors of language and of music, of the dance, and architecture, and statuary, and painting; they are the institutors of laws and the founders of civil society, and the inventors of the arts of life, and the teachers, who draw into a certain propinquity with the beautiful and the true, that partial apprehension of the agencies of the invisible world which is called religion. Hence all original religions are allegorical or susceptible of allegory, and, like Janus, have a double face of false and true. Poets, according to the circumstances of the age and nation in which they appeared, were called, in the earlier epochs of the world, legislators or prophets: a poet essentially comprises and unites both these characters. For he not only beholds intensely the present as it is, and discovers those laws according to which present things ought to be ordered, but he beholds the future in the present, and his thoughts are the germs of the flower and the fruit of latest time. Not that I assert poets to be prophets in the gross sense of the word, or that they can foretell the form as surely as they foreknow the spirit of events: such is the pretence of superstition, which would make poetry an attribute of prophecy, rather than prophecy an attribute of poetry. A poet participates in the eternal, the infinite, and the one; as far as relates to his conceptions, time and place and number are not. The grammatical forms which express the moods of time, and the difference of persons, and the distinction of place, are convertible with respect to the highest poetry without injuring it as poetry; and the choruses of Æschylus, and the book of Job, and Dante's *Paradiso*, would afford, more than any other writings, examples of this fact, if the limits of this essay did not forbid citation. The creations of sculpture, painting, and music, are illustrations still more decisive.

PERCY BYSSHE SHELLEY, *A Defence of Poetry* (1820–22).

SUSCEPTIBLE OF NOISES
(1823)

IT is hard to stand alone – in an age like this, – (constituted to the quick and critical perception of all harmonious combinations, I verily believe, beyond all preceding ages, since Jubal stumbled upon the gamut) – to remain, as it were, singly unimpressible to the magic influences of an art, which is said to have such an especial stroke at soothing, elevating, and refining the passions. – Yet rather than break the candid current of my confessions, I must avow to you, that I have received a great deal more pain than pleasure from this so cried-up faculty.

I am constitutionally susceptible of noises. A carpenter's

hammer, in a warm summer noon, will fret me into more than midsummer madness. But those unconnected, unset sounds are nothing to the measured malice of music. The ear is passive to those single strokes; willingly enduring stripes, while it hath no task to con. To music it cannot be passive. It will strive – mine at least will – spite of its inaptitude, to thrid the maze; like an unskilled eye painfully poring upon hiero-glyphics. I have sat through an Italian Opera, till, for sheer pain, and inexplicable anguish, I have rushed out into the noisiest places of the crowded streets, to solace myself with sounds, which I was not obliged to follow, and get rid of the distracting torment of endless, fruitless, barren attention! I take refuge in the unpretending assemblage of honest com-mon-life sounds; – and the purgatory of the Enraged Musician becomes my paradise.

I have sat at an Oratorio (that profanation of the purposes of the cheerful playhouse) watching the faces of the auditory in the pit (what a contrast to Hogarth's Laughing Audience!) immoveable, or affecting some faint emotion, – till (as some have said, that our occupations in the next world will be but a shadow of what delighted us in this) I have imagined myself in some cold Theatre in Hades, where some of the *forms* of the earthly one should be kept up, with none of the *enjoyment*; or like that –

> — Party in a parlour,
> All silent, and all DAMNED!

Above all, those insufferable concertos, and pieces of music, as they are called, do plague and embitter my apprehension. – Words are something; but to be exposed to an endless battery of mere sounds; to be long a dying, to lie stretched upon a rack of roses; to keep up languor by unintermitted effort; to pile honey upon sugar, and sugar upon honey, to an inter-minable tedious sweetness; to fill up sound with feeling, and strain ideas to keep pace with it; to gaze on empty frames, and be forced to make the pictures for yourself; to read a book, *all stops*, and be obliged to supply the verbal matter; to invent extempore tragedies to answer to the vague gestures of an inexplicable rambling mime – these are faint shadows of what I have undergone from a series of the ablest-executed pieces of this empty *instrumental music*.

CHARLES LAMB, *The Essays of Elia* (1823).

THE PRAISE OF CHIMNEY-SWEEPERS
(1823)

I LIKE to meet a sweep – understand me – not a grown sweeper – old chimney-sweepers are by no means attractive – but one of those tender novices, blooming through their first nigritude, the maternal washings not quite effaced from the cheek – such as come forth with the dawn, or somewhat earlier, with their little professional notes sounding like the *peep peep* of a young sparrow; or liker to the matin lark should I pronounce them, in their aerial ascents not seldom anticipating the sunrise?

I have a kindly yearning towards these dim specks – poor blots – innocent blacknesses –

I reverence these young Africans of our own growth – these almost clergy imps, who sport their cloth without assumption; and from their little pulpits (the tops of chimneys), in the nipping air of a December morning, preach a lesson of patience to mankind.

When a child, what a mysterious pleasure it was to witness their operation! to see a chit no bigger than one's-self enter, one knew not by what process, into what seemed the *fauces Averni* – to pursue him in imagination, as he went sounding on through so many dark stifling caverns, horrid shades! – to shudder with the idea that 'now, surely, he must be lost for ever!' – to revive at hearing his feeble shout of discovered day-light – and then (O fulness of delight) running out of doors, to come just in time to see the sable phenomenon emerge in safety, the brandished weapon of his art victorious like some flag waved over a conquered citadel! I seem to remember having been told, that a bad sweep was once left in a stack with his brush, to indicate which way the wind blew. It was an awful spectacle certainly; not much unlike the old stage direction in Macbeth, where the 'Apparition of a child crowned with a tree in his hand rises.'

Reader, if thou meetest one of these small gentry in thy early rambles, it is good to give him a penny. It is better to give him twopence. If it be starving weather, and to the proper troubles of his hard occupation, a pair of kibed heels (no unusual accompaniment) be superadded, the demand on thy humanity will surely rise to a tester.

There is a composition, the ground-work of which I have understood to be the sweet wood 'yclept sassafras. This wood boiled down to a kind of tea, and tempered with an infusion of milk and sugar, hath to some tastes a delicacy beyond the China luxury. I know not how thy palate may relish it; for myself, with every deference to the judicious Mr Read, who hath time out of mind kept open a shop (the only one he avers in London) for the vending of this 'wholesome and pleasant beverage', on the south side of Fleet-street, as thou approachest Bridge-street – *the only Salopian house*, – I have never yet ventured to dip my own particular lip in a basin of his commended ingredients – a cautious premonition to the olfactories constantly whispering to me, that my stomach must infallibly, with all due courtesy, decline it. Yet I have seen palates, otherwise not uninstructed in dietetical elegances, sup it up with avidity.

I know not by what particular conformation of the organ it happens, but I have always found that this composition is surprisingly gratifying to the palate of a young chimney-sweeper – whether the oily particles (sassafras is slightly oleaginous) do attenuate and soften the fuliginous concretions, which are sometimes found (in dissections) to adhere to the roof of the mouth in these unfledged practitioners; or whether Nature, sensible that she had mingled too much of bitter wood in the lot of these raw victims, caused to grow out of the earth her sassafras for a sweet lenitive – but so it is, that no possible taste or odour to the senses of a young chimney-sweeper can convey a delicate excitement comparable to this mixture. Being penniless, they will yet hang their black heads over the ascending steam, to gratify one sense if possible, seemingly no less pleased than those domestic animals – cats – when they purr over a new-found sprig of valerian. There is something more in these sympathies than philosophy can inculcate.

CHARLES LAMB, *The Essays of Elia* (1823).

A NEW MORAL WORLD
(1821)

IT has been, and still is, a received opinion among theorists in political economy, that man can provide better for himself, and more advantageously for the public, when left to his own individual exertions, opposed to and in competition with his fellows, than when aided by any social arrangement which shall unite his interests individually and generally with society.

This principle of individual interest, opposed as it is perpetually to the public good, is considered, by the most celebrated political economists, to be the corner-stone to the social system, and without which society could not subsist.

Yet when they shall know themselves, and discover the wonderful effects which combination and union can produce, they will acknowledge that the present arrangement of society is the most anti-social, impolitic, and irrational that can be devised; that under its influence all the superior and valuable qualities of human nature are repressed from infancy, and that the most unnatural means are used to bring out the most injurious propensities; in short, that the utmost pains are taken to make that which by nature is the most delightful compound for producing excellence and happiness, absurd, imbecile, and wretched.

Such is the conduct now pursued by those who are called the best and wisest of the present generation, although there is not one rational object to be gained by it.

From this principle of individual interest have arisen all the divisions of mankind, the endless errors and mischiefs of class, sect, party, and of national antipathies, creating the angry and malevolent passions, and all the crimes and misery with which the human race have been hitherto afflicted.

In short, if there be one closet doctrine more contrary to truth than another, it is the notion that individual interest, as that term is now understood, is a more advantageous principle on which to found the social system, for the benefit of all, or of any, than the principle of union and mutual co-operation.

The former acts like an immense weight to repress the most valuable faculties and dispositions, and to give a wrong direction to all human powers. It is one of those magnificent errors (if the expression may be allowed), that when enforced in practice brings ten thousand evils in its train. The principle on which these economists proceed, instead of adding to the wealth of nations or of individuals, is itself the sole cause of poverty; and but for its operation wealth would long ago have ceased to be a subject of contention in any part of the world. If, it may be asked, experience has proved that union, combination, and extensive arrangement among mankind are a thousand times more powerful to destroy than the efforts of an unconnected multitude, where each acts individually for himself, – would not a similar increased effect be produced by union, combination, and extensive arrangement, to *create and conserve*? Why should not the result be the same in the one case as in the other? But it is well known that a combination of men and of interests can effect that which it would be futile to attempt, and impossible to accomplish, by individual exertions and separate interests. Then why, it may be inquired, have men so long acted individually, and in opposition to each other? This is an important question, and merits the most serious attention.

Men have not yet been trained in principles that will permit them *to act in union*, except to defend themselves or to destroy others. For self-preservation they were early compelled to unite for these purposes in war. A necessity, however, equally powerful, will now compel men to be trained to act together to *create and conserve*, that, in like manner, they may preserve life in peace. Fortunately for mankind the system of individual opposing interests has now reached the extreme point of error and inconsistency; – in the midst of the most ample means to create wealth, all are in poverty, or in imminent danger from the effects of poverty upon others.

The reflecting part of mankind have admitted, in theory, that the characters of men are formed chiefly by the circumstances in which they are placed; yet the science of the influence of circumstances, which is the most important of all the sciences, remains unknown for the great practical business of life. When it shall be fully developed it will be discovered that to unite the mental faculties of men for the attainment of pacific and civil objects will be a far more easy task than it has been to combine their physical powers to carry on extensive warlike preparations.

The discovery of the distance and movements of the heavenly bodies, – of the timepiece, – of a vessel to navigate the most distant parts of the ocean, – of the steam engine, which performs under the easy control of one man the labour of many thousands, – and of the press, by which knowledge and improvement may be speedily given to the most ignorant in all parts of the earth, – these have, indeed, been discoveries of high import to mankind; but, important as these and others have been in their effects on the condition of human society, their combined benefits in practice will fall far short of those which will be speedily attained by the new intellectual power which men will acquire through the knowledge of 'the science of the influence of circumstances over the whole conduct, character, and proceedings of the human race.' By this latter discovery more will be accomplished in one year, for the well-being of human nature, including, without any exceptions, all ranks and descriptions of men, than has ever yet been effected in one or in many centuries. Strange as this language may seem to those whose minds have not yet had a glimpse of the real state in which society now is, it will prove to be not more strange than true.

Are not the mental energies of the world at this moment in a state of high effervescence? – Is not society at a stand, incompetent to proceed in its present course? – And do not all men cry out that 'something must be done'? – That 'something', to produce the effect desired, must be a complete renovation of the whole social compact; one not forced on prematurely, by confusion and violence; not one to be brought about by the futile measures of the Radicals, Whigs, or Tories of Britain, – the Liberals or Royalists of France, – the Illuminati of Germany, or the mere party proceedings of any little local portion of human beings, trained as they have hitherto been in almost every kind of error, and without any true knowledge of themselves.

No! The change sought for must be preceded by the clear development of a great and universal principle which shall unite in one all the petty jarring interests by which, till now, human nature has been made a most inveterate enemy to itself.

ROBERT OWEN, *Report to the County of Lanark* (1821).

HAZLITT ON MALTHUS

(1825)

Mr Malthus's 'gospel is preached to the poor'. He lectures them on economy, on morality, the regulation of their passions (which, he says, at other times, are amenable to no restraint) and on the ungracious topic, that 'the laws of nature, which are the laws of God, have doomed them and their families to starve for want of a right to the smallest portion of food beyond what their labour will supply, or some charitable hand may hold out in compassion.' This is illiberal, and it is not philosophical. The laws of nature or of God, to which the author appeals, are no other than a limited fertility and a limited earth. Within those bounds, the rest is regulated by the laws of man. The division of the produce of the soil, the price of labour, the relief afforded to the poor, are matters of human arrangement: while any charitable hand can extend relief, it is a proof that the means of subsistence are not exhausted in themselves, that the 'tables are not full!' Mr Malthus says that the laws of nature, which are the laws of God, have rendered that relief physically impossible; and yet he would abrogate the poor-laws by an act of the legislature, in order to take away that *impossible* relief, which the laws of God deny, and which the laws of man *actually* afford. We cannot think that this view of his subject, which is prominent and dwelt on at great length and with much pertinacity, is dictated either by rigid logic or melting charity! A labouring man is not allowed to knock down a hare or a partridge that spoils his garden: a country-squire keeps a pack of hounds: a lady of quality rides out with a footman behind her, on two sleek, well-fed horses. We have not a word to say against all this as exemplifying the spirit of the English Constitution, as a part of the law of the land, or as an artful distribution of light and shade in the social picture; but if any one insists at the same time that 'the laws of nature, which are the laws of God, have doomed the poor and their families to starve,' because the principle of population has encroached upon and swallowed up the means of subsistence, so that not a mouthful of food is left *by the grinding law of necessity* for the poor, we beg leave to deny both fact and inference – and we put it to Mr Malthus whether we are not, in strictness, justified in doing so?

We have, perhaps, said enough to explain our feeling on the subject of Mr Malthus's merits and defects. We think he had the opportunity and the means in his hands of producing a great work on the principle of population; but we believe he has let it slip from his having an eye to other things besides that broad and unexplored question. He wished not merely to advance to the discovery of certain great and valuable truths, but at the same time to overthrow certain unfashionable paradoxes by exaggerated statements – to curry favour with existing prejudices and interests by garbled representations. He has, in a word, as it appears to us on a candid retrospect and without any feelings of controversial asperity rankling in our minds, sunk the philosopher and the friend of his species (a character to which he might have aspired) in the sophist and party-writer. The period at which Mr Malthus came forward teemed with answers to Modern Philosophy, with antidotes to liberty and humanity, with abusive Histories of the Greek and Roman republics, with fulsome panegyrics on the Roman Emperors (at the very time when we were reviling Buonaparte for his strides to universal empire) with the slime and offal of desperate servility – and we cannot but consider the Essay as one of the poisonous ingredients thrown into the cauldron of Legitimacy 'to make it thick and slab'. Our author has, indeed, so far done service to the cause of truth, that he has counteracted many capital errors formerly prevailing as to the universal and indiscriminate encouragement of population under all circumstances; but he has countenanced opposite errors, which if adopted in theory and practice would be even more mischievous, and has left it to future philosophers to follow up the principle, that some check must be provided for the unrestrained progress of population, into a set of wiser and more humane consequences.

WILLIAM HAZLITT, *The Spirit of the Age* (1825).

LAISSEZ-FAIRE
(*c.* 1830)

IT is not uncommon for 100,000 *operatives* (mark this word, for words *in this sense* are things) to be out of employment at once in the cotton districts, and, thrown upon parochial relief, to be dependent upon hard-hearted taskmasters for food. The Malthusian doctrine would indeed afford a certain means of relief, if this were not a twofold question. If, when you say to a man, – 'You have no claim upon me: you have your allotted part to perform in the world, so have I. In a state of nature, indeed, had I food, I should offer you a share from sympathy, from humanity; but in this advanced and artificial state of society, I cannot afford you relief; you must starve. You came into the world when it could not sustain you.' What would be this man's answer? He would say, – 'You disclaim all connection with me; I have no claims upon you? I can then have no duties towards you, and this pistol shall put me in possession of your wealth. You may leave a law behind you which shall hang me, but what man who saw assured starvation before him, ever feared hanging.' It is this accursed practice of ever considering *only* what seems *expedient* for the occasion, disjoined from all principle or enlarged systems of action, of never listening to the true and unerring impulses of our better nature, which has led the colder-hearted men to the study of political economy, which has turned our Parliament into a real committee of public safety. In it is all power vested; and in a few years we shall either be governed by an aristocracy, or, what is still more likely, by a contemptible democratical oligarchy of glib economists, compared to which the worst form of aristocracy would be a blessing.

SAMUEL TAYLOR COLERIDGE in *Letters, Conversations and Recollections of S. T. Coleridge*, T. Allsop, (1836).

THE NEW TIME
(1829)

I WOULD warn you in time, that so the whirlwind may not overtake you when you are gaily pressing forward with all sails set! I would teach you, that in the progress of society every stage has its own evils and besetting dangers, the only remedy for which is, that which is least regarded by all states, except by those in which it is least understood. See in how many things the parallel between this age and mine holds good; and how, in every instance, dangers the same in kind, but greater in degree, are awaiting yours! The art of war, which underwent its great alteration when the shield and lance were superseded by the firelock, and armour was rendered useless by artillery, is about to undergo a change not less momentous, with the same sure consequence of giving to ambition more formidable means. The invention of printing, which is to the moral world more than gunpowder or steam to the material, as it began in my days, so in yours its full effects are first beginning to unfold, when the press, which, down to the last generation, wrought only for a small part of the community, is employed with restless activity for all classes, disseminating good and evil with a rapidity and effect inconceivable in former ages, as it would have been impossible. Look, too, at manufactures; great efforts were made to encourage them then, . . . the Protector Seymour (one of those politic reformers who fished in troubled waters, and fell at last into the stream) introduced a colony of clothiers from what was then the very land of sedition, and converted the most venerable edifice in this whole island to their use. You have now, what it was then thought so desirable to obtain, ... a manufacturing population, ... and it is not found so easy to regulate as it has been to raise it. The peasantry were in my time first sensible of distress brought upon them by political causes; their condition was worsened by the changes which were taking place in society; a similar effect is now more widely and more pressingly felt. In those days, the dikes and boundaries of social order began to give way, and the poor, who till then had been safely left to the care of local and private charity, were first felt as a national evil; ... that evil has increased till it has now become a national danger. A new world was then discovered, ... for the punishment of its native inhabitants, the measure of whose iniquities was full; the colonies which have been established there are now in a condition seriously to affect the relations of the parent states, and America is reacting upon Europe. That was an age of religious, this of political revolutions. ...

ROBERT SOUTHEY, *Sir Thomas More, or Colloquies on the Progress and Prospects of Society* (1829).

1830–1895

‹‹•››

Observation

NASMYTH AT COALBROOKDALE
(c. 1830)

I LEFT Manchester and turned my steps in the direction of Coalbrookdale. I passed through a highly picturesque country, in which I enjoyed the sight of many old timber houses, most attractive subjects for my pencil. My route lay through Whitchurch, Wem, and Wellington; then past the Wrekin to Coalbrookdale. Before arriving there I saw the first iron bridge constructed in England, an object of historical interest in that class of structures. It was because of the superb quality of the castings produced at Coalbrookdale, that the ironmasters there were able to accomplish the building of a bridge of that material, which before had baffled all projectors both at home and abroad.

I possessed a letter of introduction to the manager, and was received by him most cordially. He permitted me to examine the works. I was greatly interested at the sight of the processes of casting. Many beautiful objects were turned out for architectural, domestic, and other purposes. I saw nothing particularly novel, however, in the methods and processes of moulding and casting. The excellence of the work depended for the most part upon the great care and skill exercised by the workmen of the foundry. They seemed to vie with each other in turning out the best castings, and their models or patterns were made with the utmost care. I was particularly impressed with the cheerful zeal and activity of the workmen and foremen of this justly celebrated establishment.

On leaving Coalbrookdale I trudged my way towards Wolverhampton. I rested at Shiffnal for the night. Next day

I was in the middle of the Black Country. I had no letters of introduction to employers in Wolverhampton; so that, without stopping there, I proceeded at once to Dudley. The Black Country is anything but picturesque. The earth seems to have been turned inside out. Its entrails are strewn about; nearly the entire surface of the ground is covered with cinder-heaps and mounds of scoriæ. The coal, which has been drawn from below ground, is blazing on the surface. The district is crowded with iron furnaces, puddling furnaces, and coal-pit engine furnaces. By day and by night the country is glowing with fire, and the smoke of the ironworks hovers over it. There is a rumbling and clanking of iron forges and rolling mills. Workmen covered with smut, and with fierce white eyes, are seen moving about amongst the glowing iron and the dull thud of forge-hammers.

Amidst these flaming, smoky, clanging works, I beheld the remains of what had once been happy farmhouses, now ruined and deserted. The ground underneath them had sunk by the working out of the coal, and they were falling to pieces. They had in former times been surrounded by clumps of trees; but only the skeletons of them remained, dilapidated, black, and lifeless. The grass had been parched and killed by the vapours of sulphureous acid thrown out by the chimneys; and every herbaceous object was of a ghastly gray – the emblem of vegetable death in its saddest aspect. Vulçan had driven out Ceres. In some places I heard a sort of chirruping sound, as of some forlorn bird haunting the ruins of the old farmsteads. But no! the chirrup was a vile delusion. It proceeded from the shrill creaking of the coal-winding chains, which were placed in small tunnels beneath the hedgeless road.

I went into some of the forges to see the workmen at their labours. There was no need of introduction; the works were open to all, for they were unsurrounded by walls. I saw the white-hot iron run out from the furnace; I saw it spun, as it were, into bars and iron ribbands, with an ease and rapidity which seemed marvellous. There were also the ponderous hammers and clanking rolling-mills. I wandered from one to another without restraint. I lingered among the blast furnaces, seeing the flood of molten iron run out from time to time, and remained there until it was late. When it became dark the scene was still more impressive. The workmen within seemed to be running about amidst the flames as in a pandemonium; while around and outside the horizon was a glowing belt of fire, making even the stars look pale and feeble. At last I came away with reluctance, and made my way towards Dudley. I reached the town at a late hour. I was exhausted in mind and body, yet the day had been most interesting and exciting. A sound sleep refreshed me, and I was up in the morning early, to recommence my journey of inquiry.

JAMES NASMYTH, *An Autobiography*, Ed. Samuel Smiles (1883).

A MARKET DINNER
(1843)

WHO is that young gentleman on horseback? He is one of the young Walters of Bearwood. What! He who lately stood for Nottingham? No; a younger brother. And who are those in the carriage, those ladies? Those are his sisters, Mr Walter's daughters. A fine family! Oh, bless you, yes; a large family; very good people all of them, very.

It is one o'clock. The various steeples proclaim the farmers' dinner hour. Every inn has a public ordinary; which shall we go to? The George is round here; the Angel is near at hand; here is the Broad Face; onward there is the Wheat Sheaf, the Wheel, the Elephant; and there is the White Hart, the Ship, the Black Horse, the Mitre, the Peacock, the Turk's Head, and several more to which we may go. This one round the corner will do; let us see, what is it called! Ah, never mind what its name is. Here we are in the public room, just in time. The clatter of knives and forks has just begun. Some of the guests are too busy filling themselves to speak; but the most are too full of the topics of the day to remain quiet. Let us open our ears.

'Roast beef, sir? – Robert Peel dare not – help you, Mr Jackson? – labourers' wages – potatoes? – Sir Robert Peel – salt? – waiter! – yes, sir – Robert Peel – potatoes – carve this pig – knife – cut off his head – Peel – roast pig? – roast – Peel – waiter! – Canada flour – fowl? – majority of votes – this way, gentlemen; seats disengaged here – turn them out – Conservative ministry – boiled mutton – church extension – over done – take in – glass of ale – no relief this year – coming, sir – waiter, remove – county members – help you to – parliamentary – greens – Peel – no more tongue, thank you – two thousand miles off – American wheat – cheated – petition – clear the table – thrown under and never read – petition – quite enough, thank you – Wallingford dinner, Mr Blackstone – powerless – nearly – false pretences – farmers – always suffering distress – Peel – so help me God – language in parliament – the League tracts – read – digest – old cheese – Cobden's speeches – relish – Wellington – 1815 – not the better of being too old – good port – porter with a head – ministers have, before now, lost their – Peel and Cobden – porter with a head – debate in the house – with a head – would have given something to have seen – porter with a head – in a passion, striking the table – the head – unseemly to be in a rage – Dublin stout – Conservative members in a tumult, applauding – Barclay's – the indignant manner of – porter with a head – retaliation – stout – gentlemen, silence please – silence – silence!'

And Silence having come when those who called for her held their tongues, and not before, the chairman said, that as dinner was now over those who chose a pipe and a glass would adjourn to another room. Whereupon one half, or more, of the whole adjourned; the remainder, not choosing to smoke, nor to be smoked, remained where they were. They disjoined themselves and reunited into small parties.

ALEXANDER SOMERVILLE, *The Whistler at the Plough* (1852).

ENGLISH COMFORT
(1830)

THE *comfort*, on which the English lay so much stress, is of the same character, and arises from the same source as their mirth. Both exist by contrast and a sort of contradiction. The English are certainly the most uncomfortable of all people in themselves, and therefore it is that they stand in need of every kind of comfort and accommodation. The least thing puts them out of their way, and therefore everything must be in its place. They are mightily offended at disagreeable tastes and smells, and therefore they exact the utmost neatness and nicety. They are sensible of heat and cold, and therefore they cannot exist, unless everything is snug and warm, or else open and airy, where they are. They must have 'all appliances and means to boot'. They are afraid of interruption and intrusion, and therefore they shut themselves up in indoor enjoyments and by their own firesides. It is not that they require luxuries (for that implies a high degree of epicurean indulgence and gratification), but they cannot do without *their comforts*; that is, whatever tends to supply their physical wants, and ward off physical pain and annoyance. As they have not a fund of animal spirits and enjoyments in themselves, they cling to external objects for support, and derive solid satisfaction from the ideas of order, cleanliness, plenty, property, and domestic quiet, as they seek for diversion from odd accidents and grotesque surprises, and have the highest possible relish not of voluptuous softness, but of hard knocks and dry blows, as one means of ascertaining their personal identity.

WILLIAM HAZLITT, 'Merry England' in *Sketches and Essays* (1839).

DARWIN AT CAMBRIDGE
(c. 1830)

ALTHOUGH, as we shall presently see, there were some redeeming features in my life at Cambridge, my time was sadly wasted there, and worse than wasted. From my passion for shooting and for hunting, and, when this failed, for riding across country, I got into a sporting set, including some dissipated low-minded young men. We used often to dine together in the evening, though these dinners often included men of a higher stamp, and we sometimes drank too much, with jolly singing and playing at cards afterwards. I know that I ought to feel ashamed of days and evenings thus spent, but as some of my friends were very pleasant, and we were all in the highest spirits, I cannot help looking back to these times with much pleasure.

But I am glad to think that I had many other friends of a widely different nature. I was very intimate with Whitley, who was afterwards Senior Wrangler, and we used continually to take long walks together. He inoculated me with a taste for pictures and good engravings, of which I bought some. I frequently went to the Fitzwilliam Gallery, and my taste must have been fairly good, for I certainly admired the best pictures, which I discussed with the old curator. I read also with much interest Sir Joshua Reynolds' book. This taste, though not natural to me, lasted for several years, and many of the pictures in the National Gallery in London gave me much pleasure; that of Sebastian del Piombo exciting in me a sense of sublimity.

I also got into a musical set, I believe by means of my warmhearted friend, Herbert, who took a high wrangler's degree. From associating with these men, and hearing them play, I acquired a strong taste for music, and used very often to time my walks so as to hear on week days the anthem in King's

College Chapel. This gave me intense pleasure, so that my backbone would sometimes shiver. I am sure that there was no affectation or mere imitation in this taste, for I used generally to go by myself to King's College, and I sometimes hired the chorister boys to sing in my rooms. Nevertheless I am so utterly destitute of an ear, that I cannot perceive a discord, or keep time and hum a tune correctly; and it is a mystery how I could possibly have derived pleasure from music.

My musical friends soon perceived my state, and sometimes amused themselves by making me pass an examination, which consisted in ascertaining how many tunes I could recognise, when they were played rather more quickly or slowly than usual. 'God save the King', when thus played, was a sore puzzle. There was another man with almost as bad an ear as I had, and strange to say he played a little on the flute. Once I had the triumph of beating him in one of our musical examinations.

But no pursuit at Cambridge was followed with nearly so much eagerness or gave me so much pleasure as collecting beetles. It was the mere passion for collecting, for I did not dissect them, and rarely compared their external characters with published descriptions, but got them named anyhow. I will give a proof of my zeal: one day, on tearing off some old bark, I saw two rare beetles, and seized one in each hand; then I saw a third and new kind, which I could not bear to lose, so that I popped the one which I held in my right hand into my mouth. Alas! it ejected some intensely acrid fluid, which burnt my tongue so that I was forced to spit the beetle out, which was lost, as was the third one.

I was very successful in collecting, and invented two new methods; I employed a labourer to scrape, during the winter, moss off old trees and place it in a large bag, and likewise to collect the rubbish at the bottom of the barges in which reeds are brought from the fens, and thus I got some very rare species. No poet ever felt more delighted at seeing his first poem published than I did at seeing, in Stephens' *Illustrations of British Insects*, the magic words, 'captured by C. Darwin, Esq.' I was introduced to entomology by my second cousin, W. Darwin Fox, a clever and most pleasant man, who was then at Christ's College, and with whom I became extremely intimate. Afterwards I became well acquainted, and went out collecting, with Albert Way of Trinity, who in after years became a well-known archaeologist; also with H. Thompson, of the same College, afterwards a leading agriculturist, chairman of a great railway, and Member of Parliament. It seems, therefore, that a taste for collecting beetles is some indication of future success in life!

I am surprised what an indelible impression many of the beetles which I caught at Cambridge have left on my mind. I can remember the exact appearance of certain posts, old trees and banks where I made a good capture. The pretty *Panagaeus eaux-major* was a treasure in those days, and here at Down I saw a beetle running across a walk and on picking it up instantly perceived that it differed slightly from *P. crux-major*, and it turned out to be *P. quadripunctatus*, which is only a variety or closely allied species, differing from it very slightly in outline. I had never seen in those old days Licinus alive, which to an uneducated eye hardly differs from many of the black Carabidous beetles; but my sons found here a specimen, and I instantly recognised that it was new to me; yet I had not looked at a British beetle for the last twenty years.

CHARLES DARWIN, *Autobiography*, in *Charles Darwin*, ed. F. Darwin (1892).

CHEAP CLOTHES AND NASTY
(1850)

NOT only the master tailors and their underlings, but the retail tradesmen, too, make their profit out of these abominations. By a method which smacks at first sight somewhat of benevolence, but proves itself in practice to be one of those 'precious balms which break', not 'the head' (for that would savour of violence, and might possibly give some bodily pain, a thing intolerable to the nerves of Mammon) but the heart – an organ which, being spiritual, can of course be recognised by no laws of police or commerce. The object of the State, we are told, is 'the conservation of body and goods'; there is nothing in that about broken hearts; nothing which should make it a duty to forbid such a system as a working tailor here describes –

'Fifteen or twenty years ago, such a thing as a journeyman tailor having to give security before he could get work was unknown; but now I and such as myself could not get a stitch to do first handed, if we did not either procure the security of some householder, or deposit £5 in the hands of the employer. The reason of this is, the journeymen are so badly paid that the employers know they can barely live on what they get, and consequently they are often driven to pawn the garments given out to them, in order to save themselves and their families from starving. If the journeyman can manage to scrape together £5, he has to leave it in the hands of his employer all the time that he is working for the house. I know one person who gives out the work for a fashionable West End slop-shop that will not take household security, and requires £5 from each hand. I am informed by one of the parties who worked for this man that he has as many as 150 hands in his employ, and that each of these has placed £5 in his hands, so that altogether the poor people have handed over £750 to increase the capital upon which he trades, and for which he pays no interest whatsoever.'

This recalls a similar case (mentioned by a poor staystitcher in another letter, published in the 'Morning Chronicle'), of a large wholesale staymaker in the City, who had amassed a large fortune by beginning to trade upon the 5s. which he demanded to be left in his hands by his work people before he gave them employment.

'Two or three years back one of the slop-sellers at the East End became bankrupt, and the poor people lost all the money that had been deposited as security for work in his hands. The journeymen who get the security of householders are enabled to do so by a system which is now in general practice at the East End. Several bakers, publicans, chandler-shop keepers, and coal-shed keepers, make a trade of becoming security for those seeking slop-work. They consent to be responsible for the workpeople upon the condition of the men dealing at their shops. The workpeople who require such security are generally very good customers, from the fact of their either having large families, all engaged in the same work, or else several females or males working under them, and living at their house. The parties becoming securities thus not only greatly increase their trade, but furnish a second-rate article at a first-rate price. It is useless to complain of the bad quality or high price of the articles supplied by the securities, for the shop-keepers know, as well as the workpeople, that it is impossible for the hands to leave them without losing their work. I know one baker whose security was refused at the slop-shop because he was already responsible for so many, and he begged the publican to be his deputy, so that by this means the work-people were obliged to deal at both baker's and publican's too. I never heard of a butcher making a trade of becoming security *because the slop-work people cannot afford to consume much meat.*

'The same system is also pursued by lodging-house keepers.

They will become responsible if the workmen requiring security will undertake to lodge at their house.'

But of course the men most interested in keeping up the system are those who buy the clothes of these cheap shops. And who are they? Not merely the blackguard gent – the butt of Albert Smith and Punch, who flaunts at the Casinos and Cremorne Gardens in vulgar finery wrung out of the souls and bodies of the poor; not merely the poor lawyer's clerk or reduced half-pay officer who has to struggle to look as respectable as his class commands him to look on a pittance often no larger than that of the day labourer – no, strange to say – and yet not strange, considering our modern eleventh commandment – 'Buy cheap and sell dear,' the richest as well as the poorest imitate the example of King Ryence and the tanners of Meudon. At a great show establishment – to take one instance out of many – the very one where, as we heard just now, 'however strong and healthy a man may be when he goes to work at that shop, in a month's time he will be a complete shadow, and have almost all his clothes in pawn' –

'We have also made garments for Sir — —, Sir — —, Alderman —, Dr —, and Dr —. We make for several of the aristocracy. We cannot say whom, because the tickets frequently come to us as Lord — and the Marquis of —. This could not be a Jew's trick, because the buttons on the liveries had coronets upon them. And again, we know the house is patronised largely by the aristocracy, clergy, and gentry, by the number of court-suits and liveries, surplices, regimentals, and ladies' riding-habits that we continually have to make up. *There are more clergymen among the customers than any other class, and often we have to work at home upon the Sunday at their clothes, in order to get a living.* The customers are mostly ashamed of dealing at this house, for the men who take the clothes to the customers' houses in the cart have directions to pull up at the corner of the street. We had a good proof of the dislike of gentlefolks to have it known that they dealt at that shop for their clothes, for when the trousers buttons were stamped with the name of the firm, we used to have the garments returned, daily, to have other buttons put on them, and now the buttons are unstamped'!!!

We shall make no comment on this extract. It needs none. If these men know how their clothes are made, they are past contempt. Afraid of man, and not afraid of God! As if His eye could not see the cart laden with the plunder of the poor, because it stopped round the corner? If, on the other hand, they do *not* know these things, and doubtless the majority do not, – it is their sin that they do not know it. Woe to a society whose only apology to God and man is, 'Am I my brother's keeper?' Men ought to know the condition of those by whose labour they live. Had the question been the investment of a few pounds in a speculation, these gentlemen would have been careful enough about good security. Ought they to take no security, when they invest their money in clothes, that they are not putting on their backs accursed garments, offered in sacrifice to devils, reeking with the sighs of the starving, tainted – yes, tainted, indeed, for it comes out now that diseases numberless are carried home in these same garments from the miserable abodes where they are made. Evidence to this effect was given in 1844; but Mammon was too busy to attend to it. These wretched creatures, when they have pawned their own clothes and bedding, will use as substitutes the very garments they are making. So Lord —'s coat has been seen covering a group of children blotched with small-pox. The Rev. D— finds himself suddenly unpresentable from a cutaneous disease, which it is not polite to mention on the south of Tweed, little dreaming that the shivering dirty being who made his coat has been sitting with his arms in the sleeves for warmth while he stitched at the tails. The charming Miss C— is swept off by typhus or scarlatina, and her parents talk about 'God's heavy judgment and visitation' – had they tracked the girl's new riding-habit back to the stifling undrained hovel where it served as a blanket to the fever-stricken slop-worker, they would have seen *why* God had visited them, seen that His judgments are true judgments, and give His plain opinion of the system which 'speaketh good of the covetous whom God abhorreth' – a system, to use the words of the 'Morning Chronicle's' correspondent, 'unheard of and unparalleled in the history of any country – a scheme so deeply laid for the introduction and supply of underpaid labour to the market, that it is impossible for the working man not to sink and be degraded by it into the lowest depths of wretchedness and infamy – a system which is steadily and gradually increasing, and sucking more and more victims out of the honourable trade, who are really intelligent artisans, living in comparative comfort and civilisation, into the dishonourable or sweating trade in which the slop-workers are generally almost brutified by their incessant toil, wretched pay, miserable food, and filthy homes.'

But to us, almost the worst feature in the whole matter is, that the Government are not merely parties to, but actually the originators of this system. The contract system, as a working tailor stated in the name of the rest, 'had been mainly instrumental in destroying the living wages of the working man. Now the Government were the sole originators of the system of contracts and of sweating. Forty years ago there was nothing known of contracts, except Government contracts; and at that period the contractors were confined to making slops for the navy, the army, and the West India slaves. It was never dreamt of then that such a system was to come into operation in the better classes of trade, till ultimately it was destructive of masters as well as men. The Government having been the cause of the contract system, and consequently of the sweating system, he called upon them to abandon it. The sweating system had established the show-shops and the ticket system, both of which were countenanced by the Government, till it had become a fashion to support them.'

CHARLES KINGSLEY, Preface to *Alton Locke* (1850).

A REGULAR SCAVENGER

(1851)

THE following statement of his business, his sentiments, and, indeed, of the subjects which concerned him, or about which he was questioned, was given to me by a street-sweeper, so he called himself, for I have found some of these men not to relish the appellation of 'scavager'. He was a short, sturdy, somewhat red-faced man, without anything particular in his appearance to distinguish him from the mass of mere labourers, but with the sodden and sometimes dogged look of a man contented in his ignorance, and – for it is not a very uncommon case – rather proud of it.

'I don't know how old I am,' he said – I have observed, by the by, that there is not any excessive vulgarity in these men's tones or accent so much as grossness in some of their expressions – 'and I can't see what that consarns any one, as I 's old enough to have a jolly rough beard, and so can take care of myself. I should think so. My father was a sweeper, and I wanted to be a waterman, but father – he hasn't been dead long – didn't like the thoughts on it, as he said they was all drownded one time or 'nother; so I ran away and tried my hand as a Jack-in-the-water, but I was starved back in a week, and got a h— of a clouting. After that I sifted a bit in a dust-yard, and helped in any way; and I was sent to help at and larn honey-pot and other pot making, at Deptford; but honey-pots was a great thing in the business. Master's foreman married a relation of mine, some way or other. I never tasted honey, but I 've heered it 's like sugar and butter mixed. The pots was often wanted to look like foreign pots; I don't know nothing what was meant by it; some b— dodge or other. No, the trade didn't suit me at all, master, so I left. I don't know why it didn't suit me; cause it didn't. Just then, father had hurt his hand and arm, in a jam again' a cart, and so, as I was a big lad, I got to take his place, and gave every satisfaction to Mr —. Yes, he was a contractor and a great man. I can't say as I knows how contracting's done; but it's a bargain atween man and man. So I got on. I'm now looked on as a stunning good workman, I can tell you.

'Well, I can't say as I thinks sweeping the streets is hard work. I'd rather sweep two hours than shovel one. It tires one's arms and back so, to go on shovelling. You can't change, you see, sir, and the same parts keeps getting gripped more and more. Then you must mind your eye, if you're shovelling slop into a cart, perticler so; or some feller may run off with a complaint that he's been splashed o' purpose. *Is* a man ever splashed o' purpose? No, sir, not as I knows on, in course not. [Laughing.] Why should he?

'The streets *must* be done as they're done now. It always was so, and will always be so. Did I ever hear what London streets were like a thousand years ago? It's nothing to me, but they must have been like what they is now. Yes, there was always streets, or how was people that has tin to get their coals taken to them, and how was the public-houses to get their beer? It's talking nonsense, talking that way, a-asking sich questions.' [As the scavenger seemed likely to lose his temper, I changed the subject of conversation.]

'Yes,' he continued, 'I have good health. I never had a doctor but twice; once was for a hurt, and the t'other I won't tell on. Well, I think nightwork's healthful enough, but I'll not say so much for it as you may hear some on 'em say. I don't like it, but I do it when I's obligated, under a necessity. It pays one as overwork; and werry like more one's in it, more one may be suited. I reckon no men works harder nor sich as me. O, as to poor journeymen tailors and sich like, I knows they're stunning badly off, and many of their masters is the hardest of beggers. I have a nephew as works for a Jew slop, but I don't reckon that *work*; anybody might do it. You think not, sir? Werry well, it's all the same. No, I won't say as I could make a veskit, but I 've sowed my own buttons on to one afore now.

'Yes, I 've heered on the Board of Health. They 've put down some night-yards, and if they goes on putting down more, what 's to become of the night-soil? I can't think what they 're up to; but if they don't touch wages, it may be all right in the end on it. I don't know that them there consarns does touch wages, but one 's naterally afeard on 'em. I could read a little when I was a child, but I can't now for want of practice, or I might know more about it. I yarns my money gallows hard, and requires support to do hard work, and if wages goes down, one 's strength goes down. I'm a man as understands what things belongs. I was once out of work, through a mistake, for a good many weeks, perhaps five or six or more; I larned then what short grub meant. I got a drop of beer and a crust sometimes with men as I knowed, or I might have dropped in the street. What did I do to pass my time when I was out of work? Sartinly the days seemed very long; but I went about and called at dust-yards, till I didn't like to go too often; and I met men I 'd know'd at tap-rooms, and spent time that way, and axed if there was any openings for work. I 've been out of collar odd weeks now and then, but when this happened, I 'd been on slack work a goodish bit, and was bad for rent three weeks and more. My rent was 2s. a week then; its 1s. 9d. now, and my own traps.

'No, I can't say I was sorry when I was forced to be idle that way, that I hadn't kept up my reading, nor tried to keep it up, because I couldn't then have settled down my mind to read; I know I couldn't. I likes to hear the paper read well enough, if I 's resting; but old Bill, as often wolunteers to read, has to spell the hard words so, that one can't tell what the devil he 's reading about. I never heers anything about books; I never heered of Robinson Crusoe, if it wasn't once at the Wic. [Victoria Theatre]; I think there was some sich a name there. He lived on a deserted island, did he, sir, all by hisself? Well,

I think, now you mentions it, I have heered on him. But one needn't believe all one hears, whether out of books or not. I don't know much good that ever anybody as I knows ever got out of books; they're fittest for idle people. Sartinly I've seen working people reading in coffee-shops; but they might as well be resting theirselves to keep up their strength. Do I think so? I'm sure on it, master. I sometimes spends a few browns a-going to the play; mostly about Christmas. It's werry fine and grand at the Wic., that's the place I goes to most; both the pantomimers and t' other things is werry stunning. I can't say how much I spends a year in plays; I keeps no account; perhaps 5s. or so in a year, including expenses, sich as beer, when one goes out after a stopper on the stage. I don't keep no accounts of what I gets, or what I spends, it would be no use; money comes and it goes, and it often goes a d—d sight faster than it comes; so it seems to me, though I ain't in debt just at this time.

'I never goes to any church or chapel. Sometimes I hasn't clothes as is fit, and I s'pose I couldn't be admitted into sich fine places in my working dress. I was once in a church, but felt queer, as one does in them strange places, and never went again. They're fittest for rich people. Yes, I've heered about religion and about God Almighty. *What* religion have I heered on? Why, the regular religion. I'm satisfied with what I knows and feels about it, and that's enough about it. I came to tell you about trade and work, because Mr — told me it might do good; but religion hasn't nothing to do with it. Yes, Mr —'s a good master, and a religious man; but I've known masters as didn't care a d—n for religion, as good as him; and so you see it comes to much the same thing. I cares nothing about politics neither; but I'm a chartist.

'I'm not a married man. I was a-going to be married to a young woman as lived with me a goodish bit as my house-keeper' [this he said very demurely]; 'but she went to the hopping to yarn a few shillings for herself, and never came back. I heered that she'd taken up with an Irish hawker, but

I can't say as to the rights on it. Did I fret about her? Perhaps not; but I was wexed.

'I'm sure I can't say what I spends my wages in. I sometimes makes 12s. 6d. a week, and sometimes better than 21s. with nightwork. I suppose grub costs 1s. a day, and beer 6d.; but I keeps no accounts. I buy ready-cooked meat; often cold b'iled beef, and eats it at any tap-room. I have meat every day; mostly more than once a day. Wegetables I don't care about, only ingans and cabbage, if you can get it smoking hot, with plenty of pepper. The rest of my tin goes for rent and baccy and togs, and a little drop of gin now and then.'

There are yet accounts of habitations, statements of wages, &c., &c., to be given in connection with men working for the honourable masters, before proceeding to the scurf-traders.

The working scavengers usually reside in the neighbourhood of the dusty-yards, occupying 'second-floor backs', kitchens (where the entire house is sublet, a system often fraught with great extortion), or garrets; they usually, and perhaps always, when married, or what they consider 'as good', have their own furniture. The rent runs from 1s. 6d. to 2s. 3d. weekly, an average being 1s. 9d. or 1s. 10d. One room which I was in was but barely furnished, – a sort of dresser, serving also for a table; a chest; three chairs (one almost bottomless); an old turn-up bedstead, a Dutch clock, with the minute-hand broken, or as the scavenger very well called it when he saw me looking at it, 'a stump', an old 'corner cupboard', and some pots and domestic utensils in a closet without a door, but retaining a portion of the hinges on which a door had swung. The rent was 1s. 10d. with a frequent intimation that it ought to be 2s. The place was clean enough, and the scavenger seemed proud of it, assuring me that his old woman (wife or concubine) was 'a good sort', and kept things as nice as ever she could, washing everything herself, where 'other old women lushed'. The only ornaments in the room were three profiles of children, cut in black paper and pasted upon white card, tacked to the wall over the fire-place, for mantel-shelf there was none, while one of the three profiles, that of the eldest child (then dead), was 'framed', with a glass, and a sort of bronze or 'cast' frame, costing, I was told, 15d. This was the apartment of a man in regular employ (with but a few exceptions).

The diet of the regular working scavenger (or nightman) seems generally to differ from that of mechanics, and perhaps of other working men, in the respect of his being fonder of salt and *strong-flavoured* food. I have before made the same remark concerning the diet of the poor generally. I do not mean, however, that the scavengers are fond of such animal food as is called 'high', for I did not hear that nightmen or scavengers were more tolerant of what approached putridity than other labouring men, despite their calling, might sicken at the rankness of some haunches of venison; but they have a great relish for highly-salted cold boiled beef, bacon, or pork, with a saucer-full of red pickled cabbage, or dingy-looking pickled onions, or one or two big, strong, raw onions, of which most of them seem as fond as Spaniards of garlic. This sort of meat, sometimes profusely mustarded, is often eaten in the beer-shops with thick 'shives' of bread, cut into big mouthfuls with a clasp pocket-knife, while vegetables, unless indeed the beer-shop can supply a plate of smoking hot potatoes, are uncared for. The drink is usually beer. The same style of eating and the same kind of food characterize the scavenger and nightman, when taking his meal at home with his wife and family; but so irregular, and often of necessity, are these men's hours, that they may be said to have no homes, merely places to sleep or doze in.

A working scavenger and nightman calculated for me his expenses in eating and drinking, and other necessaries, for the previous week. He had earned 15s., but 1s. of this went to pay off an advance of 5s. made to him by the keeper of a beer-shop, or, as he called it, a 'jerry'.

	Daily. d.	Weekly. s.	d.
Rent of an unfurnished room		1	9
Washing (average)			3
[The man himself washed the dress in which he worked, and generally washed his own stockings.]			
Shaving (when twice a week)			1
Tobacco	1		7
[Short pipes are given to these men at the beer-shops, or public-houses which they 'use'.]			
Beer	4	2	4
[He usually spent more than 4d. a day in beer, he said, 'it was only a pot'; but this week more beer than usual had been given to him in nightwork.]			
Gin	2	1	2
[The same with gin.]			
Cocoa (pint at a coffee-shop)	1½		10½
Bread (quartern loaf) (sometimes 5½d.)	6	3	6
Boiled salt beef (¾ lb. or ½ lb. daily, 'as happened', for two meals, 6d. per pound, average	4	2	4
Pickles or Onions	0¼		1¾
Butter			1
Soap			1
		13	2¼

Perhaps this informant was excessive in his drink. I believe he was so; the others not drinking so much regularly. The odd 9d., he told me, he paid to 'a snob', because he said he was going to send his half-boots to be mended.

HENRY MAYHEW, *London Labour and the London Poor* (1851).

ONE OF THE NEW VOTERS
(1885)

THE reaper had risen early to his labour, but the birds had preceded him hours. Before the sun was up the swallows had left their beams in the cowshed and twittered out into the air. The rooks and wood-pigeons and doves had gone to the corn, the blackbird to the stream, the finch to the hedgerow, the bees to the heath on the hills, the humble-bees to the clover in the plain. Butterflies rose from the flowers by the footpath, and fluttered before him to and fro and round and back again to the place whence they had been driven. Goldfinches tasting the first thistledown rose from the corner where the thistles grew thickly. A hundred sparrows came rushing up into the hedge, suddenly filling the boughs with brown fruit; they chirped and quarrelled in their talk, and rushed away again back to the corn as he stepped nearer. The boughs were stripped of their winged brown berries as quickly as they had grown. Starlings ran before the cows feeding in the aftermath, so close to their mouths as to seem in danger of being licked up by their broad tongues. All creatures, from the tiniest insect upward, were in reality busy under that curtain of white-heat haze. It looked so still, so quiet, from afar; entering it and passing among the fields, all that lived was found busy at its long day's work. Roger did not interest himself in these things, in the wasps that left the gate as he approached – they were making *papier-maché* from the wood of the top bar, – in the bright poppies brushing against his drab unpolished boots, in the hue of the wheat or the white convolvulus; they were nothing to him.

Why should they be? His life was work without skill or thought, the work of the horse, of the crane that lifts stones and timber. His food was rough, his drink rougher, his lodging dry planks. His books were – none; his picture-gallery a coloured print at the alehouse – a dog, dead, by a barrel, 'Trust is dead; Bad Pay killed him.' Of thought he thought nothing; of hope his idea was a shilling a week more wages; of any future for himself of comfort such as even a good cottage can give – of any future whatever – he had no more conception than the horse in the shafts of the waggon. A human animal simply in all this, yet if you reckoned upon him as simply an animal – as has been done these centuries – you would now be mistaken. But why should he note the colour of the butterfly, the bright light of the sun, the hue of the wheat? This loveliness gave him no cheese for breakfast; of beauty in itself, for itself, he had no idea. How should he? To many of us the harvest – the summer – is a time of joy in light and colour; to him it was a time for adding yet another crust of hardness to the thick skin of his hands.

Though the haze looked like a mist it was perfectly dry; the wheat was as dry as noon; not a speck of dew, and the pimpernels wide open for a burning day. The reaping-machine began to rattle as he came up, and work was ready for him. At breakfast-time his fellows lent him a quarter of a loaf, some young onions, and a drink from their tea. He ate little, and the tea slipped from his hot tongue like water from the bars of a grate; his tongue was like the heated iron the housemaid tries before using it on the linen. As the reaping-machine went about the gradually decreasing square of corn, narrowing it by a broad band each time, the wheat fell flat on the short stubble. Roger stooped, and, gathering sufficient together, took a few straws, knotted them to another handful as you might tie two pieces of string, and twisted the band round the sheaf. He worked stooping to gather the wheat, bending to tie it in sheaves; stooping, bending – stooping, bending, – and so across the field. Upon his head and back the fiery sun poured down the ceaseless and increasing heat of the August day. His face grew red, his neck black; the drought of the dry ground rose up and entered his mouth and nostrils, a warm air seemed to rise from the earth and fill his chest. His body ached from the ferment of the vile beer, his back ached with stooping, his forehead was bound tight with a brazen band. They brought some beer at last; it was like the spring in the desert to him. The vicious liquor – 'a hair of the dog that bit him' – sank down his throat, grateful and refreshing to his disordered palate as if he had drunk the very shadow of green boughs. Good ale would have seemed nauseous to him at that moment, his taste and stomach destroyed by so many gallons of this. He was 'pulled together', and worked easier; the slow hours went on, and it was luncheon. He could have borrowed more food, but he was content instead with a screw of tobacco for his pipe and his allowance of beer.

They sat in the corner of the field. There were no trees for shade; they had been cut down as injurious to corn, but there were a few maple bushes and thin ash sprays, which seemed better than the open. The bushes cast no shade at all, the sun being so nearly overhead, but they formed a kind of enclosure, an open-air home, for men seldom sit down if they can help it on the bare and level plain; they go to the bushes, to the corner, or even to some hollow. It is not really any advantage; it is habit; or shall we not rather say that it is nature? Brought back as it were in the open field to the primitive conditions of life, they resumed the same instincts that controlled man in the ages past. Ancient man sought the shelter of trees and banks, of caves and hollows, and so the labourers under somewhat the same conditions came to the corner where the bushes grew. There they left their coats and slung up their luncheon-bundles to the branches; there the children played and took charge of the infants; there the women had their hearth and hung their kettle over a fire of sticks.

RICHARD JEFFERIES, 'One of the New Voters' from *The Open Air* (1885).

DARWIN AT WORK
(1876)

MY *Variation of Animals and Plants under Domestication* was begun, as already stated, in the beginning of 1860, but was not published until the beginning of 1868. It was a big book, and cost me four years and two months' hard labour. It gives all my observations and an immense number of facts collected from various sources, about our domestic productions. In the second volume the causes and laws of variation, inheritance, etc., are discussed, as far as our present state of knowledge permits. Towards the end of the work I give my well-abused hypothesis of Pangenesis. An unverified hypothesis is of little or no value; but if any one should hereafter be led to make observations by which some such hypothesis could be established, I shall have done good service, as an astonishing number of isolated facts can be thus connected together and rendered intelligible. In 1875 a second and largely corrected edition, which cost me a good deal of labour, was brought out.

My *Descent of Man* was published in February 1871. As soon as I had become, in the year 1837 or 1838, convinced that species were mutable productions, I could not avoid the belief that man must come under the same law. Accordingly I collected notes on the subject for my own satisfaction, and not for a long time with any intention of publishing. Although in the *Origin of Species* the derivation of any particular species is never discussed, yet I thought it best, in order that no honourable man should accuse me of concealing my views, to add that by the work 'light would be thrown on the origin of man and his history.' It would have been useless, and injurious to the success of the book to have paraded, without giving any evidence, my conviction with respect to his origin.

But when I found that many naturalists fully accepted the doctrine of the evolution of species, it seemed to me advisable to work up such notes as I possessed, and to publish a special treatise on the origin of man. I was the more glad to do so, as it gave me an opportunity of fully discussing sexual selection – a subject which had always greatly interested me. This subject, and that of the variation of our domestic productions, together with the causes and laws of variation, inheritance, and the intercrossing of plants, are the sole subjects which I have been able to write about in full, so as to use all the materials which I have collected. The *Descent of Man* took me three years to write, but then as usual some of this time was lost by ill-health, and some was consumed by preparing new editions and other minor works. A second and largely corrected edition of the *Descent* appeared in 1874.

My book on the *Expression of the Emotions in Men and Animals* was published in the autumn of 1872. I had intended to give only a chapter on the subject in the *Descent of Man*, but as soon as I began to put my notes together, I saw that it would require a separate treatise.

My first child was born on December 27th, 1839, and I at once commenced to make notes on the first dawn of the various expressions which he exhibited, for I felt convinced, even at this early period, that the most complex and fine shades of expression must all have had a gradual and natural origin. During the summer of the following year, 1840, I read Sir C. Bell's admirable work on expression, and this greatly increased the interest which I felt in the subject, though I could not at all agree with his belief that various muscles had been specially created for the sake of expression. From this time forward I occasionally attended to the subject, both with respect to man and our domesticated animals. My book sold largely; 5267 copies having been disposed of on the day of publication.

In the summer of 1860 I was idling and resting near Hartfield, where two species of [Sundew] abound; and I noticed that numerous insects had been entrapped by the leaves. I carried home some plants, and on giving them insects saw the movements of the tentacles, and this made me think it probable that the insects were caught for some special purpose. Fortunately a crucial test occurred to me, that of placing a large number of leaves in various nitrogenous and non-nitrogenous fluids of equal density; and as soon as I found that the former alone excited energetic movements, it was obvious that here was a fine new field for investigation.

During subsequent years, whenever I had leisure, I pursued my experiments, and my book on *Insectivorous Plants* was published in July 1875 – that is sixteen years after my first observations. The delay in this case, as with all my other books, has been a great advantage to me; for a man after a long interval can criticise his own work, almost as well as if it were that of another person. The fact that a plant should secrete, when properly excited, a fluid containing an acid and ferment, closely analogous to the digestive fluid of an animal, was certainly a remarkable discovery.

During this autumn of 1876 I shall publish on the *Effects of Cross- and Self-Fertilisation in the Vegetable Kingdom*. This book will form a complement to that on the *Fertilisation of Orchids*, in which I showed how perfect were the means for cross-fertilisation, and here I shall show how important are the results. I was led to make, during eleven years, the numerous experiments recorded in this volume, by a mere accidental observation; and indeed it required the accident to be repeated before my attention was thoroughly aroused to the remarkable fact that seedlings of self-fertilised parentage are inferior, even in the first generation, in height and vigour to seedlings of cross-fertilised parentage. I hope also to republish a revised edition of my book on Orchids, and hereafter my papers on dimorphic and trimorphic plants, together with some additional observations on allied points which I never have had time to arrange. My strength will then probably be exhausted, and I shall be ready to exclaim 'Nunc dimittis.'

CHARLES DARWIN, *Autobiography* in *Charles Darwin*, ed. F. Darwin (1892).

A DREAM WITHIN A DREAM
(Monday, 14 October 1872)

LAST night I had a strange and horrible dream. It was one of those curious things, a dream within a dream, like a picture within a picture. I dreamt that I dreamt that Mr and Mrs Venables tried to murder me. We were all together in a small room and they were both trying to poison me, but I was aware of their intention and baffled them repeatedly. At length, Mr Venables put me off my guard, came round fondling me, and suddenly clapped his hand on my neck behind said, 'It's of no use, Mr Kilvert. You're done for.'

I felt the poison beginning to work and burn in my neck. I knew it was all over and started up in fury and despair. I flew at him savagely. The scene suddenly changed to the organ loft in Hardenhuish Church. Mr Venables, seeing me coming at him, burst out at the door. Close outside the door was standing the Holy Ghost. He knocked him from the top to the bottom of the stairs, rolling over head over heels, rushed downstairs himself, mounted his horse and fled away, I after him.

This dream within a dream excited me to such a state of fury, that in the outer dream I determined to murder Mr Venables. Accordingly I lay in wait for him with a pickaxe on the Vicarage lawn at Clyro, hewed an immense and hideous hole through his head, and kicked his face till it was so horribly mutilated, crushed and disfigured as to be past recognition. Then the spirit of the dream changed. Mrs Venables became her old natural self again. 'Wasn't it enough,' she said, looking at me reproachfully, 'that you should have hewed that hole through his head, but you must go and kick his face so that I don't know him again?'

At this moment, Mr Bevan, the Vicar of Hay, came in. 'Well,' he said to me, 'you *have* done it now. You have made a pretty mess of it.'

All this time I was going about visiting the sick at Clyro and preaching in Clyro Church. But I saw that people were beginning to look shy at me and suspect me of the murder which had just been discovered. I became so wretched and conscience-stricken that I could bear my remorse no longer in secret and I went to give myself up to a policeman, who immediately took me to prison where I was kept in chains. Then the full misery of my position burst upon me and the ruin and disgrace I had brought on my family. 'It will kill my father,' I cried in an agony of remorse and despair.

I knew it was no dream. This at last was a reality from which I should never awake. I had awaked from many evil dreams and horrors and found them unreal, but this was a reality and horror from which I should never awake. It was all true at last. I had committed a murder. I calculated the time. I knew the Autumn Assizes were over and I could not be tried till the Spring. 'The Assizes,' I said, 'will come on in March and I shall be hung early in April.' And at the words I saw Mrs Venables give a shudder of horror.

When I woke I was so persuaded of the reality of what I had seen and felt and done in my dreams that I felt for the hand-cuffs on my wrists and could not believe I was in bed at home till I heard the old clock on the stairs warn and then strike five.

Nothing now seems to me so real and tangible as that dream was, and it seems to me as I might wake up at any moment and find everything shadowy, fleeting and unreal. I feel as if life is a dream from which at any moment I may awake.

When I came down to breakfast I found on the table a letter from Mr Venables announcing the death of old Mr

Thomas, the Rector of Disserth, which took place last Friday. Mr Thomas's son immediately wrote to Mr Venables to beg that he would ask the Bishop to give him the living. This Mr Venables says he at once declined to do and adds that he has written strongly to the Bishop of St David's in my favour to ask him to give Disserth to me. A kind note accompanied his from Mrs Venables who is as usual hopeful and sanguine about everything and thinks Mrs Thomas of Pencerrig would do a good deal for the parish. There is no house nor glebe and the living is saddled with Bettws Disserth, a chapelry where service must be performed every Sunday, 5 or 6 miles from Disserth Church. Mr Venables thinks notwithstanding that I should be unwise to decline the offer of Disserth should it be made to me. I hope the question may not arise. I am divided in opinion, and should be in great difficulty how to decide. Now I am settled here I do not want to leave my Father and this place and people to whom I am much attached, but yet I feel that I might throw away a fair chance of making myself a home and run the risk of finding myself adrift in the world, still a curate in middle age.

I have a sort of lingering longing for the old country and its beauty and romance, and it would be pleasant to be settled again among my old friends and the dear old scenes and memories.

However, sufficient unto the day is the evil thereof.

FRANCIS KILVERT, *Diary*, in *Kilvert's Diary*, Vol. 2, ed. Plomer (1944).

THE STORM CLOUD

(1884)

THE first time I recognized the clouds brought by the plague-wind as distinct in character was in walking back from Oxford, after a hard day's work, to Abingdon, in the early spring of 1871: it would take too long to give you any account this evening of the particulars which drew my attention to them; but during the following months I had too frequent opportunities of verifying my first thoughts of them, and on the first of July in that year wrote the description of them which begins the *Fors Clavigera* of August, thus:

It is the first of July, and I sit down to write by the dismallest light that ever yet I wrote by; namely, the light of this midsummer morning, in mid-England (Matlock, Derbyshire), in the year 1871.

For the sky is covered with grey cloud; – not rain-cloud, but a dry black veil, which no ray of sunshine can pierce; partly diffused in mist, feeble mist, enough to make distant objects unintelligible, yet without any substance, or wreathing, or colour of its own. And everywhere the leaves of the trees are shaking fitfully, as they do before a thunderstorm; only not violently, but enough to show the passing to and fro of a strange, bitter, blighting wind. Dismal enough, had it been the first morning of its kind that summer had sent. But during all this spring, in London, and at Oxford, through meagre March, through changelessly sullen April, through despondent May, and darkened June, morning after morning has come grey-shrouded thus.

And it is a new thing to me, and a very dreadful one. I am fifty years old, and more; and since I was five, have gleaned the best hours of my life in the sun of spring and summer mornings; and I never saw such as these, till now.

And the scientific men are busy as ants, examining the sun and the moon, and the seven stars, and can tell me all about *them*, I believe, by this time; and how they move, and what they are made of.

And I do not care, for my part, two copper spangles how they move, nor what they are made of. I can't move them any other way than they go, nor make them of anything else, better than they are made. But I would care much and give much, if I could be told where this bitter wind comes from, and what *it* is made of.

For, perhaps, with forethought, and fine laboratory science, one might make it of something else.

It looks partly as if it were made of poisonous smoke; very possibly it may be: there are at least two hundred furnace chimneys in a square of two miles on every side of me. But mere smoke would not blow to and fro in that wild way. It looks more to me as if it were made of dead men's souls – such of them as are not gone yet where they have to go, and may be flitting hither and thither, doubting, themselves, of the fittest place for them.

You know, if there *are* such things as souls, and if ever any of them haunt places where they have been hurt, there must be many above us, just now, displeased enough!

The last sentence refers of course to the battles of the Franco-German campaign, which was especially horrible to me, in its digging, as the Germans should have known, a moat flooded with waters of death between the two nations for a century to come.

Since that Midsummer day, my attention, however otherwise occupied, has never relaxed in its record of the phenomena characteristic of the plague-wind; and I now define for you, as briefly as possible, the essential signs of it.

(1) It is a wind of darkness, – all the former conditions of tormenting winds, whether from the north or east, were more or less capable of co-existing with sunlight, and often with steady and bright sunlight; but whenever, and wherever the plague-wind blows, be it but for ten minutes, the sky is darkened instantly.

(2) It is a malignant *quality* of wind, unconnected with any one quarter of the compass; it blows indifferently from all, attaching its own bitterness and malice to the worst characters of the proper winds of each quarter. It will blow either with drenching rain, or dry rage, from the south, – with ruinous blasts from the west, – with bitterest chills from the north, – and with venomous blight from the east.

Its own favourite quarter, however, is the south-west, so that it is distinguished in its malignity equally from the Bise of Provence, which is a north wind always, and from our own old friend, the east.

(3) It always blows *tremulously*, making the leaves of the trees shudder as if they were all aspens, but with a peculiar

fitfulness which gives them – and I watch them this moment as I write – an expression of anger as well as of fear and distress. You may see the kind of quivering, and hear the ominous whimpering, in the gusts that precede a great thunderstorm; but plague-wind is more panic-struck, and feverish; and its sound is a hiss instead of a wail.

When I was last at Avallon, in South France, I went to see *Faust* played at the little country theatre: it was done with scarcely any means of pictorial effect, except a few old curtains, and a blue light or two. But the night on the Brocken was nevertheless extremely appalling to me, – a strange ghastliness being obtained in some of the witch scenes merely by fine management of gesture and drapery; and in the phantom scenes, by the half-palsied, half-furious, faltering or fluttering past of phantoms stumbling as into graves; as if of not only soulless, but senseless, Dead, moving with the very action, the rage, the decrepitude, and the trembling of the plague-wind.

(4) Not only tremulous at every moment, it is also *intermittent* with a rapidity quite unexampled in former weather. There are, indeed, days – and weeks, on which it blows without cessation, and is as inevitable as the Gulf Stream; but also there are days when it is contending with healthy weather, and on such days it will remit for half an hour, and the sun will begin to show itself, and then the wind will come back and cover the whole sky with clouds in ten minutes; and so on, every half-hour, through the whole day; so that it is often impossible to go on with any kind of drawing in colour, the light being never for two seconds the same from morning till evening.

(5) It degrades, while it intensifies, ordinary storm; but before I read you any description of its efforts in this kind, I must correct an impression which has got abroad through the papers, that I speak as if the plague-wind blew now always, and there were no more any natural weather. On the contrary,

the winter of 1878–9 was one of the most healthy and lovely
I ever saw ice in; – Coniston lake shone under the calm clear
frost in one marble field, as strong as the floor of Milan
Cathedral, half a mile across and four miles down; and the
first entries in my diary which I read you shall be from the
22nd to 26th June, 1876, of perfectly lovely and natural
weather: . . .

JOHN RUSKIN, *The Storm Cloud of the Nineteenth Century.* Lecture
delivered at the London Institution 4 February 1884.

Imagination

THE URBAN POOR
(1848)

'GOING – art thou going to work this time o' day?'

'No, stupid, to be sure not. Going to see the chap thou spoke on.' So they put on their hats and set out. On the way Wilson said Davenport was a good fellow, though too much of the Methodee; that his children were too young to work, but not too young to be cold and hungry; that they had sunk lower and lower, and pawned thing after thing, and that they now lived in a cellar in Berry Street, off Store Street. Barton growled inarticulate words of no benevolent import to a large class of mankind, and so they went along till they arrived in Berry Street. It was unpaved: and down the middle a gutter forced its way, every now and then forming pools in the holes with which the street abounded. Never was the old Edinburgh cry of *Gardez l'eau!* more necessary than in this street. As they passed, women from their doors tossed household slops of *every* description into the gutter; they ran into the next pool, which overflowed and stagnated. Heaps of ashes were the stepping-stones, on which the passer-by, who cared in the least for cleanliness, took care not to put his foot. Our friends were not dainty, but even they picked their way, till they got to some steps leading down to a small area, where a person standing would have his head about one foot below the level of the street, and might at the same time, without the least motion of his body, touch the window of the cellar and the damp muddy wall right opposite. You went down one step even from the foul area into the cellar in which a family of human beings lived. It was very dark inside. The window-panes, many of them, were broken and stuffed with rags, which was reason enough for the dusky light that pervaded the place even at midday. After the account I have given of the state of the street, no one can be surprised that on going into the cellar inhabited by Davenport, the smell was so foetid as almost to knock the two men down. Quickly recovering themselves, as those inured to such things do, they began to penetrate the thick darkness of the place, and to see three or four little children rolling on the damp, nay wet brick floor, through which the stagnant, filthy moisture of the street oozed up; the fire-place was empty and black; the wife sat on her husband's lair, and cried in the dark loneliness.

'See, missis, I'm back again. – Hold your noise, children, and don't mither your mammy for bread; here's a chap as has got some for you.'

In that dim light, which was darkness to strangers, they clustered round Barton, and tore from him the food he had brought with him. It was a large hunch of bread, but it vanished in an instant.

'We mun do summut for 'em,' said he to Wilson. 'Yo stop here, and I'll be back in half-an-hour.'

So he strode, and ran, and hurried home. He emptied into the ever-useful pocket-handkerchief the little meal remaining in the mug. Mary would have her tea at Miss Simmonds'; her food for the day was safe. Then he went upstairs for his better coat, and his one, gay red-and-yellow silk pocket-handkerchief – his jewels, his plate, his valuables, these were. He went to the pawn-shop; he pawned them for five shillings; he stopped not, nor stayed, till he was once more in London Road, within five minutes' walk of Berry Street – then he loitered in his gait, in order to discover the shops he wanted. He bought meat, and a loaf of bread, candles, chips, and from a little retail yard he purchased a couple of hundredweights of coal. Some money still remained – all destined for them, but he did not yet know how best to spend it. Food, light, and warmth, he had instantly seen were necessary; for luxuries he would wait. Wilson's eyes filled with tears when he saw Barton enter with his purchases. He understood it all, and longed to be once more in work that he might help in some of these material ways, without feeling that he was using his son's money. But though 'silver and gold he had none', he gave heart-service and love-works of far more value. Nor was John Barton behind in these. 'The fever' was (as it usually is in Manchester) of a low, putrid, typhoid kind; brought on by miserable living, filthy neighbourhood, and great depression of mind and body. It is virulent, malignant, and highly infectious. But the poor are fatalists with regard to infection! and well for them it is so, for in their crowded dwellings no invalid can be isolated. Wilson asked Barton if he thought he should catch it, and was laughed at for his idea.

The two men, rough, tender nurses as they were, lighted the fire, which smoked and puffed into the room as if it did not know the way up the damp, unused chimney. The very smoke seemed purifying and healthy in the thick clammy air. The children clamoured again for bread; but this time Barton took a piece first to the poor, helpless, hopeless woman, who still sat by the side of her husband, listening to his anxious miserable mutterings. She took the bread, when it was put into her hand, and broke a bit, but could not eat. She was past hunger. She fell down on the floor with a heavy unresisting bang. The men looked puzzled. 'She's well-nigh clemmed,' said Barton. 'Folk do say one mustn't give clemmed people much to eat; but, bless us, she'll eat nought.'

'I'll tell yo what I'll do,' said Wilson. 'I'll take these two big lads, as does nought but fight, home to my missis for tonight, and I'll get a jug o' tea. Them women always does best with tea, and such-like slop.'

So Barton was now left alone with a little child, crying (when it had done eating) for mammy; with a fainting, dead-like woman; and with the sick man, whose mutterings were rising up to screams and shrieks of agonised anxiety. He carried the woman to the fire, and chafed her hands. He looked around for something to raise her head. There was literally nothing but some loose bricks. However, these he got; and taking off his coat he covered them with it as well as he could. He pulled her feet to the fire, which now began to emit some faint heat. He looked round for water, but the poor woman had been too weak to drag herself out to the distant pump, and water there was none. He snatched the child, and ran up the area-steps to the room above, and borrowed their only sauce-pan with some water in it. Then he began, with the useful skill of a workingman, to make some gruel; and when it was hastily made, he seized a battered iron table-spoon (kept when many other little things had been sold in a lot, in order to feed baby), and with it he forced one or two drops between her clenched teeth. The mouth opened mechanically to receive more, and gradually she revived. She sat up and looked round; and recollecting all, fell down again in weak and passive despair. Her little child crawled to her, and wiped with its fingers the thick-coming tears which she now had strength to weep. It was now high time to attend to the man. He lay on straw, so damp and mouldy, no dog would have chosen it in preference to flags; over it was a piece of sacking, coming next to his worn skeleton of a body; above him was mustered every article of clothing that could be spared by mother or children this bitter weather; and in addition to his own, these might have given as much warmth as one blanket, could they have been kept on him; but as he restlessly tossed to and fro, they fell off and left him shivering in spite of the burning heat of his skin. Every now and then he started up in his naked mad-ness, looking like the prophet of woe in the fearful plague-picture; but he soon fell again in exhaustion, and Barton found he must be closely watched, lest in these falls he should injure himself against the hard brick floor. He was thankful when Wilson re-appeared, carrying in both hands a jug of steaming tea, intended for the poor wife; but when the delirious husband saw drink, he snatched at it with animal instinct, with a selfishness he had never shown in health.

Then the two men consulted together. It seemed decided, without a word being spoken on the subject, that both should spend the night with the forlorn couple; that was settled. But could no doctor be had? In all probability, no; the next day an Infirmary order must be begged, but meanwhile the only medical advice they could have must be from a druggist's. So Barton (being the moneyed man) set out to find a shop in London Road.

It is a pretty sight to walk through a street with lighted shops; the gas is so brilliant, the display of goods so much more vividly shown than by day, and of all shops a druggist's looks the most like the tales of our childhood, from Aladdin's garden of enchanted fruits to the charming Rosamond with her purple jar. No such associations had Barton; yet he felt the contrast between the well-filled, well-lighted shops and the dim gloomy cellar, and it made him moody that such contrasts should exist. They are the mysterious problem of life to more than him. He wondered if any in all the hurrying crowd had come from such a house of mourning. He thought they all looked joyous, and he was angry with them. But he could not, you cannot, read the lot of those who daily pass you by in the street. How do you know the wild romances of their lives; the trials, the temptations they are even now enduring, resisting, sinking under? You may be elbowed one instant by the girl desperate in her abandonment, laughing in mad merriment with her outward gesture, while her soul is longing for the rest of the dead, and bringing itself to think of the cold flowing river as the only mercy of God remaining to her here. You may pass the criminal, meditating crimes at which you will tomorrow shudder with horror as you read them. You may push against one, humble and unnoticed, the last upon earth, who in heaven will for ever be in the immediate light of God's countenance. Errands of mercy – errands of sin – did you ever think where all the thousands of people you daily meet are bound? Barton's was an errand of mercy; but the thoughts of his heart were touched by sin, by bitter hatred of the happy, whom he, for the time, confounded with the selfish.

He reached a druggist's shop, and entered. The druggist (whose smooth manners seemed to have been salved over with his own spermaceti) listened attentively to Barton's description of Davenport's illness; concluded it was typhus fever, very prevalent in that neighbourhood; and proceeded to make up a bottle of medicine, sweet spirits of nitre, or some such innocent potion, very good for slight colds, but utterly powerless to stop, for an instant, the raging fever of the poor man it was intended to relieve. He recommended the same course they had previously determined to adopt, applying the next morning for an Infirmary order; and Barton left the shop with comfortable faith in the physic given him; for men of his class, if they believe in physic at all, believe that every description is equally efficacious.

Meanwhile, Wilson had done what he could at Davenport's home. He had soothed, and covered the man many a time; he had fed and hushed the little child, and spoken tenderly to the woman, who lay still in her weakness and her weariness. He had opened a door, but only for an instant; it led into a back cellar, with a grating instead of a window, down which dropped the moisture from pigsties, and worse abominations. It was not paved; the floor was one mass of bad smelling mud. It had never been used, for there was not an article of furniture in it; nor could a human being, much less a pig, have lived there many days. Yet the 'back apartment' made a difference in the rent. The Davenports paid threepence more for having two rooms. When he turned round again, he saw the woman suckling the child from her dry, withered breast.

'Surely the lad is weaned!' exclaimed he, in surprise. 'Why, how old is he?'

'Going on two year,' she faintly answered. 'But, oh! it keeps him quiet when I've nought else to gi' him, and he'll get a bit of sleep lying there, if he's getten nought beside. We han done our best to gi' the childer food, howe'er we pinch ourselves.'

'Han ye had no money fra' th' town?'

'No; my master is Buckinghamshire born; and he's feared the town would send him back to his parish, if he went to th' board; so we've just borne on in hope o' better times. But I think they'll never come in my day,' and the poor woman began her weak high-pitched cry again.

'Here, sup this drop o' gruel, and then try and get a bit o' sleep. John and I will watch by your master tonight.'

'God's blessing be on you.'

She finished the gruel, and fell into a deep sleep. Wilson covered her with his coat as well as he could, and tried to move lightly for fear of disturbing her; but there need have been no such dread, for her sleep was profound and heavy with exhaustion. Once only she roused to pull the coat round her little child.

And now Wilson's care, and Barton's to boot, was wanted to restrain the wild mad agony of the fevered man. He started up, he yelled, he seemed infuriated by overwhelming anxiety. He cursed and swore, which surprised Wilson, who knew his piety in health, and who did not know the unbridled tongue of delirium. At length he seemed exhausted, and fell asleep; and Barton and Wilson drew near the fire, and talked together in whispers. They sat on the floor, for chairs there were none; the sole table was an old tub turned upside down. They put out the candle and conversed by the flickering firelight.

ELIZABETH GASKELL, *Mary Barton* (1848).

A COUNTRY TOWN
(1845)

THE situation of the rural town of Marney was one of the most delightful easily to be imagined. In a spreading dale, contiguous to the margin of a clear and lively stream, surrounded by meadows and gardens, and backed by lofty hills, undulating and richly wooded, the traveller on the opposite heights of the dale would often stop to admire the merry prospect that recalled to him the traditional epithet of his country.

Beautiful illusion! For behind that laughing landscape, penury and disease fed upon the vitals of a miserable population.

The contrast between the interior of the town and its external aspect was as striking as it was full of pain. With the exception of the dull high street, which had the usual characteristics of a small agricultural market town, some sombre mansions, a dingy inn, and a petty bourse, Marney mainly consisted of a variety of narrow and crowded lanes formed by cottages built of rubble, or unhewn stones without cement, and, from age or badness of the material, looking as if they could scarcely hold together. The gaping chinks admitted every blast; the leaning chimneys had lost half their original height; the rotten rafters were evidently misplaced; while in many instances the thatch, yawning in some parts to admit the wind and wet, and in all utterly unfit for its original purpose of giving protection from the weather, looked more like the top of a dunghill than a cottage. Before the doors of these dwellings, and often surrounding them, ran open drains full of animal and vegetable refuse, decomposing into disease, or sometimes in their imperfect course filling foul pits or spreading into stagnant pools, while a concentrated solution of every species of dissolving filth was allowed to soak through, and thoroughly impregnate, the walls and ground adjoining.

These wretched tenements seldom consisted of more than two rooms, in one of which the whole family, however numerous, were obliged to sleep, without distinction of age, or sex, or suffering. With the water streaming down the walls, the light distinguished through the roof, with no hearth even in winter, the virtuous mother in the sacred pangs of child-birth gives forth another victim to our thoughtless civilisation; surrounded by three generations whose inevitable presence is more painful than her sufferings in that hour of travail; while the father of her coming child, in another corner of the sordid chamber, lies stricken by that typhus which his contaminating dwelling has breathed into his veins, and for whose next prey is perhaps destined his new-born child. These swarming walls had neither windows nor doors sufficient to keep out the weather, or admit the sun, or supply the means of ventilation; the humid and putrid roof of thatch exhaling malaria like all other decaying vegetable matter. The dwelling-rooms were neither boarded nor paved; and whether it were that some were situate in low and damp places, occasionally flooded by the river, and usually much below the level of the road; or that the springs, as was often the case, would burst through the mud floor; the ground was at no time better than so much clay, while sometimes you might see little channels cut from the centre under the doorways to carry off the water, the door itself removed from its hinges; a resting-place for infancy in its deluged home. These hovels were in many instances not provided with the commonest conveniences of the rudest police; contiguous to every door might be observed the dung-heap on which every kind of filth was accumulated, for the purpose of being disposed of for manure, so that, when the poor man opened his narrow habitation in the hope of refreshing it with the breeze of summer, he was met with a mixture of gases from reeking dung-hills.

This town of Marney was a metropolis of agricultural labour, for the proprietors of the neighbourhood having for the last half-century acted on the system of destroying the cottages on their estates, in order to become exempted from the maintenance of the population, the expelled people had flocked to Marney, where, during the war, a manufactory had afforded them some relief, though its wheels had long ceased to disturb the waters of the Mar.

Deprived of this resource, they had again gradually spread themselves over that land which had, as it were, rejected them; and obtained from its churlish breast a niggardly subsistence. Their re-entrance into the surrounding parishes was viewed with great suspicion; their renewed settlement opposed by every ingenious contrivance. Those who availed themselves of their labour were careful that they should not become dwellers on the soil; and though, from the excessive competition, there were few districts in the kingdom where the rate of wages was more depressed, those who were fortunate enough to obtain the scant remuneration had, in addition to their toil, to endure, each morn and even, a weary journey before they could reach the scene of their labour, or return to the squalid hovel which profaned the name of home. To that home, over which malaria hovered, and round whose shivering hearth were clustered other guests besides the exhausted family of toil, Fever, in every form, pale Consumption, exhausting Synochus, and trembling Ague, returned, after cultivating the broad fields of merry England, the bold British peasant, returned to encounter the worst of diseases, with a frame the least qualified to oppose them; a frame that, subdued by toil, was never sustained by animal food; drenched by the tempest, could not change its dripping rags; and was indebted for its scanty fuel to the windfalls of the woods.

BENJAMIN DISRAELI, *Sybil* (1845).

THE NEW RAILWAY
(1848)

The first shock of a great earthquake had, just at that period, rent the whole neighbourhood to its centre. Traces of its course were visible on every side. Houses were knocked down; streets broken through and stopped; deep pits and trenches dug in the ground; enormous heaps of earth and clay thrown up; buildings that were undermined and shaking, propped by great beams of wood. Here, a chaos of carts, overthrown and jumbled together, lay topsy-turvy at the bottom of a steep unnatural hill; there, confused treasures of iron soaked and rusted in something that had accidentally become a pond. Everywhere were bridges that led nowhere; thoroughfares that were wholly impassable; Babel towers of chimneys, wanting half their height; temporary wooden houses and enclosures, in the most unlikely situations; carcases of ragged tenements, and fragments of unfinished walls and arches, and piles of scaffolding, and wildernesses of bricks, and giant forms of cranes, and tripods straddling above nothing. There were a hundred thousand shapes and substances of incompleteness, wildly mingled out of their places, upside down, burrowing in the earth, aspiring in the air, mouldering in the water, and unintelligible as any dream. Hot springs and fiery eruptions, the usual attendants upon earthquakes, lent their contributions of confusion to the scene. Boiling water hissed and heaved within dilapidated walls; whence also, the glare and roar of flames came issuing forth; and mounds of ashes blocked up rights of way, and wholly changed the law and custom of the neighbourhood.

In short, the yet unfinished and unopened railroad was in progress; and from the very core of all this dire disorder, trailed smoothly away, upon its mighty course of civilization and improvement.

But as yet, the neighbourhood was shy to own the railroad, one or two bold speculators had projected streets; and one had built a little, but had stopped among the mud and ashes to consider farther of it. A bran-new tavern, redolent of fresh mortar and size, and fronting nothing at all, had taken for its sign The Railway Arms; but that might be rash enterprise – and then it hoped to sell drink to the workmen. So, the Excavator's House of Call had sprung up from a beer shop; and the old-established ham and beef shop had become The Railway Eating House, with a roast leg of pork daily, through interested motives of a similar immediate and popular description. Lodging-house keepers were favourable in like manner; and for the like reasons were not to be trusted. The general belief was very slow. There were frowzy fields, and cowhouses, and dunghills, and dustheaps, and ditches, and gardens, and summer-houses, and carpet-beating grounds, at the very door of the railway. Little tumuli of oyster shells in the oyster season, and of lobster shells in the lobster season, and of broken crockery and faded cabbage leaves in all seasons, encroached upon its high places. Posts, and rails, and old cautions to trespassers, and backs of mean houses, and patches of vegetation stared it out of countenance. Nothing was the better for it, or thought of being so. If the miserable waste ground lying near it could have laughed, it would have laughed it to scorn, like many of the miserable neighbours.

Staggs's Gardens was uncommonly incredulous. It was a little row of houses, with little squalid patches of ground before them, fenced off with old doors, barrel staves, scraps of tarpauling and dead bushes; with bottomless tin kettles and exhausted iron fenders, thrust into the gaps. Here, the Staggs's Gardeners trained scarlet beans, kept fowls and rabbits, erected rotten summer-houses (one was an old boat), dried clothes, and smoked pipes. Some were of opinion that Staggs's Gardens derived its name from a deceased capitalist, one Mr Staggs, who had built it for his delectation. Others, who had a natural taste for the country, held that it dated from those rural times when the antlered herd, under the familiar denomination of Staggses, had resorted to its shady precincts. Be this as it may, Staggs's Gardens was regarded by its population as a sacred grove not to be withered by railroads; and so confident were they generally of its long outliving any such ridiculous inventions, that the master chimney-sweeper at the corner, who was understood to take the lead in the local politics of the Gardens, had publicly declared that on the occasion of the railroad opening, if ever it did open, two of his boys should ascend the flues of his dwelling, with instructions to hail the failure with derisive jeers from the chimney-pots.

*

There was no such place as Staggs's Gardens. It had vanished from the earth. Where the old rotten summer-houses once had stood, palaces now reared their heads, and granite columns of gigantic girth opened a vista to the railway world beyond. The miserable waste ground, where the refuse-matter had been heaped of yore, was swallowed up and gone; and in its frowsy stead were tiers of warehouses, crammed with rich goods and costly merchandise. The old by-streets now swarmed with passengers and vehicles of every kind; the new streets that had stopped disheartened in the mud and waggon-ruts, formed towns within themselves, originating wholesome comforts and conveniences belonging to themselves, and never tried nor thought of until they sprung into existence. Bridges that had led to nothing, led to villas, gardens, churches, healthy public walks. The carcasses of houses, and beginnings of new thoroughfares, had started off upon the line at steam's own speed, and shot away into the country in a monster train.

As to the neighbourhood which had hesitated to acknowledge the railroad in its struggling days, that had grown wise and penitent, as any Christian might in such a case, and now boasted of its powerful and prosperous relation. There were railway patterns in its drapers' shops, and railway journals in the windows of its newsmen. There were railway hotels, coffee-houses, lodging-houses, boarding-houses; railway plans, maps, views, wrappers, bottles, sandwich-boxes, and time-tables; railway hackney-coach and cabstands; railway omni-buses, railway streets and buildings, railway hangers-on and parasites, and flatterers out of all calculation. There was even railway time observed in clocks, as if the sun itself had given in. Among the vanquished was the master chimney-sweeper, whilom incredulous at Staggs's Gardens, who now lived in a stuccoed house three stories high, and gave himself out, with golden flourishes upon a varnished board, as contractor for the cleansing of railway chimneys by machinery.

To and from the heart of this great change, all day and night, throbbing currents rushed and returned, incessantly like its life's blood. Crowds of people and mountains of goods, departing and arriving scores upon scores of times in every four-and-twenty hours, produced a fermentation in the place that was always in action. The very houses seemed disposed to pack up and take trips. Wonderful Members of Parliament, who, little more than twenty years before, had made themselves merry with the wild railroad theories of engineers, and given them the liveliest rubs in cross-examination, went down into the north with their watches in their hands, and sent on messages before by the electric telegraph, to say that they were coming. Night and day the conquering engines rumbled at their distant work, or, advancing smoothly to their journey's end, and gliding like tame dragons into the allotted corners grooved out to the inch for their reception, stood bubbling and trembling there, making the walls quake, as if they were dilating with the secret knowledge of great powers yet un-suspected in them, and strong purposes not yet achieved.

CHARLES DICKENS, *Dombey and Son* (1848).

PARTIES IN THE COUNTRY
(1852)

WHY, yes. It cannot be disguised. There *are*, at Chesney Wold this January week, some ladies and gentlemen of the newest fashion, who have set up a Dandyism – in Religion, for instance. Who, in mere lackadaisical want of an emotion, have agreed upon a little dandy talk about the Vulgar wanting faith in things in general; meaning, in the things that have been tried and found wanting, as though a low fellow should unaccountably lose faith in a bad shilling, after finding it out! Who would make the Vulgar very picturesque and faithful, by putting back the hands upon the Clock of Time, and cancelling a few hundred years of history.

There are also ladies and gentlemen of another fashion, not so new, but very elegant, who have agreed to put a smooth glaze on the world and to keep down all its realities. For whom everything must be languid and pretty. Who have found out the perpetual stoppage. Who are to rejoice at nothing, and be sorry for nothing. Who are not to be disturbed by ideas. On whom even the Fine Arts, attending in powder and walking backward like the Lord Chamberlain, must array themselves in the milliners' and tailors' patterns of past generations, and be particularly careful not to be in earnest, or to receive any impress from the moving age.

Then there is my Lord Boodle, of considerable reputation with his party, who has known what office is, and who tells Sir Leicester Dedlock with much gravity, after dinner, that he really does not see to what the present age is tending. A debate is not what a debate used to be; the House is not what the House used to be; even a Cabinet is not what it formerly was. He perceives with astonishment, that supposing the present Government to be overthrown, the limited choice of the Crown, in the formation of a new Ministry, would lie between Lord Coodle and Sir Thomas Doodle – supposing it to be impossible for the Duke of Foodle to act with Goodle, which may be assumed to be the case in consequence of the breach arising out of that affair with Hoodle. Then, giving the Home Department and the Leadership of the House of Commons to Joodle, the Exchequer to Koodle, the Colonies to Loodle, and the Foreign Office to Moodle, what are you to do with Noodle? You can't offer him the Presidency of the Council; that is reserved for Poodle. You can't put him in the Woods and Forests; that is hardly good enough for Quoodle. What follows? That the country is shipwrecked, lost, and gone to pieces (as is made manifest to the patriotism of Sir Leicester Dedlock), because you can't provide for Noodle!

On the other hand, the Right Honourable William Buffy, M.P., contends across the table with some one else, that the shipwreck of the country – about which there is no doubt; it is only the manner of it that is in question – is attributable to Cuffy. If you had done with Cuffy what you ought to have done when he first came into Parliament, and had prevented him from going over to Duffy, you would have got him into an alliance with Fuffy, you would have had with you the weight attaching as a smart debater to Guffy, you would have brought to bear upon the elections the wealth of Huffy, you would have got in for three counties Juffy, Kuffy, and Luffy; and you would have strengthened your administration by the official knowledge and the business habits of Muffy. All this, instead of being, as you now are, dependent on the mere caprice of Puffy!

As to this point, and as to some minor topics, there are differences of opinion; but it is perfectly clear to the brilliant and distinguished circle, all round, that nobody is in question but Boodle and his retinue, and Buffy and *his* retinue. These are the great actors for whom the stage is reserved. A People there are, no doubt – a certain large number of supernumeraries, who are to be occasionally addressed, and relied upon for shouts and choruses, as on the theatrical stage; but Boodle and Buffy, their followers and families, their heirs, executors, administrators, and assigns, are the born first-actors, managers, and leaders, and no others can appear upon the scene for ever and ever.

CHARLES DICKENS, *Bleak House* (1852–3).

FLORA
(1855)

THERE was no one with Flora but Mr F's Aunt, which respectable gentlewoman, basking in a balmy atmosphere of tea and toast, was ensconced in an easy-chair by the fireside, with a little table at her elbow, and a clean white handkerchief spread over her lap, on which two pieces of toast at that moment awaited consumption. Bending over a steaming vessel of tea, and looking through the steam, and breathing forth the steam, like a malignant Chinese enchantress engaged in the performance of unholy rites, Mr F's Aunt put down her great teacup, and exclaimed, 'Drat him, if he an't come back again!'

It would seem from the foregoing exclamation that this uncompromising relative of the lamented Mr F, measuring time by the acuteness of her sensations and not by the clock, supposed Clennam to have lately gone away; whereas at least a quarter of a year had elapsed since he had had the temerity to present himself before her.

'My goodness Arthur!' cried Flora, rising to give him a cordial reception, 'Doyce and Clennam what a start and a surprise for though not far from the machinery and foundry business and surely might be taken sometimes if at no other time about mid-day when a glass of sherry and a humble sandwich of whatever cold meat in the larder might not come amiss nor taste the worse for being friendly for you know you buy it somewhere and wherever bought a profit must be made or they would never keep the place it stands to reason without a motive still never seen and learnt now not to be expected, for as Mr F himself said if seeing is believing not seeing is believing too and when you don't see you may fully believe you're not remembered not that I expect you Arthur Doyce and Clennam to remember me why should I for the days are gone but bring another teacup here directly and tell her fresh toast and pray sit near the fire.'

Arthur was in the greatest anxiety to explain the object of his visit; but was put off for the moment, in spite of himself, by what he understood of the reproachful purport of these words, and by the genuine pleasure she testified in seeing him.

'And now pray tell me something all you know,' said Flora, drawing her chair near to his, 'about the good dear quiet little thing and all the changes of her fortunes carriage people now no doubt and horses without number most romantic, a coat of arms of course and wild beasts on their hind legs showing it as if it was a copy they had done with mouths from ear to ear good gracious, and has she her health which is the first consideration after all for what is wealth without it Mr F himself so often saying when his twinges came that sixpence a day and find yourself and no gout so much preferable, not that he could have lived on anything like it being the last man or that the precious little thing though far too familiar an expression now had any tendency of that sort much too slight and small but looked so fragile bless her!'

Mr F's Aunt, who had eaten a piece of toast down to the crust, here solemnly handed the crust to Flora, who ate it for her as a matter of business. Mr F's Aunt then moistened her ten fingers in slow succession at her lips, and wiped them in exactly the same order on the white handkerchief; then took the other piece of toast, and fell to work upon it. While pursuing this routine, she looked at Clennam with an expression of such intense severity that he felt obliged to look at her in return, against his personal inclinations.

'She is in Italy, with all her family, Flora,' he said, when the dread lady was occupied again.

'In Italy is she really?' said Flora, 'with the grapes and figs growing everywhere and lava necklaces and bracelets too that land of poetry with burning mountains picturesque beyond belief though if the organ-boys come away from the neighbourhood not to be scorched nobody can wonder being so young and bringing their white mice with them most humane, and is she really in that favoured land with nothing but blue about her and dying gladiators and Belvederas though Mr F himself did not believe for his objection when in spirits was that the images could not be true there being no medium between expensive quantities of linen badly got up and all in creases and none whatever, which certainly does not seem probable though perhaps in consequence of the extremes of rich and poor which may account for it.'

Arthur tried to edge a word in, but Flora hurried on again.

CHARLES DICKENS, *Little Dorrit* (1855-7).

MAKING FRIENDS
(1848)

WITH Mr Crawley Miss Sharp was respectful and obedient. She used to consult him on passages of French which she could not understand, though her mother was a Frenchwoman, and which he would construe to her satisfaction: and, besides giving her his aid in profane literature, he was kind enough to select for her books of a more serious tendency, and address to her much of his conversation. She admired, beyond measure, his speech at the Quashimaboo-Aid Society; took an interest in his pamphlet on malt; was often affected, even to tears, by his discourses of an evening, and would say – 'Oh, thank you' sir,' with a sigh, and a look up to heaven, that made him occasionally condescend to shake hands with her. 'Blood is everything, after all,' would that aristocratic religionist say. 'How Miss Sharp is awakened by my words, when not one of the people here is touched. I am too fine for them – too delicate. I must familiarize my style – but she understands it. Her mother was a Montmorency.'

Indeed it was from this famous family, as it appears, that Miss Sharp, by the mother's side, was descended. Of course she did not say that her mother had been on the stage; it would have shocked Mr Crawley's religious scruples. How many noble *emigrées* had this horrid revolution plunged in poverty! She had several stories about her ancestors ere she had been many months in the house; some of which Mr Crawley happened to find in D'Hozier's dictionary, which was in the library, and which strengthened his belief in their truth, and in the high-breeding of Rebecca. Are we to suppose from this curiosity and prying into dictionaries, could our heroine suppose, that Mr Crawley was interested in her? – no, only in a friendly way. Have we not stated that he was attached to Lady Jane Sheepshanks?

He took Rebecca to task once or twice about the propriety of playing at backgammon with Sir Pitt, saying that it was a godless amusement, and that she would be much better engaged in reading *Thrump's Legacy*, or *The Blind Washerwoman of Moorfields*, or any work of a more serious nature; but Miss Sharp said her dear mother used often to play the same game with the old Count de Trictrac and the venerable Abbé du Cornet, and so found an excuse for this and other worldly amusement.

But it was not only by playing at backgammon with the baronet that the little governess rendered herself agreeable to her employer. She found many different ways of being useful to him. She read over, with indefatigable patience, all those

law papers, with which, before she came to Queen's Crawley'
he had promised to entertain her. She volunteered to copy
many of his letters, and adroitly altered the spelling of them so
as to suit the usages of the present day. She became interested
in everything appertaining to the estate, to the farm, the park,
the garden, and the stables; and so delightful a companion was
she, that the baronet would seldom take his after-breakfast
walk without her (and the children of course), when she would
give her advice as to the trees which were to be lopped in the
shrubberies, the garden-beds to be dug, the crops which were
to be cut, the horses which were to go to cart or plough.
Before she had been a year at Queen's Crawley she had quite
won the baronet's confidence; and the conversation at the
dinner-table, which before used to be held between him and
Mr Horrocks the butler, was now almost exclusively between
Sir Pitt and Miss Sharp. She was almost mistress of the house
when Mr Crawley was absent, but conducted herself in her
new and exalted situation with such circumspection and
modesty as not to offend the authorities of the kitchen and
stable, among whom her behaviour was always exceedingly
modest and affable. She was quite a different person from the
haughty, shy, dissatisfied little girl whom we have known
previously, and this change of temper proved great prudence,
a sincere desire of amendment, or at any rate great moral
courage on her part. Whether it was the heart which dictated
this new system of complaisance and humility adopted by our
Rebecca, is to be proved by her after-history. A system of
hypocrisy, which lasts through whole years, is one seldom
satisfactorily practised by a person of one-and-twenty; however, our readers will recollect, that, though young in years,
our heroine was old in life and experience, and we have written
to no purpose if they have not discovered that she was a very
clever woman.

The elder and younger son of the house of Crawley were,
like the gentleman and lady in the weather-box, never at

home together – they hated each other cordially: indeed·
Rawdon Crawley, the dragoon, had a great contempt for the
establishment altogether, and seldom came thither except
when his aunt paid her annual visit.

The great good quality of this old lady has been mentioned.
She possessed seventy thousand pounds, and had almost
adopted Rawdon. She disliked her elder nephew exceedingly,
and despised him as a milksop. In return he did not hesitate
to state that her soul was irretrievably lost, and was of opinion
that his brother's chance in the next world was not a whit
better. 'She is a godless woman of the world,' would Mr Crawley say; 'she lives with atheists and Frenchmen. My mind
shudders when I think of her awful, awful situation, and that,
near as she is to the grave, she should be so given up to vanity,
licentiousness, profaneness, and folly.' In fact, the old lady
declined altogether to hear his hour's lecture of an evening;
and when she came to Queen's Crawley alone, he was
obliged to pretermit his usual devotional exercises.

'Shut up your sarmons, Pitt, when Miss Crawley comes
down,' said his father; 'she has written to say that she won't
stand the preachifying.'

'Oh, sir! consider the servants.'

'The servants be hanged,' said Sir Pitt; and his son thought
even worse would happen were they deprived of the benefit
of his instruction.

'Why, hang it, Pitt!' said the father to his remonstrance.
'You wouldn't be such a flat as to let three thousand a year
go out of the family?'

'What is money compared to our souls, sir?' continued
Crawley.

'You mean that the old lady won't leave the money to you?'
– and who knows but it *was* Mr Crawley's meaning?

Old Miss Crawley was certainly one of the reprobate. She
had a snug little house in Park Lane, and, as she ate and drank
a great deal too much during the season in London, she went

to Harrogate or Cheltenham for the summer. She was the most hospitable and jovial of old vestals, and had been a beauty in her day, she said. (All old women were beauties once, we very well know.) She was a *bel esprit*, and a dreadful Radical for those days. She had been in France (where St Just, they say, inspired her with an unfortunate passion), and loved, ever after, French novels, French cookery, and French wines. She read Voltaire, and had Rousseau by heart; talked very lightly about divorce, and most energetically of the rights of women. She had pictures of Mr Fox in every room in the house: when that statesman was in opposition, I am not sure that she had not flung a main with him; and when he came into office, she took great credit for bringing over to him Sir Pitt and his colleague for Queen's Crawley, although Sir Pitt would have come over himself, without any trouble on the honest lady's part. It is needless to say that Sir Pitt was brought to change his views after the death of the great Whig statesman.

This worthy old lady took a fancy to Rawdon Crawley when a boy, sent him to Cambridge (in opposition to his brother at Oxford), and, when the young man was requested by the authorities of the first-named University to quit after a residence of two years, she bought him his commission in the Life Guards Green.

A perfect and celebrated 'blood', or dandy about town, was this young officer. Boxing, rat-hunting, the fives-court, and four-in-hand driving were then the fashion of our British aristocracy; and he was an adept in all these noble sciences. And though he belonged to the household troops, who, as it was their duty to rally round the Prince Regent, had not shown their valour in foreign service yet, Rawdon Crawley had already (à propos of play, of which he was immoderately fond) fought three bloody duels in which he gave ample proofs of his contempt for death.

'And for what follows after death,' would Mr Crawley

observe, throwing his gooseberry-coloured eyes up to the ceiling. He was always thinking of his brother's soul, or of the souls of those who differed with him in opinion: it is a sort of comfort which many of the serious give themselves.

Silly, romantic Miss Crawley, far from being horrified at the courage of her favourite, always used to pay his debts after his duels; and would not listen to a word that was whispered against his morality. 'He will sow his wild oats,' she would say, 'and is worth far more than that puling hypocrite of a brother of his.'

Besides these honest folks at the Hall (whose simplicity and sweet rural purity surely show the advantage of a country life over a town one), we must introduce the reader to their relatives and neighbours at the Rectory, Bute Crawley and his wife.

The Reverend Bute Crawley was a tall, stately, jolly, shovel-hatted man, far more popular in his county than the baronet his brother. At college he pulled stroke-oar in the Christchurch boat, and had thrashed all the best bruisers of the 'town'. He carried his taste for boxing and athletic exercises into private life; there was not a fight within twenty miles at which he was not present, nor a race, nor a coursing match, nor a regatta, nor a ball, nor an election, nor a visitation dinner, nor indeed a good dinner in the whole county, but he found means to attend it. You might see his bay mare and gig-lamps a score of miles away from his rectory house, whenever there was any dinner-party at Fuddleston, or at Roxby, or at Wapshot Hall, or at the great lords of the county, with all of whom he was intimate. He had a fine voice; sang 'A southerly wind and a cloudy sky'; and gave the 'whoop' in chorus with general applause. He rode to hounds in a pepper-and-salt frock, and was one of the best fishermen in the county.

Mrs Crawley, the rector's wife, was a smart little body, who wrote this worthy divine's sermons. Being of a domestic turn, and keeping the house a great deal with her daughters, she ruled absolutely within the Rectory, wisely giving her husband full liberty without. He was welcome to come and go, and dine abroad as many days as his fancy dictated, for Mrs Crawley was a saving woman and knew the price of port wine. Ever since Mrs Bute carried off the young rector of Queen's Crawley (she was of a good family, daughter of the late Lieut-Colonel Hector MacTavish, and she and her mother played for Bute and won him at Harrogate), she had been a prudent and thrifty wife to him. In spite of her care, however, he was always in debt. It took him at least ten years to pay off his college bills contracted during his father's lifetime. In the year 179-, when he was just clear of these incumbrances, he gave the odds of 100 to 1 (in twenties) against Kangaroo, who won the Derby. The rector was obliged to take up the money at a ruinous interest, and had been struggling ever since. His sister helped him with a hundred now and then, but of course his great hope was in her death – when 'hang it' (as he would say), 'Matilda *must* leave me half her money.'

So that the baronet and his brother had every reason which two brothers possibly can have for being by the ears. Sir Pitt had had the better of Bute in innumerable family transactions. Young Pitt not only did not hunt, but set up a meeting-house under his uncle's very nose. Rawdon, it was known, was to come in for the bulk of Miss Crawley's property. These money transactions – these speculations in life and death – these silent battles for reversionary spoil – make brothers very loving towards each other in Vanity Fair. I, for my part, have known a five-pound note to interpose and knock up a half-century's attachment between two brethren; and can't but admire, as I think what a fine and durable thing Love is among wordly people.

It cannot be supposed that the arrival of such a personage as Rebecca at Queen's Crawley, and her gradual establishment in the good graces of all people there, could be unremarked by Mrs Bute Crawley. Mrs Bute, who knew how many days the sirloin of beef lasted at the Hall; how much linen was got ready at the great wash; how many peaches were on the south wall; how many doses her ladyship took when she was ill – for such points are matters of intense interest to certain persons in the country – Mrs Bute, I say, could not pass over the Hall governess without making every inquiry respecting her history and character. There was always the best understanding between the servants at the Rectory and the Hall. There was always a good glass of ale in the kitchen of the former place for the Hall people, whose ordinary drink was very small – and, indeed, the rector's lady knew exactly how much malt went to every barrel of Hall beer – ties of relationship existed between the Hall and Rectory domestics, as between their masters; and through these channels each family was perfectly well acquainted with the doings of the other. That, by the way, may be set down as a general remark. When you and your brother are friends, his doings are indifferent to you. When you have quarrelled, all his outgoings and incomings you know, as if you were his spy.

Very soon then after her arrival, Rebecca began to take a regular place in Mrs Crawley's bulletin from the Hall. It was to this effect: – 'The black porker's killed – weighed x stone – salted the sides – pig's pudding and leg of pork for dinner. Mr Cramp from Mudbury, over with Sir Pitt about putting John Blackmore in gaol – Mr Pitt at meeting (with all the names of the people who attended) – my lady as usual – the young ladies with the governess.'

Then the report would come – the new governess be a rare manager – Sir Pitt be very sweet on her – Mr Crawley too – He be reading tracts to her – 'What an abandoned wretch!' said little, eager, active, black-faced Mrs Bute Crawley.

Finally, the reports were that the governess had 'come round' everybody, wrote Sir Pitt's letters, did his business, managed his accounts – had the upper hand of the whole house, my lady, Mr Crawley, the girls and all – at which Mrs

Crawley declared she was an artful hussy, and had some dreadful designs in view.

WILLIAM MAKEPEACE THACKERAY, *Vanity Fair* (1848).

THE MEANINGS OF LOVE
(1847)

I WAS superstitious about dreams then, and am still; and Catherine had an unusual gloom in her aspect, that made me dread something from which I might shape a prophecy, and foresee a fearful catastrophe. She was vexed, but she did not proceed. Apparently taking up another subject, she recommenced in a short time.

'If I were in heaven, Nelly, I should be extremely miserable.'

'Because you are not fit to go there,' I answered. 'All sinners would be miserable in heaven.'

'But it is not for that. I dreamt once that I was there.'

'I tell you I won't hearken to your dreams, Miss Catherine! I'll go to bed,' I interrupted again.

She laughed, and held me down; for I made a motion to leave my chair.

'This is nothing,' cried she: 'I was only going to say that heaven did not seem to be my home; and I broke my heart with weeping to come back to earth; and the angels were so angry that they flung me out into the middle of the heath on the top of Wuthering Heights; where I woke sobbing for joy. That will do to explain my secret, as well as the other. I've no more business to marry Edgar Linton than I have to be in heaven; and if the wicked man in there had not brought Heathcliff so low, I shouldn't have thought of it. It would degrade me to marry Heathcliff now; so he shall never know how I love him: and that, not because he's handsome, Nelly, but because he's more myself than I am. Whatever our souls are made of, his and mine are the same; and Linton's is as different as a moonbeam from lightning, or frost from fire.'

Ere this speech ended, I became sensible of Heathcliff's presence. Having noticed a slight movement, I turned my head, and saw him rise from the bench, and steal out noiselessly. He had listened till he heard Catherine say it would degrade her to marry him, and then he stayed to hear no further. My companion, sitting on the ground, was prevented by the back of the settle from remarking his presence or departure; but I started, and bade her hush.

'Why?' she asked, gazing nervously round.

'Joseph is here,' I answered, catching opportunely the roll of his cart-wheels up the road; 'and Heathcliff will come in with him. I'm not sure whether he were not at the door this moment.'

'Oh, he couldn't overhear me at the door!' said she. 'Give me Hareton, while you get the supper, and when it is ready ask me to sup with you. I want to cheat my uncomfortable conscience, and be convinced that Heathcliff has no notion of these things. He has not, has he? He does not know what being in love is?'

'I see no reason that he should not know, as well as you,' I returned; 'and if *you* are his choice, he will be the most unfortunate creature that ever was born! As soon as you become Mrs Linton, he loses friend, and love, and all! Have you considered how you'll bear the separation, and how he'll bear to be quite deserted in the world? Because, Miss Catherine—'

'He quite deserted! We separated!' she exclaimed, with an accent of indignation. 'Who is to separate us, pray? They'll meet the fate of Milo! Not so long as I live, Ellen: for no mortal creature. Every Linton on the face of the earth might melt into nothing, before I could consent to forsake Heathcliff. Oh, that's not what I intend – that's not what I mean! I shouldn't be Mrs Linton were such a price demanded! He'll be as much to me as he has been all his lifetime. Edgar must shake off his antipathy, and tolerate him, at least. He will, when he learns my true feelings towards him. Nelly, I see now, you think me a selfish wretch; but did it never strike you that if Heathcliff and I married, we should be beggars? Whereas, if I marry Linton, I can aid Heathcliff to rise, and place him out of my brother's power.'

'With your husband's money, Miss Catherine?' I asked. 'You'll find him not so pliable as you calculate upon: and though I'm hardly a judge, I think that's the worst motive you've given yet for being the wife of young Linton.'

'It is not,' retorted she; 'it is the best! The others were the satisfaction of my whims: and for Edgar's sake, too, to satisfy him. This is for the sake of one who comprehends in his person my feelings to Edgar and myself. I cannot express it; but surely you and everybody have a notion that there is or should be an existence of yours beyond you. What were the use of my creation, if I were entirely contained here? My great miseries in this world have been Heathcliff's miseries, and I watched and felt each from the beginning: my great thought in living is himself. If all else perished, and *he* remained, *I* should still continue to be; and if all else remained, and he were annihilated, the universe would turn to a mighty stranger: I should not seem a part of it. My love for Linton is like the foliage in the woods: time will change it, I'm well aware, as winter changes the trees. My love for Heathcliff resembles the eternal rocks beneath: a source of little visible delight, but necessary. Nelly, I *am* Heathcliff! He's always, always in my mind: not as a pleasure, any more than I am always a pleasure to myself, but as my own being. So don't talk of our separation again: it is impracticable; and —'

She paused, and hid her face in the folds of my gown; but I jerked it forcibly away. I was out of patience with her folly!

EMILY BRONTË, *Wuthering Heights* (1847).

'WHERE AM I?'

(1853)

I COULD only think of the pensionnat in the Rue Fossette. Still half dreaming, I tried hard to discover in what room they had put me; whether the greater dormitory or one of the little dormitories. I was puzzled, because I could not make the glimpses of furniture I saw accord with my knowledge of any of these apartments. The empty white beds were wanting, and the long line of large windows. 'Surely,' thought I, 'it is not to Madame Beck's own chamber they have carried me!' And here my eye fell on an easy chair covered with blue damask. Other seats, cushioned to match, dawned on me by degrees; and at last I took in the complete fact of a pleasant parlour, with a wood fire on a clear shining hearth, a carpet where arabesques of bright blue relieved a ground of shaded fawn; pale walls over which a slight but endless garland of azure forget-me-nots ran mazed and bewildered amongst myriad gold leaves and tendrils. A gilded mirror filled up the space between two windows, curtained amply with blue damask. In this mirror I saw myself laid, not in bed, but on a sofa. I looked spectral; my eyes larger and more hollow, my hair darker than was natural, by contrast with my thin and ashen face. It was obvious, not only from the furniture, but from the position of windows, doors and fireplace that this was an unknown room in an unknown house.

Hardly less plain was it that my brain was not yet settled; for, as I gazed at the blue armchair, it appeared to grow familiar; so did a certain scroll couch, and not less so the round centre table, with a blue covering bordered with autumn-tinted foliage; and, above all, two little footstools with worked covers, and a small ebony-framed chair, of which the seat and back were also worked with groups of brilliant flowers on a dark ground.

Struck with these things, I explored further. Strange to say, old acquaintance were all about me, and 'auld lang syne' smiled out of every nook. There were two oval miniatures over the mantelpiece, of which I knew by heart the pearls about the high and powdered 'heads'; the velvet circling the white throats; the swell of the full muslin kerchiefs; the pattern of the lace sleeve ruffles. Upon the mantelshelf there were two china vases, some relics of a diminutive tea service, as smooth as enamel and as thin as egg shell, and a white centre ornament, a classic group in alabaster, preserved under glass. Of all these things I could have told the peculiarities, numbered the flaws or cracks, like any *clairvoyante*. Above all, there was a pair of hand-screens, with elaborate pencil drawings finished like line engravings: these, my very eyes ached at beholding again, recalling hours when they had followed, stroke by stroke and touch by touch, a tedious, feeble, finical, schoolgirl pencil held in these fingers, now so skeleton-like.

Where was I? Not only in what spot of the world, but in what year of our Lord? For all these objects were of past days and of a distant country. Ten years ago I bade them goodbye; since my fourteenth year they and I had never met. I gasped audibly, 'Where am I?'

A shape hitherto unnoticed, stirred, rose, came forward: a shape inharmonious with the environment, serving only to complicate the riddle further. This was no more than a sort of native bonne, in a commonplace bonne's cap and print dress. She spoke neither French nor English, and I could get no intelligence from her, not understanding her phrases of dialect. But she bathed my temples and forehead with some cool and perfumed water, and then she heightened the cushion on which I reclined, made signs that I was not to speak, and resumed her post at the foot of the sofa.

She was busy knitting; her eyes thus drawn from me, I could gaze on her without interruption. I did mightily wonder how she came there, or what she could have to do among the scenes, or with the days of my girlhood. Still more I marvelled what those scenes and days could now have to do with me.

Too weak to scrutinise thoroughly the mystery, I tried to settle it by saying it was a mistake, a dream, a fever-fit; and yet I knew there could be no mistake, and that I was not sleeping, and I believed I was sane. I wished the room had not been so well lighted, that I might not so clearly have seen the little pictures, the ornaments, the screens, the worked chair. All these objects, as well as the blue damask furniture, were, in fact, precisely the same, in every minutest detail, with those I so well remembered, and with which I had been so thoroughly intimate, in the drawing-room of my godmother's house at Bretton. Methought the apartment only was changed, being of different proportions and dimensions.

I thought of Bedreddin Hassan, transported in his sleep from Cairo to the gates of Damascus. Had a Genius stooped his dark wing down the storm to whose stress I had succumbed, and gathering me from the church steps, and 'rising high into the air,' as the eastern tale said, had he borne me over land and ocean, and laid me quietly down beside a hearth of Old England? But no: I knew the fire of that hearth burned before its Lares no more – it went out long ago, and the household gods had been carried elsewhere.

The bonne turned again to survey me, and seeing my eyes wide open, and, I suppose, deeming their expression perturbed and excited, she put down her knitting. I saw her busied for a moment at a little stand; she poured out water, and measured drops from a phial: glass in hand, she approached me. What dark-tinged draught might she now be offering? what Genii-elixir of Magi-distillation?

It was too late to inquire – I had swallowed it passively, and at once. A tide of quiet thought now came gently caressing my brain; softer and softer rose the flow, with tepid undulations smoother than balm. The pain of weakness left my limbs, my muscles slept. I lost power to move; but, losing at the same time wish, it was no privation. That kind bonne placed a screen between me and the lamp; I saw her rise to do this, but do not remember seeing her resume her place: in the interval between the two acts, I 'fell on sleep'.

CHARLOTTE BRONTË, *Villette* (1853).

THE EMPHASIS OF WANT
(1860)

MAGGIE drew a long breath and pushed her heavy hair back, as if to see a sudden vision more clearly. Here, then, was a secret of life that would enable her to renounce all other secrets – here was a sublime height to be reached without the help of outward things – here was insight, and strength, and conquest, to be won by means entirely within her own soul, where a supreme Teacher was waiting to be heard. It flashed through her like the suddenly apprehended solution of a problem, that all the miseries of her young life had come from fixing her heart on her own pleasure, as if that were the central necessity of the universe; and for the first time she saw the possibility of shifting the position from which she looked at the gratification of her own desires – of taking her stand out of herself, and looking at her own life as an insignificant part of a divinely-guided whole. She read on and on in the old book, devouring eagerly the dialogues with the invisible Teacher, the pattern of sorrow, the source of all strength; returning to it after she had been called away, and reading till the sun went down behind the willows. With all the hurry of an imagination that could never rest in the present, she sat in the deepening twilight forming plans of self-humiliation and entire devotedness; and, in the ardour of first discovery, renunciation seemed to her the entrance into that satisfaction which she had so long been craving in vain. She had not perceived – how could she until she had lived longer? – the inmost truth of the old monk's outpourings, that renunciation remains sorrow, though a sorrow borne willingly. Maggie was still panting for happiness, and was in ecstasy because she had found the key to it. She knew nothing of doctrines and systems – of mysticism or quietism; but this voice out of the far-off Middle Ages was the direct communication of a human soul's belief and experience, and came to Maggie as an unquestioned message.

I suppose that is the reason why the small old-fashioned book, for which you need only pay sixpence at a bookstall, works miracles to this day, turning bitter waters into sweetness: while expensive sermons and treatises, newly issued, leave all things as they were before. It was written down by a hand that waited for the heart's prompting; it is the chronicle of a solitary, hidden anguish, struggle, trust and triumph – not written on velvet cushions to teach endurance to those who are treading with bleeding feet on the stones. And so it remains to all time a lasting record of human needs and human consolations: the voice of a brother who, ages ago, felt and suffered and renounced – in the cloister, perhaps, with serge gown and tonsured head, with much chanting and long fasts, and with a fashion of speech different from ours – but under the same silent far-off heavens, and with the same passionate desires, the same strivings, the same failures, the same weariness.

In writing the history of unfashionable families, one is apt to fall into a tone of emphasis which is very far from being the tone of good society, where principles and beliefs are not only of an extremely moderate kind, but are always presupposed, no subjects being eligible but such as can be touched with a light and graceful irony. But then, good society has its claret and its velvet carpets, its dinner-engagements six weeks deep, its opera and its fairy ballrooms; rides off its *ennui* on thorough-bred horses, lounges at the club, has to keep clear of crinoline vortices, gets its science done by Faraday, and its religion by the superior clergy who are to be met in the best houses: how should it have time or need for belief and emphasis? But good society, floated on gossamer wings of light irony, is of very expensive production; requiring nothing less than a wide and arduous national life condensed in unfragrant, deafening factories, cramping itself in mines, sweating at furnaces, grinding, hammering, weaving under more or less oppression of carbonic acid – or else, spread over sheep-walks, and scattered in lonely houses and huts on the clayey or chalky corn-lands, where the rainy days look dreary. This wide national life is based entirely on emphasis – the emphasis of want, which urges it into all the activities necessary for the maintenance of good society and light irony: it spends its heavy years often in a chill, uncarpeted fashion, amidst family discord unsoftened by long corridors. Under such circumstances, there are many among its myriads of souls who have absolutely needed an emphatic belief: life in this unpleasurable shape demanding some solution even to unspeculative minds; just as you inquire into the stuffing of your couch when anything galls you there, whereas eider-down and perfect French springs excite no question. Some have an emphatic belief in alcohol, and seek their *ekstasis* or outside standing-ground in gin; but the rest require something that good society calls 'enthusiasm', something that will present motives in an entire absence of high prizes, something that will give patience and feed human love when the limbs ache with weariness, and human looks are hard upon us – something, clearly, that lies outside personal desires, that includes resignation for ourselves and active love for what is not ourselves. Now and then, that sort of enthusiasm finds a far-echoing voice that comes from an experience springing out of the deepest need.

GEORGE ELIOT, *The Mill on the Floss* (1860).

A VOTE AT A COMMITTEE

(1871)

SOME weeks passed after this conversation before the question of the chaplaincy gathered any practical import for Lydgate, and without telling himself the reason, he deferred the pre-determination on which side he should give his vote. It would really have been a matter of total indifference to him – that is to say, he would have taken the more convenient side, and given his vote for the appointment of Tyke without any hesitation – if he had not cared personally for Mr Farebrother.

But his liking for the Vicar of St Botolph's grew with growing acquaintanceship. That, entering into Lydgate's position as a newcomer who had his own professional objects to secure, Mr Farebrother should have taken pains rather to warn off than to obtain his interest, showed an unusual delicacy and generosity, which Lydgate's nature was keenly alive to. It went along with other points of conduct in Mr Farebrother which were exceptionally fine, and made his character re-semble those southern landscapes which seem divided between natural grandeur and social slovenliness. Very few men could have been as filial and chivalrous as he was to the mother, aunt, and sister, whose dependence on him had in many ways shaped his life rather uneasily for himself; few men who feel the pressure of small needs are so nobly resolute not to dress up their inevitably self-interested desires in a pretext of better motives. In these matters he was conscious that his life would bear the closest scrutiny; and perhaps the consciousness en-couraged a little defiance towards the critical strictness of per-sons whose celestial intimacies seemed not to improve their domestic manners, and whose lofty aims were not needed to account for their actions. Then, his preaching was ingenious and pithy, like the preaching of the English Church in its robust age, and his sermons were delivered without book.

People outside his parish went to hear him; and, since to fill the church was always the most difficult part of a clergyman's function, here was another ground for a careless sense of superiority. Besides, he was a likeable man: sweet-tempered, ready-witted, frank, without grins of suppressed bitterness or other conversational flavours which make half of us an affliction to our friends. Lydgate liked him heartily, and wished for his friendship.

With this feeling uppermost, he continued to waive the question of the chaplaincy, and to persuade himself that it was not only no proper business of his, but likely enough never to vex him with a demand for his vote. Lydgate, at Mr Bulstrode's request, was laying down plans for the internal arrangements of the new hospital, and the two were often in consultation. The banker was always presupposing that he could count in general on Lydgate as a coadjutor, but made no special recurrence to the coming decision between Tyke and Farebrother. When the General Board of the Infirmary had met, however, and Lydgate had notice that the question of the chaplaincy was thrown on a council of the directors and medical men, to meet on the following Friday, he had a vexed sense that he must make up his mind on this trivial Middlemarch business. He could not help hearing within him the distinct declaration that Bulstrode was prime minister, and that the Tyke affair was a question of office or no office; and he could not help an equally pronounced dislike to giving up the prospect of office. For his observation was constantly confirming Mr Farebrother's assurance that the banker would not overlook opposition. 'Confound their petty politics!' was one of his thoughts for three mornings in the meditative process of shaving, when he had begun to feel that he must really hold a court of conscience on this matter. Certainly there were valid things to be said against the election of Mr Farebrother: he had too much on his hands already, especially considering how much time he spent on non-clerical occupations. Then again it was a continually repeated shock, disturbing Lydgate's esteem, that the Vicar should obviously play for the sake of money, liking the play indeed, but evidently liking some end which it served. Mr Farebrother contended on theory for the desirability of all games, and said that Englishmen's wit was stagnant for want of them; but Lydgate felt certain that he would have played very much less but for the money. There was a billiard-room at the Green Dragon, which some anxious mothers and wives regarded as the chief temptation in Middlemarch. The Vicar was a first-rate billiard-player, and though he did not frequent the Green Dragon, there were reports that he had sometimes been there in the daytime and had won money. And as to the chaplaincy, he did not pretend that he cared for it, except for the sake of the forty pounds. Lydgate was no Puritan, but he did not care for play, and winning money at it had always seemed a meanness to him; besides, he had an ideal of life which made this subservience of conduct to the gaining of small sums thoroughly hateful to him. Hitherto in his own life his wants had been supplied without any trouble to himself, and his first impulse was always to be liberal with half-crowns as matters of no importance to a gentleman; it had never occurred to him to devise a plan for getting half-crowns. He had always known in a general way that he was not rich, but he had never felt poor, and he had no power of imagining the part which the want of money plays in determining the actions of men. Money had never been a motive to him. Hence he was not ready to frame excuses for this deliberate pursuit of small gains. It was altogether repulsive to him, and he never entered into any calculation of the ratio between the Vicar's income and his more or less necessary expenditure. It was possible that he would not have made such a calculation in his own case.

And now, when the question of voting had come, this repulsive fact told more strongly against Mr Farebrother than it had done before. One would know much better what to do if men's characters were more consistent, and especially if one's friends were invariably fit for any function they desired to undertake! Lydgate was convinced that if there had been no valid objection to Mr Farebrother, he would have voted for him, whatever Bulstrode might have felt on the subject: he did not intend to be a vassal of Bulstrode's. On the other hand, there was Tyke, a man entirely given to his clerical office, who was simply a curate at a chapel of ease in St Peter's parish, and had time for extra duty. Nobody had anything to say against Mr Tyke, except that they could not bear him, and suspected him of cant. Really, from his point of view, Bulstrode was thoroughly justified.

But whichever way Lydgate began to incline, there was something to make him wince; and being a proud man, he was a little exasperated at being obliged to wince. He did not like frustrating his own best purposes by getting on bad terms with Bulstrode; he did not like voting against Farebrother, and helping to deprive him of function and salary; and the question occurred whether the additional forty pounds might not leave the Vicar free from that ignoble care about winning at cards. Moreover, Lydgate did not like the consciousness that in voting for Tyke he should be voting on the side obviously convenient for himself. But would the end really be his own convenience? Other people would say so, and would allege that he was currying favour with Bulstrode for the sake of making himself important and getting on in the world. What then? He for his own part knew that if his personal prospects simply had been concerned, he would not have cared a rotten nut for the banker's friendship or enmity. What he really cared for was a medium for his work, a vehicle for his ideas; and after all, was he not bound to prefer the object of getting a good hospital, where he could demonstrate the specific distinctions of fever and test therapeutic results, before anything else connected with this chaplaincy? For the first time Lydgate was feeling the hampering threadlike pressure of small social conditions, and their frustrating complexity. At the end of his inward debate, when he set out for the hospital, his hope was really in the chance that discussion might somehow give a new aspect to the question, and make the scale dip so as to exclude the necessity for voting. I think he trusted a little also to the energy which is begotten by circumstances – some feeling rushing warmly and making resolve easy, while debate in cool blood had only made it more difficult. However it was, he did not distinctly say to himself on which side he would vote; and all the while he was inwardly resenting the subjection which had been forced upon him. It would have seemed beforehand like a ridiculous piece of bad logic that he, with his unmixed resolutions of independence and his select purposes, would find himself at the very outset in the grasp of petty alternatives, each of which was repugnant to him. In his student's chambers, he had pre-arranged his social action quite differently.

Lydgate was late in setting out, but Dr Sprague, the two other surgeons, and several of the directors had arrived early; Mr Bulstrode, treasurer and chairman, being among those who were still absent. The conversation seemed to imply that the issue was problematical, and that a majority for Tyke was not so certain as had been generally supposed. The two physicians, for a wonder, turned out to be unanimous, or rather, though of different minds, they concurred in action. Dr Sprague, the rugged and weighty, was, as every one had foreseen, an adherent of Mr Farebrother. The Doctor was more than suspected of having no religion, but somehow Middlemarch tolerated this deficiency in him as if he had been a Lord Chancellor; indeed it is probable that his professional weight was the more believed in, the world-old association of cleverness with the evil principle being still potent in the minds even of lady-patients who had the strictest ideas of frilling and sentiment. It was perhaps this negation in the Doctor which made his neighbours call him hard-headed and dry-witted;

conditions of texture which were also held favourable to the storing of judgments connected with drugs. At all events, it is certain that if any medical man had come to Middlemarch with the reputation of having very definite religious views, of being given to prayer, and of otherwise showing an active piety, there would have been a general presumption against his medical skill.

On this ground it was (professionally speaking) fortunate for Dr Minchin that his religious sympathies were of a general kind, and such as gave a distant medical sanction to all serious sentiment, whether of Church or Dissent, rather than any adhesion to particular tenets. If Mr Bulstrode insisted, as he was apt to do, on the Lutheran doctrine of justification, as that by which a Church must stand or fall, Dr Minchin in return was quite sure that man was not a mere machine or a fortuitous conjunction of atoms; if Mrs Wimple insisted on a particular providence in relation to her stomach complaint, Dr Minchin for his part liked to keep the mental windows open and objected to fixed limits; if the Unitarian brewer jested about the Athanasian Creed, Dr Minchin quoted Pope's 'Essay on Man'. He objected to the rather free style of anecdote in which Dr Sprague indulged, preferring well-sanctioned quotations, and liking refinement of all kinds: it was generally known that he had some kinship to a bishop, and sometimes spent his holidays at 'the palace'.

Dr Minchin was soft-handed, pale-complexioned, and of rounded outline, not to be distinguished from a mild clergyman in appearance: whereas Dr Sprague was superfluously tall; his trousers got creased at the knees, and showed an excess of boot at a time when straps seemed necessary to any dignity of bearing; you heard him go in and out, and up and down, as if he had come to see after the roofing. In short, he had weight, and might be expected to grapple with a disease and throw it; while Dr Minchin might be better able to detect it lurking and to circumvent it. They enjoyed about equally the mysterious privilege of medical reputation, and concealed with much etiquette their contempt for each other's skill. Regarding themselves as Middlemarch institutions, they were ready to combine against all innovators, and against non-professionals given to interference. On this ground they were both in their hearts equally averse to Mr Bulstrode, though Dr Minchin had never been in open hostility with him, and never differed from him without elaborate explanation to Mrs Bulstrode, who had found that Dr Minchin alone understood her constitution. A layman who pried into the professional conduct of medical men, and was always obtruding his reforms, – though he was less directly embarrassing to the two physicians than to the surgeon-apothecaries who attended paupers by contract, was nevertheless offensive to the professional nostril as such; and Dr Minchin shared fully in the new pique against Bulstrode, excited by his apparent determination to patronise Lydgate. The long-established practitioners, Mr Wrench and Mr Toller, were just now standing apart and having a friendly colloquy, in which they agreed that Lydgate was a jackanapes, just made to serve Bulstrode's purpose. To non-medical friends they had already concurred in praising the other young practitioner, who had come into the town on Mr Peacock's retirement without further recommendation than his own merits and such argument for solid professional acquirement as might be gathered from his having apparently wasted no time on other branches of knowledge. It was clear that Lydgate, by not dispensing drugs, intended to cast imputations on his equals, and also to obscure the limit between his own rank as a general practitioner and that of the physicians, who, in the interest of the profession, felt bound to maintain its various grades. Especially against a man who had not been to either of the English universities and enjoyed the absence of anatomical and bedside study there, but came with a libellous pretension to experience in Edinburgh and Paris, where observation might be abundant indeed, but hardly sound.

Thus it happened that on this occasion Bulstrode became identified with Lydgate, and Lydgate with Tyke; and owing to this variety of interchangeable names for the chaplaincy question, diverse minds were enabled to form the same judgment concerning it.

Dr Sprague said at once bluntly to the group assembled when he entered, 'I go for Farebrother. A salary, with all my heart. But why take it from the Vicar? He has none too much – has to insure his life, besides keeping house, and doing a vicar's charities. Put forty pounds in his pocket and you'll do no harm. He's a good fellow, is Farebrother, with as little of the parson about him as will serve to carry orders.'

'Ho, ho! Doctor,' said old Mr Powderell, a retired ironmonger of some standing – his interjection being something between a laugh and a Parliamentary disapproval. 'We must let you have your say. But what we have to consider is not anybody's income – it's the souls of the poor sick people' – here Mr Powderell's voice and face had a sincere pathos in them. 'He is a real Gospel preacher, is Mr Tyke. I should vote against my conscience if I voted against Mr Tyke – I should indeed.'

'Mr Tyke's opponents have not asked any one to vote against his conscience, I believe,' said Mr Hackbutt, a rich tanner of fluent speech, whose glittering spectacles and erect hair were turned with some severity towards innocent Mr Powderell. 'But in my judgment it behoves us, as Directors, to consider whether we will regard it as our whole business to carry out propositions emanating from a single quarter. Will any member of the committee aver that he would have entertained the idea of displacing the gentleman who has always discharged the function of chaplain here, if it had not been suggested to him by parties whose disposition it is to regard every institution of this town as a machinery for carrying out their own views? I tax no man's motives: let them lie between himself and a higher Power; but I do say, that there are influences at work here which are incompatible with genuine independence, and that a crawling servility is usually dictated by circumstances which gentlemen so conducting themselves could not afford either morally or financially to avow. I myself am a layman, but I have given no inconsiderable attention to the divisions in the Church and . . .'

'Oh, damn the divisions!' burst in Mr Frank Hawley, lawyer and town-clerk, who rarely presented himself at the board, but now looked in hurriedly, whip in hand. 'We have nothing to do with them here. Farebrother has been doing the work – what there was – without pay, and if pay is to be given, it should be given to him. I call it a confounded job to take the thing away from Farebrother.'

'I think it would be as well for gentlemen not to give their remarks a personal bearing,' said Mr Plymdale. 'I shall vote for the appointment of Mr Tyke, but I should not have known, if Mr Hackbutt hadn't hinted it, that I was a Servile Crawler.'

'I disclaim any personalities. I expressly said, if I may be allowed to repeat, or even to conclude what I was about to say —'

'Ah, here's Minchin!' said Mr Frank Hawley; at which everybody turned away from Mr Hackbutt, leaving him to feel the uselessness of superior gifts in Middlemarch. 'Come, Doctor, I must have you on the right side, eh?'

'I hope so,' said Dr Minchin, nodding and shaking hands here and there. 'At whatever cost to my feelings.'

'If there's any feeling here, it should be feeling for the man who is turned out, I think,' said Mr Frank Hawley.

'I confess I have feelings on the other side also. I have a divided esteem,' said Dr Minchin, rubbing his hands. 'I consider Mr Tyke an exemplary man – none more so – and I believe him to be proposed from unimpeachable motives. I, for my part, wish that I could give him my vote. But I am constrained to take a view of the case which gives the preponderance to Mr Farebrother's claims. He is an amiable man, an able preacher, and has been longer among us.'

Old Mr Powderell looked on, sad and silent. Mr Plymdale settled his cravat, uneasily.

'You don't set up Farebrother as a pattern of what a clergyman ought to be, I hope,' said Mr Larcher, the eminent carrier, who had just come in. 'I have no ill-will towards him, but I think we owe something to the public, not to speak of anything higher, in these appointments. In my opinion Farebrother is too lax for a clergyman. I don't wish to bring up particulars against him; but he will make a little attendance here go as far as he can.'

'And a devilish deal better than too much,' said Mr Hawley, whose bad language was notorious in that part of the county. 'Sick people can't bear so much praying and preaching. And that methodistical sort of religion is bad for the spirits – bad for the inside, eh?' he added, turning quickly round to the four medical men who were assembled.

But any answer was dispensed with by the entrance of three gentlemen, with whom there were greetings more or less cordial. These were the Reverend Edward Thesiger, Rector of St Peter's, Mr Bulstrode, and our friend Mr Brooke of Tipton, who had lately allowed himself to be put on the board of directors in his turn, but had never before attended, his attendance now being due to Mr Bulstrode's exertions. Lydgate was the only person still expected.

Every one now sat down, Mr Bulstrode presiding, pale and self-restrained as usual. Mr Thesiger, a moderate evangelical, wished for the appointment of his friend Mr Tyke, a zealous able man, who, officiating at a chapel of ease, had not a cure of souls too extensive to leave him ample time for the new duty. It was desirable that chaplaincies of this kind should be entered on with a fervent intention: they were peculiar opportunities for spiritual influence; and while it was good that a salary should be allotted, there was the more need for scrupulous watching lest the office should be perverted into a mere question of salary. Mr Thesiger's manner had so much quiet propriety that objectors could only simmer in silence.

Mr Brooke believed that everybody meant well in the matter. He had not himself attended to the affairs of the Infirmary, though he had a strong interest in whatever was for the benefit of Middlemarch, and was most happy to meet the gentlemen present on any public question – 'any public question, you know,' Mr Brooke repeated, with his nod of perfect understanding. 'I am a good deal occupied as a magistrate, and in the collection of documentary evidence, but I regard my time as being at the disposal of the public – and, in short, my friends have convinced me that a chaplain with a salary – a salary, you know – is a very good thing, and I am happy to be able to come here and vote for the appointment of Mr Tyke, who, I understand, is an unexceptionable man, apostolic and eloquent and everything of that kind – and I am the last man to withhold my vote – under the circumstances, you know.'

'It seems to me that you have been crammed with one side of the question, Mr Brooke,' said Mr Frank Hawley, who was afraid of nobody, and was a Tory suspicious of electioneering intentions. 'You don't seem to know that one of the worthiest men we have has been doing duty as chaplain here for years without pay, and that Mr Tyke is proposed to supersede him.'

'Excuse me, Mr Hawley,' said Mr Bulstrode. 'Mr Brooke has been fully informed of Mr Farebrother's character and position.'

'By his enemies,' flashed out Mr Hawley.

'I trust there is no personal hostility concerned here,' said Mr Thesiger.

'I'll swear there is, though,' retorted Mr Hawley.

'Gentlemen,' said Mr Bulstrode, in a subdued tone, 'the merits of the question may be very briefly stated, and if any one present doubts that every gentleman who is about to give his vote has not been fully informed, I can now recapitulate the considerations that should weigh on either side.'

'I don't see the good of that,' said Mr Hawley. 'I suppose we all know whom we mean to vote for. Any man who wants to do justice does not wait till the last minute to hear both sides of the question. I have no time to lose, and I propose that the matter be put to the vote at once.'

A brief but still hot discussion followed before each person wrote 'Tyke' or 'Farebrother' on a piece of paper and slipped it into a glass tumbler; and in the mean time Mr Bulstrode saw Lydgate enter.

'I perceive that the votes are equally divided at present,' said Mr Bulstrode, in a clear biting voice. Then, looking up at Lydgate –

'There is a casting-vote still to be given. It is yours, Mr Lydgate: will you be good enough to write?'

'The thing is settled now,' said Mr Wrench, rising. 'We all know how Mr Lydgate will vote.'

'You seem to speak with some peculiar meaning, sir,' said Lydgate, rather defiantly, and keeping his pencil suspended.

'I merely mean that you are expected to vote with Mr Bulstrode. Do you regard that meaning as offensive?'

'It may be offensive to others. But I shall not desist from voting with him on that account.'

Lydgate immediately wrote down 'Tyke'.

GEORGE ELIOT, *Middlemarch* (1871-2).

GETTING MARRIED
(1876)

THE sails of the schooner filled. On a fair frosty day, with a light wind ruffling from the North-west, she swept away, out of sight of Bevisham, and the island, into the Channel, to within view of the coast of France. England once below the water-line, alone with Beauchamp and Dr Shrapnel, Jenny Denham knew her fate.

As soon as that grew distinctly visible in shape and colour, she ceased to be reluctant. All about her, in air and sea and unknown coast, was fresh and prompting. And if she looked on Beauchamp, the thought – my husband! palpitated, and destroyed and re-made her. Rapidly she underwent her transformation from doubtfully-minded woman to woman awakening clear-eyed, and with new sweet shivers in her temperate blood, like the tremulous light seen running to the morn upon a quiet sea. She fell under the charm of Beauchamp at sea.

In view of the island of Madeira, Jenny noticed that some trouble had come upon Dr Shrapnel and Beauchamp, both of whom had been hilarious during the gales; but sailing into summer they began to wear that look which indicated one of their serious deliberations. She was not taken into their confidence, and after a while they recovered partially.

The truth was, they had been forced back upon old English ground by a recognition of the absolute necessity, for her sake, of handing themselves over to a parson. In England, possibly, a civil marriage might have been proposed to the poor girl. In a foreign island, they would be driven not simply to accept the services of a parson, but to seek him and solicit him: otherwise the knot, faster than any sailor's in binding, could not be tied. Decidedly it could not; and how submit? Neither Dr Shrapnel nor Beauchamp were of a temper to deceive the clerical gentleman; only they had to think of Jenny's feelings. Alas for us! – this our awful baggage in the rear of humanity, these women who have not moved on their own feet one step since the primal mother taught them to suckle, are perpetually pulling us backward on the march. Slaves of custom, forms, shows and superstitions, they are slaves of the priests. 'They are so in gratitude perchance, as the matter works,' Dr Shrapnel admitted. For at one period the priests did cherish and protect the weak from animal man. But we have entered a broader daylight now, when the sun of high heaven has crowned our structure with the flower of brain, like him to scatter mists, and penetrate darkness, and shoot from end to end of earth; and must we still be grinning subserviently to ancient usages and stale forms, because of a baggage that it is, woe to us! too true, we cannot cut ourselves loose from? Lydiard might say we are compelling the priests to fight, and that they are compact foeman, not always passive. Battle, then! – The cry was valiant. Nevertheless, Jenny would certainly insist upon the presence of a parson, in spite of her bridegroom's 'natural repugnance'. Dr Shrapnel offered to argue it with her, being of opinion that a British consul could satisfactorily perform the ceremony. Beauchamp knew her too well. Moreover, though tongue-tied as to love-making, he was in a hurry to be married. Jenny's eyes were lovely, her smiles were soft; the fair promise of her was in bloom on her face and figure. He could not wait; he must off to the parson.

Then came the question as to whether honesty and honour did not impose it on them to deal openly with that gentle, and on such occasions unobtrusive official, by means of a candid statement to him overnight, to the effect that they were the avowed antagonists of his Church, which would put him on his defence, and lead to an argument that would accomplish his overthrow. – You parsons, whose cause is good, marshal out the poor of the land, that we may see the sort of army your stewardship has gained for you. What! no army? only women and hoary men? And in the rear rank, to support you as an institution, none but fanatics, cowards, white-eyeballed dogmatists, timeservers, money-changers, mockers in their sleeves? What is this?

But the prospect of so completely confounding the unfortunate parson warned Beauchamp that he might have a shot in his locker: the parson heavily trodden on will turn. 'I suppose we must be hypocrites,' he said in dejection. Dr Shrapnel was even more melancholy. He again offered to try his persuasiveness upon Jenny, Beauchamp declined to let her be disturbed.

She did not yield so very lightly to the invitation to go before a parson. She had to be wooed after all; a Harry Hotspur's wooing. Three clergymen of the Established Church were on the island: 'And where won't they be, where there's fine scenery and comforts abound?' Beauchamp said to the doctor ungratefully.

'Whether a celibate clergy ruins the Faith faster than a non-celibate, I won't dispute,' replied the doctor; 'but a non-celibate interwinds with us, and is likely to keep up a one-storied edifice longer.'

Jenny hesitated. She was a faltering unit against an ardent and imperative two in the council. And Beauchamp had shown her a letter of Lady Romfrey's very clearly signifying that she and her lord anticipated tidings of the union. Marrying Beauchamp was no simple adventure. She feared in her bosom, and resigned herself.

She had a taste of what it was to be, at the conclusion of the service. Beauchamp thanked the good-natured clergyman, and spoke approvingly of him to his bride, as an agreeable well-bred gentlemanly person. Then, fronting her and taking both her hands: 'Now, my darling,' he said: 'You must pledge me your word to this: I have stooped my head to the parson, and I am content to have done that to win you, though I don't think much of myself for doing it. I can't look so happy as I am. And this idle ceremony – however, I thank God I have you, and I thank you for taking me. But you won't expect me to give in to the parson again.'

'But, Nevil,' she said, fearing what was to come: 'They are gentlemen, good men.'

'Yes, yes.'

'They are educated men, Nevil.'

'Jenny! Jenny Beauchamp, they're not men, they're Church-men. My experience of the priest in our country is, that he has abandoned – he's dead against the only cause that can justify and keep up a Church: the cause of the poor – the people. He is a creature of the moneyed class. I look on him as a pretender. I go through his forms, to save my wife from annoyance, but there's the end of it: and if ever I'm helpless, unable to resist him, I rely on your word not to let him intrude; he's to have nothing to do with the burial of me. He's against the cause of the people. Very well: I make my protest to the death against him. When he's a Christian instead of a Churchman, then may my example not be followed. It's little use looking for that.'

Jenny dropped some tears on her bridal day. She sighed her submission. 'So long as you do not change,' said she.

'Change!' cried Nevil. 'That's for the parson. Now it's over: we start fair. My darling! I have you. I don't mean to bother you. I'm sure you'll see that the enemies of Reason are the enemies of the human race; you will see that. I can wait.'

'If we can be sure that we ourselves are using reason rightly, Nevil! – not prejudice.'

'Of course. But don't you see, my Jenny, *we* have no interest in opposing reason?'

'But have we not all grown up together? And is it just or wise to direct our efforts to overthrow a solid structure that is a part . . .?'

He put his legal right in force to shut her mouth, telling her presently she might *Lydiardize* as much as she liked. While practising this mastery, he assured her he would always listen to her: yes, whether she Lydiardized, or what Dr Shrapnel called Jennyprated.

'That is to say, dear Nevil, that you have quite made up your mind to a toddling chattering little nursery wife?'

Very much the contrary to anything of the sort, he declared; and he proved his honesty by announcing an immediate reflection that had come to him: 'How oddly things are settled! Cecilia Halkett and Tuckham; you and I! Now, I know for certain that I have brought Cecilia Halkett out of her woman's Toryism, and given her at least liberal views, and she goes and marries an arrant Tory; while you, a bit of a Tory at heart, more than anything else, have married an ultra.'

'Perhaps we may hope that the conflict will be seasonable on both sides? – if you give me fair play, Nevil!'

As fair play as a woman's lord could give her, she was to have; with which, adieu to argumentation and controversy, and all the thanks in life to the parson! On a lovely island, free from the seductions of care, possessing a wife who, instead of starting out of romance and poetry with him to the supreme honeymoon, led him back to those forsaken valleys of his youth, and taught him the joys of colour and sweet companionship, simple delights, a sister mind, with a loveliness of person and nature unimagined by him, Beauchamp drank of a happiness that neither Renée nor Cecilia had promised. His wooing of Jenny Beauchamp was a flattery richer than any the maiden Jenny Denham could have deemed her due; and if his wonder in experiencing such strange gladness was quaintly ingenuous, it was delicious to her to see and know full surely that he who was at little pains to court, or please, independently of the urgency of the truth in him, had come to be her lover through being her husband.

GEORGE MEREDITH, *Beauchamp's Career* (1876).

THE FORTUNE OF THE COMPANY
(1875)

THE scheme in question was the grand proposal for a South Central Pacific and Mexican railway, which was to run from the Salt Lake City, thus branching off from the San Francisco and Chicago line, – and pass down through the fertile lands of New Mexico and Arizona, into the territory of the Mexican Republic, run by the city of Mexico, and come out on the gulf at the port of Vera Cruz. Mr Fisker admitted at once that it was a great undertaking, acknowledged that the distance might be perhaps something over 2,000 miles, acknowledged that no computation had or perhaps could be made as to the probable cost of the railway; but seemed to think that questions such as these were beside the mark and childish. Melmotte, if he would go into the matter at all, would ask no such questions.

But we must go back a little. Paul Montague had received a telegram from his partner, Hamilton K. Fisker, sent on shore at Queenstown from one of the New York liners, requesting him to meet Fisker at Liverpool immediately. With this request he had felt himself bound to comply. Personally he had disliked Fisker, – and perhaps not the less so because when in California he had never found himself able to resist the man's good humour, audacity, and cleverness combined. He had found himself talked into agreeing with any project which Mr Fisker might have in hand. It was altogether against the grain with him, and yet by his own consent, that the flour-mill had been opened at Fiskerville. He trembled for his money and never wished to see Fisker again; but still, when Fisker came to England, he was proud to remember that Fisker was his partner, and he obeyed the order and went down to Liverpool.

If the flour-mill had frightened him, what must the present project have done! Fisker explained that he had come with two objects, – first to ask the consent of the English partner to the proposed change in their business, and secondly to obtain the co-operation of English capitalists. The proposed change in the business meant simply the entire sale of the establishment at Fiskerville, and the absorption of the whole capital in the work of getting up the railway. 'If you could realise all the money it wouldn't make a mile of the railway,' said Paul. Mr Fisker laughed at him. The object of Fisker, Montague, and Montague was not to make a railway to Vera Cruz, but to float a company. Paul thought that Mr Fisker seemed to be indifferent whether the railway should ever be constructed or not. It was clearly his idea that fortunes were to be made out of the concern before a spadeful of earth had been moved. If brilliantly printed programmes might avail anything, with gorgeous maps, and beautiful little pictures of trains running into tunnels beneath snowy mountains and coming out of them on the margin of sunlit lakes, Mr Fisker had certainly done much. But Paul, when he saw all these pretty things, could not keep his mind from thinking whence had come the money to pay for them. Mr Fisker had declared that he had come over to obtain his partner's consent, but it seemed to that partner that a great deal had been done without any consent. And Paul's fears on this hand were not allayed by finding that on all these beautiful papers he himself was described as one of the agents and general managers of the company. Each document was signed Fisker, Montague, and Montague. References on all matters were to be made to Fisker, Montague, and Montague, – and in one of the documents it was stated that a member of the firm had proceeded to London with the view of attending to British interests in the matter. Fisker had seemed to think that his young partner would express unbounded satisfaction at the greatness which was thus falling upon him. A certain feeling of importance, not altogether unpleasant, was produced, but at the same time there was another conviction forced upon Montague's mind, not altogether pleasant, that his money was being made to disappear without any consent given by him, and that it behoved him to be cautious lest such consent should be extracted from him unawares.

'What has become of the mill?' he asked.

'We have put an agent into it?'

'Is not that dangerous? What check have you on him?'

'He pays us a fixed sum, sir. But, my word! when there is such a thing as this on hand a trumpery mill like that is not worth speaking of.'

'You haven't sold it?'

'Well; – no. But we've arranged a price for a sale.'

'You haven't taken the money for it?'

'Well; – yes; we have. We've raised money on it, you know. You see you weren't there, and so the two resident partners acted for the firm. But Mr Montague, you'd better go with us. You had indeed.'

'And about my own income?'

'That's a flea-bite. When we've got a little ahead with this it won't matter, sir, whether you spend twenty thousand or forty thousand dollars a year. We've got the concession from the United States Government through the territories, and we're in correspondence with the President of the Mexican Republic. I've no doubt we've an office open already in Mexico and another at Vera Cruz.'

'Where's the money to come from?'

'Money to come from, sir? Where do you suppose the money comes from in all these undertakings? If we can float the shares, the money'll come in quick enough. We hold three million dollars of the stock ourselves.'

'Six hundred thousand pounds!' said Montague.

'We take them at par, of course, – and as we sell we shall pay for them. But of course we shall only sell at a premium. If we can run them up even to 110, there would be three hundred thousand dollars. But we'll do better than that. I must try and see Melmotte at once. You had better write a letter now.'

'I don't know the man.'

'Never mind. Look here – I'll write it, and you can sign it.' Whereupon Mr Fisker did write the following letter:

Langham Hotel, London. March 4, 18—

Dear Sir,

I have the pleasure of informing you that my partner Mr Fisker, – of Fisker, Montague, and Montague, of San Francisco, – is now in London with the view of allowing British capitalists to assist in carrying out perhaps the greatest work of the age, – namely, the South Central Pacific and Mexican Railway, which is to give direct communication between San Francisco and the Gulf of Mexico. He is very anxious to see you upon his arrival, as he is aware that your co-operation would be desirable. We feel assured that with your matured judgment in such matters you would see at once the magnificence of the enterprise. If you will name a day and an hour, Mr Fisker will call upon you.

I have to thank you and Madame Melmotte for a very pleasant evening spent at your house last week.

Mr Fisker proposes returning to New York. I shall remain here, superintending the British interests which may be involved.

I have the honour to be,

Dear Sir,

Most faithfully yours,

– –.

'But I have never said that I would superintend the interests,' said Montague.

'You can say so now. It binds you to nothing. You regular John Bull Englishmen are so full of scruples that you lose as much of life as should serve to make an additional fortune.'

After some further conversation Paul Montague recopied the letter and signed it. He did it with doubt, – almost with dismay. But he told himself that he could do no good by refusing. If this wretched American, with his hat on one side and rings on his fingers, had so far got the upper hand of Paul's uncle as to have been allowed to do what he liked with the funds of the partnership, Paul could not stop it. On the following morning they went up to London together, and in the course of the afternoon Mr Fisker presented himself in Abchurch Lane. The letter written at Liverpool, but dated from the Langham Hotel, had been posted at the Euston Square Railway Station at the moment of Fisker's arrival. Fisker sent in his card, and was asked to wait. In the course of twenty minutes he was ushered into the great man's presence by no less a person than Miles Grendall.

It has been already said that Mr Melmotte was a big man with large whiskers, rough hair, and with an expression of mental power on a harsh vulgar face. He was certainly a man to repel you by his presence unless attracted to him by some internal consideration. He was magnificent in his expenditure, powerful in his doings, successful in his business, and the world around him therefore was not repelled. Fisker, on the other hand, was a shining little man, – perhaps about forty years of age, with a well-twisted moustache, greasy brown hair, which was becoming bald at the top, good-looking if his features were analysed, but insignificant in appearance. He was gorgeously dressed, with a silk waistcoat and chains, and he carried a little stick. One would at first be inclined to say that Fisker was not much of a man; but after a little conversation most men would own that there was something in Fisker. He was troubled by no shyness, by no scruples, and by no fears. His mind was not capacious, but such as it was it was his own, and he knew how to use it.

Abchurch Lane is not a grand site for the offices of a merchant prince. Here, at a small corner house, there was a small brass plate on a swing door, bearing the words 'Melmotte & Co.' Of whom the Co. was composed no one knew. In one sense Mr Melmotte might be said to be in company with all the commercial world, for there was no business to which he would refuse his co-operation on certain terms. But he had never burthened himself with a partner in the usual sense of the term. Here Fisker found three or four clerks seated at desks, and was desired to walk upstairs. The steps were narrow and crooked, and the rooms were small and irregular. Here he stayed for a while in a small dark apartment in which 'The Daily Telegraph' was left for the amusement of its occupant till Miles Grendall announced to him that Mr Melmotte would see him. The millionaire looked at him for a moment or two, just condescending to touch with his fingers the hand which Fisker had projected.

'I don't seem to remember,' he said, 'the gentleman who has done me the honour of writing to me about you.'

'I dare say not, Mr Melmotte. When I'm at home in San Francisco, I make acquaintance with a great many gents whom I don't remember afterwards. My partner I think told me that he went to your house with his friend, Sir Felix Carbury.'

'I know a young man called Sir Felix Carbury.'

'That's it. I could have got any amount of introductions to you if I had thought this would not have sufficed.' Mr Melmotte bowed. 'Our account here in London is kept with the City and West End Joint Stock. But I have only just arrived, and as my chief object in coming to London is to see you, and as I met my partner, Mr Montague, in Liverpool, I took a note from him and came on straight.'

'And what can I do for you, Mr Fisker?'

Then Mr Fisker began his account of the Great South Central Pacific and Mexican Railway, and exhibited considerable skill by telling it all in comparatively few words. And yet he was gorgeous and florid. In two minutes he had displayed his programme, his maps, and his pictures before Mr Melmotte's eyes, taking care that Mr Melmotte should see how often the names of Fisker, Montague, and Montague, reappeared upon them. As Mr Melmotte read the documents, Fisker from time to time put in a word. But the words had no reference at all to the future profits of the railway, or to the benefit which such means of communication would confer upon the world at large; but applied solely to the appetite for such stock as theirs, which might certainly be produced in the speculating world by a proper manipulation of the affairs.

'You seem to think you couldn't get it taken up in your own country,' said Melmotte.

'There's not a doubt about getting it all taken up there. Our folk, sir, are quick enough at the game; but you don't want me to teach you, Mr Melmotte, that nothing encourages this kind of thing like competition. When they hear at St Louis and Chicago that the thing is alive in London, they'll be alive there. And it's the same here, sir. When they know that the stock is running like wildfire in America, they'll make it run here too.'

'How far have you got?'

'What we've gone to work upon is a concession for making the line from the United States Congress. We're to have the land for nothing, of course, and a grant of one thousand acres round every station, the stations to be twenty-five miles apart.'

'And the land is to be made over to you, – when?'

'When we have made the line up to the station.' Fisker understood perfectly that Mr Melmotte did not ask the question in reference to any value that he might attach to the possession of such lands, but to the attractiveness of such a prospectus in the eyes of the outside world of speculators.

'And what do you want me to do, Mr Fisker?'

'I want to have your name there,' he said. And he placed his finger down on a spot on which it was indicated that there was, or was to be, a chairman of an English Board of Directors, but with a space for the name, hitherto blank.

'Who are to be your directors here, Mr Fisker?'

'We should ask you to choose them, sir. Mr Paul Montague should be one, and perhaps his friend Sir Felix Carbury might be another. We could get probably one of the Directors of the City and West End. But we would leave it all to you, – as also the amount of stock you would like to take yourself. If you gave yourself to it, heart and soul, Mr Melmotte, it would be the finest thing that there has been out for a long time. There would be such a mass of stock!'

'You have to back that with a certain amount of paid-up capital?'

'We take care, sir, in the West not to cripple commerce too closely by old-fashioned bandages. Look at what we've done already, sir, by having our limbs pretty free. Look at our line, sir, right across the continent, from San Francisco to New York. Look at —'

'Never mind that, Mr Fisker. People wanted to go from New York to San Francisco, and I don't know that they do want to go to Vera Cruz. But I will look at it, and you shall hear from me.' The interview was over, and Mr Fisker was contented with it. Had Mr Melmotte not intended at least to think of it he would not have given ten minutes to the subject. After all, what was wanted from Mr Melmotte was little more than his name, for the use of which Mr Fisker proposed that he should receive from the speculative public two or three hundred thousand pounds.

At the end of a fortnight from the date of Mr Fisker's arrival in London, the company was fully launched in England, with a body of London directors, of whom Mr Melmotte was the chairman. Among the directors were Lord Alfred Grendall, Sir Felix Carbury, Samuel Cohenlupe, Esq., Member of Parliament for Staines, a gentleman of the Jewish persuasion, Lord Nidderdale, who was also in Parliament, and Mr Paul Montague. It may be thought that the directory was not strong, and that but little help could be given to any commercial enterprise by the assistance of Lord Alfred or Sir Felix; – but it was felt that Mr Melmotte was himself so great a tower of strength that the fortune of the Company, – as a company, – was made.

ANTHONY TROLLOPE, *The Way We Live Now* (1875).

FOR YOUR AMUSEMENT
(1872)

'IN that case we start afresh,' said Humpty Dumpty, 'and it's my turn to choose a subject —' ('He talks about it just as if it was a game!' thought Alice.) 'So here's a question for you. How old did you say you were?'

Alice made a short calculation, and said 'Seven years and six months.'

'Wrong!' Humpty Dumpty exclaimed triumphantly. 'You never said a word like it!'

'I thought you meant "How old *are* you?"' Alice explained.

'If I'd meant that, I'd have said it,' said Humpty Dumpty.

Alice didn't want to begin another argument, so she said nothing.

'Seven years and six months!' Humpty Dumpty repeated thoughtfully. 'An uncomfortable sort of age. Now if you'd asked *my* advice, I'd have said "Leave off at seven" – but it's too late now.'

'I never ask advice about growing,' Alice said indignantly.

'Too proud?' the other enquired.

Alice felt even more indignant at this suggestion. 'I mean,' she said, 'that one ca'n't help growing older.'

'*One* ca'n't, perhaps,' said Humpty Dumpty; 'but *two* can. With proper assistance, you might have left off at seven.'

'What a beautiful belt you've got on!' Alice suddenly remarked. (They had had quite enough of the subject of age, she thought: and, if they really were to take turns in choosing subjects, it was *her* turn now.) 'At least,' she corrected herself on second thoughts, 'a beautiful cravat, I should have said – no, a belt, I mean – I beg your pardon!' she added in dismay, for Humpty Dumpty looked thoroughly offended, and she began to wish she hadn't chosen that subject. 'If only I knew,' she thought to herself, 'which was neck and which was waist!'

Evidently Humpty Dumpty was very angry, though he said nothing for a minute or two. When he *did* speak again, it was in a deep growl.

'It is a – *most* – *provoking* – thing,' he said at last, 'when a person doesn't know a cravat from a belt!'

'I know it's very ignorant of me,' Alice said, in so humble a tone that Humpty Dumpty relented.

'It's a cravat, child, and a beautiful one, as you say. It's a present from the White King and Queen. There now!'

'Is it really?' said Alice, quite pleased to find that she *had* chosen a good subject after all.

'They gave it me,' Humpty Dumpty continued thoughtfully as he crossed one knee over the other and clasped his hands round it, 'they gave it me – for an un-birthday present.'

'I beg your pardon?' Alice said with a puzzled air.

'I'm not offended,' said Humpty Dumpty.

'I mean, what *is* an un-birthday present?'

'A present given when it isn't your birthday, of course.'

Alice considered a little. 'I like birthday presents best,' she said at last.

'You don't know what you're talking about!' cried Humpty Dumpty. 'How many days are there in a year?'

'Three hundred and sixty-five,' said Alice.

'And how many birthdays have you?'

'One.'

'And if you take one from three hundred and sixty-five what remains?'

'Three hundred and sixty-four, of course.'

Humpty Dumpty looked doubtful. 'I'd rather see that done on paper,' he said.

Alice couldn't help smiling as she took out her memorandum-book, and worked the sum for him:

$$365$$
$$1$$
$$\overline{364}$$

Humpty Dumpty took the book and looked at it carefully. 'That seems to be done right —' he began.

'You're holding it upside down!' Alice interrupted.

'To be sure I was!' Humpty Dumpty said gaily as she turned it round for him. 'I thought it looked a little queer. As I was saying, that *seems* to be done right – though I haven't time to look it over thoroughly just now – and that shows that there are three hundred and sixty-four days when you might get un-birthday presents –'

'Certainly,' said Alice.

'And only *one* for birthday presents, you know. There's glory for you!'

'I don't know what you mean by "glory",' Alice said.

Humpty Dumpty smiled contemptuously. 'Of course you don't – till I tell you. I meant "there's a nice knock-down argument for you!"'

'But "glory" doesn't mean "a nice knock-down argument",' Alice objected.

'When *I* use a word,' Humpty Dumpty said, in rather a scornful tone, 'it means just what I choose it to mean – neither more nor less.'

'The question is,' said Alice, 'whether you *can* make words mean so many different things.'

'The question is,' said Humpty Dumpty, 'which is to be master – that's all.'

Alice was too much puzzled to say anything; so after a minute Humpty Dumpty began again. 'They've a temper, some of them – particularly verbs: they're the proudest – adjectives you can do anything with, but not verbs – however, *I* can manage the whole lot of them! Impenetrability! That's what *I* say!'

'Would you tell me please,' said Alice, 'what that means?'

'Now you talk like a reasonable child,' said Humpty Dumpty, looking very much pleased. 'I meant by "impenetrability" that we've had enough of that subject, and it would be just as well if you'd mention what you mean to do next, as I suppose you don't mean to stop here all the rest of your life.'

'That's a great deal to make one word mean,' Alice said in a thoughtful tone.

'When I make a word do a lot of work like that,' said Humpty Dumpty, 'I always pay it extra.'

'Oh!' said Alice. She was too much puzzled to make any other remark.

'Ah, you should see 'em come round me of a Saturday night,' Humpty Dumpty went on, wagging his head gravely from side to side, 'for to get their wages, you know.'

(Alice didn't venture to ask what he paid them with; and so you see I ca'n't tell *you*.)

'You seem very clever at explaining words, Sir,' said Alice. 'Would you kindly tell me the meaning of the poem called "Jabberwocky"?'

'Let's hear it,' said Humpty Dumpty. 'I can explain all the poems that ever were invented – and a good many that haven't been invented just yet.'

This sounded very hopeful, so Alice repeated the first verse:

> "*Twas brillig, and the slithy toves*
> *Did gyre and gimble in the wabe:*
> *All mimsy were the borogoves,*
> *And the mome raths outgrabe.*'

'That's enough to begin with,' Humpty Dumpty interrupted: 'there are plenty of hard words there. '*Brillig*' means four o'clock in the afternoon – the time when you begin *broiling* things for dinner.'

'That'll do very well,' said Alice: 'and "*slithy*"?'

'Well, "*slithy*" means "lithe and slimy". "Lithe" is the same as "active". You see it's like a portmanteau – there are two meanings packed up into one word.'

'I see it now,' Alice remarked thoughtfully: 'and what are "*toves*"?'

'Well, "*toves*" are something like badgers – they're something like lizards – and they're something like corkscrews.'

'They must be very curious-looking creatures.'

'They are that,' said Humpty Dumpty: 'also they make their nests under sun-dials – also they live on cheese.'

'And what's to "*gyre*" and to "*gimble*"?'

'To "*gyre*" is to go round and round like a gyroscope. To "*gimble*" is to make holes like a gimlet.'

'And "*the wabe*" is the grass-plot round a sundial, I suppose?' said Alice, surprised at her own ingenuity.

'Of course it is. It's called "*wabe*" you know, because it goes a long way before it, and a long way behind it —'

'And a long way beyond it on each side,' Alice added.

'Exactly so. Well then, "*mimsy*" is "flimsy and miserable" (there's another portmanteau for you). And a "*borogove*" is a thin shabby-looking bird with its feathers sticking out all round – something like a live mop.'

'And then "*mome raths*"?' said Alice. 'I'm afraid I'm giving you a great deal of trouble.'

'Well, a "*rath*" is a sort of green pig: but "*mome*" I'm not certain about. I think it's short for "from home" – meaning that they'd lost their way, you know.'

'And what does "*outgrabe*" mean?'

'Well, "*outgribing*" is something between bellowing and whistling, with a kind of sneeze in the middle: however, you'll hear it done, maybe – down in the wood yonder – and, when you've once heard it, you'll be *quite* content. Who's been repeating all that hard stuff to you?'

'I read it in a book' said Alice. 'But I *had* some poetry repeated to me much easier than that, by – Tweedledee, I think it was.'

'As to poetry, you know,' said Humpty Dumpty, stretching out one of his great hands, '*I* can repeat poetry as well as other folk, if it comes to that —'

'Oh, it needn't come to that!' Alice hastily said, hoping to keep him from beginning.

'The piece I'm going to repeat,' he went on without

noticing her remark, 'was written entirely for your amusement.'

LEWIS CARROLL, *Through the Looking-Glass* (1872).

A COUNTY POLLING DAY
(1887)

THE county polling day meanwhile drew near, and with its approach party spirit rose and the mutual exasperation of both sides increased. George and his father were out every evening at the Institute or canvassing, and George's first attempts at public speaking were a success. At length the day dawned which was to decide their fate. Cowfold was the polling station for a large district, and both sides fully recognised its importance. The Democratic colour was orange, and the Tory was purple. Everybody wore rosettes and bands of music went about the town, carrying flags and banners, which had such an effect upon the Cowfold population, more particularly upon that portion of it which knew nothing whatever of the questions at issue, that the mere sound of the instruments or sight of a bit of bunting tied to a pole was sufficient to enable them to dare a broken head, or even death. Beer may have been partly the cause of this peculiar mental condition, but not entirely, for sober persons felt the contagion. We may laugh at it if we please, and no doubt it is evidence of the weakness of human nature; but, like much more evidence of the same order, it is double-voiced, and testifies also to our strength.

Priscilla was staying that night with her mother. Mr Broad's house, at the end of the town, was very quiet, and George did not care to leave her alone with the servant. Those were the days when the state of the poll was published every hour, and as Cowfold lay near the centre of the county, a very fair opinion could be formed of the progress of the voting. By three o'clock it was known that up to eleven parties were neck and neck, and the excitement grew more and more intense. Every public-house in Cowfold was free, and soon after dinner-time there was not a single person in the place who was ever drunk before who had not found it necessary to get drunk then in order to support the strain on his nerves. Four o'clock came, and the polling-booth was shut; the numbers were made up, and the two committees now anxiously awaited the news from the outlying districts. The general impression seemed to be that the popular candidate would win by about a dozen, and by eight o'clock a crowd had assembled before the 'Cross Keys' to give due welcome to the desired announcement. Ten o'clock came, and the mob began to get impatient and unruly. Then there was a stir and a roar, and the whole assemblage rushed off to the 'Angel', in the square. On the balcony was a huge placard, with the purple hero at the top – 1837 – and below was the orange favourite, in small and ignominious figures – 1831. Bushel stood at the open window waving his hat, apparently half frantic. Just underneath him was a smaller crowd of the purple faction, who were cheering and bawling with all their might as the enemy came in sight. In an instant the conflict had begun. The purple banners were the first objects of attack, and disappeared every one of them, in less than five minutes, under foot. Seen from one of the upper storeys of the houses, the square looked like a great pot full of boiling confusion. By degrees the wearers of purple were driven hard against the 'Angel' yard-gates, which opened to receive them; some who were not successful in securing admittance escaping, with bloody heads, down the side lane, and so out across the fields. There was great difficulty in shutting the gates again; but the 'Angel' hostlers appeared on the scene with pitchforks and other weapons, which caused an ebb of the tide for a moment. They managed in the nick of time to swing the gates together, and the heavy wooden bar was thrown across them. The orange party was now triumphant, but very unhappy, because it was able to do no further mischief. Suddenly Bushel was seen again at the window, and, as it was afterwards averred, made some insulting gesture. A stone was the prompt response, and in five minutes there was not a whole pane of glass left in the front of the building. 'Have old Bushel out! Smoke 'em out!' was shouted, and a rush followed towards the door. But the insurgents had no siege train for such a fortress, and the sight of two or three fowling-pieces somewhat damped their courage. They therefore turned off, wrecked the brewer's house, and forced the 'Angel' tap, which was separated from the main building. The spirit-casks were broached, and men turned the gin and brandy taps into their mouths without waiting for glasses. Many of them, especially those who first entered, were at once overcome and dropped, lying about in the room and in the gutter perfectly insensible. The remainder, who could only drink what was left, became more and more riotous, and a general sack of all purple property was imminent. Mr Allen was at the 'Cross Keys', but George was at home, and as he watched the scene he saw the mob take a kind of lurch and sway along the street which led to Mr Broad's. He thought he heard Mr Broad's name, and in an instant he had buttoned up his coat, taken the heaviest stick he could find, and was off. He had the greatest difficulty in forcing his way, and he did not reach the front of the crowd till it was opposite Mr Broad's and the destruction of the windows had begun. He leaped over the iron railing, and presented himself at the gate with the orange rosette on his coat and the stick in his right hand. He was just in time, for yells of 'Psalm-singing old hypocrite!' were already in the air, and the fence was being stormed. George administered to the foremost ruffian a blow on the shoulder which felled him on the path outside, and then, standing on the low brick wall on which the railings rested, showed his rosette, brandished his club, and made some kind of inarticulate expostulation, which, happily for him and Mr Broad, was received with cheers. Whether taken by itself it would have been effectual or not cannot be said, for just at that moment a more powerful auxiliary appeared. When the 'Angel' was abandoned the imprisoned garrison, amongst whom were one or two county magistrates, held a brief consultation. They organised their forces and marched out, the well-to-do folk in front and abreast, armed with bludgeons, the 'Angel' dependents and about fifty more of the refugees coming in the rear, every garden and stable weapon of offence being distributed amongst them. They had the advantage, of course, of being sober. They advanced at a run, and their tramp was heard just as George was beginning to try the effect of his eloquence. Panic and scattering flight at once followed, not, however, before some dozen or so of the fugitives had recovered what little sense they ever had by virtue of sundry hard knocks on their skulls, and a dozen more or so had been captured. By twelve o'clock Cowfold was quiet and peaceable. Citizens were left to wonder how their town, lying usually so sleepily still, like a farmyard on a summer Sunday afternoon, could ever transform itself after this fashion. Men unknown and never before seen seemed suddenly to spring out of the earth, and as suddenly to disappear. Who were they? Respectable Cowfold, which thought it knew everybody in the place, could not tell. There was no sign of their existence on the next day. People gathered together and looked at the mischief wrought the night before, and talked everlastingly about it; but the doers of it vanished, wrapt away apparently into an invisible world. On Sunday next, at one o'clock, Cowfold Square, save for a few windows not yet mended, looked just as it always looked; that is to say, not a soul was visible in it, and the pump was, as usual, chained.

MARK RUTHERFORD, *The Revolution in Tanner's Lane* (1887).

LIFE AND EDUCATION
(1891)

ANGEL sat down, and the place felt like home; yet he did not so much as formerly feel himself one of the family gathered there. Every time that he returned hither he was conscious of this divergence, and since he had last shared in the Vicarage life it had grown even more distinctly foreign to his own than usual. Its transcendental aspirations – still unconsciously based on the geocentric view of things, a zenithal paradise, a nadiral hell – were as foreign to his own as if they had been the dreams of people on another planet. Latterly he had seen only Life, felt only the great passionate pulse of existence, unwarped, uncontorted, untrammelled by those creeds which futilely attempt to check what wisdom would be content to regulate.

On their part they saw a great difference in him, a growing divergence from the Angel Clare of former times. It was chiefly a difference in his manner that they noticed just now, particularly his brothers. He was getting to behave like a farmer; he flung his legs about; the muscles of his face had grown more expressive; his eyes looked as much information as his tongue spoke, and more. The manner of the scholar had nearly disappeared; still more the manner of the drawing-room young man. A prig would have said that he had lost culture, and a prude that he had become coarse. Such was the contagion of domiciliary fellowship with the Talbothays nymphs and swains.

After breakfast he walked with his two brothers, non-evangelical, well-educated, hall-marked young men, correct to their remotest fibre; such unimpeachable models as are turned out yearly by the lathe of a systematic tuition. They were both somewhat short-sighted, and when it was the custom to wear a single eyeglass and string they wore a single eyeglass and string; when it was the custom to wear a double glass they wore a double glass; when it was the custom to wear spectacles they wore spectacles straightway, all without reference to the particular variety of defect in their own vision. When Wordsworth was enthroned they carried pocket copies; and when Shelley was belittled they allowed him to grow dusty on their shelves. When Correggio's Holy Families were admired, they admired Correggio's Holy Families; when he was decried in favour of Velasquez, they sedulously followed suit without any personal objection.

If these two noticed Angel's growing social ineptness, he noticed their growing mental limitations. Felix seemed to him all Church; Cuthbert all College. His Diocesan Synod and Visitations were the mainsprings of the world to the one; Cambridge to the other. Each brother candidly recognized that there were a few unimportant scores of millions of outsiders in civilized society, persons who were neither University men nor churchmen; but they were to be tolerated rather than reckoned with and respected.

They were both dutiful and attentive sons, and were regular in their visits to their parents. Felix, though an offshoot from a far more recent point in the devolution of theology than his father, was less self-sacrificing and disinterested. More tolerant than his father of a contradictory opinion, in its aspect as a danger to its holder, he was less ready than his father to pardon it as a slight to his own teaching. Cuthbert was, upon the whole, the more liberal-minded, though, with greater subtlety, he had not so much heart.

As they walked along the hillside Angel's former feeling revived in him – that whatever their advantages by comparison with himself, neither saw or set forth life as it really was lived. Perhaps, as with many men, their opportunities of observation were not so good as their opportunities of expression. Neither had an adequate conception of the complicated forces at work outside the smooth and gentle current in which they and their associates floated. Neither saw the difference between local truth and universal truth; that what the inner world said in their clerical and academic hearing was quite a different thing from what the outer world was thinking.

THOMAS HARDY, *Tess of the D'Urbervilles* (1891).

LIFE AND WORK
(1887)

'MARTY,' she said, 'we both loved him. We will go to his grave together.'

The church stood somewhat outside the village, and could be reached without passing through the street. In the dusk of the late September day they went thither by secret ways, walking mostly in silence side by side, each busied with her own thoughts. Grace had a trouble exceeding Marty's, that haunting sense of having put out the light of his life by her own hasty doings. She had tried to persuade herself that he might have died of his illness, even if she had not taken possession of his house. Sometimes she succeeded in her attempt; sometimes she did not.

They stood by the grave together, and though the sun had gone down they could get glimpses over the woodland for miles, and along the vale in which he had been accustomed to descend every year with his portable mill and press to make cider about this time.

Perhaps Grace's first grief, the discovery that if he had lived he could never have claimed her, had some power in softening this, the second. On Marty's part there was the same consideration; never would she have been his. As no anticipation of gratified affection had been in existence while he was with them there was none to be disappointed now that he had gone.

Grace was abased when, by degrees, she found that she had

never understood Giles as Marty had done. Marty South alone, of all the women in Hintock and the world, had approximated to Winterborne's level of intelligent intercourse with Nature. In that respect she had formed his true complement in the other sex, had lived as his counterpart, had subjoined her thoughts to his as a corollary.

The casual glimpses which the ordinary population bestowed upon that wondrous world of sap and leaves called the Hintock woods had been with these two, Giles and Marty, a clear gaze. They had been possessed of its finer mysteries as of commonplace knowledge; had been able to read its hieroglyphs as ordinary writing; to them the sights and sounds of night, winter, wind, storm, amid those dense boughs, which had to Grace a touch of the uncanny, and even of the supernatural, were simple occurrences whose origin, continuance, and laws they foreknew. They had planted together, and together they had felled; together they had, with the run of the years, mentally collected those remoter signs and symbols which seen in few were of runic obscurity, but all together made an alphabet. From the light lashing of the twigs upon their faces when brushing through them in the dark either could pronounce upon the species of the tree whence they stretched; from the quality of the wind's murmur through a bough either could in like manner name its sort afar off. They knew by a glance at a trunk if its heart were sound, or tainted with incipient decay; and by the state of its upper twigs the stratum that had been reached by its roots. The artifices of the seasons were seen by them from the conjuror's own point of view, and not from that of the spectator.

'He ought to have married *you*, Marty, and nobody else in the world!' said Grace with conviction, after thinking in the above strain.

Marty shook her head. 'In all our outdoor days and years together, ma'am,' she replied, 'the one thing he never spoke of to me was love; nor I to him.'

'Yet you and he could speak in a tongue that nobody else knew – not even my father, though he came nearest knowing – the tongue of the trees and fruits and flowers themselves.'

She could indulge in mournful fancies like this to Marty; but the hard core to her grief – which Marty's had not – remained. Had she been sure that Giles's death resulted entirely from his exposure, it would have driven her well-nigh to insanity; but there was always the bare possibility that his exposure had only precipitated what was inevitable. She longed to believe that it had not done even this.

THOMAS HARDY, *The Woodlanders* (1887).

ON THE MARGIN
(1892)

IN the prosperous year of 1856, incomes of between a hundred and a hundred and fifty pounds were chargeable with a tax of elevenpence halfpenny in the pound: persons who enjoyed a revenue of a hundred and fifty or more had the honour of paying one and fourpence. Abatements there were none, and families supporting life on two pounds a week might in some cases, perchance, be reconciled to the mulct by considering how equitably its incidence was graduated.

Some, on the other hand, were less philosophical; for instance, the household consisting of Nicholas Peak, his wife, their three-year-old daughter, their newly-born son, and a blind sister of Nicholas, dependent upon him for sustenance. Mr Peak, aged thirty and now four years wedded, had a small cottage on the outskirts of Greenwich. He was employed as dispenser, at a salary of thirty-five shillings a week, by a medical man with a large practice. His income, therefore, fell considerably within the hundred pound limit; and, all things considered, it was not unreasonable that he should be allowed to expend the whole of this sum on domestic necessities. But it came to pass that Nicholas, in his greed of wealth, obtained supplementary employment, which benefited him to the extent of a yearly ten pounds. Called upon to render his statement to the surveyor of income-tax, he declared himself in possession of a hundred and one pounds per annum; consequently, he stood indebted to the Exchequer in the sum of four pounds, sixteen shillings, and ninepence. His countenance darkened, as also did that of Mrs Peak.

'This is wrong and cruel – dreadfully cruel!' cried the latter, with tears in her eyes.

'It is; but that's no new thing,' was the bitter reply.

'I think it's wrong of *you*, Nicholas. What need is there to say anything about that ten pounds? It's taking the food out of our mouths.'

Knowing only the letter of the law, Mr Peak answered sternly:

'My income is a hundred and one pounds. I can't sign my name to a lie.'

Picture the man. Tall, gaunt, with sharp intellectual features, and eyes of singular beauty, the face of an enthusiast – under given circumstances, of a hero. Poorly clad, of course, but with rigorous self-respect; his boots polished, *propria manu*, to the point of perfection; his linen washed and ironed by the indefatigable wife. Of simplest tastes, of most frugal habits, a few books the only luxury which he deemed indispensable; yet a most difficult man to live with, for to him applied precisely the description which Robert Burns gave of his own father; he was 'of stubborn, ungainly integrity and headlong irascibility'.

Ungainly, for his strong impulses towards culture were powerless to obliterate the traces of his rude origin. Born in a London alley, the son of a labourer burdened with a large family, he had made his way by sheer force of character to a position which would have seemed proud success but for the difficulty with which he kept himself alive. His parents were dead. Of his brothers, two had disappeared in the abyss, and one, Andrew, earned a hard livelihood as a journeyman baker; the elder of his sisters had married poorly, and the younger was his blind pensioner. Nicholas had found a wife of better birth than his own, a young woman with country kindred in decent circumstances, though she herself served as nursemaid in the house of the medical man who employed her future husband. He had taught himself the English language, so far as grammar went, but could not cast off the London accent; Mrs Peak was fortunate enough to speak with nothing worse than the note of the Midlands.

His bent led him to the study of history, politics, economics, and in that time of military outbreak he was frenzied by the conflict of his ideals with the state of things about him. A book frequently in his hands was Godwin's *Political Justice*, and when a son had been born to him he decided to name the child after that favourite author. In this way, at all events, he could find some expression for his hot defiance of iniquity.

He paid his income-tax, and felt a savage joy in the privation thus imposed upon his family. Mrs Peak could not forgive her husband, and in this case, though she had but dim appreciation of the point of honour involved, her censures doubtless fell on Nicholas's vulnerable spot; it was the perversity of arrogance, at least as much as honesty, that impelled him to incur taxation. His wife's perseverance in complaint drove him to stern impatience, and for a long time the peace of the household suffered.

When the boy Godwin was five years old, the death of his blind aunt came as a relief to means which were in every sense overtaxed. Twelve months later, a piece of unprecedented good fortune seemed to place the Peaks beyond fear of want, and at the same time to supply Nicholas with a fulfilment of hopeless desires. By the death of Mrs Peak's brother, they came into possession of a freehold house and about nine hundred pounds. The property was situated some twelve miles from the Midland town of Twybridge, and thither they at once removed. At Twybridge lived Mrs Peak's elder sister, Miss Cadman; but between this lady and her nearest kinsfolk there had been but slight correspondence – the deceased Cadman left her only a couple of hundred pounds. With capital at command, Nicholar Peak took a lease of certain fields near his house, and turned farmer. The study of chemistry had given a special bent to his economic speculations; he fancied himself endowed with exceptional aptitude for agriculture, and the scent of the furrow brought all his energies into feverish activity – activity which soon impoverished him: that was in the order of things. 'Ungainly integrity' and 'headlong irascibility' wrought the same results for the ex-dispenser as for the Ayrshire husbandman. His farming came to a chaotic end; and, when the struggling man died, worn out at forty-three, his wife and children (there was now a younger boy, Oliver, named after the Protector) had no very bright prospects.

Things went better with them than might have been anticipated. To Mrs Peak her husband's death was not an occasion of unmingled mourning. For the last few years she had suffered severely from domestic discord, and when left at peace by bereavement she turned with a sense of liberation to the task of caring for her children's future. Godwin was just thirteen, Oliver was eleven; both had been well schooled, and with the help of friends they might soon be put in the way of self-support. The daughter, Charlotte, sixteen years of age, had accomplishments which would perhaps be profitable. The widow decided to make a home in Twybridge, where Miss Cadman kept a millinery shop. By means of this connection, Charlotte presently found employment for her skill in fine needlework. Mrs Peak was incapable of earning money, but the experiences of her early married life enabled her to make more than the most of the pittance at her disposal.

Miss Cadman was a woman of active mind, something of a busy-body – dogmatic, punctilious in her claims to respect, proud of the acknowledgment by her acquaintances that she was not as other tradespeople; her chief weakness was a fanatical ecclesiasticism, the common blight of English womanhood. Circumstances had allowed her a better education than generally falls to women of that standing, and in spite of her shop she succeeded in retaining the friendship of certain ladies long ago her schoolfellows. Among these were the Misses Lumb – middle-aged sisters, who lived at Twybridge on a small independence, their time chiefly devoted to the support of the Anglican Church. An eldest Miss Lumb had been fortunate enough to marry that growing potentate of the Midlands, Mr Job Whitelaw. Now Lady Whitelaw, she dwelt at Kingsmill, but her sisters frequently enjoyed the honour of entertaining her, and even Miss Cadman the milliner occasionally held converse with the baronet's wife. In this way it came to pass that the Widow Peak and her children were brought under the notice of persons who sooner or later might be of assistance to them.

GEORGE GISSING, *Born in Exile* (1892).

COLLEGES OF UNREASON

(1872)

WE drove to an inn in the middle of the town, and then, while it was still light, my friend the cashier, whose name was Thims, took me for a stroll in the streets and in the court-yards of the principal colleges. Their beauty and interest were extreme; it was impossible to see them without being attracted towards them; and I thought to myself that he must be indeed an ill-grained and ungrateful person who can have been a member of one of these colleges without retaining an affectionate feeling towards it for the rest of his life. All my misgivings gave way at once when I saw the beauty and venerable appearance of this delightful city. For half an hour I forgot both myself and Arowhena.

After supper Mr Thims told me a good deal about the system of education which is here practised. I already knew a part of what I heard, but much was new to me, and I obtained a better idea of the Erewhonian position than I had done hitherto; nevertheless there were parts of the scheme of which I could not comprehend the fitness, although I fully admit that this inability was probably the result of my having been trained so very differently and to my being then much out of sorts.

The main feature in their system is the prominence which they give to a study which I can only translate by the word 'hypothetics'. They argue thus – that to teach a boy merely the nature of the things which exist in the world around him, and about which he will have to be conversant during his whole life, would be giving him but a narrow and shallow conception of the universe, which it is urged might contain all manner of things which are not now to be found therein. To open his eyes to these possibilities, and so to prepare him for all sorts of emergencies, is the object of this system of hypothetics. To imagine a set of utterly strange and impossible contigencies, and require the youths to give intelligent answers to the questions that arise therefrom, is reckoned the fittest conceivable way of preparing them for the actual conduct of their affairs in after life.

Thus they are taught what is called the hypothetical language for many of their best years – a language which was originally composed at a time when the country was in a very different state of civilization to what it is at present, a state which has long since disappeared and been superseded. Many valuable maxims and noble thoughts which were at one time concealed in it have become current in their modern literature, and have been translated over and over again into the language now spoken. Surely, then, it would seem enough that the study of the original language should be confined to the few whose instincts led them naturally to pursue it.

But the Erewhonians think differently; the store they set by this hypothetical language can hardly be believed; they will even give anyone a maintenance for life if he attains a considerable proficiency in the study of it; nay, they will spend years in learning to translate some of their own good poetry into the hypothetical language – to do so with fluency being reckoned a distinguishing mark of a scholar and a gentleman. Heaven forbid that I should be flippant, but it appeared to me to be a wanton waste of good human energy that men should spend years and years in the perfection of so barren an exercise, when their own civilization presented problems by the hundred which cried aloud for solution and would have paid the solver handsomely; but people know their own affairs best. If the youths chose it for themselves I should have wondered less; but they did not choose it; they have it thrust upon them, and for the most part are disinclined towards it. I can only say that all I heard in defence of the system was insufficient to make me think very highly of its advantages.

The arguments in favour of the deliberate development of the unreasoning faculties were much more cogent. But here they depart from the principles on which they justify their study of hypothetics; for they base the importance which they assign to hypothetics upon the fact of their being a preparation for the extraordinary, while their study of Unreason rests upon its developing those faculties which are required for the daily conduct of affairs. Hence their professorships of Inconsistency and Evasion, in both of which studies the youths are examined before being allowed to proceed to their degree in hypothetics. The more earnest and conscientious students attain to a proficiency in these subjects which is quite surprising; there is hardly any inconsistency so glaring but they soon learn to defend it, or injunction so clear that they cannot find some pretext for disregarding it.

Life, they urge, would be intolerable if men were to be guided in all they did by reason and reason only. Reason betrays men into the drawing of hard-and-fast lines, and to the defining by language – language being like the sun, which rears and then scorches. Extremes are alone logical, but they are always absurd; the mean is illogical, but an illogical mean is better than the sheer absurdity of an extreme. There are no follies and no unreasonablenesses so great as those which can apparently be irrefragably defended by reason itself, and there is hardly an error into which men may not easily be led if they base their conduct upon reason only.

Reason might very possibly abolish the double currency; it might even attack the personality of Hope and Justice. Besides, people have such a strong natural bias towards it that they will seek it for themselves and act upon it quite as much as or more than is good for them; there is no need of encouraging reason. With unreason the case is different. She is the natural complement of reason without whose existence reason itself were non-existent.

If, then, reason would be non-existent were there no such thing as unreason, surely it follows that the more unreason there is, the more reason there must be also? Hence the necessity for the development of unreason, even in the interests of reason herself. The Professors of Unreason deny that they undervalue reason; none can be more convinced than they are that if the double currency cannot be rigorously deduced as a necessary consequence of human reason, the double currency should cease forthwith; but they say that it must be deduced from no narrow and exclusive view of reason which should deprive that admirable faculty of the one-half of its own existence. Unreason is a part of reason; it must therefore be allowed its full share in stating the initial conditions.

SAMUEL BUTLER, *Erewhon* (1872).

Argument

◄◄◄►►►

PAINTING IS A SCIENCE
(1836)

As your kind attention has so long been given to my description of pictures, it may now be well to consider in what estimation we are to hold them, and in what class we are to place the men who have produced them. – It appears to me that pictures have been over-valued; held up by a blind admiration as ideal things, and almost as standards by which nature is to be judged rather than the reverse; and this false estimate has been sanctioned by the extravagant epithets that have been applied to painters, as 'the divine', 'the inspired', and so forth. Yet, in reality, what are the most sublime productions of the pencil, but selections of some of the forms of nature, and copies of a few of her evanescent effects; and this is the result, not of inspiration, but of long and patient study, under the direction of much good sense. – It was said by Sir Thomas Lawrence, that 'we can never hope to compete with nature in the beauty and delicacy of her separate forms or colours, – our only chance lies in selection and combination.' Nothing can be more true, – and it may be added, that selection and combination are learned from nature herself, who constantly presents us with compositions of her own, far more beautiful than the happiest arranged by human skill. I have endeavoured to draw a line between genuine art and mannerism, but even the greatest painters have never been wholly untainted by manner. – Painting is a science, and should be pursued as an inquiry into the laws of nature. Why, then, may not landscape painting be considered as a branch of natural philosophy, of which pictures are but the experiments?

JOHN CONSTABLE, *Fourth Lecture at the Royal Institution* (1836).

AN IDEA OF PROGRESS
(1830)

THE cure which Mr Southey thinks that he has discovered is worthy of the sagacity which he has shown in detecting the evil. The calamities arising from the collection of wealth in the hands of a few capitalists are to be remedied by collecting it in the hands of one great capitalist, who has no conceivable motive to use it better than other capitalists, the all-devouring state.

It is not strange that, differing so widely from Mr Southey as to the past progress of society, we should differ from him also as to its probable destiny. He thinks, that to all outward appearance, the country is hastening to destruction; but he relies firmly on the goodness of God. We do not see either the piety or the rationality of thus confidently expecting that the Supreme Being will interfere to disturb the common succession of causes and effects. We, too, rely on his goodness, on his goodness as manifested, not in extraordinary interpositions, but in those general laws which it has pleased him to establish in the physical and in the moral world. We rely on the natural tendency of the human intellect to truth, and on the natural tendency of society to improvement. We know no well authenticated instance of a people which has decidedly retrograded in civilisation and prosperity, except from the influence of violent and terrible calamities, such as those which laid the Roman empire in ruins, or those which, about the beginning of the sixteenth century, desolated Italy. We know of no country which, at the end of fifty years of peace and tolerably good government, has been less prosperous than at the beginning of that period. The political importance of a state may decline, as the balance of power is disturbed by the introduction of new forces. Thus the influence of Holland and of Spain is much diminished. But are Holland and Spain poorer than formerly? We doubt it. Other countries have outrun them. But we suspect that they have been positively, though not relatively, advancing. We suspect that Holland is richer than when she sent her navies up the Thames, that Spain is richer than when a French king was brought captive to the footstool of Charles the Fifth.

History is full of the signs of this natural progress of society. We see in almost every part of the annals of mankind how the industry of individuals, struggling up against wars, taxes, famines, conflagrations, mischievous prohibitions, and more mischievous protections, creates faster than governments can squander, and repairs whatever invaders can destroy. We see the wealth of nations increasing, and all the arts of life approaching nearer and nearer to perfection, in spite of the grossest corruption and the wildest profusion on the part of rulers.

The present moment is one of great distress. But how small will that distress appear when we think over the history of the last forty years; a war, compared with which all other wars sink into insignificance; taxation, such as the most heavily taxed people of former times could not have conceived; a debt larger than all the public debts that ever existed in the world added together; the food of the people studiously rendered dear; the currency imprudently debased, and imprudently restored. Yet is the country poorer than in 1790? We firmly believe that, in spite of all the misgovernment of her rulers, she has been almost constantly becoming richer and richer. Now and then there has been a stoppage, now and then a short retrogression; but as to the general tendency there can be no doubt. A single breaker may recede; but the tide is evidently coming in.

If we were to prophesy that in the year 1930 a population of fifty millions, better fed, clad and lodged than the English of our time, will cover these islands, that Sussex and Huntingdonshire will be wealthier than the wealthiest parts of the

West Riding of Yorkshire now are, that cultivation, rich as that of a flowering-garden, will be carried up to the very tops of Ben Nevis and Helvellyn, that machines constructed on principles yet undiscovered, will be in every house, that there will be no highways but railroads, no travelling but by steam, that our debt, vast as it seems to us, will appear to our great-grandchildren a trifling incumbrance, which might easily be paid off in a year or two, many people would think us insane. We prophesy nothing; but this we say: If any person had told the Parliament which met in perplexity and terror after the crash in 1720 that in 1830 the wealth of England would surpass all their wildest dreams, that the annual revenue would equal the principal of that debt which they considered as an intolerable burden, that for one man of ten thousand pounds then living there would be five men of fifty thousand pounds, that London would be twice as large and twice as populous, and that nevertheless the rate of mortality would have diminished to one half of what it then was, that the post-office would bring more into the exchequer than the excise and customs had brought in together under Charles the Second, that stagecoaches would run from London to York in twenty-four hours, that men would be in the habit of sailing without wind, and would be beginning to ride without horses, our ancestors would have given as much credit to the prediction as they gave to Gulliver's Travels. Yet the prediction would have been true; and they would have perceived that it was not altogether absurd, if they had considered that the country was then raising every year a sum which would have purchased the fee-simple of the revenue of the Plantagenets, ten times what supported the government of Elizabeth, three times what, in the time of Oliver Cromwell, had been thought intolerably oppressive. To almost all men the state of things under which they have been used to live seems to be the necessary state of things. We have heard it said that five per cent is the natural interest of money, that twelve is the natural number of a jury, that forty shillings is the natural qualification of a county voter. Hence it is that, though in every age everybody knows that up to his own time progressive improvement has been taking place, nobody seems to reckon on any improvement during the next generation. We cannot absolutely prove that those are in error who tell us that society has reached a turning point, that we have seen our best days. But so said all who came before us, and with just as much apparent reason. 'A million a year will beggar us,' said the patriots of 1640. 'Two millions a year will grind the country to powder,' was the cry in 1660. 'Six millions a year, and a debt of fifty millions!' exclaimed Swift; 'the high allies have been the ruin of us.' 'A hundred and forty millions of debt!' said Junius; 'well may we say that we owe Lord Chatham more than we shall ever pay, if we owe him such a load as this.' 'Two hundred and forty millions of debt!' cried all the statesmen of 1783 in chorus; 'what abilities, or what economy on the part of a minister, can save a country so burdened?' We know that if, since 1783, no fresh debt had been incurred, the increased resources of the country would have enabled us to defray that debt at which Pitt, Fox, and Burke stood aghast, nay, to defray it over and over again, and that with much lighter taxation than what we have actually borne. On what principle is it that, when we see nothing but improvement behind us, we are to expect nothing but deterioration before us?

It is not by the intermeddling of Mr Southey's idol, the omniscient and omnipotent State, but by the prudence and energy of the people, that England has hitherto been carried forward in civilisation; and it is to the same prudence and the same energy that we now look with comfort and good hope. Our rulers will best promote the improvement of the nation by strictly confining themselves to their own legitimate duties, by leaving capital to find its most lucrative course, commodities their fair price, industry and intelligence their natural reward, idleness and folly their natural punishment, by maintaining peace, by defending property, by diminishing the price of law, and by observing strict economy in every department of the state. Let the Government do this: the People will assuredly do the rest.

T. B. MACAULAY, 'Southey's Colloquies on Society', in *Critical and Historical Essays* (1830).

A VIEW OF LIBERALISM
(1843)

WHEN, in the beginning of the present century, not very long before my own time, after many years of moral and intellectual declension, the University of Oxford woke up to a sense of its duties, and began to reform itself, the first instruments of this change, to whose zeal and courage we all owe so much, were naturally thrown together for mutual support, against the numerous obstacles which lay in their path, and soon stood out in relief from the body of residents, who, though many of them men of talent themselves, cared little for the object which the others had at heart. These Reformers, as they may be called, were for some years members of scarcely more than three or four Colleges; and their own Colleges, as being under their direct influence, of course had the benefit of those stricter views of discipline and teaching, which they themselves were urging on the University. They had, in no long time, enough of real progress in their several spheres of exertion, and enough of reputation out of doors, to warrant them in considering themselves the *élite* of the place; and it is not wonderful if they were in consequence led to look down upon the majority of Colleges, which had not kept pace with the reform, or which had been hostile to it. And, when those rivalries of one man with another arose, whether personal or collegiate, which befall literary and scientific societies, such disturbances did but tend to raise in their eyes the value which they had already set upon academical distinction, and increase their zeal in pursuing it. Thus was formed an intellectual circle or class in the University, – men, who felt they had a career before them, as soon as the pupils, whom they were forming, came into public life; men, whom non-residents, whether country parsons or preachers of the Low Church, on coming up from time to time to the old place, would look at, partly with admiration, partly with suspicion, as being an honour indeed to Oxford, but withal exposed to the temptation of ambitious views, and to the spiritual evils signified in what is called the 'pride of reason'.

Nor was this imputation altogether unjust; for, as they were following out the proper idea of a University, of course they suffered more or less from the moral malady incident to such a pursuit. The very object of such great institutions lies in the cultivation of the mind and the spread of knowledge: if this object, as all human objects, has its dangers at all times, much more would these exist in the case of men, who were engaged in a work of reformation, and had the opportunity of measuring themselves, not only with those who were their equals in intellect, but with the many, who were below them. In this select circle or class of men, in various Colleges, the direct instruments and the choice fruit of real University Reform, we see the rudiments of the Liberal party.

Whenever men are able to act at all, there is the chance of extreme and intemperate action; and therefore, when there is exercise of mind, there is the chance of wayward or mistaken exercise. Liberty of thought is in itself a good; but it gives an opening to false liberty. Now by Liberalism I mean false liberty of thought, or the exercise of thought upon matters, in which, from the constitution of the human mind, thought cannot be brought to any successful issue, and therefore is out of place. Among such matters are first principles of whatever kind; and of these the most sacred and momentous are especially to be reckoned the truths of Revelation. Liberalism then is the mistake of subjecting to human judgment those revealed doctrines which are in their nature beyond and independent of it, and of claiming to determine on intrinsic grounds the truth and value of propositions which rest for their reception simply on the external authority of the Divine Word.

Now certainly the party of whom I have been speaking, taken as a whole, were of a character of mind out of which Liberalism might easily grow up, as in fact it did; certainly they breathed around an influence which made men of religious seriousness shrink into themselves. But, while I say as much as this, I have no intention whatever of implying that the talent of the University, in the years before and after 1820, was liberal in its theology, in the sense in which the bulk of the educated classes through the country are liberal now. I would not for the world be supposed to detract from the Christian earnestness, and the activity in religious works, above the average of men, of many of the persons in question. They would have protested against their being supposed to place reason before faith, or knowledge before devotion; yet I do consider that they unconsciously encouraged and successfully introduced into Oxford a licence of opinion which went far beyond them. In their day they did little more than take credit to themselves for enlightened views, largeness of mind, liberality of sentiment, without drawing the line between what was just and what was inadmissible in speculation, and without seeing the tendency of their own principles; and engrossing, as they did, the mental energy of the University, they met for a time with no effectual hindrance to the spread of their influence, except (what indeed at the moment was most effectual, but not of an intellectual character) the thorough-going Toryism and traditionary Church-of-England-ism of the great body of the Colleges and Convocation.

Now and then a man of note appeared in the Pulpit or Lecture Rooms of the University, who was a worthy representative of the more religious and devout Anglicans. These belonged chiefly to the High-Church party; for the party called Evangelical never has been able to breathe freely in the atmosphere of Oxford, and at no time has been conspicuous, as a party, for talent or learning. But of the old High Churchmen several exerted some sort of Anti-liberal influence in the place, at least from time to time, and that influence of an intellectual nature. Among these especially may be mentioned Mr John Miller, of Worcester College, who preached the Bampton Lecture in the year 1817. But, as far as I know, he who turned the tide, and brought the talent of the University round to the side of the old theology, and against what was familiarly called 'march-of-mind', was Mr Keble. In and from Keble the mental activity of Oxford took that contrary direction which issued in what was called Tractarianism.

Keble was young in years, when he became a University celebrity, and younger in mind. He had the purity and simplicity of a child. He had few sympathies with the intellectual party, who sincerely welcomed him as a brilliant specimen of young Oxford. He instinctively shut up before literary display, and pomp and donnishness of manner, faults which always will beset academical notabilities. He did not respond to their advances. His collision with them (if it may be so called) was thus described by Hurrell Froude in his own way. 'Poor Keble!' he used gravely to say, 'he was asked to join the aristocracy of talent, but he soon found his level.' He went into the country, but his instance serves to prove that men need not, in the event, lose that influence which is rightly theirs, because they happen to be thwarted in the use of the channels natural and proper to its exercise. He did not lose his place in the minds of men because he was out of their sight.

Keble was a man who guided himself and formed his judgments, not by processes of reason, by inquiry or by argument, but, to use the word in a broad sense, by authority. Conscience is an authority; the Bible is an authority; such is the

Church; such is Antiquity; such are the words of the wise; such are hereditary lessons; such are ethical truths; such are historical memories, such are legal saws and state maxims; such are proverbs; such are sentiments, presages, and prepossessions. It seemed to me as if he ever felt happier, when he could speak or act under some such primary or external sanction; and could use argument mainly as a means of recommending or explaining what had claims on his reception prior to proof. He even felt a tenderness, I think, in spite of Bacon, for the Idols of the Tribe and the Den, of the Market and the Theatre. What he hated instinctively was heresy, insubordination, resistance to things established, claims of independence, disloyalty, innovation, a critical, censorious spirit. And such was the main principle of the school which in the course of years was formed around him.

J. H. NEWMAN, *Apologia Pro Vita Sua – Note on Liberalism* (1843–4).

UTILITY AND FEELING
(1873)

I CONCEIVE that the description so often given of a Benthamite, as a mere reasoning machine, though extremely inapplicable to most of those who have been designated by that title, was during two or three years of my life not altogether untrue of me. It was perhaps as applicable to me as it can well be to any one just entering into life, to whom the common objects of desire must in general have at least the attraction of novelty. There is nothing very extraordinary in this fact: no youth of the age I then was, can be expected to be more than one thing, and this was the thing I happened to be. Ambition and desire of distinction, I had in abundance; and zeal for what I thought the good of mankind was my strongest sentiment, mixing with and colouring all others. But my zeal was as yet little else, at that period of my life, than zeal for speculative opinions. It had not its root in genuine benevolence, or sympathy with mankind; though these qualities held their due place in my ethical standard. Nor was it connected with any high enthusiasm for ideal nobleness. Yet of this feeling I was imaginatively very susceptible; but there was at that time an intermission of its natural aliment, poetical culture, while there was a superabundance of the discipline antagonistic to it, that of mere logic and analysis. Add to this that, as already mentioned, my father's teachings tended to the undervaluing of feeling. It was not that he was himself cold-hearted or insensible; I believe it was rather from the contrary quality; he thought that feeling could take care of itself; that there was sure to be enough of it if actions were properly cared about. Offended by the frequency with which, in ethical and philosophical controversy, feeling is made the ultimate reason and justification of conduct, instead of being itself called on for a justification, while, in practice, actions the effect of which on human happiness is mischievous, are defended as being required by feeling, and the character of a person of feeling obtains a credit for desert, which he thought only due to actions, he had a real impatience of attributing praise to feeling, or of any but the most sparing reference to it, either in the estimation of persons or in the discussion of things. In addition to the influence which this characteristic in him, had on me and others, we found all the opinions to which we attached most importance, constantly attacked on the ground of feeling. Utility was denounced as cold calculation; political economy as hard-hearted; anti-population doctrines as repulsive to the natural feelings of mankind. We retorted by the word 'sentimentality', which, along with 'declamation' and 'vague generalities', served us as common terms of opprobrium. Although we were generally in the right, as against those who were opposed to us, the effect was that the cultivation of feeling (except the feelings of public and private duty), was not in much esteem among us, and had very little place in the thoughts of most of us, myself in particular. What we principally thought of, was to alter people's opinions; to make them believe according to evidence, and know what was their real interest, which when they once knew, they would, we thought, by the instrument of opinion, enforce a regard to it upon one another. While fully recognising the superior excellence of unselfish benevolence and love of justice, we did not expect the regeneration of mankind from any direct action on those sentiments, but from the effect of educated intellect, enlightening the selfish feelings. Although this last is prodigiously important as a means of improvement in the hands of those who are themselves impelled by nobler principles of action, I do not believe that any one of the survivors of the Benthamites or Utilitarians of that day, now relies mainly upon it for the general amendment of human conduct.

From this neglect both in theory and in practice of the cultivation of feeling, naturally resulted, among other things, an undervaluing of poetry, and of Imagination generally, as an element of human nature. It is, or was, part of the popular notion of Benthamites, that they are enemies of poetry: this was partly true of Bentham himself; he used to say that 'all poetry is misrepresentation': but in the sense in which he said it, the same might have been said of all impressive speech; of all representation or inculcation more oratorical in its character than a sum in arithmetic. An article of Bingham's in the first number of the Westminster Review, in which he offered as an explanation of something which he disliked in Moore, that 'Mr Moore *is* a poet, and therefore is *not* a reasoner,' did a good deal to attach the notion of hating poetry to the writers in the Review. But the truth was that many of us were great readers of poetry; Bingham himself had been a writer of it, while as regards me (and the same thing might be said of my father), the correct statement would be, not that I disliked poetry, but that I was theoretically indifferent to it. I disliked any sentiments in poetry which I should have disliked in prose; and that included a great deal. And I was wholly blind to its place in human culture, as a means of educating the feelings. But I was always personally very susceptible to some kinds of it. In the most sectarian period of my Benthamism, I happened to look into Pope's Essay on Man, and though every opinion in it was contrary to mine, I well remember how powerfully it acted on my imagination. Perhaps at that time poetical composition of any higher type than eloquent discussion in verse, might not have produced a similar effect on me: at all events I seldom gave it an opportunity. This, however, was a mere passive state. Long before I had enlarged in any considerable degree, the basis of my intellectual creed, I had obtained in the natural course of my mental progress, poetic culture of the most valuable kind, by means of reverential admiration for the lives and characters of heroic persons; especially the heroes of philosophy. The same inspiring effect which so many of the benefactors of mankind have left on record that they had experienced from Plutarch's Lives, was produced on me by Plato's pictures of Socrates, and by some modern biographies, above all by Condorcet's Life of Turgot; a book well calculated to rouse the best sort of enthusiasm, since it contains one of the wisest and noblest of lives, delineated by one of the wisest and noblest of men. The heroic virtue of these glorious representatives of the opinions with which I sympathized, deeply affected me, and I perpetually recurred to them as others do to a favourite poet, when needing to be carried up into the more elevated regions of feeling and thought. I may observe by the way that this book cured me of my sectarian follies. The two or three pages beginning 'Il regardait toute secte comme nuisible,' and explaining why Turgot always kept himself perfectly distinct from the Encyclopedists, sank deeply into my mind. I left off designating myself and others as Utilitarians, and by the pronoun 'we' or any other collective designation, I ceased to *afficher* sectarianism. My real inward sectarianism I did not get rid of till later, and much more gradually.

JOHN STUART MILL, *Autobiography* (1873).

REVOLUTIONARY ARDOUR
(1848)

WRITE and tell you that I join you in your happiness about the French Revolution? Very fine, my good friend. If I made you wait for a letter as long as you do me, our little *échantillon* of a millennium would be over: Satan would be let loose again: and I should have to share your humiliation instead of your triumph.

Nevertheless I absolve you, for the sole merit of thinking rightly (that is, of course, just as I do) about *la grande nation* and its doings. You and Carlyle (have you seen his article in last week's 'Examiner'?) are the only two people who feel just as I would have them – who can glory in what is actually great and beautiful without putting forth any cold reservations and incredulities to save their credit for wisdom. I am all the more delighted with your enthusiasm because I didn't expect it. I feared that you lacked revolutionary ardour. But no – you are just as *sans-culottish* and rash as I would have you. You are not one of those sages whose reason keeps so tight a reign on their emotions that they are too constantly occupied in calculating consequences to rejoice in any great manifestation of the forces that underlie our everyday existence. I should have written a soprano to your Jubilate the very next day, but that, lest I should be exalted above measure, a messenger of Satan was sent in the form of a headache, and directly on the back of that a face-ache, so that I have been a mere victim of sensations, memories, and visions for the last week. I am even now, as you may imagine, in a very shattered, limbo-like mental condition.

I thought we had fallen on such evil days that we were to see no really great movement – that ours was what St Simon calls a purely critical epoch, not at all an organic one; but I begin to be glad of my date. I would consent, however, to have a year clipt off my life for the sake of witnessing such a scene as that of the men of the barricades bowing to the image of Christ, 'who first taught fraternity to men'. One trembles to look into every fresh newspaper lest there should be something to mar the picture; but hitherto even the scoffing newspaper critics have been compelled into a tone of genuine respect for the French people and the Provisional Government. Lamartine can act a poem if he cannot write one of the very first order. I hope that beautiful face given to him in the pictorial newspaper is really his: it is worthy of an aureole. I am chiefly anxious about Albert, the operative, but his picture is not to be seen. I have little patience with people who can find time to pity Louis Philippe and his moustachioed sons. Certainly our decayed monarchs should be pensioned off: we should have a hospital for them, or a sort of zoological garden, where these worn-out humbugs may be preserved. It is but justice that we should keep them, since we have spoiled them for any honest trade. Let them sit on soft cushions, and have their dinner regularly, but, for heaven's sake, preserve me from sentimentalising over a pampered old man when the earth has its millions of unfed souls and bodies. Surely he is not so Ahab-like as to wish that the revolution had been deferred till his son's days: and I think the shades of the Stuarts would have some reason to complain if the Bourbons, who are so little better than they, had been allowed to reign much longer.

I should have no hope of good from any imitative movement at home. Our working classes are eminently inferior to the mass of the French people. In France the *mind* of the people is highly electrified; they are full of ideas on social subjects; they really desire social *reform* – not merely an acting out of

Sancho Panza's favourite proverb, 'Yesterday for you, to-day for me.' The revolutionary animus extended over the whole nation, and embraced the rural population – not merely, as with us, the artisans of the towns. Here there is so much larger a proportion of selfish radicalism and unsatisfied brute sensuality (in the agricultural and mining districts especially) than of perception or desire of justice, that a revolutionary movement would be simply destructive, not constructive. Besides, it would be put down. Our military have no notion of 'fraternising'. They have the same sort of inveteracy as dogs have for the ill-drest *canaille*. They are as mere a brute force as a battering-ram; and the aristocracy have got firm hold of them. And there is nothing in our Constitution to obstruct the slow progress of *political* reform. This is all we are fit for at present. The social reform which may prepare us for great changes is more and more the object of effort both in Parliament and out of it. But we English are slow crawlers. The sympathy in Ireland seems at present only of the water-toast kind. The Glasgow riots are more serious; but one cannot believe in a Scotch Reign of Terror in these days. I should not be sorry to hear that the Italians had risen *en masse*, and chased the odious Austrians out of beautiful Lombardy. But this they could hardly do without help, and that involves another European war.

GEORGE ELIOT, *Letter to J. Sibree* (February 1848).

THE UNIVERSITY OF BOOKS
(1841)

COMPLAINT is often made, in these times, of what we call the disorganised condition of society: how ill many arranged forces of society fulfil their work; how many powerful forces are seen working in a wasteful, chaotic, altogether un-arranged manner. It is too just a complaint, as we all know.

But perhaps if we look at this of Books and the Writers of Books, we shall find here, as it were, the summary of all other disorganisation; – a sort of *heart*, from which, and to which, all other confusion circulates in the world! Considering what Book-writers do in the world, and what the world does with Book-writers, I should say, It is the most anomalous thing the world at present has to show. – We should get into a sea far beyond sounding, did we attempt to give account of this: but we must glance at it for the sake of our subject. The worst element in the life of these three Literary Heroes was, that they found their business and position such a chaos. On the beaten road there is tolerable travelling; but it is sore work, and many have to perish, fashioning a path through the impassable!

Our pious Fathers, feeling well what importance lay in the speaking of man to men, founded churches, made endowments, regulations; everywhere in the civilized world there is a Pulpit, environed with all manner of complex dignified appurtenances and furtherances, that therefrom a man with the tongue may, to best advantage, address his fellow-men. They felt that this was the most important thing; that without this there was no good thing. It is a right pious work, that of theirs; beautiful to behold! But now with the art of Writing, with the art of Printing, a total change has come over that business. The Writer of a Book, is not he a Preacher preaching not to this parish or that, on this day or that, but to all men in all times and places? Surely it is of the last importance that *he* do his work right, whoever do it wrong; – that the *eye* report not falsely, for then all the other members are astray! Well; how he may do his work, whether he do it right or wrong, or do it at all, is a point which no man in the world has taken the pains to think of. To a certain shopkeeper, trying to get some money for his books, if lucky, he is of some importance; to no other man of any. Whence he came, whither he is bound, by what ways he arrived, by what he might be furthered on his course, no one asks. He is an accident in society. He wanders like a wild Ishmaelite, in a world of which he is as the spiritual light, either the guidance or the misguidance!

Certainly the art of writing is the most miraculous of all things man has devised. Odin's *Runes* were the first form of the work of a Hero; *Books*, written words, are still miraculous *Runes*, of the latest form! In Books lies the *soul* of the whole Past Time; the articulate audible voice of the Past, when the body and material substance of it has altogether vanished like a dream. Mighty fleets and armies, harbours and arsenals, vast cities, high-domed, many-engined, – they are precious, great: but what do they become? Agamemnon, the many Agamemnons, Pericleses, and their Greece; all is gone now to some ruined fragments, dumb mournful wrecks and blocks: but the Books of Greece! There Greece, to every thinker, still very literally lives; can be called-up again into life. No magic *Rune* is stranger than a Book. All that Mankind has done, thought, gained or been: it is lying as in magic preservation in the pages of Books. They are the chosen possession of men.

Do not Books still accomplish *miracles* as *Runes* were fabled to do? They persuade men. Not the wretchedest circulating-library novel, which foolish girls thumb and con in remote villages but will help to regulate the actual practical weddings and households of those foolish girls. So 'Celia' felt, so 'Clifford' acted: the foolish Theorem of Life, stamped into those young brains, comes out as a solid Practice one day. Consider whether any *Rune* in the wildest imagination of Mythologist ever did such wonders as, on the actual firm Earth, some Books have done! What built St Paul's Cathedral? Look at the heart of the matter, it was that divine Hebrew Book, – the word partly of the man Moses, an outlaw tending his Midianitish herds, four thousand years ago, in the wildernesses of Sinai! It is the strangest of things, yet nothing is truer. With the art of Writing, of which Printing is a simple, an inevitable and comparatively insignificant corollary, the true reign of miracles for mankind commenced. It related, with a wondrous new contiguity and perpetual closeness, the Past and Distant with the Present in time and place; all times and all places with this our actual Here and Now. All things were altered for men; all modes of important work of men: teaching, preaching, governing, and all else.

To look at Teaching, for instance. Universities are a notable, respectable product of the modern ages. Their existence too is modified, to the very basis of it, by the existence of Books. Universities arose while there were yet no Books procurable; while a man, for a single Book, had to give an estate of land. That, in those circumstances, when a man had some knowledge to communicate, he should do it by gathering the learners round him, face to face, was a necessity for him. If you wanted to know what Abelard knew, you must go and listen to Abelard. Thousands, as many as thirty-thousand, went to hear Abelard and that metaphysical theology of his. And now for any other teacher who had something of his own to teach, there was a great convenience opened: so many thousands eager to learn were already assembled yonder; of all places the best place for him was that. For any third teacher it was better still; and grew ever the better, the more teachers there came. It only needed now that the King took notice of this new phenomenon; combined or agglomerated the various schools into one school; gave it edifices, privileges, encouragements, and named it *Universitas*, or School of all Sciences: the University of Paris, in its essential characters, was there. The model of all subsequent Universities; which down even to these days, for six centuries now, have gone on to found themselves. Such, I conceive, was the origin of Universities.

It is clear, however, that with this simple circumstance, facility of getting Books, the whole conditions of the business from top to bottom were changed. Once invent Printing, you metamorphosed all Universities, or superseded them! The Teacher needed not now to gather men personally round him, that he might *speak* to them what he knew: print it in a Book, and all learners far and wide, for a trifle, had it each at his own fireside, much more effectually to learn it! – Doubtless there is still peculiar virtue in Speech; even writers of Books may still, in some circumstances, find it convenient to speak also, – witness our present meeting here! There is, one would say, and must ever remain while man has a tongue, a distinct province for Speech as well as for Writing and Printing. In regard to all things this must remain; to Universities among others. But the limits of the two have nowhere yet been pointed out, ascertained; much less put in practice: the University which would completely take-in that great new fact, of the existence of Printed Books, and stand on a clear footing for the Nineteenth Century as the Paris one did for the Thirteenth, has not yet come into existence. If we think of it, all that a University, or final highest School can do for us, is still but what the first School began doing, – teach us to *read*. We learn to *read*, in various languages, in various sciences; we learn the alphabet and letters of all manners of Books. But the place where we go to get knowledge, even theoretic knowledge, is the Books themselves! It depends on what we read, after all manner of Professors have done their best for us. The true University of these days is a Collection of Books.

THOMAS CARLYLE, *On Heroes, Hero-Worship and the Heroic in History* (1841).

LABOUR AND CIVILIZATION
(1851)

AND now, reader, look round this English room of yours, about which you have been proud so often, because the work of it was so good and strong, and the ornaments of it so finished. Examine again all those accurate mouldings, and perfect polishings, and unerring adjustments of the seasoned wood and tempered steel. Many a time you have exulted over them, and thought how great England was, because her slightest work was done so thoroughly. Alas! if read rightly, these perfectnesses are signs of a slavery in our England a thousand times more bitter and more degrading than that of the scourged African, or helot Greek. Men may be beaten, chained, tormented, yoked like cattle, slaughtered like summer flies, and yet remain in one sense, and the best sense, free. But to smother their souls with them, to blight and hew into rotting pollards the suckling branches of their human intelligence, to make the flesh and skin which, after the worm's work on it, is to see God, into leathern thongs to yoke machinery with, – this is to be slave-masters indeed; and there might be more freedom in England, though her feudal lords' lightest words were worth men's lives, and though the blood of the vexed husbandman dropped in the furrows of her fields, than there is while the animation of her multitudes is sent like fuel to feed the factory smoke, and the strength of them is given daily to be wasted into the fineness of a web, or racked into the exactness of a line.

And, on the other hand, go forth again to gaze upon the old cathedral front, where you have smiled so often at the fantastic ignorance of the old sculptors: examine once more those ugly goblins, and formless monsters, and stern statues, anatomiless and rigid; but do not mock at them, for they are signs of the life and liberty of every workman who struck the stone; a freedom of thought, and rank in scale of being, such as no laws, no charters, no charities can secure; but which it must be the first aim of all Europe at this day to regain for her children.

Let me not be thought to speak wildly or extravagantly. It is verily this degradation of the operative into a machine, which, more than any other evil of the times, is leading the mass of the nations everywhere into vain, incoherent, destructive struggling for a freedom of which they cannot explain the nature to themselves. Their universal outcry against wealth, and against nobility, is not forced from them either by the pressure of famine, or the sting of mortified pride. These do much, and have done much in all ages; but the foundations of society were never yet shaken as they are at this day. It is not that men are ill fed, but that they have no pleasure in the work by which they make their bread, and therefore look to wealth as the only means of pleasure. It is not that men are pained by the scorn of the upper classes, but they cannot endure their own; for they feel that the kind of labour to which they are condemned is verily a degrading one, and makes them less than men. Never had the upper classes so much sympathy with the lower, or charity for them, as they have at this day, and yet never were they so much hated by them: for, of old, the separation between the noble and the poor was merely a wall built by law; now it is a veritable difference in level of standing, a precipice between upper and lower grounds in the field of humanity, and there is pestilential air at the bottom of it.

*

We have much studied and much perfected, of late, the great civilized invention of the division of labour; only we give it a false name. It is not, truly speaking, the labour that is divided; but the men: – Divided into mere segments of men – broken into small fragments and crumbs of life; so that all the little piece of intelligence that is left in a man is not enough to make a pin, or a nail, but exhausts itself in making the point of a pin or the head of a nail. Now it is a good and desirable thing, truly, to make many pins in a day; but if we could only see with what crystal sand their points were polished, – sand of human soul, much to be magnified before it can be discerned for what it is – we should think there might be some loss in it also. And the great cry that rises from all our manufacturing cities, louder than their furnace blast, is all in very deed for this, – that we manufacture everything there except men; we blanch cotton, and strengthen steel, and refine sugar, and shape pottery; but to brighten, to strengthen, to refine, or to form a single living spirit, never enters into our estimate of advantages. And all the evil to which that cry is urging our myriads can be met only in one way: not by teaching nor preaching, for to teach them is but to show them their misery, and to preach to them, if we do nothing more than preach, is to mock at it. It can be met only by a right understanding, on the part of all classes, of what kinds of labour are good for men, raising them, and making them happy; by a determined sacrifice of such convenience, or beauty, or cheapness as is to be got only by the degradation of the workman; and by equally determined demand for the products and results of healthy and ennobling labour.

JOHN RUSKIN, *The Stones of Venice* (1851).

MATERIAL AND MORAL PROGRESS
(1861)

WHILE, however, in regard to the material world, the narrow notions formerly entertained, are, in the most enlightened countries, almost extinct, it must be confessed that, in regard to the moral world, the progress of opinion is less rapid. The same men who believe that Nature is undisturbed by miraculous interposition, refuse to believe that Man is equally undisturbed. In the one case, they assert the scientific doctrine of regularity; in the other, they assert the theological doctrine of irregularity. The reason of this difference of opinion is, that the movements of nature are less complex than the movements of man. Being less complex, they are more easily studied, and more quickly understood. Hence we find, that while natural science has long been cultivated, historical science hardly yet exists. Our knowledge of the circumstances which determine the course of mankind, is still so imperfect, and has been so badly digested, that it has produced scarcely any effect on popular ideas. Philosophers, indeed, are aware, that here, as elsewhere, there must be a necessary connexion between even the most remote and dissimilar events. They know that every discrepancy is capable of being reconciled, though we, in the present state of knowledge, may be unequal to the task. This is their faith, and nothing can wean them from it. But the great majority of people have a different faith. They believe that what is unexplained is inexplicable, and that what is inexplicable is supernatural. Science has explained an immense number of physical phenomena, and therefore, even to the vulgar, those phenomena no longer seem supernatural, but are ascribed to natural causes. On the other hand, science has not yet explained the phenomena of history; consequently, the theological spirit lays hold of them, and presses them into its own service. In this way, there has arisen that famous and ancient theory, which has received the name of the moral government of the world. It is a high-sounding title, and imposes on many, who, if they examined its pretensions, would never be duped by them. For, like that other notion which we have just considered, it is not only unscientific, but it is eminently irreligious. It is, in fact, an impeachment of one of the noblest attributes of the Deity. It is a slur on the Omniscience of God. It assumes that the fate of nations, instead of being the result of preceding and surrounding events, is specially subject to the control and interference of Providence. It assumes, that there are great public emergencies, in which such interference is needed. It assumes, that without the interference, the course of affairs could not run smoothly; that they would be jangled and out of tune; that the play and harmony of the whole would be incomplete. And thus it is, that the very men who, at one moment, proclaim the Divine

Omniscience, do, at the next moment, advocate a theory which reduces that Omniscience to nothing, since it imputes to an All-Wise Being, that the scheme of human affairs, of which He must, from the beginning, have foreseen every issue and every consequence, is so weakly contrived as to be liable to be frustrated; that it has not turned out as He could have wished; that it has been baffled by His own creatures, and that, to preserve its integrity, its operations must be tampered with, and its disorders redressed. The great Architect of the universe, the Creator and Designer of all existing things, is likened to some clumsy mechanic, who knows his trade so ill, that he has to be called in to alter the working of his own machine, to supply its deficiencies, to fill up its flaws, and to rectify its errors.

It is time that such unworthy notions should come to an end. It is time that what has long been known to philosophers, should also be known to historians, and that the history of mankind should cease to be troubled by what, to those who are imbued with the scientific spirit, must seem little better than arrant trifling. Of two things, choose one. Either deny the Omniscience of the Creator, or else admit it. If you deny it, you deny what, to my mind at least, is a fundamental truth, and, on these matters, there can be no sympathy between us. But if you admit the Omniscience of God, beware of libelling what you profess to defend. For when you assert what is termed the moral government of the world, you slander Omniscience, inasmuch as you declare that the mechanism of the entire universe, including the actions both of Nature and of Man, planned as it is by Infinite Wisdom, is unequal to its duties, unless that same Wisdom does from time to time interfere with it. You assert, in fact, either that Omniscience has been deceived, or that Omnipotence has been defeated. Surely, they who believe, and whose pride and happiness it is to believe, that there is a Power above all and before all, knowing all and creating all, ought not to fall into such a snare as this. They who, dissatisfied with this little world of sense, seek to raise their minds to something which the senses are unable to grasp, can hardly fail, on deeper reflection, to perceive how coarse and material is that theological prejudice, which ascribes to such a Power the vulgar functions of a temporal ruler, arrays him in the garb of an earthly potentate, and represents him as meddling here and meddling there, uttering threats, inflicting punishments, bestowing rewards. These are base and grovelling conceptions, the offspring of ignorance and of darkness. Such gross and sordid notions are but one remove from actual idolatry. They are the draff and offal of a bygone age, and we will not have them obtruded here. Well suited they were to those old and barbarous times, when men, being unable to refine their ideas, were, therefore, unable to purify their creed. Now, however, they jar upon us; they do not assimilate with other parts of our knowledge; they are incongruous; their concord is gone. Everything is against them. They stand alone; there is nothing left with which they harmonize. The whole scope and tendency of modern thought force upon our minds conceptions of regularity and of law, to which they are diametrically opposed. Even those who cling to them, do so from the influence of tradition, rather than from complete and unswerving belief. That child-like and unhesitating faith, with which the doctrine of interposition was once received, is succeeded by a cold and lifeless assent, very different from the enthusiasm of former times. Soon, too, this will vanish, and men will cease to be terrified by phantoms which their own ignorance has reared. This age, haply, may not witness the emancipation; but, so surely as the human mind advances, so surely will that emancipation come. It may come quicker than anyone expects. For, we are stepping on far and fast. The signs of the time are all around, and they who list may read.

H. T. BUCKLE, *History of Civilization in England* (1861).

A DEFERENTIAL SOCIETY
(1867)

ENGLAND is the type of deferential countries, and the manner in which it is so, and has become so, is extremely curious. The middle classes – the ordinary majority of educated men – are in the present day the despotic power in England. 'Public opinion', nowadays, 'is the opinion of the bald-headed man at the back of the omnibus.' It is *not* the opinion of the aristocratical classes as such; or of the most educated or refined classes as such; it is simply the opinion of the ordinary mass of educated, but still commonplace mankind. If you look at the mass of the constituencies, you will see that they are not very interesting people; and perhaps if you look behind the scenes and see the people who manipulate and work the constituencies, you will find that these are yet more uninteresting. The English constitution in its palpable form is this – the mass of the people yield obedience to a select few; and when you see this select few, you perceive that though not of the lowest class, nor of an unrespectable class, they are yet of a heavy sensible class – the last people in the world to whom, if they were drawn up in a row, an immense nation would ever give an exclusive preference.

In fact, the mass of the English people yield a deference rather to something else than to their rulers. They defer to what we may call the *theatrical show* of society. A certain state passes before them; a certain pomp of great men; a certain spectacle of beautiful women; a wonderful scene of wealth and enjoyment is displayed, and they are coerced by it. Their imagination is bowed down; they feel they are not equal to the life which is revealed to them. Courts and aristocracies have the great quality which rules the multitude, though philosophers can see nothing in it – visibility. Courtiers can do what others cannot. A common man may as well try to rival the actors on the stage in their acting, as the aristocracy in *their* acting. The higher world, as it looks from without, is a stage on which the actors walk their parts much better than the spectators can. This play is played in every district. Every rustic feels that his house is not like my lord's house; his life like my lord's life; his wife like my lady. The climax of the play is the Queen: nobody supposes that their house is like the court; their life like her life; her orders like their orders. There is in England a certain charmed spectacle which imposes on the many, and guides their fancies as it will. As a rustic on coming to London finds himself in the presence of a great show and vast exhibition of inconceivable mechanical things, so by the structure of our society, he finds himself face to face with a great exhibition of political things which he could not have imagined, which he could not make – to which he feels in himself scarcely anything analogous.

Philosophers may deride this superstition, but its results are inestimable. By the spectacle of this august society, countless ignorant men and women are induced to obey the few nominal electors – the £10 borough renters, and the £50 county renters – who have nothing imposing about them, nothing which would attract the eye or fascinate the fancy. What impresses men is not mind, but the result of mind. And the greatest of these results is this wonderful spectacle of society, which is ever new, and yet ever the same; in which accidents pass and essence remains; in which one generation dies and another succeeds, as if they were birds in a cage, or animals in a menagerie; or which it seems almost more than a metaphor to treat the parts as limbs of a perpetual living thing, so silently do they seem to change, so wonderfully and so perfectly does the conspicuous life of the new year take the place of the conspicuous life of last year. The apparent rulers of the English nation are like the most imposing personages of a splendid procession: it is by them the mob are influenced; it is they whom the spectators cheer. The real rulers are secreted in second-rate carriages; no one cares for them or asks about them, but they are obeyed implicitly and unconsciously by reason of the splendour of those who eclipsed and preceded them.

It is quite true that this imaginative sentiment is supported by a sensation of political satisfaction. It cannot be said that the mass of the English people are well off. There are whole classes who have not a conception of what the higher orders call comfort; who have not the prerequisites of moral existence; who cannot lead the life that becomes a man. But the most miserable of these classes do not impute their misery to politics. If a political agitator were to lecture to the peasants of Dorsetshire, and try to excite political dissatisfaction, it is much more likely that he would be pelted than that he would succeed. Of Parliament these miserable creatures know scarcely anything; of the Cabinet they never heard. But they would say that, 'for all they have heard, the Queen is very good'; and rebelling against the structure of society is to their minds rebelling against the Queen, who rules that society, in whom all its most impressive part – the part that they know – culminates. The mass of the English people are politically contented as well as politically deferential.

A deferential community, even though its lowest classes are not intelligent, is far more suited to a Cabinet government than any kind of democratic country, because it is more suited to political excellence. The highest classes can rule in it; and the highest classes must, as such, have more political ability than the lower classes. A life of labour, an incomplete education, a montonous occupation, a career in which the hands are used much and the judgment is used little, cannot create as much flexible thought, as much applicable intelligence, as a life of leisure, a long culture, a varied experience, an existence by which the judgment is incessantly exercised, and by which it may be incessantly improved. A country of respectful poor, though far less happy than where there are no poor to be respectful, is nevertheless far more fitted for the best government. You can use the best classes of the respectful country; you can only use the worst where every man thinks he is as good as every other.

WALTER BAGEHOT, *The English Constitution* (1867).

PROGRESS AND HAPPINESS
(1869)

WE have already seen how these things, – trade, business, and population, – are mechanically pursued by us as ends precious in themselves, and are worshipped as what we call fetishes; and Mr Bright, I have already said, when he wishes to give the working class a true sense of what makes glory and greatness, tells it to look at the cities it has built, the railroads it has made, the manufactures it has produced. So to this idea of glory and greatness the free-trade which our Liberal friends extol so solemnly and devoutly has served, – to the increase of trade, business, and population; and for this it is prized. Therefore, the untaxing of the poor man's bread has, with this view of national happiness, been used not so much to make the existing poor man's bread cheaper or more abundant, but rather to create more poor men to eat it; so that we cannot precisely say that we have fewer poor men than we had before free-trade, but we can say with truth that we have many more centres of industry, as they are called, and much more business, population, and manufactures. And if we are sometimes a little troubled by our multitude of poor men, yet we know the increase of manufactures and population to be such a salutary thing in itself, and our free-trade policy begets such an admirable movement, creating fresh centres of industry and fresh poor men here, while we were thinking about our poor men there, that we are quite dazzled and borne away, and more and more industrial movement is called for, and our social progress seems to become one triumphant and enjoyable course of what is sometimes called, vulgarly, outrunning the constable.

If, however, taking some other criterion of man's well-being than the cities he has built and the manufactures he has produced, we persist in thinking that our social progress would be happier if there were not so many of us so very poor, and in busying ourselves with notions of in some way or other adjusting the poor man and business one to the other, and not multiplying the one and the other mechanically and blindly, then our Liberal friends, the appointed doctors of free-trade, take us up very sharply. 'Art is long,' says the *Times*, 'and life is short; for the most part we settle things first and understand them afterwards. Let us have as few theories as possible; what is wanted is not the light of speculation. If nothing worked well of which the theory was not perfectly understood, we should be in sad confusion. The relations of labour and capital, we are told, are not understood, yet trade and commerce, on the whole, work satisfactorily.' I quote from the *Times* of only the other day. But thoughts like these, as I have often pointed out, are thoroughly British thoughts, and we have been familiar with them for years.

Or, if we want more of a philosophy of the matter than this, our free-trade friends have two axioms for us, axioms laid down by their justly esteemed doctors, which they think ought to satisfy us entirely. One is, that, other things being equal, the more population increases, the more does production increase to keep pace with it; because men by their numbers and contact call forth all manner of activities and resources in one another and in nature, which, when men are few and sparse, are never developed. The other is, that, although population always tends to equal the means of sub-sistence, yet people's notions of what subsistence is enlarge as civilisation advances, and take in a number of things beyond the bare necessaries of life; and thus, therefore, is supplied whatever check on population is needed. But the error of our friends is, perhaps, that they apply axioms of this sort as if they were self-acting laws which will put themselves into operation without trouble or planning on our part, if we will only pursue free-trade, business, and population zealously and staunchly. Whereas the real truth is, that, however the case might be under other circumstances, yet in fact, as we now manage the matter, the enlarged conception of what is included in *subsistence* does not operate to prevent the bringing into the world of numbers of people who but just attain to the barest necessaries of life or who even fail to attain to them; while, again, though production may increase as population increases, yet it seems that the production may be of such a kind, and so related, or rather non-related, to population, that the population may be little the better for it.

For instance, with the increase of population since Queen Elizabeth's time the production of silk-stockings has wonderfully increased, and silk-stockings have become much cheaper, and procurable in greater abundance by many more people, and tend perhaps, as population and manufactures increase, to get cheaper and cheaper, and at last to become, according to Bastiat's favourite image, a common free property of the human race, like light and air. But bread and bacon have not become much cheaper with the increase of population since Queen Elizabeth's time, nor procurable in much greater abundance by many more people; neither do they seem at all to promise to become, like light and air, a common free property of the human race. And if bread and bacon have not kept pace with our population, and we have many more people in want of them now than in Queen Elizabeth's time, it seems vain to tell us that silk-stockings have kept pace with our population, or even more than kept pace with it, and that we are to get our comfort out of that.

In short, it turns out that our pursuit of free-trade, as of so many other things, has been too mechanical. We fix upon some object, which in this case is the production of wealth, and the increase of manufactures, population, and commerce through free-trade, as a kind of one thing needful or end in itself; and then we pursue it staunchly and mechanically, and say that it is our duty to pursue it staunchly and mechanically, not to see how it is related to the whole intelligible law of things and to full human perfection, or to treat it as the piece of machinery, of varying value as its relations to the intelligible law of things vary, which it really is.

MATTHEW ARNOLD, *Culture and Anarchy* (1869).

SCIENCE AND CULTURE
(1880)

THE representatives of the Humanists, in the nineteenth century, take their stand upon classical education as the sole avenue to culture, as firmly as if we were still in the age of Renascence. Yet, surely, the present intellectual relations of the modern and the ancient worlds are profoundly different from those which obtained three centuries ago. Leaving aside the existence of a great and characteristically modern literature, of modern painting, and, especially, of modern music, there is one feature of the present state of the civilised world which separates it more widely from the Renascence, than the Renascence was separated from the middle ages.

This distinctive character of our own times lies in the vast and constantly increasing part which is played by natural knowledge. Not only is our daily life shaped by it, not only does the prosperity of millions of men depend upon it, but our whole theory of life has long been influenced, consciously or unconsciously, by the general conceptions of the universe, which have been forced upon us by physical science.

In fact, the most elementary acquaintance with the results of scientific investigation shows us that they offer a broad and striking contradiction to the opinion so implicitly credited and taught in the middle ages.

The notions of the beginning and the end of the world entertained by our forefathers are no longer credible. It is very certain that the earth is not the chief body in the material universe, and that the world is not subordinated to man's use. It is even more certain that nature is the expression of a definite order with which nothing interferes, and that the chief business of mankind is to learn that order and govern themselves accordingly. Moreover this scientific 'criticism of life' presents itself to us with different credentials from any other. It appeals not to authority, nor to what anybody may have thought or said, but to nature. It admits that all our interpretations of natural fact are more or less imperfect and symbolic, and bids the learner seek for truth not among words but among things. It warns us that the assertion which outstrips evidence is not only a blunder but a crime.

The purely classical education advocated by the representatives of the Humanists in our day, gives no inkling of all this. A man may be a better scholar than Erasmus, and know no more of the chief causes of the present intellectual fermentation than Erasmus did. Scholarly and pious persons, worthy of all respect, favour us with allocutions upon the sadness of the antagonism of science to their mediæval way of thinking, which betray an ignorance of the first principles of scientific investigation, an incapacity for understanding what a man of science means by veracity, and an unconsciousness of the weight of established scientific truths, which is almost comical.

There is no great force in the *tu quoque* argument, or else the advocates of scientific education might fairly enough retort upon the modern Humanists that they may be learned specialists, but that they possess no such sound foundation for a criticism of life as deserves the name of culture. And, indeed, if we were disposed to be cruel, we might urge that the Humanists have brought this reproach upon themselves, not because they are too full of the spirit of the ancient Greek, but because they lack it.

The period of the Renascence is commonly called that of the 'Revival of Letters', as if the influences then brought to bear upon the mind of Western Europe had been wholly exhausted in the field of literature. I think it is very commonly forgotten that the revival of science, effected by the same agency, although less conspicuous, was not less momentous.

In fact, the few and scattered students of nature of that day picked up the clue to her secrets exactly as it fell from the hands of the Greeks a thousand years before. The foundations of mathematics were so well laid by them, that our children learn their geometry from a book written for the schools of Alexandria two thousand years ago. Modern astronomy is the natural continuation and development of the work of Hipparchus and of Ptolemy; modern physics of that of Democritus and of Archimedes; it was long before modern biological science outgrew the knowledge bequeathed to us by Aristotle, by Theophrastus, and by Galen.

We cannot know all the best thoughts and sayings of the Greeks unless we know what they thought about natural phænomena. We cannot fully apprehend their criticism of life unless we understand the extent to which that criticism was affected by scientific conceptions. We falsely pretend to be the inheritors of their culture, unless we are penetrated, as the best minds among them were, with an unhesitating faith that the free employment of reason, in accordance with scientific method, is the sole method of reaching truth.

Thus I venture to think that the pretensions of our modern Humanists to the possession of the monopoly of culture and to the exclusive inheritance of the spirit of antiquity must be abated, if not abandoned. But I should be very sorry that anything I have said should be taken to imply a desire on my part to depreciate the value of classical education, as it might be and as it sometimes is. The native capacities of mankind vary no less than their opportunities; and while culture is one, the road by which one man may best reach it is widely different from that which is most advantageous to another. Again, while scientific education is yet inchoate and tentative, classical education is thoroughly well organised upon the practical experience of generations of teachers. So that, given ample time for learning and destination for ordinary life, or for a literary career, I do not think that a young Englishman in search of culture can do better than follow the course usually marked out for him, supplementing its deficiencies by his own efforts.

But for those who mean to make science their serious occupation; or who intend to follow the profession of medicine; or who have to enter early upon the business of life; for all these, in my opinion, classical education is a mistake; and it is for this reason that I am glad to see 'mere literary education and instruction' shut out from the curriculum of Sir Josiah Mason's College, seeing that its inclusion would probably lead to the introduction of the ordinary smattering of Latin and Greek.

Nevertheless, I am the last person to question the importance of genuine literary education, or to suppose that intellectual culture can be complete without it. An exclusively scientific training will bring about a mental twist as surely as an exclusively literary training. The value of the cargo does not compensate for a ship's being out of trim; and I should be very sorry to think that the Scientific College would turn out none but lop-sided men.

There is no need, however, that such a catastrophe should happen. Instruction in English, French and German is provided, and thus the three greatest literatures of the modern world are made accessible to the student.

French and German, and especially the latter language, are absolutely indispensable to those who desire full knowledge in any department of science. But even supposing that the knowledge of these languages acquired is not more than sufficient for purely scientific purposes, every Englishman has, in his native tongue, an almost perfect instrument of literary expression; and, in his own literature, models of every kind of literary excellence. If an Englishman cannot get literary culture out of his Bible, his Shakespeare, his Milton, neither, in my belief, will the profoundest study of Homer and Sophocles, Virgil and Horace, give it to him.

Thus, since the constitution of the College makes sufficient provision for literary as well as for scientific education, and since artistic instruction is also contemplated, it seems to me that a fairly complete culture is offered to all who are willing to take advantage of it.

But I am not sure that at this point the 'practical' man, scotched but not slain, may ask what all this talk about culture has to do with an Institution, the object of which is defined to be 'to promote the prosperity of the manufactures and the industry of the country'. He may suggest that what is wanted for this end is not culture, nor even a purely scientific discipline, but simply a knowledge of applied science.

I often wish that this phrase, 'applied science', had never been invented. For it suggests that there is a sort of scientific knowledge of direct practical use, which can be studied apart from another sort of scientific knowledge, which is of no practical utility, and which is termed 'pure science'. But there is no more complete fallacy than this. What people call applied science is nothing but the application of pure science to particular classes of problems. It consists of deductions from those general principles, established by reasoning and observation, which constitute pure science. No one can safely make these deductions until he has a firm grasp of the principles; and he can obtain that grasp only by personal experience of the operations of observation and of reasoning on which they are founded.

Almost all the processes employed in the arts and manufactures fall within the range either of physics or of chemistry. In order to improve them, one must thoroughly understand them; and no one has a chance of really understanding them, unless he has obtained that mastery of principles and that habit of dealing with facts, which is given by long-continued and well-directed purely scientific training in the physical and the chemical laboratory. So that there really is no question as to the necessity of purely scientific discipline, even if the work of the College were limited by the narrowest interpretation of its stated aims.

And, as to the desirableness of a wider culture than that yielded by science alone, it is to be recollected that the improvement of manufacturing processes is only one of the conditions which contribute to the prosperity of industry. Industry is a means and not an end; and mankind work only to get something which they want. What that something is depends partly on their innate, and partly on their acquired, desires.

If the wealth resulting from prosperous industry is to be spent upon the gratification of unworthy desires, if the increasing perfection of manufacturing processes is to be accompanied by an increasing debasement of those who carry them on, I do not see the good of industry and prosperity.

T. H. HUXLEY, *Science and Culture* (1880).

AN AGNOSTIC'S APOLOGY
(1893)

THE name Agnostic, originally coined by Professor Huxley about 1869, has gained general acceptance. It is sometimes used to indicate the philosophical theory which Mr Herbert Spencer, as he tells us, developed from the doctrine of Hamilton and Mansel. Upon that theory I express no opinion. I take the word in a vaguer sense, and am glad to believe that its use indicates an advance in the courtesies of controversy. The old theological phrase for an intellectual opponent was Atheist – a name which still retains a certain flavour as of the stake in this world and hell-fire in the next, and which, moreover, implies an inaccuracy of some importance. Dogmatic Atheism – the doctrine that there is no God, whatever may be meant by God – is, to say the least, a rare phase of opinion. The word Agnosticism, on the other hand, seems to imply a fairly accurate appreciation of a form of creed already common and daily spreading. The Agnostic is one who asserts – what no one denies – that there are limits to the sphere of human intelligence. He asserts, further, what many theologians have expressly maintained, that those limits are such as to exclude at least what Lewes called 'metempirical' knowledge. But he goes further, and asserts, in opposition to theologians, that theology lies within this forbidden sphere. This last assertion raises the important issue; and, though I have no pretension to invent an opposition nickname, I may venture, for the purposes of this article, to describe the rival school as Gnostics.

The Gnostic holds that our reason can, in some sense, transcend the narrow limits of experience. He holds that we can attain truths not capable of verification, and not needing verification, by actual experiment or observation. He holds, further, that a knowledge of those truths is essential to the highest interests of mankind, and enables us in some sort to solve the dark riddle of the universe. A complete solution, as everyone admits, is beyond our power. But some answer may be given to the doubts which harass and perplex us when we try to frame any adequate conception of the vast order of which we form an insignificant portion. We cannot say why this or that arrangement is what it is; we can say, though obscurely, that some answer exists, and would be satisfactory, if we could only find it. Overpowered, as every honest and serious thinker is at times overpowered, by the sight of pain, folly, and helplessness, by the jarring discords which run through the vast harmony of the universe, we are yet enabled to hear at times a whisper that all is well, to trust to it as coming from the most authentic source, and to know that only the temporary bars of sense prevent us from recognising with certainty that the harmony beneath the discords is a reality and not a dream. This knowledge is embodied in the central dogma of theology. God is the name of the harmony; and God is knowable. Who would not be happy in accepting this belief, if he could accept it honestly? Who would not be glad if he could say with confidence: 'The evil is transitory, the good eternal: our doubts are due to limitations destined to be abolished, and the world is really an embodiment of love and wisdom, however dark it may appear to our faculties'? And yet, if the so-called knowledge be illusory, are we not bound by the most sacred obligations to recognise the facts? Our brief path is dark enough on any hypothesis. We cannot afford to turn aside after every *ignis fatuus* without asking whether it leads to sounder footing or to hopeless quagmires. Dreams may be pleasanter for the moment than realities; but happiness must be won by adapting our lives to the realities. And who that has felt the burden of existence, and suffered under well-meant efforts at consolation, will deny that such consolations are the bitterest of mockeries? Pain is not an evil; death is not a separation; sickness is but a blessing in disguise. Have the gloomiest speculations of avowed pessimists ever tortured sufferers like those kindly platitudes? Is there a more cutting piece of satire in the language than the reference in our funeral service to the 'sure and certain hope of a blessed resurrection'? To dispel genuine hopes might be painful, however salutary. To suppress these spasmodic efforts to fly in the face of facts would be some comfort, even in the distress which they are meant to alleviate.

Besides the important question whether the Gnostic can

prove his dogmas, there is, therefore, the further question, whether the dogmas, if granted, have any meaning. Do they answer our doubts, or mock us with the appearance of an answer? The Gnostics rejoice in their knowledge. Have they anything to tell us? They rebuke what they call the 'pride of reason' in the name of a still more exalted pride. The scientific reasoner is arrogant because he sets limits to the faculty in which he trusts, and denies the existence of any other faculty. They are humble because they dare to tread in the regions which he declares to be inaccessible. But without bandying such accusations, or asking which pride is the greatest, the Gnostics are at least bound to show some ostensible justification for their complacency. Have they discovered a firm resting-place from which they are entitled to look down in compassion or contempt upon those who hold it to be a mere edifice of moonshine? If they have diminished by a scruple the weight of one passing doubt, we should be grateful: perhaps we should be converts. If not, why condemn Agnosticism?

I have said that our knowledge is in any case limited. I may add that, on any showing, there is a danger in failing to recognise the limits of possible knowledge. The word Gnostic has some awkward associations. It once described certain heretics who got into trouble from fancying that men could frame theories of the Divine mode of existence. The sects have been dead for many centuries. Their fundamental assumptions can hardly be quite extinct. Not long ago, at least, there appeared in the papers a string of propositions framed – so we were assured – by some of the most candid and most learned of living theologians. These propositions defined by the help of various languages the precise relations which exist between the persons of the Trinity. It is an odd, though far from an unprecedented, circumstance that the unbeliever cannot quote them for fear of profanity. If they were transplanted into the pages of the *Fortnightly Review*, it would be impossible to convince anyone that the intention was not to mock the simple-minded persons who, we must suppose, were not themselves intentionally irreverent. It is enough to say that they defined the nature of God Almighty with an accuracy from which modest naturalists would shrink in describing the genesis of a black-beetle. I know not whether these dogmas were put forward as articles of faith, as pious conjectures, or as tentative contributions to a sound theory. At any rate, it was supposed that they were interesting to beings of flesh and blood. If so, one can only ask in wonder whether an utter want of reverence is most strongly implied in this mode of dealing with sacred mysteries; or an utter ignorance of the existing state of the world in the assumption that the question which really divides mankind is the double procession of the Holy Ghost; or an utter incapacity for speculation in the confusion of these dead exuviæ of long-past modes of thought with living intellectual tissue; or an utter want of imagination, or of even a rudimentary sense of humour, in the hypothesis that the promulgation of such dogmas could produce anything but the laughter of sceptics and the contempt of the healthy human intellect?

LESLIE STEPHEN, *An Agnostic's Apology* (1893).

THE DIRECTIONS OF ART
(1873)

IT is the mistake of much popular criticism to regard poetry, music, and painting – all the various products of art – as but translations into different languages of one and the same fixed quantity of imaginative thought, supplemented by certain technical qualities of colour, in painting; of sound, in music; of rhythmical words, in poetry. In this way, the sensuous element in art, and with it almost everything in art that is essentially artistic, is made a matter of indifference; and a clear apprehension of the opposite principle – that the sensuous material of each art brings with it a special phase or quality of beauty, untranslatable into the forms of any other, an order of impressions distinct in kind – is the beginning of all true aesthetic criticism. For, as art addresses not pure sense, still less the pure intellect, but the 'imaginative reason' through the senses, there are differences of kind in aesthetic beauty, corresponding to the differences in kind of the gifts of sense themselves. Each art, therefore, having its own peculiar and untranslatable sensuous charm, has its own special mode of reaching the imagination, its own special responsibilities to its material. One of the functions of aesthetic criticism is to define these limitations; to estimate the degree of which a given work of art fulfils its responsibilities to its special material; to note in a picture that true pictorial charm, which is neither a mere poetical thought or sentiment, on the one hand, nor a mere result of communicable technical skill in colour or design, on the other; to define in a poem that true poetical quality, which is neither descriptive nor meditative merely, but comes of an inventive handling of rhythmical language, the element of song in the singing; to note in music the musical charm, that essential music, which presents no words, no matter of sentiment or thought, separable from the special form in which it is conveyed to use.

To such a philosophy of the variations of the beautiful, Lessing's analysis of the spheres of sculpture and poetry, in the *Laocoon*, was an important contribution. But a true appreciation of these things is possible only in the light of a whole system of such art-casuistries. Now painting is the art in the criticism of which this truth most needs enforcing, for it is in popular judgments on pictures that the false generalisation of all art into forms of poetry is most prevalent. To suppose that all is mere technical acquirement in delineation or touch, working through and addressing itself to the intelligence, on the one side, or a merely poetical, or what may be called literary interest, addressed also to the pure intelligence, on the other: – this is the way of most spectators, and of many critics, who have never caught sight all the time of that true pictorial quality which lies between, unique pledge, as it is, of the possession of the pictorial gift, that inventive or creative handling of pure line and colour, which, as almost always in Dutch painting, as often also in the works of Titian or Veronese, is quite independent of anything definitely poetical in the subject it accompanies. It is the *drawing* – the design projected from the peculiar pictorial temperament or constitution, in which, while it may possibly be ignorant of true anatomical proportions, all things whatever, all poetry, all ideas however abstract or obscure, float up as visible scene or image: it is the *colouring* – that weaving of light as of just perceptible gold threads, through the dress, the flesh, the atmosphere, in Titian's *Lace-girl*, that staining of the whole fabric of the thing with a new, delightful physical quality. This *drawing*, then – the arabesque traced in the air by Tintoret's flying figures, by Titian's forest branches; this colouring – the magic conditions of light and hue in the atmosphere of Titian's *Lace-girl*, or Rubens's *Descent from the Cross*: – these essential pictorial qualities must first of all delight the sense, delight it as directly and sensuously as a fragment of Venetian glass; and through this delight alone become the vehicle of whatever poetry or science may lie beyond them in the intention of the composer. In its primary aspect, a great picture has no more definite message for us than an accidental play of sunlight and shadow for a few moments on the wall or floor: is itself, in truth, a space of such fallen light, caught as the colours are in an Eastern carpet, but refined upon, and dealt with more subtly and exquisitely than by nature itself. And this primary and essential condition fulfilled, we may trace the coming of poetry into painting, by fine gradations upwards; from Japanese fan-painting, for instance, where we get, first, only abstract colour; then, just a little interfused sense of the poetry of flowers; then, sometimes, perfect flower-painting; and so, on-wards, until in Titian we have, as his poetry in the *Ariadne*, so actually a touch of true childlike humour in the diminutive, quaint figure with its silk gown, which ascends the temple stairs, in his picture of the *Presentation of the Virgin*, at Venice.

But although each art has thus its own specific order of impressions, and an untranslatable charm, while a just apprehension of the ultimate differences of the arts is the beginning of aesthetic criticism; yet it is noticeable that, in its special mode of handling its given material, each art may be observed to pass into the condition of some other art, by what German critics term an *Anders-streben* – a partial alienation from its own limitations, through which the arts are able, not indeed to supply the place of each other, but reciprocally to lend each other new forces.

Thus some of the most delightful music seems to be always approaching to figure, to pictorial definition. Architecture, again, though it has its own laws – laws esoteric enough, as the true architect knows only too well – yet sometimes aims at fulfilling the conditions of a picture, as in the *Arena* chapel; or of sculpture, as in the flawless unity of Giotto's tower at Florence; and often finds a true poetry, as in those strangely twisted staircases of the *châteaux* of the country of the Loire, as if it were intended that among their odd turnings the actors in a theatrical mode of life might pass each other unseen; there being a poetry also of memory and of the mere effect of time, by which architecture often profits greatly. Thus, again, sculpture aspires out of the hard limitation of pure form towards colour, or its equivalent, poetry also, in many ways, finding guidance from the other arts, the analogy between a Greek tragedy and a work of Greek sculpture, between a sonnet and a relief, of French poetry generally with the art of engraving, being more than mere figures of speech; and all the arts in common aspiring towards the principle of music; music being the typical, or ideally consummate art, the object of the great *Anders-streben* of all art, of all that is artistic, or partakes of artistic qualities.

All art constantly aspires towards the condition of music. For while in all other kinds of art it is possible to distinguish the matter from the form, and the understanding can always make this distinction, yet it is the constant effort of art to obliterate it. That the mere matter of a poem, for instance, its subject, namely, its given incidents or situation – that the mere matter of a picture, the actual circumstances of an event, the actual topography of a landscape – should be nothing without the form, the spirit, of the handling, that this form, this mode of handling, should become an end in itself, should penetrate every part of the matter: this is what all art constantly strives after, and achieves in different degrees.

WALTER PATER, *The School of Giorgione* (1873).

1895–Present

Observation

A BUSINESS FAMILY IN THE LATE NINETEENTH CENTURY

THE same note of perpetual change characterised our social relationships. We had no intercourse either in the country or in London with our nearest neighbours; nor did we belong to any organised profession or church; and my father, who had been brought up a Radical and had become a Conservative, took little part in local politics beyond subscribing handsomely to his party's funds. It is true that there was, somewhere in the background of our Gloucestershire life, a social entity called 'county society', consisting for the most part of a monotonous level of fox-hunting squires and the better-off incumbents; this plain of dull conventionality being broken here and there by the social peaks of peer or baronet, by the outstanding opulence of a retired manufacturer or trader, or, and this was the most invigorating variety, by the wider culture and more heterodox opinions of the Bishop and the Dean of Gloucester of the period. But the attachments of the family of the timber merchant of Gloucester to county society had always been loose and undefined; and as I grew up and the family became more nomadic, these more stationary ties fell to the ground. The world of human intercourse in which I was brought up was in fact an endless series of human beings, unrelated one to the other, and only casually connected with the family group – a miscellaneous crowd who came into and went out of our lives, rapidly and unexpectedly. Servants came and went; governesses and tutors came and went; business men of all sorts and degrees, from American railway presidents to Scandinavian timber growers, from British

Imperial company promoters to managers and technicians of local works, came and went; perpetually changing circles of 'London Society' acquaintances came and went; intellectuals of all schools of thought, religious, scientific and literary, came and went; my elder sisters' suitors, a series extensive and peculiar, came and went, leaving it is true, in the course of my girlhood, a permanent residue of seven brothers-in-law, who brought with them yet other business, professional and political affiliations, extending and diversifying the perpetually shifting panorama of human nature in society which opened to my view. Our social relations had no roots in neighbourhood, in vocation, in creed, or for that matter in race; they likened a series of moving pictures – surface impressions without depth – restlessly stimulating in their glittering variety. How expressive of the circumstance of modern profit-making machine enterprises is now its culminating attempt to entertain the world – the ubiquitous cinema!

There was, however, one section of humanity wholly unrepresented in these moving pictures, the world of labour. With the word labour I was, of course, familiar. Coupled mysteriously with its mate capital, this abstract term was always turning up in my father's conversation, and it occurred and reoccurred in the technical journals and reports of companies which lay on the library table. 'Water plentiful and labour docile', 'The wages of labour are falling to their natural level', 'To raise artificially the wage of labour is like forcing water up hill: when the pressure is removed the wage, like the water, falls down hill', were phrases which puzzled me: the allusion to water and its ways giving a queer physico-mechanical twist to my conception of the labouring classes of the current history books. Indeed, I never visualised labour as separate men and women of different sorts and kinds. Right down to the time when I became interested in social science and began to train as a social investigator, labour was an abstraction, which seemed to denote an arithmetically calculable mass of human beings, each individual a repetition of the other, very much in the same way that the capital of my father's companies consisted, I imagined, of gold sovereigns identical with all other gold sovereigns in form, weight and colour, and also in value, except 'when the capital is watered' explained my father. Again this mysterious allusion to water! Was it because water was the most monotonous and most easily manipulated of the elements? I enquired.

This ignorance about the world of labour, did it imply class consciousness, the feeling of belonging to a superior caste? A frank answer seems worth giving. There was no consciousness of superior riches: on the contrary, owing to my mother's utilitarian expenditure (a discriminating penuriousness which I think was traditional in families rising to industrial power during the Napoleonic wars) the Potter girls were brought up to 'feel poor'. 'You girls,' grumbled a brother-in-law, as he glanced from a not too luxurious breakfast table at the unexpectedly large credit in his bank-book, 'have neither the habit nor the desire for comfortable expenditure.' The consciousness that was present, I speak for my own analytic mind, was the consciousness of superior power. As life unfolded itself I became aware that I belonged to a class of persons who habitually gave orders, but who seldom, if ever, executed the orders of other people. My mother sat in her boudoir and gave orders – orders that brooked neither delay nor evasion. My father, by temperament the least autocratic and most accommodating of men, spent his whole life giving orders. He ordered his stockbroker to buy and sell shares, his solicitor to prepare contracts and undertake legal proceedings. In the running of the timber yards, his intervention took the form of final decisions with regard to the new developments in buying and selling, and new agreements with railway companies as to rates and transport facilities. When those maps of continents were unrolled before him I listened with fascinated interest to eager discussions, whether a line of railway should run through this section or that; at what exact point the station or junction should be placed; what land should be purchased for the contingent town; whether this patch or that, of forest, coalfield or mineral ore, should be opened up or left for future generations to exploit. And these manifold decisions seemed to me to be made without reference to any superior authority, without consideration of the desires or needs of the multitudes of lives which would, in fact, be governed by them; without, in short, any other consideration than that of the profit of the promoters. As for the shareholders' control (with what bewildered curiosity I watched the preparation for these meetings!), I knew it was a myth as far as human beings were concerned; it was patently the shares that were counted and not the holders; and share certificates, like all other forms of capital, could be easily manipulated. And when, one after the other, my sisters' husbands joined the family group, they also were giving orders: the country gentleman on his estate and at sessions; the manufacturer in his mill; the shipowner to his fleet of ships on the high seas; the city financier in the money market floating or refusing to float foreign government loans; the Member of Parliament as Financial Secretary of the Treasury; the surgeon and the barrister well on their way to leadership in their respective professions. It remains to be added, though this is forestalling my tale, that on the death of my mother I found myself giving orders and never executing them. Reared in this atmosphere of giving orders it was not altogether surprising that I apparently acquired the marks of the caste. When, in search of facts, I found myself working as a trouser hand in a low-grade Jewish shop, I overheard the wife of the sub-contractor, as she examined my bungled buttonholes, remark to her husband, 'She's no good at the sewing: if I keep her I will put her to look after the outworkers – she's got the voice and manner to deal with that bloody lot.' Alas! to be recognised – not as a scholar, not even as a 'r-e-e-l lidee' unaccustomed to earn her livelihood – but as a person particularly fitted by nature or nurture 'to give work out' and to 'take work in' in such a manner and in such a voice as to make the biggest profit, for (I say it as a justifiable retort) that bloody sweater!

BEATRICE WEBB, *My Apprenticeship* (1926).

DEFYING THE LIGHTNING
(1921, retrospective)

ONE evening in 1878 or thereabouts, I, being then in my earliest twenties, was at a bachelor party of young men of the professional class in the house of a rising young London physician. We fell to talking about religious revivals; and an anecdote was related of an 'infidel' who, having incautiously scoffed at the mission of Messrs Moody and Sankey, a then famous firm of American evangelists, was subsequently carried home on a shutter, slain by divine vengeance as a blasphemer. A timid minority, without quite venturing to question the truth of the incident – for they naturally did not care to run the risk of going home on shutters themselves – nevertheless shewed a certain disposition to cavil at those who exulted in it; and something approaching to an argument began. At last it was alleged by the most evangelical of the disputants that Charles Bradlaugh, the most formidable atheist on the Secularist platform, had taken out his watch publicly and challenged the Almighty to strike him dead in five minutes if he really existed and disapproved of atheism. The leader of the cavillers, with great heat, repudiated this as a gross calumny, declaring that Bradlaugh had repeatedly and indignantly contradicted it, and implying that the atheist champion was far too pious a man to commit such a blasphemy. This exquisite confusion of ideas roused my sense of comedy. It was clear to me that the challenge attributed to Charles Bradlaugh was a scientific experiment of a quite simple, straightforward, and proper kind to ascertain whether the expression of atheistic opinions really did involve any personal risk. It was certainly the method taught in the Bible, Elijah having confuted the prophets of Baal in precisely that way, with every circumstance of bitter mockery of their god when he failed to send down fire from heaven. Accordingly I said that if the question at issue were whether the penalty of questioning the theology of Messrs Moody and Sankey was to be struck dead on the spot by an incensed deity, nothing could effect a more convincing settlement of it than the very obvious experiment attributed to Mr Bradlaugh, and that consequently if he had not tried it, he ought to have tried it. The omission, I added, was one which could easily be remedied there and then, as I happened to share Mr Bradlaugh's views as to the absurdity of the belief in these violent interferences with the order of nature by a short-tempered and thin-skinned supernatural deity. Therefore – and at that point I took out my watch.

The effect was electrical. Neither sceptics nor devotees were prepared to abide the result of the experiment. In vain did I urge the pious to trust in the accuracy of their deity's aim with a thunderbolt, and the justice of his discrimination between the innocent and the guilty. In vain did I appeal to the sceptics to accept the logical outcome of their scepticism: it soon appeared that when thunderbolts were in question there were no sceptics. Our host, seeing that his guests would vanish precipitately if the impious challenge were uttered, leaving him alone with a solitary infidel under sentence of extermination in five minutes, interposed and forbade the experiment, pleading at the same time for a change of subject. I of course complied, but could not refrain from remarking that though the dreadful words had not been uttered, yet, as the thought had been formulated in my mind, it was very doubtful whether the consequences could be averted by sealing my lips. However, the rest appeared to feel that the game would be played according to the rules, and that it mattered very little what I thought so long as I said nothing.

Only the leader of the evangelical party, I thought, was a little preoccupied until five minutes had elapsed and the weather was still calm.

BERNARD SHAW, Preface to *Back to Methuselah* (1921).

THE GENTLENESS OF NATURE
(1927)

To the Englishman Nature is a thing of spring, of lambs gambolling in snakeless meadows, of wild flowers and the song of larks. In our towns we have covered her over completely with paving-stones, and asphalt, and houses; in the fields we cover her up with corn and turnips and fat sheep and shiny domesticated cows; in the rich man's park we cover her up with ridiculous hand-fed pheasants.

But elsewhere, in the East for example, where Nature rules man and not man Nature, the depth of her melancholy and her iron ruthlessness become apparent. The curious forgotten fact is that even in England not so many generations back she was like that. Today in our churches we still pray anachronistically to be delivered from the scourge of cattle murrain. Some years ago in Ceylon, I saw what it really was that our forefathers so fervently prayed God for protection against. It was Nature – pitiless, untamed, and all-powerful – appearing in the form not of violets and cowslips, but of pain and destruction and wholesale death. There is a district in the south of Ceylon consisting principally of jungle. The chief population consists of wild pig, deer, buffaloes, leopards, and elephants. But there is also a human population of about 100,000 living in scattered villages. Such wealth as these men have lies in their herds of cattle, in the bulls which draw their carts, and the domesticated buffaloes which, treading the round of the rice-fields in primeval fashion, take the place of ploughs, and treading the grain upon the threshing-floor serve the purpose of the flail and threshing-machine.

Upon this district there descended suddenly murrain or rinderpest. It was the season when the crops were on the ground, and the cattle had therefore been driven out from the villages to graze in the jungles or the great open spaces of dry lagoons. The disease first appeared in a herd of 150 buffaloes grazing in such a lagoon. When I went to the place, the ground was covered with great beasts lying dead or dying, and the flies were swarming over the dead and dying alike. Out of the clouds of far-off Colombo, that mysterious entity, 'the Government', sent down its orders that all cattle should be tethered or impounded, that all 'suspected' beasts should be segregated and the 'infected' shot. But it was all useless. The disease had spread already into the jungle, to the wild buffaloes, and the jungle was soon full of death. The carcasses lay thick in the lagoons, and on the game tracks, and around the water-holes. The herds of wild pig came and fed upon the infected bodies, sickened, carried the disease back to the domestic cattle of the villages, and died everywhere in hundreds. In the thickest jungle you came upon even the great sambhur deer dying. And the villager, after the manner of the East, prepared to watch ruin descend upon him silently and patiently. He would do nothing. He had never tethered a buffalo or put his half-wild bulls within fences, and therefore to tether a buffalo now or to impound his cattle was not only useless but impossible. He had never killed his own animals, and therefore nothing on earth would induce him now to kill a plague-stricken beast, though it were a mere living mass of flies and maggots. Even on the few main roads bulls dropped and died, and were left to rot where they had fallen. Herds of two hundred dwindled in a few months to two or three head of cattle, and many a village saw almost its entire wealth swept away in a week.

Around the village the grim cruelty of Nature had full sway. There was a village of some forty huts, a little Government school, a tank, and a stretch of rice-fields, set in the jungle. A villager told me that there was a plague-stricken buffalo near the tank. I went through a little patch of jungle and came out upon the bund of the tank. It was a pleasant sight after the dry, scrubby, barren jungle. Great kumbuk and tamarind trees grew upon the bund, the sheet of water was starred with lotus flowers, a great flight of teal flew whirring round and round high overhead. I sat down for a moment, and then far off across the tank in the water caught sight of a black patch, clearly a wallowing buffalo. And almost immediately it stirred, and, as I sat there, I saw that it was very slowly moving towards me. This in itself was strange, for a buffalo will always move away from you, and I had expected a long, hot chase. As it came nearer, even at 250 yards, you could see from its slow gait that it was plague-stricken, and as I sat there in the sun watching it drag itself towards me I felt as if it was deliberately coming to be killed, to be put out of some intolerable agony. At 100 yards I fired at it with a rifle and missed completely, but it paid no attention and continued to plod straight towards me. I fired again and it fell dead. And when I went up to it I found that the whole of one side of its face, including the eye, had been eaten away by maggots.

LEONARD WOOLF, 'The Gentleness of Nature', in *Essays on Literature, history, politics etc.* (1927).

IN THE LINE
(1916)

AFTER resting for a day and a half we were sent to relieve the lads who had landed. Our baptism, and a severe one it seemed to me at the time, but was only a fleabite to later on. We were all posted thus. The trenches are very high, and to get on your post you have to step up. Then standing straight up, an average man's head would be level with the top. For protection sand-bags are stacked two deep with a loop hole. The loop hole is about 2 or 3 feet long by 2 feet of sheet steel, and a hole large enough to put the rifle through with a door which you close when not in use. The steel is about an inch thick. Two men mount a post, two hours on, two hours sitting on the step, ready with a blanket or overcoat to throw over bombs should they come over, and two hours sleep. For six days and nights we did this without a spell, and then when we had what they call a spell, we had to go and deepen a trench with pick and shovel – 48 hours in the trenches and 48 hours out. So we worked after, but it was just as bad out as in, and as dangerous. At first we used to sleep at the bottom of the trench, and being only a little over 2 feet wide, and N.C.O.s walking about all night, we were walked all over; but nature must have its way, and we slept.

You would see bloodstains all over your post where perhaps the soldier on before you was hit, and pieces of a rifle smashed to atoms. Things were fairly quiet for awhile, and then they gave us a demonstration. The never ceasing crack of the thousands of rifles, and the boom boom of the bigger guns. The bursting of the shells, – a moan telling that some poor unfortunate soldier was hit, made up for the quietness. The hand bombs were worse than anything excepting shells. We were in places only a few yards from the Turks and hand bombs did the most damage. The night is the worst and busiest part of the twenty-four hours. Each side is looking and waiting for an attack. Every man in the trenches has to 'stand to' with bayonets fixed in case the Turks attack, from an hour before dawn till daylight. Firing over 100 shots in a night I think caused me to go a bit deaf, or else the explosion of a bomb. Be that as it may, the fact remains I went deaf, and was put on assisting the engineers. You said in one of your letters that the rest behind the firing line would do me good. At Gallipoli, Mum, there is no such thing as behind the firing line. Down the beach – in your dugout, it is all the same, and the man that has set foot on Gallipoli, in my opinion, has done his bit. The Engineers work right in the firing [line], and I would just as soon be at my post. The Engineers sap towards the Turks' trenches, and the Turks sap towards us. Should we hear the Turks picking we locate whereabouts they are, and try to get underneath them and blow them up, and they do the same. It is just like a race. To give you an idea what a sap is, try and imagine a tunnel going in about 10 to 15 ft, then down 20 feet, another drive about 12 feet and then another shaft sunk another 10 ft.

I was in one when it was blown up, and will never forget the experience. I was only just in the mouth at the time, but the force of the charge caused me to stagger against the opposite side of the trench, and I had to feel if my nose was on and my eyes correct. They were alright. I might here say that when a sap is blown up the charge is so strong that it shakes the earth, and the feeling is just as if a huge giant tilted the earth from underneath. What I did not like about sapping was that should the Turks charge or anything else happen you were caught in a trap, being as it were, in the bowels of the earth. Just before I left it snowed and became bitterly cold, and was the cause of a lot of us being sent away sick. Men were getting frost bitten feet, and when they removed their boots, they could not put them on again, on account of the swelling. Men were wearing socks as gloves, and here it was where Grandma's gloves came handy. On top of this snow, bitterly cold, as it was, the Turks opened up a heavy bombardment. The heaviest bombardment the Peninsula has known, so some who were at the landing tell us. They kept their fire on Lonesome Pine only, and the 23rd and 24th were holding Lonesome Pine and bore the brunt of it all. Shells of all descriptions were poured into us. You would feel the earth quake as a shell would bore its way into the earth. Men were ordered to take cover in the tunnels, but of what avail? A shell would come crashing through the tunnel and bury unknown numbers alive. Stretcher bearers running past with their dead or wounded, Officers giving orders, and Hell was let loose. How I escaped I know not – shrapnel was falling by me, shells passing overhead on their deadly mission, and there I lay with never a scratch. The worst of all this was the fact that the warships, artillery and big guns answered never a shot. Here were we getting bowled over like ninepins, and us taking it like so many sheep. Every man there waited for the order to charge, and have some of their own back. As far as is known, between the 23rd and 24th over 200 men were lost in that bombardment without as much as one shot in self defence. Then came the calm. Our trenches were all knocked about. Dirt piled up like the pyramids. We had to go and dig out who we could, and a gruesome game it was. Pieces of flesh, scalp, legs, tunics tattered and parts of soldiers carried away in blankets. By God, to stand by and see your own boys dug out in pieces and do nothing is almost unbearable.

Such is war, and the curse to the ones who are the cause of it. Many a brave man had tears in his eyes, as, gazing on some friend in almost unrecognizable masses, he had but a minute before his death been joking with him. Imagine you are all sitting down to a meal with friends around you, when all of a sudden by some unseen hand the person to whom you are speaking drops dead by your side. Before you have recovered a head flies off another of your friends, and you then look around, and seeing nothing, you gaze on what is before you. Then the feeling would come over you that you would like to avenge their death. We do not blame the Turks as, unseen by us, they no doubt have suffered more than we have, and all is fair in war. The Turks from what I have seen of them are fair fighters, and from the appearance of the prisoners we captured are glad to be out of the fight. They wear all sorts of clothing, and seem fond of gay colours. Some were coming in to us to surrender, but as soon as our fellows saw them they shot them dead. This is due to their treachery early in the war. They are big men, and one we pulled over the parapet had a chest on him like an ox. At night they sometimes would creep up to our trenches and throw bombs into us, or wait until you opened the loop-hole and then shoot at you. I never struck any on my post, but others told me that is what they used to do.

THE MISERIES OF GALLIPOLI

Now we come to the hardships of Gallipoli. It is reckoned that Gallipoli is one of the hardest fronts to fight on. Unlike France, there are no friendly villages to get a little comfort or food, neither is there any flat country with farms. Nothing but mountains, and barren at that, save for a little scrub here and there, to say nothing of the flies with which we had to contend. These pests would be on your face, hands, down your throat, and if you were eating biscuits with jam on, it was more like biscuits and flies. We slept in dugouts, which is a place dug out of the side of a trench, with sufficient width and length to lie in with ease. The lower they were the better protection for the occupier. Here was another misery. You would turn in your sleep and knock your head or arm against the top, and the soil, being of a sandy nature, would fall down on your face, and if you happened to have your mouth open you would get it full, but we soon got used to that, and after a while got very comfortable. These are as nothing compared to the lice. For a week I did not feel them, but after that I suffered the tortures of hell, and to use the only expression, became 'lousey'. Each day I would kill about 50, and woe to him who neglected going through himself each day. He would not sleep that night.

There was no getting rid of them. They would breed on you, and no matter how often you changed yourself, you would be just as bad next day. We could not wash ourselves, as there was a scarcity of water. The only chance to wash yourself was to go down to the beach, but so dangerous did this become, owing to the havoc caused by the gun known as 'Beachy Bill', that it was not worth the risk. In fact, they had police there to prevent anyone so doing. This may seem to you overdrawn, but it is the truth. My skin was red raw through scratching myself. All were the same. One fellow said he had none on him. We took his shirt off, and it was swarming with them. When we showed him he said he did not know what they were before, but thought it was fleas that bit him at night. To read this you would think it impossible that we slept at night, but so hardened had we become that after we had a scratch or two we would fall asleep, and they would then do their worst. The fleas were not nearly so numerous.

You ask me in one of your letters how we get on for food. I dared not mention the truth, for you would never have received the letter. You may think some of my letters funny from the front not giving much news, but the fact was, we were not allowed to tell much. For instance I wrote simply saying the sights here are ghastly and I was told the censor had done his work with his masterful stroke. For breakfast we got a slice of bacon with either biscuits or bread and plenty of tea. Dinner either rice, which was good, or stew. The stew at first was made of bully beef and dessicated vegetables. For tea, sometimes rice or stew with tea. At this time we got a fair amount of bread, but not sufficient to last a day. Jam was issued every day. A pound tin between three, and plenty of water. Later on we got fresh meat stew and steak in the morning. This was good while it lasted. Then came the change. In the first place a shell knocked some of our dixies over and made us short, and we had to suffer. Instead of getting rice and stew each day, we got for breakfast sometimes bacon. For dinner tea only, and for tea rice or stew. We were issued with a 2 lb loaf between 3 men, but could not get a biscuit on the peninsula. This bread was only sufficient for one meal, but had to last you for a day. Then we got biscuits, but could not get bread and our meals consisted of the following: 6 biscuits per man, which were as hard as iron. They taste something like cabin biscuits. A piece of bacon, which you could eat in one mouthful, and quarter ration of tea. Water was getting scarce. For dinner just a cupful of tea and bully and biscuits if you liked to eat it. For tea a little stew. Then came the starvation rations. Three biscuits a day. No bacon or sometimes a little and a very little stew. For dinner we got a little cheese but only a bite. To top the lot, we could not get water or tea to drink for nearly a fortnight. So bad did our thirst become that we had to go down to the cooks and get a drop in the middle of the night at the risk of getting into serious trouble, as they had sentries stationed all round. Then the snow came and we ate it, but it takes a lot to quench your thirst. Some, who were fortunate enough to find wood, melted a lot of snow and got water that way. So bad were things that I saw a fellow near me go round picking old pieces of bacon off the parapet and eating them, and to quench his thirst drink out of a dirty well where perhaps dead bodies had been. This is the gospel truth, as M— L— will tell you. You may not believe it, but things were that bad over there, that if fellows were carried out on a stretcher wounded some would say 'Lucky devil, I would give a limb to be there.' I would not go that far, but I often wished for a nice little wound to give me a spell. You will hear soldiers who are wounded now that they are home again exaggerate to some extent such as 'dying to get back again'. I have been through the mill, and know that all or most who were on the peninsula would not like it again. It was a great joke to us to read some of the letters by the soldiers, and many a laugh we had over them. It seems that I am appearing as a coward, but were we ordered back to Gallipoli tomorrow, I would go willingly, but not with the same enthusiasm, knowing that we cannot get the proper treatment as at other fronts. No matter where we go now it will never be as bad as Gallipoli. ....

PRIVATE THOMAS DRY, in *War Letters of Fallen Englishmen*, ed. Laurence Housman (1930).

IN THE MINE
(1937)

THE machines that keep us alive, and the machines that make the machines, are all directly or indirectly dependent upon coal. In the metabolism of the Western world the coal-miner is second in importance only to the man who ploughs the soil. He is a sort of grimy caryatid upon whose shoulders nearly everything that is *not* grimy is supported. For this reason the actual process by which coal is extracted is well worth watching, if you get the chance and are willing to take the trouble.

When you go down a coal-mine it is important to try and get to the coal face when the 'fillers' are at work. This is not easy, because when the mine is working visitors are a nuisance and are not encouraged, but if you go at any other time, it is possible to come away with a totally wrong impression. On a Sunday, for instance, a mine seems almost peaceful. The time to go there is when the machines are roaring and the air is black with coal dust, and when you can actually see what the miners have to do. At those times the place is like hell, or at any rate like my own mental picture of hell. Most of the things one imagines in hell are there – heat, noise, confusion, darkness, foul air, and, above all, unbearably cramped space. Everything except the fire, for there is no fire down there except the feeble beams of Davy lamps and electric torches which scarcely penetrate the clouds of coal dust.

When you have finally got there – and getting there is a job in itself: I will explain that in a moment – you crawl through the last line of pit props and see opposite you a shiny black wall three or four feet high. This is the coal face. Overhead is the smooth ceiling made by the rock from which the coal has been cut; underneath is the rock again, so that the gallery you are in is only as high as the ledge of coal itself, probably not much more than a yard. The first impression of all, overmastering everything else for a while, is the frightful, deafening din from the conveyor belt which carries the coal away. You cannot see very far, because the fog of coal dust throws back the beam of your lamp, but you can see on either side of you the line of half-naked kneeling men, one to every four or five yards, driving their shovels under the fallen coal and flinging it swiftly over their left shoulders. They are feeding it on to the conveyor belt, a moving rubber belt a couple of feet wide which runs a yard or two behind them. Down this belt a glittering river of coal races constantly. In a big mine it is carrying away several tons of coal every minute. It bears it off to some place in the main roads where it is shot into tubs holding half a ton, and thence dragged to the cages and hoisted to the outer air.

It is impossible to watch the 'fillers' at work without feeling a pang of envy for their toughness. It is a dreadful job that they do, an almost superhuman job by the standards of an ordinary person. For they are not only shifting monstrous quantities of coal, they are also doing it in a position that doubles or trebles the work. They have got to remain kneeling all the while – they could hardly rise from their knees without hitting the ceiling – and you can easily see by trying it what a tremendous effort this means. Shovelling is comparatively easy when you are standing up, because you can use your knee and thigh to drive the shovel along; kneeling down, the whole of the strain is thrown upon your arm and belly muscles. And the other conditions do not exactly make things easier. There is the heat – it varies, but in some mines it is suffocating – and the coal dust that stuffs up your throat and nostrils and collects along your eyelids, and the unending rattle of the conveyor belt, which in that confined space is rather like the rattle of a machine gun. But the fillers look and work as though they were made of iron. They really do look like iron – hammered iron statues – under the smooth coat of coal dust which clings to them from head to foot. It is only when you see miners down the mine and naked that you realise what splendid men they are. Most of them are small (big men are at a disadvantage in that job) but nearly all of them have the most noble bodies; wide shoulders tapering to slender supple waists, and small pronounced buttocks and sinewy thighs, with not an ounce of waste flesh anywhere. In the hotter mines they wear only a pair of thin drawers, clogs and knee-pads; in the hottest mines of all, only the clogs and knee-pads. You can hardly tell by the look of them whether they are young or old. They may be any age up to sixty or even sixty-five, but when they are black and naked they all look alike. No one could do their work who had not a young man's body, and a figure fit for a guardsman at that; just a few pounds of extra flesh on the waist-line, and the constant bending would be impossible. You can never forget that spectacle once you have seen it – the line of bowed, kneeling figures, sooty black all over, driving their huge shovels under the coal with stupendous force and speed. They are on the job for seven and a half hours, theoretically without a break, for there is no time 'off'. Actually they snatch a quarter of an hour or so at some time during the shift to eat the food they have brought with them, usually a hunk of bread and dripping and a bottle of cold tea. The first time I was watching the 'fillers' at work I put my hand upon some dreadful slimy thing among the coal dust. It was a chewed quid of tobacco. Nearly all the miners chew tobacco, which is said to be good against thirst.

Probably you have to go down several coal-mines before you can get much grasp of the processes that are going on round you. This is chiefly because the mere effort of getting from place to place makes it difficult to notice anything else. In some ways it is even disappointing, or at least is unlike what you have expected. You get into the cage, which is a steel box about as wide as a telephone box and two or three times as long. It holds ten men, but they pack it like pilchards in a tin, and a tall man cannot stand upright in it. The steel door shuts upon you, and somebody working the winding gear above drops you into the void. You have the usual momentary qualm in your belly and a bursting sensation in the ears, but not much sensation of movement till you get near the bottom, when the cage slows down so abruptly that you could swear it is going upwards again. In the middle of the run the cage probably touches sixty miles an hour; in some of the deeper mines it touches even more. When you crawl out at the bottom you are perhaps four hundred yards under ground. That is to say you have a tolerable-sized mountain on top of you; hundreds of yards of solid rock, bones of extinct beasts, subsoil, flints, roots of growing things, green grass and cows grazing on it – all this suspended over your head and held back only by wooden props as thick as the calf of your leg. But because of the speed at which the cage has brought you down, and the complete blackness through which you have travelled, you hardly feel yourself deeper down than you would at the bottom of the Piccadilly tube.

What *is* surprising, on the other hand, is the immense horizontal distances that have to be travelled underground. Before I had been down a mine I had vaguely imagined the miner stepping out of the cage and getting to work on a ledge of coal a few yards away. I had not realised that before he even gets to his work he may have to creep through passages as long as from London Bridge to Oxford Circus. In the beginning, of course, a mine shaft is sunk somewhere near a seam of coal. But as that seam is worked out and fresh seams are followed up, the workings get further and further from the pit bottom. If it is a mile from the pit bottom to the coal face, that is probably an average distance; three miles is a fairly normal one; there are even said to be a few mines where it is as much as five miles. But these distances bear no relation to distances above ground. For in all that mile or three miles as it may be, there is hardly anywhere outside the main road, and not many places even there, where a man can stand upright.

You do not notice the effect of this till you have gone a few hundred yards. You start off, stooping slightly, down the dim-lit gallery, eight or ten feet wide and about five high, with the walls built up with slabs of shale, like the stone walls in Derbyshire. Every yard or two there are wooden props holding up the beams and girders; some of the girders have buckled into fantastic curves under which you have to duck. Usually it is bad going underfoot – thick dust or jagged chunks of shale, and in some mines where there is water it is mucky as a farmyard. Also there is the track for the coal tubs, like a miniature railway track with sleepers a foot or two apart, which is tiresome to walk on. Everything is grey with shale dust; there is a dusty fiery smell which seems to be the same in all mines. You see mysterious machines of which you never learn the purpose, and bundles of tools slung together on wires, and sometimes mice darting away from the beam of the lamps. They are surprisingly common, especially in mines where there are or have been horses. It would be interesting to know how they got there in the first place; possibly by falling down the shaft – for they say a mouse can fall any distance uninjured, owing to its surface area being so large relative to its weight. You press yourself against the wall to make way for lines of tubs jolting slowly towards the shaft, drawn by an endless steel cable operated from the surface. You creep through sacking curtains and thick wooden doors which, when they are opened, let out fierce blasts of air. These doors are an important part of the ventilation system. The exhausted air is sucked out of one shaft by means of fans, and the fresh air enters the other of its own accord. But if left to itself the air will take the shortest way round, leaving the deeper workings unventilated; so all short cuts have to be partitioned off.

At the start to walk stooping is rather a joke, but it is a joke that soon wears off. I am handicapped by being exceptionally tall, but when the roof falls to four feet or less it is a tough job for anybody except a dwarf or a child. You have not only got to bend double, you have also got to keep your head up all the while so as to see the beams and girders and dodge them when they come. You have, therefore, a constant crick in the neck, but this is nothing to the pain in your knees and thighs. After half a mile it becomes (I am not exaggerating) an unbearable agony. You begin to wonder whether you will ever get to the end – still more, how on earth you are going to get back. Your pace grows slower and slower. You come to a stretch of a couple of hundred yards where it is all exceptionally low and you have to work yourself along in a squatting position. Then suddenly the roof opens out to a mysterious height – scene of an old fall of rock, probably – and for twenty whole yards you can stand upright. The relief is overwhelming. But after this there is another low stretch of a hundred yards and then a succession of beams which you have to crawl under. You go down on all fours; even this is a relief after the squatting business. But when you come to the end of the beams and try to get up again, you find that your knees have temporarily struck work and refuse to lift you. You call a halt, ignominiously, and say that you would like to rest for a minute or two. Your guide (a miner) is sympathetic. He knows that your muscles are not the same as his. 'Only another four hundred yards,' he says encouragingly; you feel that he might as well say another four hundred miles. But finally you do somehow creep as far as the coal face. You have gone a mile and taken the best part of an hour; a miner would do it in not much more than twenty minutes. Having got there, you have to sprawl in the coal dust and get your strength back for several minutes before you can even watch the work in progress with any kind of intelligence.

GEORGE ORWELL, *The Road to Wigan Pier* (1937).

RED BLOOD
(1961)

TURNING now to red blood, and particularly to the haemoglobin of the crustacean *Daphnia*, brings us back to Ray Lankester, for again it was he who recognized with his microspectroscope, in 1871, that the red pigment sometimes present in the blood of water fleas is haemoglobin. Today we know that various species of the genus *Daphnia* have each their own specific haemoglobin, distinguishable spectroscopically with Hartridge's elegant instrument; here is a chemical specific character. Since the time of Schwammerdam, naturalists have observed that swarms of water fleas in ponds may sometimes be blood red, but no one knew until lately that this red colour is that of Lankester's haemoglobin, and is not due, as some maintained, to a carotenoid, which too can sometimes colour *Daphnia*. Aquarium keepers who feed their fishes on *Daphnia* may notice that red ones in a bowl become paler day by day, although they do not know the cause of this. Nor was it known until recently that pale water fleas can become red. As an evacuee (strange word, suggesting a Torricellian being) during the war in Professor James Gray's hospitable Department, I started to look into this question, and one of my greatest scientific thrills was when one night, whilst fire-watching in the zoological laboratory, I found that individuals of a *Daphnia* culture left in a dark cupboard had reddened. The control animals on a window sill were still pale, so I jumped to the wrong conclusion that darkness and light were responsible. It was not light, however, but oxygen from algal photosynthesis in the window, and its absence in the dark, that was in play. This started a decade of happy work with young Bedford College colleagues.

We found that the blood of *Daphnia* behaves like that of human mountain-dwellers: with a scarcity of oxygen in the environment more haemoglobin is acquired, and on return to well aerated water, or to normal barometric pressure at sea level, the extra blood pigment is lost. Yet a big difference between the water flea and man is in the scale of the phenomenon. In aerated water *Daphnia* has so little haemoglobin that we do not see its colour, but when oxygen becomes scarce the quantity may increase tenfold, and afterwards, in aerated water, decrease by as much, whereas in the mountaineer the gain or loss is only up to 20 per cent. *Daphnia* has haemoglobin not only in blood but in muscles too, in nerve ganglia and in its parthenogenetic eggs. In these situations the amount of haemoglobin again varies inversely as the dissolved oxygen content of the water. Concerning the eggs, the remarkable fact was discovered by Elisabeth Dresel that haemoglobin passes from the blood into the ovary and eggs, despite the large size of the molecules. Svedberg found in 1934 with his ultracentrifuge that *Daphnia* has haemoglobin molecules of two sizes, one-half and six times those of man: perhaps they dissociate into the basic haemoglobin molecule, one quarter that of man, to pass into *Daphnia's* ovary, for there is evidence that haemoglobin molecules can dissociate. It was to be expected that the additional haemoglobin acquired by *Daphnia* as a result of oxygen deficit would be of use to the water fleas and this proved indeed to be so. In poorly aerated water red animals survive longer, swim more quickly, catch more food and produce more eggs than pale ones put into such water.

This capacity of increasing the content of haemoglobin is possessed not only by species of *Daphnia* living in ponds and ditches where oxygen may fall very low, but, strange to say, also by *Daphnia hyalina* in the plankton of lakes, living where the water is always well aerated. In nature these animals have no red tinge, although they do contain traces of haemoglobin, but in artificial conditions of poorly aerated water they synthesize enough to become pink. The capacity to synthesize is indeed there although never used in nature. This is so in the

Lago Maggiore, beside which I studied the animals in the beautiful hydrobiological institute at Pallanza. Increased haemoglobin synthesis with oxygen paucity is not, however, the monopoly of *Daphnia*. Other Cladocera have the same faculty and so do branchiopods such as the uncommon British Apus (*Triops canciformis*) and fairy shrimp (*Chirocephalus diaphanus*). The brine shrimp (*Artemia salina*) is known to be redder in more saline water and Barbara Gilchrist showed that this redness too is caused by haemoglobin and that its increase is not a direct effect of salt concentration but of lessened oxygen in the stronger salt solution. Young bloodworms (*Chironomus* larvae) and young ramshorn pond snails (*Planorbis*) also possess more haemoglobin when they are raised in oxygen-poor water, and the same has been found with fish. Yet the faculty does not seem to be universal – at least, I could not succeed in getting young annelids to fall into line.

In ourselves haemoglobin of the red cells in the blood is synthesized and destroyed continuously. In the breakdown the porphyrin ring is opened at one of the links between two pyrroles, the iron atom is detached and the string of four pyrroles, now constituting a bile pigment or bilin, is excreted. The iron, however, is not thrown away. It may be temporarily stored in the liver, and it is used again to make more proto-haem and then haemoglobin in the bone marrow. What happens in *Daphnia* to the haemoglobin that is got rid of on such a big scale when animals pass from poorly aerated to well-aerated water? Some of it, as we have seen, goes into the eggs, which are produced anew and then hatch during each instar, repeated every 3–4 days. In a single instar a third of the blood pigment may thus be lost into the eggs. But what becomes of the rest? No bilin can be detected, either in the animals or in the water. No porphyrin appears, which would betray itself by its red fluorescence. One can only suppose that the breakdown of the protohaem goes further than protoporphyrin or bilin, into colourless fragments. And what becomes of the iron? Strange to say, *Daphnia*, unlike ourselves, excretes the iron. This may not be just wasteful, but necessary, since storage of such large quantities might be embarrassing, and if oxygen deficit again occurs, there is presumably always enough iron available in the pond water. This excretion of iron was discovered by Wendy Smaridge, using Prussian blue and radioautography. She found that in *Daphnia* which is losing haemoglobin, and at that time only, iron is abundant in the so-called shell glands, the maxillary excretory organs.

The next question was this: whereabouts in the body of *Daphnia* is haemoglobin synthesized and where is it broken down? The first part of the question has not been answered. Presumably the haemoglobin of muscles and nerves is synthesized *in situ*, but in view of the transference from blood to eggs this may not be so, and we do not yet know where the blood pigment originates. In vertebrates it is simple to know this, as we can see where blood cells are produced, but in *Daphnia* the blood pigment is not in cells. For the breakdown, however, we have a probable answer. When haemoglobin is being lost, iron accumulates, not only in the excretory organs, but also in the so-called fat or storage cells, easily seen, like all the organs, through the transparent body wall. J. Green has found that sometimes, during haemoglobin loss, these fat cells are coloured red by the pigment, the oxyhaemoglobin bands showing here with the microspectroscope more strongly than in the surrounding blood spaces. This occurs, however, only in poorly nourished *Daphnia*, which consequently has few eggs. Haemoglobin, as we have seen, is lost partly to the eggs, and the rest of it seems thus to go into the fat cells to be destroyed, but when there are few eggs the fat cells are overworked and they accumulate haemoglobin until it can be broken down and the products sent on through the blood stream to be excreted.

One wonders why it is that red *Daphnia* on coming into fully aerated water loses haemoglobin at all. The pigment is no longer needed, but why should it be rejected? A continuous, more or less rapid, turnover – synthesis and breakdown – of haemoglobin is, however, quite likely to go on in poorly aerated water, and if this does occur the synthesis would cease when aeration supervenes, but the breakdown would go on. Thus pallor would result. This leads on to a last question, and a fundamental one. How does oxygen deficiency favour haemoglobin synthesis? This question has not yet been fully answered for the mountain climber, but there is evidence that here the low oxygen pressure does not act directly on the synthetic cells in the bone marrow, but through a humoral factor in the blood stream. This was demonstrated by Reissmann, who subjected one member of a pair of rats, made artificially parabiotic, to an atmosphere deficient in oxygen and found increased production of red blood cells in the bone marrow of both (see Gordon, 1959). In *Daphnia* there are several different possibilities. It might be that only ferrous iron can be absorbed through the gut wall and that therefore in aerated water, with the dissolved iron in the ferric state, the animal cannot take in enough for haemoglobin manufacture. Or it may be that anaerobic conditions in cells where protohaem is synthesized favour one or more stages in the process. It has recently been found by Falk and collaborators (1959) that the synthesis of the porphyrin and haem of haemoglobin by fowl erythrocytes *in vitro* is most active at a low oxygen pressure. We await further results showing which synthetic steps are inhibited by oxygen.

H. MUNRO FOX, 'Green, Red and Blue Bloods', in *The Cell and the Organism*, ed. Ramsay and Wigglesworth (1961).

NO PLACE LIKE HOME
(1957)

WORKING-CLASS people have always hated the thought of 'ending up in the work'ouse' for several good reasons, and of these the deepest is the sense of the inalienable quality of home life. A widow will 'work 'erself to death' as a charwoman rather than accept offers of places even in a comfortable orphanage for her children. If she dies, the family, some of whom may well have done nothing for her earlier and do not much want to look after a child, will split the children between them. My mother was left with three, aged one, three and five; when she died after five years of struggle, I remember a previously unknown aunt from some distance away saying that 'orphanages are different nowadays'. She cut no ice; we were taken severally then and there by various members of the family, each of them poorer than she was.

The insistence on the privacy of home arises from this feeling, reinforced by the knowledge that, though the neighbours are 'your sort' and will rally round in trouble, they are always ready for a gossip and perhaps a mean-minded gossip. 'What will the neighbours think?' Usually they think that two and two make six; their gossip may 'mean no harm' but it can be unconscionably brutal. They may be able to 'hear everything going on' through the thin party-wall, but you can shut the front door, 'live yer own life', 'keep y'self to y'self' – that is, to the immediate members of the household which includes the married sons and daughters with their families from the streets nearby, and extends to the few friends who are on 'popping-in' terms. You want good neighbours but a good neighbour is not always 'coming in and out': if she does that, she may have to be 'frozen off'. The half-length lace curtains keep out most of what little sun there is, but they establish your privacy: the window-ledges and doorsteps scrubbed and yellowed with scouring-stone further establish that you are a 'decent' family, that you believe in 'bottoming' the house each week.

Inside, the aspidistra has gone in favour of the ragged-country-lad-eating-cherries and the little-girl-coyly-holding-her-skirt or the big-girl-in-a-picture-hat-holding-two-Borzois or a single Alsatian. Chain-store modernismus, all bad veneer and sprayed-on-varnish-stain, is replacing the old mahogany; multi-coloured plastic and chrome biscuit barrels and bird-cages have come in. This is more than keeping up with the Joneses; these things subserve the domestic values, full and rich. So, many prefabs now have leaded and coloured window-panes provided by the owners: in the older houses the deep window-sills give the opportunity for some exterior colour, for a box of rank and colourful nasturtiums or of even more dazzling geraniums.

Looking back on years of living in one, I should say that a good 'living-room' must provide three principal things; gregariousness, warmth and plenty of good food. The living-room is the warm heart of the family and therefore often slightly stuffy to a middle-class visitor. It is not a social centre but a family centre; little entertaining goes on there or in the front room, if there happens to be one: you do not entertain in anything approaching the middle-class sense. The wife's social life outside her immediate family is found over the washing-line, at the corner-shop, visiting relatives at a moderate distance occasionally, and perhaps now and again going with her husband to his pub or club. He has his pub or club, his work, his football matches. The friends of either at all these places may well not know what the inside of their house is like, may never have 'stepped across the threshold'. The hearth is reserved for the family, whether living at home or nearby, and those who are 'something to us', and look in for a talk or just to sit. Much of the free time of a man and his wife will usually be passed at that hearth; 'just staying-in' is still one of the most common leisure-time occupations.

It is a cluttered and congested setting, a burrow deeply away from the outside world. There is no telephone to ring, and knocks at the door in the evening are rare. But the group, though restricted, is not private: it is a gregarious group, in which most things are shared, including personality; 'our Mam', 'our Dad', 'our Alice' are normal forms of address. To be alone, to think alone, to read quietly is difficult. There is the wireless or television, things being done in odd bouts, or intermittent snatches of talk (but rarely a sustained conversation); the iron thumps on the table, the dog scratches and yawns or the cat miaows to be let out; the son drying himself on the family towel near the fire whistles, or rustles the communal letter from his brother in the army which has been lying on the mantelpiece behind the photo of his sister's wedding; the little girl bursts into a whine because she is too tired to be up at all, the budgerigar twitters.

In a few of the more careful homes this unity is still objectified in the making of a clip-rug by the hearth. Clippings of old clothes are prepared, sorted into rough colour groups and punched singly through a piece of harding (sacking). Patterns are traditional and simple, usually a centre circle or diamond with the remainder an unrelieved navy blue (except for the edging) or that greyish-blue which mixed shoddy usually produces; most of us knew it years ago in army blankets. The rug will replace at the fireside one made a long time ago and will have cost little more than the price of the harding, unless it is decided to have a vivid centre and colour is short. Then prepared clippings in, say, red can be bought at about half a crown the pound.

Is it to be wondered that married sons and daughters take a few years to wean themselves from their mother's hearth? Until the needs of their own children make evening visits practically impossible, and this will be a long time after a mother with views on the healthy rearing of children would think it reasonable, the son or daughter with whatever children they have will be around in the evenings. A son-in-law will tend to drop in straight from work and be fed at a table more often laid than not. He may well join Grandad and Grandma, who are permanent residents (though most old people hate the thought of 'giving up me 'ome' and only do so as a last resort; they much prefer the younger people and their children to join them).

Warmth, to be 'as snug as a bug in a rug', is of the first importance. Seventy years of cheap coal have ensured that most people have learned to use it lavishly, by most foreign standards. A good housewife knows that she must 'keep a good fire', and is likely to pay more attention to securing that than to buying the better qualities of warm woollen underclothing: a fire is shared and seen.

'A good table' is equally important, and this still means a fully-stocked table rather than one which presents a balanced diet. Thus, many families seem to buy less milk than they should and salads are not popular. Around this there clusters a whole group of attitudes, some of them plainly sensible, some founded on myth. 'Homecooking' is always better than any other; café food is almost always adulterated. Small confectioners know they will fare better if they put 'Home-made Bread and Cakes' over their windows; in a sense the claim is still likely to be true, though huge electric ovens have probably replaced the original range in what was once the family kitchen behind the shop. The mistrust of cafés has been reinforced by the knowledge that they can hardly be afforded anyway, but much the same resistance often arises to the cheap works' canteens. A husband will complain that the food there 'has no body' and the wife has to 'pack something up', which usually means a pile of sandwiches with 'something tasty' in them, and she prepares a big hot meal for the evening.

'Something tasty' is the key-phrase in feeding: something solid, preferably meaty, and with a well-defined flavour. The tastiness is increased by a liberal use of sauces and pickles, notably tomato sauce and piccalilli. I used to notice that in the flusher early years of married life my relatives were often frying at tea-times – chops, steak, kidney, chips. By contrast, poor old-age pensioners used sometimes to simulate a tasty meal by dissolving a penny Oxo in warm water, and having it with bread. Meat has been much relied upon since it first became really cheap, and any working-class wife who has known thin times will have a fine knowledge of those cuts which are inexpensive and nourishing and also tasty. The emphasis on tastiness shows itself most clearly in the need to provide 'something for tea', at weekends if not each day. There is a great range of favourite savouries, often by-products – black-puddings, pig's feet, liver, cowheel, tripe, polony, 'ducks', chitterlings (and for special occasions pork-pies, which are extremely popular); and the fishmongers' savouries – shrimps, roe, kippers and mussels. In our house we lived simply for most of the week; breakfast was usually bread and beef-dripping, dinner a good simple stew; something tasty was provided for the workers at tea-time, but nothing costing more than a few coppers. At the week-end we lived largely, like everyone else except the very poor, and Sunday tea was the peak. By six on that evening the middens up the back had a fine topcoat of empty salmon and fruit tins. Pineapple was the most popular because, in that period of what now seems extraordinarily cheap canned fruit, it could be bought for a few pence (there was a recurrent story that it was really flavoured turnip). Peaches and apricots were more expensive, and needed something approaching an occasion – a birthday or a sudden visit by relatives from a few miles away. The salmon was delicious, especially the red middle-cut; I still find it far 'tastier' than fresh salmon.

During the years in which meat was short, the newer spiced-meat products seem to have been adopted by a large public. I know a family of five where they buy their meat-loaf by the four-pound tin; one son-in-law who has his meals there will eat no fresh meat, only a version of Spam, cold or fried. It is not a cheap food, any more than boiled ham or fish-and-chips, which retain their high favour.

The insistence on food which is both solid and enjoyable is not difficult to appreciate – 'as long as y' get some good food inside y', y' can't complain'; you have to ensure plenty of bulk and protein for the heavy workers and as high a measure of tastiness as can be managed. No doubt the effects are less admirable than the aims. When I was a boy my aunts and uncles, in their thirties and forties, all seemed to have false teeth. Was this only due to neglect? (They had corn-trouble, too, from years of ill-fitting shoes.) Yet I remember also that a regular topic of conversation was this one's constipation and that one's 'heartburn': we bought bicarbonate of soda as regularly as firewood. This may be a fancy, but I am often struck by an apparent difference in the fatness of the different classes, say between that of a middle-aged working-class woman and that of a prosperous middle-aged business-man. One has a white and matt quality, the other is tightly-rounded, shiny and polished; one makes me think of gallons of tea, hundred-weights of bread, and plates of fish-and-chips; the other of steaks in station hotels.

I could continue almost endlessly recalling other individual details which give this kind of domestic life a recognisable quality of its own; the steam-and-soda-and-hashed-meat smell of washday, or the smell of clothes drying by the fireside; the Sunday smell of the *News of the World*-mingled-with-roast-beef; the intermittent reading of pieces of old newspaper in the lavatory; the waste of Sunday afternoon, relieved by occasional visits to relatives or to the cemetery, whose gates are flanked by the stalls of flower-sellers and by the workshops of those who sell expensive headstones. Like any life with a firm centre, it has a powerful hold: working-class people themselves are often sentimental about it. In the excesses of poker-work or the ornately frilled cards and hankies sold even today at fairs and seaside booths, there is still embroidered 'Home, sweet Home', or 'Home – the place where we grumble the most and are treated the best'.

This description and the later descriptive passages in this chapter are largely based on memories of twenty years ago, as I have said. I say little about the increased spending-power of working-class people and so about, for example, the effects of labour-saving devices in the home, and so on. This is chiefly because many of us assume today that the effects of these changes on our attitudes are greater than they are. It therefore seems important to stress first how large a part of the basic pattern of working-class life remains as it has been for many years.

This is in many respects a good and comely life, one founded on care, affection, a sense of the small group if not of the individual. It is elaborate and disorderly and yet sober: it is not chintzy or kittenish or whimsical or 'feminised'. The father is a part of the inner life of the home, not someone who spends most of his time miles away earning the money to keep the establishment going: the mother is the working-centre, always with too much to do and with her thoughts revolving almost entirely around the life of this family room (bedrooms are simply places you sleep in). Her 'one hope', as she puts it, is that her daughters and sons will 'soon find a nice lad or lass and make homes of their own'.

Though it may seem muddled and sprawling, the design can be seen, ensured by an unsophisticated and unconscious but still strong sense of what a home is for. Compare it with the kind of public room which may be found in many a café or small hotel today – the walls in several hostile shades of distemper, clashing strips of colour along their centres; cold and ugly plastic doorhandles; fussy and meaningless wall lamp-holders; metal tables which invite no one and have their over-vivid colours kicked and scratched away: all tawdry and gimcrack. The materials need not produce this effect; but when they are used by people who have rejected what sense of a whole they had and have no feeling for the new materials, the collapse is evident. In homes, the new things are absorbed into the kind of whole instinctively reached after. The old tradition is being encroached upon, here as in so many other areas. But the strong sense of the importance of home ensures that change is taken slowly: generations of opposing the chief home-breaker – drink – have helped to build a solid resistance to new potential destroyers.

RICHARD HOGGART, *The Uses of Literacy* (1957).

A LONDON CHILDHOOD
(1966)

ALONG the south-eastern edge of the sewage farm went the railway-line from Elmers End to Woodside, and beside this was a long double line of pines, and a narrow path, fenced high on both sides with wire. We called this the 'cinder-track' because it was black cinder underfoot. You could walk up this till you got right to the other side of the sewage farm, and then you could go home up the Albert Road. When I was small it seemed an immense way to cross the empty open space of the farm itself (it was about six hundred yards really) and then immense again to go all this way alongside the lines and the pine-trees. For many years, that view across the sewage farm was the widest view I knew. The pine-trees were exciting because in that open place a lot of wind could catch them, and they would toss and sweep to and fro, and make the sustained many-noted sound that a lot of pines always make. Between us and the rails ran the barbed-wire fence, the wired white gates inset at each level-crossing (there were two, but they were just for cart-tracks) and the notices warning us not to trespass, and especially not to touch the conductor-rail. Then we would see a train in the distance, small and still silent, but swaying with its own speed. It rocked and swayed all the more as it came nearer, and began its roaring noise. Then it faded and everything went quiet again, with just the pine-trees. There were steam-trains with white smoke or black, and sometimes slow goods-trains – we would hear their staggered clank-clank-clank, and the shunting noises from Elmers End yard, all the way across. Sometimes, clouds of white steam from the engines nearly reached us on the narrow shut-in cinder-track. (When a steam-engine went under the Goat House Bridge – called after a pub – back in South Norwood, two white clouds of smoke or steam used to billow up, one on each side, over the wall: and the game was to run right across before they met, swirling, in the middle.)

The electric trains were more exciting because they flashed sparks from their shoes on the conductor-rails. At night, of course, the train flashes could make big sudden sheets of light that lit up the sky a deep yellow, gone in an instant. You could see these from the other side of the sewage farm, or even, as just a fleeting light in the sky, from home sometimes. But it was on frosty and snowy days that all this was at its best. Then, when the white of the snow was weighing down the pine-branches, and the frost was already glinting every-where, the trains would come towards us on the cinder-track with their shoes sizzling and hissing over the ice on the live rail; and there would be brilliant white or bluish flashes from them, and showers and swirls of sparks, a deep golden colour, or purple, and the clotted ice was broken and scattered by the moving shoe, to be flung off in clouds of little chips. Once or twice we saw this by night: the play of light frightened me, and made me feel the great swift power of the train.

We saw this on one of several trips which we made after dark, when I was about eight, to a house in Eden Park. I should explain that on all these walks – at least those that went across the Sewage Farm and up the cinder-track – my mother, mindful of my supposed 'weak heart', used to see that we brought the push-chair. I wheeled it for some of the time, but if I felt tired, or if she thought the time had come, I would get in and be wheeled. But on these trips we also took the push-chair because we seemed to have a lot of things to carry. Once – I forget why – my mother knew the house would be empty and decided to get it ready for when the people there got back; so we took enough kindling and coal to make a fire. I was allowed to look after the matches as a special thing; then when she thought the time had come she would get me into the push-chair, with all the odds and ends between my feet or at my side or on my knee, and would push me along.

That time we took the coal I felt, for some reason, that there was something secret about the whole expedition; though the reason why these trips were all in the dark was that we went in late afternoon or evening and it happened to be winter. The whole journey was quite a long one, rather over two miles, and it broke up in my mind into a number of clearly divided stages – in fact, into seven. First we went through the little roads near our own house, under the gas lamps and their gentle sighing sound, until by the allotments at the end of Harrington Road we could look right across the sewage farm all at once, to the lights at Elmers End, distant but bright and sharp. Then came the last gas lamps, one at the little general shop just before the cemetery gate, and the last one of all at the beginning of the sewage farm path. Now we left the metalled pavement, and went over the gravel and the bumpy stones.

It was dark across the sewage farm. In those days there were only gas lamps along the road at the side of it, and these were several hundred yards away and there weren't many of them. Once or twice it was foggy. Then, as soon as we were out on the farm, we could see nothing at all except the dark and the fog, and hear just the streams running, and the fog-signals' occasional bang. Usually my mother wheeled me this bit. The fog made our clothes damp and the arms of the push-chair wet. I sat listening to the scrunch and rattle of the wheels, and watched for a long time to see the first lamp come in a yellow blur out of the mist. This lamp was by the gate into the yard: the kind of gate that swung in a little ring of fence, to keep motor-bikes out (you could just get a push-bike through, standing it up on its back wheel: or a strong man could hoist it up and hold it flat, well above his head, and then march straight round). It took us a long time to get the push-chair through this gate, and while we did it we could hear the little whine of the gas lamp. On a clear night, from right across the sewage farm, we could watch the whole bright line of lamps along the station platform as they shone through the fir-trees, getting slowly nearer.

The next part of the walk was right round through the empty station approach, out into the road, and up the slope to the railway bridge. Now the lights were bright all round, but there would still be no one about. A steep flight of wooden steps led up to the top of the bridge, but there was another white 'kissing-gate' there, that the push-chair wouldn't go through at all; that was why we had to take the long way round.

Next, crossing the main road that ran through Elmers End village, we went, up the slope, through the estate of little grey-walled council houses behind their trim but shabby privet. We had come well over a mile now, and I remember how the rhythm of the walk would settle in. But it would be cold too. And when the council houses stopped, we had really got to the edge of London, and the country began.

JOHN HOLLOWAY, *A London Childhood* (1966).

FREUD COMES TO ENGLAND
(1938)

THEY crossed by night on the ferryboat to Dover, and since Lord De La Warr, then Lord Privy Seal, had arranged that they be accorded diplomatic privileges, none of their luggage was examined there or in London. He also arranged with the railway authorities that the train to Victoria should arrive at an unusual platform so as to circumvent the battery of cameras and the huge crowd of welcoming or curious visitors. They were greeted and bade welcome by the Superintendent of the Southern Railway and the Station Master of Victoria. Freud's eldest children Mathilde and Martin, and of course my wife and myself, were waiting, and the reunion was a moving scene. We made a quick getaway in my car, and it was some time before the newspaper reporters caught us up; Ernst and Anna remained behind to collect the extensive luggage. I drove past Buckingham Palace and Burlington House to Piccadilly Circus and up Regent Street, Freud eagerly identifying each landmark and pointing it out to his wife. The first stop was at 39, Elsworthy Road, where Ernst Freud had rented a house while he was searching for a permanent home.

The mythopoeic faculty of the surrounding world, always so busy with Freud's personality – it has certainly not ceased with his death – pursued him to London. There is a story that a visitor to Elsworthy Road was distressed at witnessing a scene between him and his wife. It was a Friday evening and Mrs Freud was supposed therefore to be lighting the ritual candle. Freud blew it out every time she lit it until at last she cried. This is one of the myths without even a nucleus of truth; there never were such candles, and Freud's unsurpassable tenderness towards his wife was never marred in the fifty-three years of their married life.

Freud's heart had stood the journey better than he expected, though it had needed several doses of nitroglycerine and strychnine to carry him through.

During the night journey from Paris to London he dreamed that he was landing at Pevensey. When he related this to his son he had to explain that Pevensey was where William the Conqueror had landed in 1066. That does not sound like a depressed refugee, and indeed it foreshadowed the almost royal honours with which he was greeted in England.

Freud rallied well from the strain of the journey and was soon able to stroll in the garden for short spells. This garden abutted on Primrose Hill with Regent's Park beyond and a distant view of the City. On his first stroll into the garden on arriving Freud threw up his arms and made the famous remark to me: 'I am almost tempted to cry out "Heil Hitler".' The change to this pleasant prospect from his confinement to his flat in Vienna during the long winter and spring cheered him enormously, and he had moments of great happiness. This was added to by the truly remarkable evidences of the welcome with which he was received in England, no doubt somewhat to his surprise. This is what he wrote two days after his arrival: 'Here there is enough to write about, most of it pleasant, some very pleasant. The reception in Victoria Station and then in the newspapers of these first two days was most kind, indeed enthusiastic. We are buried in flowers. Interesting letters came: only three collectors of autographs, a painter who wants to make a portrait when I have rested, etc. ... Then greetings from most of the members of the English group, some scientists and Jewish societies; the *pièce de résistance* was a lengthy telegram of four pages from Cleveland signed by "the citizens of all faiths and professions", a highly respectful invitation, with all kinds of promises, for us to make our home there. (We shall have to answer that we have already unpacked!) Finally, and this is something special for England, numerous letters from strangers who only wish to say how happy they are that we have come to England and that we are in safety and peace. Really as if our concern were theirs as well. I could write like this for hours without exhausting what there is to say.'

The newspapers were for a few days full of photographs and friendly accounts of Freud's arrival, and the medical journals published short leading articles expressing welcome. The *Lancet* wrote: 'His teachings have in their time aroused controversy more acute and antagonism more bitter than any since the days of Darwin. Now, in his old age, there are few psychologists of any school who do not admit their debt to him. Some of the conceptions he formulated clearly for the first time have crept into current philosophy against the stream of wilful incredulity which he himself recognized as man's natural reaction to unbearable truth.' The *British Medical Journal* said: 'The medical profession of Great Britain will feel proud that their country has offered an asylum to Professor Freud, and that he has chosen it as his new home.'

There were even gifts of valuable antiques from people who evidently shared Freud's uncertainty about getting his collection sent from Vienna. Taxi-drivers knew where he lived, and the bank manager greeted him with the remark, 'I know all about you.'

And yet it was not entirely unmixed happiness. Apart from his concern at Minna's grave condition and at the state of his own heart, there were other emotions to move him. On the very day he arrived in London he wrote to Eitingon: 'The feeling of triumph at being freed is too strongly mingled with grief, since I always greatly loved the prison from which I have been released.' But his son Ernst was really 'what we have always called him – a tower of strength'.

That the conflicting emotions about Vienna persisted was shown by a curious occurrence a year later. In May, 1939, Indra called on Freud on his way home from America to Austria. On saying good-bye Freud said: 'So you are going back to – I can't recall the name of the city'! Indra, not being familiar with Freud's special type of humour, took this literally as an act of forgetfulness, but I have no doubt that Freud deliberately intended the pretended amnesia to convey his struggle to forget Vienna. It was probably an allusion to the Jewish curse 'let him be forgotten' so terribly described by Heine.

ERNEST JONES, *Sigmund Freud: Life and Work*, Vol. 3 (1957).

Imagination

--◄‹-›►--

THE PHOENIX FIRES
(1906)

In the end my mother died rather suddenly, and her death came as a shock to me. Diagnosis was still very inadequate at that time. The doctors were, of course, fully alive to the incredible defects of their common training and were doing all they could to supply its deficiencies, but they were still extraordinarily ignorant. Some unintelligently observed factor of her illness came into play with her, and she became feverish and sank and died very quickly. I do not know what remedial measures were attempted. I hardly knew what was happening until the whole thing was over.

At that time my attention was much engaged by the stir of the great Beltane festival that was held on May-day in the Year of Scaffolding. It was the first of the ten great rubbish burnings that opened the new age. Young people nowadays can scarcely hope to imagine the enormous quantities of pure litter and useless accumulation with which we had to deal; had we not set aside a special day and season, the whole world would have been in incessant reek of small fires; and it was, I think, a happy idea to revive this ancient festival of the May and November burnings. It was inevitable that the old idea of purification should revive with the name, it was felt to be a burning of other than material encumbrances, innumerable quasi-spiritual things, deeds, documents, debts, vindictive records, went up on those great flares. People passed praying between the fires, and it was a fine symbol of the new and wiser tolerance that had come to men, that those who still found their comfort in the orthodox faiths came hither unpersuaded, to pray that all hate might be burned out of their professions. For even in the fires of Baal, now that men have done with base hatred, one may find the living God.

Endless were the things we had to destroy in those great purgings. First, there were nearly all the houses and buildings of the old time. In the end we did not save in England one building in five thousand that were standing when the comet came. Year by year, as we made our homes afresh in accordance with the saner needs of our new social families, we swept away more and more of those horrible structures, the ancient residential houses, hastily built, without imagination, without beauty, without common honesty, without even comfort or convenience, in which the early twentieth century had sheltered until scarcely one remained; we saved nothing but what was beautiful or interesting out of all their gaunt and melancholy abundance. The actual houses, of course, we could not drag to our fires, but we brought all their ill-fitting deal doors, their dreadful window-sashes, their servant-tormenting staircases, their dank, dark cupboards, the verminous papers from their scaly walls, their dust- and dirt-sodden carpets, their ill-designed and yet pretentious tables and chairs, sideboards and chests of drawers, the old dirt-saturated books, their ornaments – their dirty, decayed, and altogether painful ornaments – amidst which I remember there were sometimes even *stuffed dead birds*! – we burned them all. The paint-plastered woodwork, with coat above coat of nasty paint, that in particular blazed finely. I have already tried to give you an impression of old-world furniture, of Parload's bedroom, my mother's room, Mr Gabbitas's sitting-room; but, thank Heaven! there is nothing in life now to convey the peculiar dinginess of it all. For one thing, there is no more imperfect combustion of coal going on everywhere, and no roadways like grassless open scars along the earth from which dust pours out perpetually. We burned and destroyed most of our private buildings and all the woodwork, all our furniture, except a few score thousand pieces of distinct and intentional beauty from which our present forms have developed, nearly all our hangings and carpets, and also we destroyed almost every scrap of old-world clothing. Only a few carefully disinfected types and vestiges of that remain now in our museums.

One writes now with a peculiar horror of the dress of the old world. The men's clothes were worn without any cleansing process at all, except an occasional superficial brushing, for periods of a year or so; they were made of dark obscurely mixed patterns to conceal the stage of defilement they had reached, and they were of a felted and porous texture admirably calculated to accumulate drifting matter. Many women wore skirts of similar substances, and of so long and inconvenient a form that they inevitably trailed among all the abomination of our horse-frequented roads. It was our boast in England that the whole of our population was booted – their feet were for the most part ugly enough to need it – but it becomes now inconceivable how they could have imprisoned their feet in the amazing cases of leather and imitations of leather they used. I have heard it said that a large part of the physical decline that was apparent in our people during the closing years of the nineteenth century, though no doubt due in part to the miscellaneous badness of the food they ate, was in the main attributable to the vileness of the common footwear. They shirked open-air exercise altogether, because their boots wore out ruinously, and pinched and hurt them if they took it. I have mentioned, I think, the part my own boots played in the squalid drama of my adolescence. I had a sense of unholy triumph over a fallen enemy when at last I found myself steering truck after truck of cheap boots and shoes (unsold stock from Swathinglea) to the run-off by the top of the Glanville blast furnaces.

'Plup!' they would drop into the cone when Beltane came, and with the roar of their burning would fill the air. Never a cold would come from the saturation of their brown-paper soles, never a corn from their foolish shapes, never a nail in them get home at last in suffering flesh. . . .

Most of our public buildings we destroyed and burned as we reshaped our plan of habitation, our theatre sheds, our banks, and inconvenient business warrens, our factories, and all the unmeaning repetition of silly little sham Gothic churches and meeting-houses, mean looking shells of stone and mortar without love, invention, or any beauty at all in them, that men had thrust into the face of their sweated God even as they thrust cheap food into the mouths of their sweated workers; all these we also swept away in the course of that first decade. Then we had the whole of the superseded steam-railway system to scrap and get rid of, stations, signals, fences, rolling-stock; a plant of ill-planned, smoke-distributing nuisance apparatus, that would, under former conditions, have maintained an offensive dwindling obstructive life for perhaps half a century. Then also there was a great harvest of fences, notice-boards, hoardings, ugly sheds, all the corrugated iron in the world, and everything that was smeared with tar, all our gas works and petroleum stores, all our horse vehicles and vans and lorries had to be erased. . . . But I have said enough now perhaps to give some idea of the bulk and quality of our great bonfires, our burnings up, our meltings down, our toil of sheer wreckage, over and above the constructive effort, in those early years.

But these were the coarse material bases of the Phoenix fires of the world. These were but the outward and visible signs of the innumerable claims, rights, adhesions, debts, bills, deeds, and charters that were cast upon the fires; a vast accumulation of insignia and uniforms neither curious enough nor beautiful enough to preserve, went to swell the blaze, and all (saving a few truly glorious trophies and memories) of our symbols, our apparatus and material of war. Then innumerable triumphs of our old, bastard, half-commercial fine-art were presently condemned, great oil paintings, done to please the half-educated middle-class, glared for a moment and were gone. Academy marbles crumbled to useful lime, a gross multitude of silly statuettes and decorative crockery, and hangings, and embroideries, and bad music, and musical instruments shared this fate. And books, countless books, too, and bales of newspapers went also to these pyres. From the private houses in Swathinglea alone – which I had deemed, perhaps not unjustly, altogether illiterate – we gathered a whole dustcart full of cheap ill-printed editions of the minor English classics – for the most part very dull stuff indeed and still clean – and about a truckload of thumbed and dog-eared penny fiction, watery base stuff, the dropsy of our nation's mind. . . . And it seemed to me that when we gathered those books and papers together, we gathered together something more than print and paper, we gathered warped and crippled ideas and contagious base suggestions, the formulae of dull tolerances and stupid impatiences, the mean defensive ingenuities of sluggish habits of thinking and timid and indolent evasions. There was more than a touch of malignant satisfaction for me in helping gather it all together.

I was so busy, I say, with my share in this dustman's work that I did not notice, as I should otherwise have done, the little indications of change in my mother's state. Indeed, I thought her stronger; she was slightly flushed, slightly more talkative. . . .

On Beltane Eve, and our Lowchester rummage being finished, I went along the valley to the far end of Swathinglea to help sort the stock of the detached group of pot-banks there – their chief output had been mantel ornaments in imitation of marble, and there was very little sorting, I found, to be done – and there it was nurse Anna found me at last by telephone, and told me my mother had died in the morning suddenly and very shortly after my departure.

For a while I did not seem to believe it; this obviously imminent event stunned me when it came, as though I had never had an anticipatory moment. For a while I went on working, and then almost apathetically, in a mood of half-reluctant curiosity, I started for Lowchester.

When I got there the last offices were over, and I was shown my old mother's peaceful white face, very still, but a little cold and stern to me, a little unfamiliar, lying among white flowers.

I went in alone to her, into that quiet room, and stood for a long time by her bedside. I sat down then and thought.

Then at last, strangely hushed, and with the deeps of my loneliness opening beneath me, I came out of that room and down into the world again, a bright-eyed, active world, very noisy, happy, and busy with its last preparations for the mighty cremation of past and superseded things.

H. G. WELLS, *In the Days of the Comet* (1906).

THE BEAST IN THE JUNGLE
(1903)

HE had thought himself, so long as nobody knew, the most disinterested person in the world, carrying his concentrated burden, his perpetual suspense, ever so quietly, holding his tongue about it, giving others no glimpse of it nor of its effect upon his life, asking of them no allowance and only making on his side all those that were asked. He hadn't disturbed people with the queerness of their having to know a haunted man, though he had had moments of rather special temptation on hearing them say they were forsooth 'unsettled'. If they were as unsettled as he was – he who had never been settled for an hour in his life – they would know what it meant. Yet it wasn't, all the same, for him to make them, and he listened to them civilly enough. This was why he had such good – though possibly such rather colourless – manners; this was why, above all, he could regard himself, in a greedy world, as decently – as in fact perhaps even a little sublimely – unselfish. Our point is accordingly that he valued this character quite sufficiently to measure his present danger of letting it lapse, against which he promised himself to be much on his guard. He was quite ready, none the less, to be selfish, just a little, since surely no more charming occasion for it had come to him. 'Just a little,' in a word, was just as much as Miss Bartram, taking one day with another, would let him. He never would be in the least coercive, and would keep well before him the lines on which consideration for her – the very highest – ought to proceed. He would thoroughly establish the heads under which her affairs, her requirements, her peculiarities – he went so far as to give them the latitude of that name – would come into their intercourse. All this naturally was a sign of how much he took the intercourse itself for granted. There was nothing more to be done about *that*. It simply existed; had sprung into being with her first penetrating question to him in the autumn light there at Weatherend. The real form it should have taken on the basis that stood out large was the form of their marrying. But the devil in this was that the very basis itself put marrying out of the question. His conviction, his apprehension, his obsession, in short, wasn't a privilege he could invite a woman to share; and that consequence of it was precisely what was the matter with him. Something or other lay in wait for him, amid the twists and the turns of the months and the years, like a crouching Beast in the Jungle. It signified little whether the crouching Beast were destined to slay him or to be slain. The definite point was the inevitable spring of the creature; and the definite lesson from that was that a man of feeling didn't cause himself to be accompanied by a lady on a tiger-hunt. Such was the image under which he had ended by figuring his life.

They had at first, none the less, in the scattered hours spent together, made no allusion to that view of it; which was a sign he was handsomely alert to give that he didn't expect, that he in fact didn't care, always to be talking about it. Such a feature in one's outlook was really like a hump on one's back. The difference it made every minute of the day existed quite independently of discussion. One discussed of course *like* a hunchback, for there was always, if nothing else, the hunchback face. That remained, and she was watching him; but people watched best, as a general thing, in silence, so that such would be predominantly the manner of their vigil. Yet he didn't want, at the same time, to be tense and solemn; tense and solemn was what he imagined he too much showed for with other people. The thing to be, with the one person who knew, was easy and natural – to make the reference rather than be seeming to avoid it, to avoid it rather than be seeming to make it, and to keep it, in any case, familiar, facetious even, rather than pedantic and portentous. Some such consideration as the latter was doubtless in his mind for instance when he wrote pleasantly to Miss Bartram that perhaps the great thing he had so long felt as in the lap of the gods was no more than this circumstance, which touched him so nearly, of her acquiring a house in London. It was the first allusion they had yet again made, needing any other hitherto so little; but when she replied, after having given him the news, that she was by no means satisfied with such a trifle as the climax to so special a suspense, she almost set him wondering if she hadn't even a larger conception of singularity for him than he had for himself. He was at all events destined to become aware little by little, as time went by, that she was all the while looking at his life, judging it, measuring it, in the light of the thing she knew, which grew to be at last, with the consecration of the years, never mentioned between them save as 'the real truth' about him. That had always been his own form of reference to it, but she adopted the form so quietly that, looking back at the end of a period, he knew there was no moment at which it was traceable that she had, as he might say, got inside his idea, or exchanged the attitude of beautifully indulging for that of still more beautifully believing him.

It was always open to him to accuse her of seeing him but as the most harmless of maniacs, and this, in the long run – since it covered so much ground – was his easiest description of their friendship. He had a screw loose for her but she liked him in spite of it and was practically, against the rest of the world, his kind wise keeper, unremunerated but fairly amused and, in the absence of other near ties, not disreputably occupied. The rest of the world of course thought him queer, but she, she only, knew how, and above all why, queer; which was precisely what enabled her to dispose the concealing veil in the right folds. She took his gaiety from him – since it had to pass with them for gaiety – as she took everything else; but she certainly so far justified by her unerring touch his finer sense of the de- gree to which he had ended by convincing her. *She* at least never spoke of the secret of his life except as 'the real truth about you,' and she had in fact a wonderful way of making it seem, as such, the secret of her own life too. That was in fine how he so constantly felt her as allowing for him; he couldn't on the whole call it anything else. He allowed for himself, but she, exactly, allowed still more; partly because, better placed for a sight of the matter, she traced his unhappy perversion through reaches of its course into which he could scarce follow it. He knew how he felt, but, besides knowing that, she knew how he *looked* as well; he knew each of the things of import- ance he was insidiously kept from doing, but she could add up the amount they made, understand how much, with a lighter weight on his spirit, he might have done, and thereby establish how, clever as he was, he fell short. Above all she was in the secret of the difference between the forms he went through – those of his little office under Government, those of caring for his modest patrimony, for his library, for his gar- den in the country, for the people in London whose invitations he accepted and repaid – and the detachment that reigned be-

neath them and that made of all behaviour, all that could in
the least be called behaviour, a long act of dissimulation. What
it had come to was that he wore a mask painted with the social
simper, out of the eye-holes of which there looked eyes of an
expression not in the least matching the other features. This
the stupid world, even after years, had never more than half
discovered. It was only May Bartram who had, and she
achieved, by an art indescribable, the feat of at once – or perhaps it was only alternately – meeting the eyes from in front
and mingling her own vision, as from over his shoulder, with
their peep through the apertures.

So while they grew older together she did watch with him,
and so she let this association give shape and colour to her
own existence. Beneath *her* forms as well detachment had
learned to sit, and behaviour had become for her, in the social
sense, a false account of herself. There was but one account of
her that would have been true all the while and that she could
give straight to nobody, least of all to John Marcher. Her whole
attitude was a virtual statement, but the perception of that only
seemed called to take its place for him as one of the many
things necessarily crowded out of his consciousness. If she had
moreover, like himself, to make sacrifices to their real truth, it
was to be granted that her compensation might have affected
her as more prompt and more natural. They had long periods,
in this London time, during which, when they were together,
a stranger might have listened to them without in the least
pricking up his ears; on the other hand the real truth was
equally liable at any moment to rise to the surface, and the
auditor would then have wondered indeed what they were
talking about. They had from an early hour made up their
mind that society was, luckily, unintelligent, and the margin
allowed them by this had fairly become one of their commonplaces. Yet there were still moments when the situation turned
almost fresh – usually under the effect of some expression
drawn from herself. Her expressions doubtless repeated them-

selves, but her intervals were generous. 'What saves us, you know, is that we answer so completely to so usual an appearance: that of the man and woman whose friendship has become such a daily habit – or almost – as to be at last indispensable.' That for instance was a remark she had frequently enough had occasion to make, though she had given it at different times different developments. What we are especially concerned with is the turn it happened to take from her one afternoon when he had come to see her in honour of her birthday. This anniversary had fallen on a Sunday, at a season of thick fog and general outward gloom; but he had brought her his customary offering, having known her now long enough to have established a hundred small traditions. It was one of his proofs to himself, the present he made her on her birthday, that he hadn't sunk into real selfishness. It was mostly nothing more than a small trinket, but it was always fine of its kind, and he was regularly careful to pay for it more than he thought he could afford. 'Our habit saves you, at least, don't you see? because it makes you, after all, for the vulgar, indistinguishable from other men. What's the most inveterate mark of men in general? Why the capacity to spend endless time with dull women – to spend it I won't say without being bored but without minding that they are, without being driven off at a tangent by it; which comes to the same thing. I'm your dull woman, a part of the daily bread for which you pray at church. That covers your tracks more than anything.'

'And what covers yours?' asked Marcher, whom his dull woman could mostly to this extent amuse. 'I see of course what you mean by your saving me, in this way and that, so far as other people are concerned – I've seen it all along. Only what is it that saves *you*? I often think, you know, of that.'

She looked as if she sometimes thought of that too, but rather in a different way. 'Where other people, you mean, are concerned?'

'Well, you're really so in with me, you know – as a sort of result of my being so in with yourself. I mean of my having such an immense regard for you, being so tremendously mindful of all you've done for me. I sometimes ask myself if it's quite fair. Fair I mean to have so involved and – since one may say it – interested you. I almost feel as if you hadn't really had time to do anything else.'

'Anything else but be interested?' she asked. 'Ah what else does one ever want to be? If I've been "watching" with you, as we long ago agreed I was to do, watching's always in itself an absorption.'

'Oh certainly,' John Marcher said, 'if you hadn't had your curiosity —! Only doesn't it sometimes come to you as time goes on that your curiosity isn't being particularly repaid?'

May Bartram had a pause. 'Do you ask that, by any chance, because you feel at all that yours isn't? I mean because you have to wait so long.'

Oh he understood what she meant! 'For the thing to happen that never does happen? For the Beast to jump out? No, I'm just where I was about it. It isn't a matter as to which I can *choose*, I can decide for a change. It isn't one as to which there *can* be a change. It's in the lap of the gods. One's in the hands of one's law – there one is. As to the form the law will take, the way it will operate, that's its own affair.'

'Yes,' Miss Bartram replied; 'of course one's fate's coming, of course it *has* come in its own form and its own way, all the while. Only, you know, the form and the way in your case were to have been – well, something so exceptional and, as one may say, so particularly *your* own.'

Something in this made him look at her with suspicion. 'You say "were to *have* been," as if in your heart you had begun to doubt.'

'Oh!' she vaguely protested.

'As if you believed,' he went on, 'that nothing will now take place.'

She shook her head slowly but rather inscrutably. 'You're far from my thought.'

He continued to look at her. 'What then is the matter with you?'

'Well,' she said after another wait, 'the matter with me is simply that I'm more sure than ever my curiosity, as you call it, will be but too well repaid.'

HENRY JAMES, *The Beast in the Jungle* (1903).

STATION ON THE CONGO
(1902)

'I CAME upon a boiler wallowing in the grass, then found a path leading up the hill. It turned aside for the boulders, and also for an undersized railway-truck lying there on its back with its wheels in the air. One was off. The thing looked as dead as the carcass of some animal. I came upon more pieces of decaying machinery, a stack of rusty rails. To the left a clump of trees made a shady spot, where dark things seemed to stir feebly. I blinked, the path was steep. A horn tooted to the right, and I saw the black people run. A heavy and dull detonation shook the ground, a puff of smoke came out of the cliff, and that was all. No change appeared on the face of the rock. They were building a railway. The cliff was not in the way or anything; but this objectless blasting was all the work going on.

'A slight clinking behind me made me turn my head. Six black men advanced in a file, toiling up the path. They walked erect and slow, balancing small baskets full of earth on their heads, and the clink kept time with their footsteps. Black rags were wound round their loins, and the short ends behind waggled to and fro like tails. I could see every rib, the joints of their limbs were like knots in a rope; each had an iron collar on his neck, and all were connected together with a chain whose bights swung between them, rhythmically clinking. Another report from the cliff made me think suddenly of that ship of war I had seen firing into a continent. It was the same kind of ominous voice; but these men could by no stretch of imagination be called enemies. They were called criminals, and the outraged law, like the bursting shells, had come to them, an insoluble mystery from the sea. All their meagre breasts panted together, the violently dilated nostrils quivered, the eyes stared stonily up-hill. They passed me within six inches, without a glance, with that complete, deathlike indifference of unhappy savages. Behind this raw matter one of the reclaimed, the product of the new forces at work, strolled despondently, carrying a rifle by its middle. He had a uniform jacket with one button off, and seeing a white man on the path, hoisted his weapon to his shoulder with alacrity. This was simple prudence, white men being so much alike at a distance that he could not tell who I might be. He was speedily reassured, and with a large, white, rascally grin, and a glance at his charge, seemed to take me into partnership in his exalted trust. After all, I also was a part of the great cause of these high and just proceedings.

'Instead of going up, I turned and descended to the left. My idea was to let that chain-gang get out of sight before I climbed the hill. You know I am not particularly tender; I've had to strike and to fend off. I've had to resist and to attack sometimes – that's only one way of resisting – without counting the exact cost, according to the demands of such sort of life as I had blundered into. I've seen the devil of violence, and the devil of greed, and the devil of hot desire; but, by all the stars! these were strong, lusty, red-eyed devils, that swayed and drove men – men, I tell you. But as I stood on this hillside, I foresaw that in the blinding sunshine of that land I would become acquainted with a flabby, pretending, weak-eyed devil of a rapacious and pitiless folly. How insidious he could be, too, I was only to find out several months later and a thousand miles farther. For a moment I stood appalled, as though by a warning. Finally I descended the hill, obliquely, towards the trees I had seen.

'I avoided a vast artificial hole somebody had been digging on the slope, the purpose of which I found it impossible to divine. It wasn't a quarry or a sandpit, anyhow. It was just a hole. It might have been connected with the philanthropic desire of giving the criminals something to do. I don't know. Then I nearly fell into a very narrow ravine, almost no more than a scar in the hillside. I discovered that a lot of imported drainage-pipes for the settlement had been tumbled in there. There wasn't one that was not broken. It was a wanton smash-up. At last I got under the trees. My purpose was to stroll into the shade for a moment; but no sooner within than it seemed to me I had stepped into the gloomy circle of some Inferno. The rapids were near, and an uninterrupted, uniform, headlong, rushing noise filled the mournful stillness of the grove, where not a breath stirred, not a leaf moved, with a mysterious sound – as though the tearing pace of the launched earth had suddenly become audible.

'Black shapes crouched, lay, sat between the trees leaning against the trunks, clinging to the earth, half coming out, half effaced within the dim light, in all the attitudes of pain, abandonment, and despair. Another mine on the cliff went off, followed by a slight shudder of the soil under my feet. The work was going on. The work! And this was the place where some of the helpers had withdrawn to die.

'They were dying slowly – it was very clear. They were not enemies, they were not criminals, they were nothing earthly now, – nothing but black shadows of disease and starvation, lying confusedly in the greenish gloom. Brought from all the recesses of the coast in all the legality of time contracts, lost in uncongenial surroundings, fed on unfamiliar food, they sickened, became inefficient, and were then allowed to crawl away and rest. These moribund shapes were free as air – and nearly as thin. I began to distinguish the gleam of the eyes under the trees. Then, glancing down, I saw a face near my hand. The black bones reclined at full length with one shoulder against the tree, and slowly the eyelids rose and the sunken eyes looked up at me, enormous and vacant, a kind of blind, white flicker in the depths of the orbs, which died out slowly. The man seemed young – almost a boy – but you know with them it's hard to tell. I found nothing else to do but to offer him one of my good Swede's ship's biscuits I had in my pocket. The fingers closed slowly on it and held – there was no other movement and no other glance. He had tied a bit of white worsted round his neck – Why? Where did he get it? Was it a badge – an ornament – a charm – a propitiatory act? Was there any idea at all connected with it? It looked startling round his black neck, this bit of white thread from beyond the seas.

'Near the same tree two more bundles of acute angles sat with their legs drawn up. One, with his chin propped on his knees, stared at nothing, in an intolerable and appalling manner: his brother phantom rested its forehead, as if overcome with a great weariness; and all about others were scattered in every pose of contorted collapse, as in some picture of a massacre or a pestilence. While I stood horror-struck, one of these creatures rose to his hands and knees, and went off on all-fours towards the river to drink. He lapped out of his hand, then sat up in the sunlight, crossing his shins in front of him, and after a time let his woolly head fall on his breastbone.

'I didn't want any more loitering in the shade, and I made haste towards the station. When near the buildings I met a white man, in such an unexpected elegance of get-up that in the first moment I took him for a sort of vision. I saw a high starched collar, white cuffs, a light alpaca jacket, snowy trousers, a clear necktie, and varnished boots. No hat. Hair parted, brushed, oiled, under a green-lined parasol held in a big white hand. He was amazing, and had a penholder behind his ear.

'I shook hands with this miracle, and I learned he was the Company's chief accountant, and that all the book-keeping was done at this station. He had come out for a moment, he said, "to get a breath of fresh air". The expression sounded wonderfully odd, with its suggestion of sedentary desk-life. I wouldn't have mentioned the fellow to you at all, only it was from his lips that I first heard the name of the man who is so indissolubly connected with the memories of that time. Moreover, I respected the fellow. Yes; I respected his collars, his vast cuffs, his brushed hair. His appearance was certainly that of a hairdresser's dummy; but in the great demoralization of the land he kept up his appearance. That's backbone. His starched collars and got-up shirt-fronts were achievements of character. He had been out nearly three years; and, later, I could not help asking him how he managed to sport such linen. He had just the faintest blush, and said modestly, "I've been teaching one of the native women about the station. It was difficult. She had a distaste for the work." Thus this man had verily accomplished something. And he was devoted to his books, which were in apple-pie order.

'Everything else in the station was in a muddle, – heads, things, buildings. Strings of dusty niggers with splay feet arrived and departed; a stream of manufactured goods, rubbishy cottons, beads, and brass-wire set into the depths of darkness, and in return came a precious trickle of ivory.

'I had to wait in the station for ten days – an eternity. I lived in a hut in the yard, but to be out of the chaos I would sometimes get into the accountant's office. It was built of horizontal planks, and so badly put together that, as he bent over his high desk, he was barred from neck to heels with narrow strips of sunlight. There was no need to open the big shutter to see. It was hot there, too; big flies buzzed fiendishly, and did not sting, but stabbed. I sat generally on the floor, while, of faultless appearance (and even slightly scented), perching on a high stool, he wrote, he wrote. Sometimes he stood up for exercise. When a truckle-bed with a sick man (some invalid agent from up-country) was put in there, he exhibited a gentle annoyance. "The groans of this sick person," he said, "distract my attention. And without that it is extremely difficult to guard against clerical errors in this climate."

'One day he remarked, without lifting his head, "In the interior you will no doubt meet Mr Kurtz." On my asking who Mr Kurtz was, he said he was a first-class agent; and seeing my disappointment at this information, he added slowly, laying down his pen, "He is a very remarkable person." Further questions elicited from him that Mr Kurtz was at present in charge of a trading post, a very important one, in the true ivory-country, at "the very bottom of there. Sends in as much ivory as all the others put together . . ." He began to write again. The sick man was too ill to groan. The flies buzzed in a great peace.

'Suddenly there was a growing murmur of voices and a great tramping of feet. A caravan had come in. A violent babble of uncouth sounds burst out on the other side of the planks. All the carriers were speaking together, and in the midst of the uproar the lamentable voice of the chief agent was heard "giving it up" tearfully for the twentieth time that day. . . . He rose slowly. "What a frightful row," he said. He crossed the room gently to look at the sick man, and returning, said to me, "He does not hear." "What! Dead?" I asked, startled. "No, not yet," he answered, with great composure. Then, alluding with a toss of the head to the tumult in the station-yard, "When one has got to make correct entries, one comes to hate those savages – hate them to the death." He remained thoughtful for a moment. "When you see Mr Kurtz," he went on, "tell him from me that everything here" – he glanced at the desk – "is very satisfactory. I don't like to write to him – with those messengers of ours you never know who may get hold of your letter – at that Central Station.' He stared at me for a moment with his mild, bulging eyes. 'Oh, he will go far, very far,' he began again. 'He will be a some-body in the Administration before long. They, above – the Council in Europe, you know – mean him to be."

'He turned to his work. The noise outside had ceased, and presently in going out I stopped at the door. In the steady buzz of flies, the homeward-bound agent was lying flushed and insensible; the other bent over his books, was making correct entries of perfectly correct transactions; and fifty feet below the doorstep I could see the still tree-tops of the grove of death.'

JOSEPH CONRAD, *Heart of Darkness* (1902).

THE LAST OF A SCHOOLBOY
(1910)

THEY climbed the long bank from the canal up to the Manor Farm, at which high point their roads diverged, one path leading direct to Bleakridge where Orgreave lived, and the other zigzagging down through neglected pasturage into Bursley proper. Usually they parted here without a word, taking pride in such Spartan taciturnity, and they would doubtless have done the same this morning also, though it were fiftyfold their last walk together as two schoolboys. But an incident intervened.

'Hold on!' cried the Sunday.

To the south of them, a mile and a half off, in the wreathing mist of the Cauldon Bar Ironworks, there was a yellow gleam that even the capricious sunlight could not kill, and then two rivers of fire sprang from the gleam and ran in a thousand delicate and lovely hues down the side of a mountain of refuse. They were emptying a few tons of molten slag at the

Cauldon Bar Ironworks. The two rivers hung slowly dying in the mists of smoke. They reddened and faded, and you thought they had vanished, and you could see them yet, and then they escaped the baffled eye, unless a cloud aided them for a moment against the sun; and their ephemeral but enchanting beauty had expired for ever.

'Now!' said Edwin sharply.

'One minute ten seconds,' said the Sunday, who had snatched out his watch, an inestimable contrivance with a centre-seconds hand. 'By Jove! That was a good 'un.'

A moment later two smaller boys, both laden with satchels, appeared over the brow from the canal.

'Let's wait a jiff,' said the Sunday to Edwin, and as the smaller boys showed no hurry he bawled out to them across the intervening cinder-waste: 'Run!' They ran. They were his younger brothers, Johnnie and Jimmie. 'Take this and hook it!' he commanded, passing the strap of his satchel over his head as they came up. In fatalistic silence they obeyed the smiling tyrant.

'What are you going to do?' Edwin asked.

'I'm coming down your way a bit.'

'But I thought you said you were peckish.'

'I shall eat three slices of beef instead of my usual brace,' said the Sunday carelessly.

Edwin was touched. And the Sunday was touched, because he knew he had touched Edwin. After all, this was a solemn occasion. But neither would overtly admit that its solemnity had affected him. Hence, first one and then the other began to skim stones with vicious force over the surface of the largest of the three ponds that gave interest to the Manor Farm. When they had thus proved to themselves that the day differed in no manner from any other breaking-up day, they went forward.

On their left were two pitheads whose double wheels revolved rapidly in smooth silence, and the puffing engine-house and all the trucks and gear of a large ironstone mine. On their right was the astonishing farm, with barns and ricks and cornfields complete, seemingly quite unaware of its forlorn oddness in that foul arena of manufacture. In front, on a little hill in the vast valley, was spread out the Indian-red architecture of Bursley – tall chimneys and rounded ovens, schools, the new scarlet market, the grey tower of the old church, the high spire of the evangelical church, the low spire of the church of genuflexions, and the crimson chapels, and rows of little red houses with amber chimney-pots, and the gold angel of the blackened Town Hall topping the whole. The sedate reddish browns and reds of the composition, all netted in flowing scarves of smoke, harmonized exquisitely with the chill blues of the chequered sky. Beauty was achieved, and none saw it.

The boys descended without a word through the brick-strewn pastures, where a horse or two cropped the short grass. At the railway bridge, which carried a branch mineral line over the path, they exchanged a brief volley of words with the working-lads who always played pitch-and-toss there in the dinner-hour; and the Sunday added to the collection of shawds and stones lodged on the under ledges of the low iron girders. A strange boy, he had sworn to put ten thousand stones on those ledges before he died, or perish in the attempt. Hence Edwin sometimes called him 'Old Perish-in-the-attempt'. A little farther on the open gates of a manufactory disclosed six men playing the noble game of rinkers on a smooth patch of ground near the weighing machine. These six men were Messieurs Ford, Carter, and Udall, the three partners owning the works, and three of their employees. They were celebrated marble-players, and the boys stayed to watch them as, bending with one knee almost touching the earth, they shot the rinkers from their stubby thumbs with a canon-like force and precision that no boy could ever hope to equal. 'By gum!' mumbled Edwin involuntarily, when an impossible shot was accomplished; and the bearded shooter, pleased by this tribute from youth, twisted his white apron into a still narrower ring round his waist. Yet Edwin was not thinking about the game. He was thinking about a battle that lay before him, and how he would be weakened in the fight by the fact that in the last school examination, Charlie Orgreave, younger than himself by a year, had ousted him from the second place in the school. The report in his pocket said: 'Position in class next term: third'; whereas he had been second since the beginning of the year. There would of course be no 'next term' for him, but the report remained. A youth who has come to grips with that powerful enemy, his father, cannot afford to be handicapped by even such a trifle as a report entirely irrelevant to the struggle.

Suddenly Charlie Orgreave gave a curt nod, and departed, in nonchalant good-humour, doubtless considering that to accompany his chum any farther would be to be guilty of girlish sentimentality. And Edwin nodded with equal curtness and made off slowly into the maze of Bursley. The thought in his heart was: 'I'm on my own, now. I've got to face it now, by myself.' And he felt that not merely his father, but the leagued universe, was against him.

ARNOLD BENNETT, *Clayhanger* (1910).

HOUSE HUNTING
(1910)

THE Age of Property holds bitter moments even for a proprietor. When a move is imminent, furniture becomes ridiculous, and Margaret now lay awake at nights wondering where, where on earth they and all their belongings would be deposited in September next. Chairs, tables, pictures, books, that had rumbled down to them through the generations, must rumble forward again like a slide of rubbish to which she longed to give the final push, and send toppling into the sea. But there were all their father's books – they never read them, but they were their father's, and must be kept. There was the marble-topped chiffonier – their mother had set store by it, they could not remember why. Round every knob and cushion in the house sentiment gathered, a sentiment that was at times personal, but more often a faint piety to the dead, a prolongation of rites that might have ended at the grave.

It was absurd, if you came to think of it. Helen and Tibby came to think of it: Margaret was too busy with the house-agents. The feudal ownership of land did bring dignity, whereas the modern ownership of movables is reducing us again to a nomadic horde. We are reverting to the civilization of luggage, and historians of the future will note how the middle classes accreted possessions without taking root in the earth, and may find in this the secret of their imaginative poverty. The Schlegels were certainly the poorer for the loss of Wickham Place. It had helped to balance their lives, and almost to counsel them. Nor is their ground-landlord spiritually the richer. He has built flats on its site, his motor-cars grow swifter, his exposures of Socialism more trenchant. But he has spilt the precious distillation of the years, and no chemistry of his can give it back to society again.

Margaret grew depressed; she was anxious to settle on a house before they left town to pay their annual visit to Mrs Munt. She enjoyed this visit, and wanted to have her mind at ease for it. Swanage, though dull, was stable, and this year she longed more than usual for its fresh air and for the magnificent downs that guard it on the north. But London thwarted her; in its atmosphere she could not concentrate. London only stimulates, it cannot sustain; and Margaret, hurrying over its surface for a house without knowing what sort of a house she wanted, was paying for many a thrilling sensation in the past. She could not even break loose from culture, and her time was wasted by concerts which it would be a sin to miss, and invitations which it would never do to refuse. At last she grew desperate; she resolved that she would go nowhere and be at home to no one until she found a house, and broke the resolution in half an hour.

Once she had humorously lamented that she had never been to Simpson's restaurant in the Strand. Now a note arrived from Miss Wilcox, asking her to lunch there. Mr Cahill was coming, and the three would have such a jolly chat, and perhaps end up at the Hippodrome. Margaret had no strong regard for Evie, and no desire to meet her fiancé, and she was surprised that Helen, who had been far funnier about Simpson's, had not been asked instead. But the invitation touched her by its intimate tone. She must know Evie Wilcox better than she supposed, and declaring that she 'simply must', she accepted.

But when she saw Evie at the entrance of the restaurant, staring fiercely at nothing after the fashion of athletic women, her heart failed her anew. Miss Wilcox had changed perceptibly since her engagement. Her voice was gruffer, her manner more downright, and she was inclined to patronize the more foolish virgin. Margaret was silly enough to be pained at this. Depressed at her isolation, she saw not only houses and furniture, but the vessel of life slipping past her, with people like Evie and Mr Cahill on board.

There are moments when virtue and wisdom fail us, and one of them came to her at Simpson's in the Strand. As she trod the staircase, narrow, but carpeted thickly, as she entered the eating-room, where saddles of mutton were being trundled up to expectant clergymen, she had a strong, if erroneous, conviction of her own futility, and wished she had never come out of her backwater, where nothing happened except art and literature, and where no one ever got married or succeeded in remaining engaged. Then came a little surprise. 'Father might be of the party – yes, father was.' With a smile of pleasure she moved forward to greet him, and her feeling of loneliness vanished.

'I thought I'd get round if I could,' said he. 'Evie told me of her little plan, so I just slipped in and secured a table. Always secure a table first. Evie, don't pretend you want to sit by your old father, because you don't. Miss Schlegel, come in my side, out of pity. My goodness, but you look tired! Been worrying round after your young clerks?'

'No, after houses,' said Margaret, edging past him into the box. 'I'm hungry, not tired; I want to eat heaps.'

'That's good. What'll you have?'

'Fish pie,' said she, with a glance at the menu.

'Fish pie! Fancy coming for fish pie to Simpson's. It's not a bit the thing to go for here.'

'Go for something for me, then,' said Margaret, pulling off her gloves. Her spirits were rising, and his reference to Leonard Bast had warmed her curiously.

'Saddle of mutton,' said he after profound reflection; 'and cider to drink. That's the type of thing. I like this place, for a joke, once in a way. It is so thoroughly Old English. Don't you agree?'

'Yes,' said Margaret, who didn't. The order was given, the joint rolled up, and the carver, under Mr Wilcox's direction, cut the meat where it was succulent, and piled their plates high. Mr Cahill insisted on sirloin, but admitted that he had made a mistake later on. He and Evie soon fell into a conversation of the 'No, I didn't; yes, you did' type – conversation which, though fascinating to those who are engaged in it, neither desires nor deserves the attention of others.

'It's a golden rule to tip the carver. Tip everywhere's my motto.'

'Perhaps it does make life more human.'

'Then the fellows know one again. Especially in the East, if you tip, they remember you from year's end to year's end.'

'Have you been in the East?'

'Oh, Greece and the Levant. I used to go out for sport and business to Cyprus; some military society of a sort there. A few piastres, properly distributed, help to keep one's memory green. But you, of course, think this shockingly cynical. How's your discussion society getting on? Any new Utopias lately?'

'No, I'm house-hunting, Mr Wilcox, as I've already told you once. Do you know of any houses?'

'Afraid I don't.'

'Well, what's the point of being practical if you can't find two distressed females a house? We merely want a small house with large rooms, and plenty of them.'

'Evie, I like that! Miss Schlegel expects me to turn house agent for her!'

'What's that, father?'

'I want a new home in September, and someone must find it, I can't.'

'Percy, do you know of anything?'

'I can't say I do,' said Mr Cahill.

'How like you! You're never any good.'

'Never any good. Just listen to her! Never any good. Oh, come!'

'Well, you aren't. Miss Schlegel, is he?'

The torrent of their love, having splashed these drops at Margaret, swept away on its habitual course. She sympathized with it now, for a little comfort had restored her geniality. Speech and silence pleased her equally, and while Mr Wilcox made some preliminary inquiries about cheese, her eyes surveyed the restaurant, and admired its well-calculated tributes to the solidity of our past. Though no more Old English than the works of Kipling, it had selected its reminiscences so adroitly that her criticism was lulled, and the guests whom it was nourishing for imperial purposes bore the outer semblance of Parson Adams or Tom Jones. Scraps of their talk jarred oddly on the ear. 'Right you are! I'll cable out to Uganda this evening,' came from the table behind. 'Their

Emperor wants war; well, let him have it,' was the opinion of a clergyman. She smiled at such incongruities. 'Next time,' she said to Mr Wilcox, 'you shall come to lunch with me at Mr Eustace Miles's.'

'With pleasure.'

'No, you'd hate it,' she said, pushing her glass towards him for some more cider. 'It's all proteins and body buildings, and people come up to you and beg your pardon, but you have such a beautiful aura.'

'A what?'

'Never heard of an aura? Oh, happy, happy man! I scrub at mine for hours. Nor of an astral plane?'

He had heard of astral planes, and censured them.

'Just so. Luckily it was Helen's aura, not mine, and she had to chaperon it and do the politeness. I just sat with my handkerchief in my mouth till the man went.'

'Funny experiences seem to come to you two girls. No one's ever asked me about my – what d'ye call it? Perhaps I've not got one.'

'You're bound to have one, but it may be such a terrible colour that no one dares mention it.'

'Tell me, though, Miss Schlegel, do you really believe in the supernatural and all that?'

'Too difficult a question.'

'Why's that? Gruyère or Stilton?'

'Gruyère, please.'

'Better have Stilton.'

'Stilton. Because, though I don't believe in auras, and think Theosophy's only a half-way house —'

'— Yet there may be something in it all the same,' he concluded, with a frown.

'Not even that. It may be half-way in the wrong direction. I can't explain. I don't believe in all these fads, and yet I don't like saying that I don't believe in them.'

He seemed unsatisfied, and said: 'So you wouldn't give me

your word that you *don't* hold with astral bodies and all the rest of it?'

'I could,' said Margaret, surprised that the point was of any importance to him. 'Indeed, I will. When I talked about scrubbing my aura, I was only trying to be funny. But why do you want this settled?'

'I don't know.'

'Now, Mr Wilcox, you do know.'

'Yes, I am,' 'No, you're not,' burst from the lovers opposite. Margaret was silent for a moment, and then changed the subject.

'How's your house?'

'Much the same as when you honoured it last week.'

'I don't mean Ducie Street. Howards End, of course.'

'Why "of course"?'

'Can't you turn out your tenant and let it to us? We're nearly demented.'

'Let me think. I wish I could help you. But I thought you wanted to be in town. One bit of advice: fix your district, then fix your price, and then don't budge. That's how I got both Ducie Street and Oniton. I said to myself, "I mean to be exactly here," and I was, and Oniton's a place in a thousand.'

'But I do budge. Gentlemen seem to mesmerize houses – cow them with an eye, and up they come, trembling. Ladies can't. It's the houses that are mesmerizing me. I've no control over the saucy things. Houses are alive. No?'

'I'm out of my depth,' he said, and added: 'Didn't you talk rather like that to your office boy?'

'Did I? – I mean I did, more or less. I talk the same way to everyone – or try to.'

'Yes, I know. And how much do you suppose that he understood of it?'

'That's his lookout. I don't believe in suiting my conversation to my company. One can doubtless hit upon some medium of exchange that seems to do well enough, but it's no more like the real thing than money is like food. There's no nourishment in it. You pass it to the lower classes, and they pass it back to you, and this you call "social intercourse" or "mutual endeavour," when it's mutual priggishness if it's anything. Our friends at Chelsea don't see this. They say one ought to be at all costs intelligible, and sacrifice—'

'Lower classes,' interrupted Mr Wilcox, as it were thrusting his hand into her speech. 'Well, you do admit that there are rich and poor. That's something.'

Margaret could not reply. Was he incredibly stupid, or did he understand her better than she understood herself?

'You do admit that, if wealth was divided up equally, in a few years there would be rich and poor again just the same. The hard-working man would come to the top, the wastrel sink to the bottom.'

'Everyone admits that.'

'Your Socialists don't.'

'My Socialists do. Yours mayn't; but I strongly suspect yours of being not Socialists, but ninepins, which you have constructed for your own amusement. I can't imagine any living creature who would bowl over quite so easily.'

He would have resented this had she not been a woman. But women may say anything – it was one of his holiest beliefs – and he only retorted, with a gay smile: 'I don't care. You've made two damaging admissions, and I'm heartily with you in both.'

In time they finished lunch, and Margaret, who had excused herself from the Hippodrome, took her leave. Evie had scarcely addressed her, and she suspected that the entertainment had been planned by the father. He and she were advancing out of their respective families towards a more intimate acquaintance. It had begun long ago. She had been his wife's friend, and, as such, he had given her that silver vinaigrette as a memento. It was pretty of him to have given that vinaigrette, and he had always preferred her to Helen –

unlike most men. But the advance had been astonishing lately. They had done more in a week than in two years, and were beginning to know each other.

She did not forget his promise to sample Eustace Miles, and asked him as soon as she could secure Tibby as his chaperon. He came, and partook of body-building dishes with humility.

Next morning the Schlegels left for Swanage. They had not succeeded in finding a new home.

E. M. FORSTER, *Howards End* (1910).

A WORKING DEATH
(1914)

THE old woman continued to muse aloud, a monotonous irritating sound, while Elizabeth thought concentratedly, startled once, when she heard the winding-engine chuff quickly, and the brakes skirr with a shriek. Then she heard the engine more slowly, and the brakes made no sound. The old woman did not notice. Elizabeth waited in suspense. The mother-in-law talked, with lapses into silence.

'But he wasn't your son, Lizzie, an' it makes a difference. Whatever he was, I remember him when he was little, an' I learned to understand him and to make allowances. You've got to make allowances for them –'

It was half-past ten, and the old woman was saying: 'But it's trouble from beginning to end; you're never too old for trouble, never too old for that –' when the gate banged back, and there were heavy feet on the steps.

'I'll go, Lizzie, let me go', cried the old woman, rising. But Elizabeth was at the door. It was a man in pit-clothes.

'They're bringin' 'im, Missis,' he said. Elizabeth's heart halted a moment. Then it surged on again, almost suffocating her.

'Is he – is it bad?' she asked.

The man turned away, looking at the darkness:

'The doctor says 'e'd been dead hours. 'E saw 'im i' th' lamp-cabin.'

The old woman, who stood just behind Elizabeth, dropped into a chair, and folded her hands, crying: 'Oh, my boy, my boy!'

'Hush!' said Elizabeth, with a sharp twitch of a frown. 'Be still, mother, don't waken th' children: I wouldn't have them down for anything?'

The old woman moaned softly, rocking herself. The man was drawing away. Elizabeth took a step forward.

'How was it?' she asked.

'Well, I couldn't say for sure,' the man replied, very ill at ease. ' 'E wor finishin' a stint an' th' butties 'ad gone, an' a lot o' stuff come down atop 'n 'im.'

'And crushed him?' cried the widow, with a shudder.

'No,' said the man, 'it fell at th' back of 'im. 'E wor under th' face, an' it niver touched 'im. It shut 'im in. It seems 'e wor smothered.'

Elizabeth shrank back. She heard the old woman behind her cry:

'What? – what did 'e say it was?'

The man replied, more loudly: ' 'E wor smothered!'

Then the old woman wailed aloud, and this relieved Elizabeth.

'Oh, mother,' she said, putting her hand on the old woman, 'don't waken th' children, don't waken th' children.'

She wept a little, unknowing, while the old mother rocked herself and moaned. Elizabeth remembered that they were bringing him home, and she must be ready. 'They'll lay him in the parlour,' she said to herself, standing a moment pale and perplexed.

Then she lighted a candle and went into the tiny room. The air was cold and damp, but she could not make a fire, there was no fireplace. She set down the candle and looked round.

The candle-light glittered on the lustre-glasses, on the two vases that held some of the pink chrysanthemums, and on the dark mahogany. There was a cold, deathly smell of chrysanthemums in the room. Elizabeth stood looking at the flowers. She turned away, and calculated whether there would be room to lay him on the floor, between the couch and the chiffonier. She pushed the chairs aside. There would be room to lay him down and to step round him. Then she fetched the old red tablecloth, and another old cloth, spreading them down to save her bit of carpet. She shivered on leaving the parlour; so, from the dresser-drawer she took a clean shirt and put it at the fire to air. All the time her mother-in-law was rocking herself in the chair and moaning.

'You'll have to move from there, mother,' said Elizabeth. 'They'll be bringing him in. Come in the rocker.'

The old mother rose mechanically, and seated herself by the fire, continuing to lament. Elizabeth went into the pantry for another candle, and there, in the little penthouse under the naked tiles, she heard them coming. She stood still in the pantry doorway, listening. She heard them pass the end of the house, and come awkwardly down the three steps, a jumble of shuffling footsteps and muttering voices. The old woman was silent. The men were in the yard.

Then Elizabeth heard Matthews, the manager of the pit, say: 'You go in first, Jim. Mind!'

· The door came open, and the two women saw a collier backing into the room, holding one end of a stretcher, on which they could see the nailed pit-boots of the dead man. The two carriers halted, the man at the head stooping to the lintel of the door.

'Wheer will you have him?' asked the manager, a short, white-bearded man.

Elizabeth roused herself and came from the pantry carrying the unlighted candle.

'In the parlour,' she said.

'In there, Jim!' pointed the manager, and the carriers backed round into the tiny room. The coat with which they had covered the body fell off as they awkwardly turned through the two doorways, and the women saw their man, naked to the waist, lying stripped for work. The old woman began to moan in a low voice of horror.

'Lay th' stretcher at th' side,' snapped the manager, 'an' put 'im on th' cloths. Mind now, mind! Look you now –!'

One of the men had knocked off a vase of chrysanthemums. He stared awkwardly, then they set down the stretcher. Elizabeth did not look at her husband. As soon as she could get in the room, she went and picked up the broken vase and the flowers.

'Wait a minute!' she said.

The three men waited in silence while she mopped up the water with a duster.

'Eh, what a job, what a job, to be sure!' the manager was saying, rubbing his brow with trouble and perplexity. 'Never knew such a thing in my life, never! He'd no business to ha' been left. I never knew such a thing in my life! Fell over him clean as a whistle, an' shut him in. Not four foot of space, there wasn't – yet it scarce bruised him.'

He looked down at the dead man, lying prone, half naked, all grimed with coal-dust.

'"'Sphyxiated,"' the doctor said. It *is* the most terrible job I've ever known. Seems as if it was done o' purpose. Clean over him, an' shut 'im in, like a mouse-trap' – he made a sharp, descending gesture with his hand.

The colliers standing by jerked aside their heads in hopeless comment.

The horror of the thing bristled upon them all.

Then they heard the girl's voice upstairs calling shrilly: 'Mother, mother – who is it? Mother, who is it?'

Elizabeth hurried to the foot of the stairs and opened the door:

'Go to sleep!' she commanded sharply. 'What are you shouting about? Go to sleep at once – there's nothing –'

Then she began to mount the stairs. They could hear her on the boards, and on the plaster floor of the little bedroom. They could hear her distinctly:

'What's the matter now? – what's the matter with you, silly thing?' – her voice was much agitated, with an unreal gentleness.

'I thought it was some men come,' said the plaintive voice of the child. 'Has he come?'

'Yes, they've brought him. There's nothing to make a fuss about. Go to sleep now, like a good child.'

They could hear her voice in the bedroom, they waited whilst she covered the children under the bedclothes.

'Is he drunk?' asked the girl, timidly, faintly.

'No! No – he's not! He – he's asleep.'

'Is he asleep downstairs?'

'Yes – and don't make a noise.'

There was silence for a moment, then the men heard the frightened child again:

'What's that noise?'

'It's nothing, I tell you, what are you bothering for?'

The noise was the grandmother moaning. She was oblivious of everything, sitting on her chair rocking and moaning. The manager put his hand on her arm and bade her 'Sh – sh!!'

The old woman opened her eyes and looked at him. She was shocked by this interruption, and seemed to wonder.

'What time is it?' – the plaintive thin voice of the child, sinking back unhappily into sleep, asked this last question.

'Ten o'clock,' answered the mother more softly. Then she must have bent down and kissed the children.

Matthews beckoned to the men to come away. They put on their caps and took up the stretcher. Stepping over the body, they tiptoed out of the house. None of them spoke till they were far from the wakeful children.

When Elizabeth came down she found her mother alone on the parlour floor, leaning over the dead man, the tears dropping on him.

'We must lay him out,' the wife said. She put on the kettle, then returning knelt at the feet, and began to unfasten the knotted leather laces. The room was clammy and dim with only one candle, so that she had to bend her face almost to the floor. At last she got off the heavy boots and put them away.

'You must help me now,' she whispered to the old woman. Together they stripped the man.

When they arose, saw him lying in the naïve dignity of death, the women stood arrested in fear and respect. For a few moments they remained still, looking down, the old mother whimpering. Elizabeth felt countermanded. She saw him, how utterly inviolable he lay in himself. She had nothing to do with him. She could not accept it. Stooping, she laid her hand on him, in claim. He was still warm, for the mine was hot where he had died. His mother had his face between her hands, and was murmuring incoherently. The old tears fell in succession as drops from wet leaves; the mother was not weeping, merely her tears flowed. Elizabeth embraced the body of her husband, with cheek and lips. She seemed to be listening, inquiring, trying to get some connection. But she could not. She was driven away. He was impregnable.

She rose, went into the kitchen, where she poured warm water into a bowl, brought soap and flannel and a soft towel.

'I must wash him,' she said.

Then the old mother rose stiffly, and watched Elizabeth as she carefully washed his face, carefully brushing the big blonde moustache from his mouth with the flannel. She was afraid with a bottomless fear, so she ministered to him. The old woman, jealous, said:

'Let me wipe him!' – and she kneeled on the other side drying slowly as Elizabeth washed, her big black bonnet sometimes brushing the dark head of her daughter. They worked thus in silence for a long time. They never forgot it was death, and the touch of the man's dead body gave them strange emotions, different in each of the women; a great dread possessed them both, the mother felt the lie was given to her womb, she was denied; the wife felt the utter isolation of the human soul, the child within her was a weight apart from her.

At last it was finished. He was a man of handsome body, and his face showed no traces of drink. He was blonde, full-fleshed, with fine limbs. But he was dead.

'Bless him,' whispered his mother, looking always at his face, and speaking out of sheer terror. 'Dear lad – bless him!' She spoke in a faint, sibilant ecstasy of fear and mother love.

Elizabeth sank down again to the floor, and put her face against his neck, and trembled and shuddered. But she had to draw away again. He was dead, and her living flesh had no place against his. A great dread and weariness held her: she was so unavailing. Her life was gone like this.

'White as milk he is, clear as a twelve-month baby, bless him, the darling!' the old mother murmured to herself. 'Not a mark on him, clear and clean and white, beautiful as ever a child was made,' she murmured with pride. Elizabeth kept her face hidden.

'He went peaceful, Lizzie – peaceful as sleep. Isn't he beautiful, the lamb? Ay – he must ha' made his peace, Lizzie. 'Appen he made it all right, Lizzie, shut in there. He'd have time. He wouldn't look like this if he hadn't made his peace. The lamb, the dear lamb. Eh, but he had a hearty laugh. I loved to hear it. He had the heartiest laugh, Lizzie, as a lad —'

Elizabeth looked up. The man's mouth was fallen back, slightly open under the cover of the moustache. The eyes, half shut, did not show glazed in the obscurity. Life with its smoky burning gone from him, had left him apart and utterly alien to her. And she knew what a stranger he was to her. In her womb was ice of fear, because of this separate stranger with whom she had been living as one flesh. Was this what it all meant – utter, intact separateness, obscured by heat of living? In dread she turned her face away. The fact was too deadly. There had been nothing between them, and yet they had come together, exchanging their nakedness repeatedly. Each time he had taken her, they had been two isolated beings, far apart as now. He was no more responsible than she. The child was like ice in her womb. For as she looked at the dead man, her mind, cold and detached, said clearly: 'Who am I? What have I been doing? I have been fighting a husband who did not exist. *He* existed all the time. What wrong have I done? What was that I have been living with? There lies the reality, this man.' – And her soul died in her for fear: she knew she had never seen him, he had never seen her, they had met in the dark and had fought in the dark, not knowing whom they met nor whom they fought. And now she saw, and turned silent in seeing. For she had been wrong. She had said he was something he was not; she had felt familiar with him. Whereas he was apart all the while, living as she never lived, feeling as she never felt.

In fear and shame she looked at his naked body, that she had known falsely. And he was the father of her children. Her soul was torn from her body and stood apart. She looked at his naked body and was ashamed, as if she had denied it. After all, it was itself. It seemed awful to her. She looked at his face, and she turned her own face to the wall. For his look was other than hers, his way was not her way. She had denied him what he was – she saw it now. She had refused him as himself. – And this had been her life, and his life. – She was grateful to death, which restored the truth. And she knew she was not dead.

And all the while her heart was bursting with grief and pity for him. What had he suffered? What stretch of horror for this helpless man! She was rigid with agony. She had not been able to help him. He had been cruelly injured, this naked man, this other being, and she could make no reparation. There were the children – but the children belonged to life. This dead man had nothing to do with them. He and she were only channels through which life had flowed to issue in the children. She was a mother – but how awful she knew it now to have been a wife. And he, dead now, how awful he must have felt it to be a husband. She felt that in the next world he would be a stranger to her. If they met there, in the beyond, they would only be ashamed of what had been before. The children had come, for some mysterious reason, out of both of them. But the children did not unite them. Now he was dead, she knew how eternally he was apart from her, how eternally he had nothing more to do with her. She saw this episode of her life closed. They had denied each other in life. Now he had withdrawn. An anguish came over her. It was finished then: it had become hopeless between them long before he died. Yet he had been her husband. But how little!

'Have you got his shirt, 'Lizabeth?'

Elizabeth turned without answering, though she strove to weep and behave as her mother-in-law expected. But she could not, she was silenced. She went into the kitchen and returned with the garment.

'It is aired,' she said, grasping the cotton shirt here and there to try. She was almost ashamed to handle him; what right had she or anyone to lay hands on him; but her touch was humble on his body. It was hard work to clothe him. He was so heavy and inert. A terrible dread gripped her all the while: that he could be so heavy and utterly inert, unresponsive, apart. The horror of the distance between them was almost too much for her – it was so infinite a gap she must look across.

At last it was finished. They covered him with a sheet and left him lying, with his face bound. And she fastened the door of the little parlour, lest the children should see what was lying there. Then, with peace sunk heavy on her heart, she went about making tidy the kitchen. She knew she submitted to life, which was her immediate master. But from death, her ultimate master, she winced with fear and shame.

D. H. LAWRENCE, 'Odour of Chrysanthemums' in *The Prussian Officer and Other Stories* (1914).

A FARMER ON LEAVE
(1932)

CHAE sat up in his bed to reach for his pipe when he looked from the window and he gave a great roar; and he louped from his bed in his sark so that Kirsty came running and crying *What is't? Is't a wound?*

But she found Chae standing by the window then, cursing himself black in the face he was, and he asked how long had *this* been going? So Mistress Strachan looked out the way he looked and she saw it was only the long bit wood that ran by the Peesie's Knapp that vexed him, it was nearly down the whole stretch of it, now. It made a gey difference to the lookout faith! but fine for Kinraddie the woodmen had been, they'd lodged at the Knapp and paid high for their board. But Chae cried out *To hell with their board, the bastards, they're ruining my land, do you hear!* And he pulled on his trousers and boots and would fair have run over the park and been at them; but Kirsty caught at his sark and held him back and cried *Have you fair gone mad with the killing of Germans?*

And he asked her hadn't she got eyes in her head, the fool, not telling him before that the wood was cut? It would lay the whole Knapp open to the north-east now, and was fair the end of a living here. And Mistress Strachan answered up that she wasn't a fool, and they'd be no worse than the other folk, would they? all the woods in Kinraddie were due to come down. Chae shouted *What, others?* and went out to look; and when he came back he didn't shout at all, he said he'd often minded of them out there in France, the woods, so bonny they were, and thick and grave, fine shelter and lithe for the cattle. Nor more than that would he say, it seemed then to Kirsty that he quietened down, and was quiet and queer all his leave, it was daft to let a bit wood go vex him like that.

But the last night of his leave he climbed to Blawearie and he said there was nothing but the woods and their fate that could draw his eyes. For over by the Mains he'd come on the woodmen, teams and teams of them hard at work on the long bit forest that ran up the high brae, sparing nothing they were but the yews of the Manse. And up above Upperhill they had cut down the larch, and the wood was down that lay back of old Pooty's.

Folk had told him the trustees had sold it well, they got awful high prices, the trustees did, it was wanted for aeroplanes and such-like things. And over at the office he had found the factor and the creature had peeked at Chae through his horn-rimmed glasses and said that the Government would replant all the trees when the War was won. And Chae had said that would console him a bloody lot, sure, if he'd the chance of living two hundred years and seeing the woods grow up as some shelter for beast and man: but he doubted he'd not last so long. Then the factor said they must all do their bit at a sacrifice, and Chae asked *And what sacrifices have you made, tell me, you scrawny wee mucker?*

LEWIS GRASSIC GIBBON, *Sunset Song* (1932).

BLOOM IN THE STREET
(1921)

MR LEOPOLD BLOOM ate with relish the inner organs of beasts and fowls. He liked thick giblet soup, nutty gizzards, a stuffed roast heart, liver slices fried with crustcrumbs, fried hencod's roes. Most of all he liked grilled mutton kidneys which gave to his palate a fine tang of faintly scented urine.

Kidneys were in his mind as he moved about the kitchen softly, righting her breakfast things on the humpy tray. Gelid light and air were in the kitchen but out of doors gentle summer morning everywhere. Made him feel a bit peckish.

The coals were reddening.

Another slice of bread and butter: three, four: right. She didn't like her plate full. Right. He turned from the tray, lifted the kettle off the hob and set it sideways on the fire. It sat there, dull and squat, its spout stuck out. Cup of tea soon. Good. Mouth dry. The cat walked stiffly round a leg of the table with tail on high.

– Mkgnao!

– O, there you are, Mr Bloom said, turning from the fire.

The cat mewed in answer and stalked again stiffly round a leg of the table, mewing. Just how she stalks over my writing-table. Prr. Scratch my head. Prr.

Mr Bloom watched curiously, kindly, the lithe black form. Clean to see: the gloss of her sleek hide, the white button under the butt of her tail, the green flashing eyes. He bent down to her, his hands on his knees.

– Milk for the pussens, he said.

– Mrkgnao! the cat cried.

They call them stupid. They understand what we say better than we understand them. She understands all she wants to. Vindictive too. Wonder what I look like to her. Height of a tower? No, she can jump me.

– Afraid of the chickens she is, he said mockingly. Afraid of the chookchooks. I never saw such a stupid pussens as the pussens.

Cruel. Her nature. Curious mice never squeal. Seem to like it.

– Mrkrgnao! the cat said loudly.

She blinked up out of her avid shameclosing eyes, mewing plaintively and long, showing him her milkwhite teeth. He watched the dark eyeslits narrowing with greed till her eyes were green stones. Then he went to the dresser, took the jug Hanlon's milkman had just filled for him, poured warm-bubbled milk on a saucer and set it slowly on the floor.

– Gurrhr! she cried, running to lap.

He watched the bristles shining wirily in the weak light as she tipped three times and licked lightly. Wonder is it true if you clip them they can't mouse after. Why? They shine in the dark, perhaps, the tips. Or kind of feelers in the dark, perhaps.

He listened to her licking lap. Ham and eggs, no. No good eggs with this drouth. Want pure fresh water. Thursday: not a good day either for a mutton kidney at Buckley's. Fried with butter, a shake of pepper. Better a pork kidney at Dlugacz's. While the kettle is boiling. She lapped slower, then licking the saucer clean. Why are their tongues so rough? To lap better, all porous holes. Nothing she can eat? He glanced round him. No.

On quietly creaky boots he went up the staircase to the hall, paused by the bedroom door. She might like something tasty. Thin bread and butter she likes in the morning. Still perhaps: once in a way.

He said softly in the bare hall:

– I am going round the corner. Be back in a minute.

And when he had heard his voice say it he added:

– You don't want anything for breakfast?

A sleepy soft grunt answered:

– Mn.

No. She did not want anything. He heard then a warm heavy sigh, softer, as she turned over and the loose brass quoits of the bedstead jingled. Must get those settled really. Pity. All the way from Gibraltar. Forgotten any little Spanish she knew. Wonder what her father gave for it. Old style. Ah yes, of course. Bought it at the governor's auction. Got a short knock. Hard as nails at a bargain, old Tweedy. Yes, sir. At Plevna that was. I rose from the ranks, sir, and I'm proud of it. Still he had brains enough to make that corner in stamps. Now that was farseeing.

His hand took his hat from the peg over his initialled heavy overcoat, and his lost property office secondhand waterproof. Stamps: sticky-back pictures. Daresay lots of officers are in the swim too. Course they do. The sweated legend in the crown of his hat told him mutely: Plasto's high grade ha. He peeped quickly inside the leather headband. White slip of paper. Quite safe.

On the doorstep he felt in his hip pocket for the latchkey. Not there. In the trousers I left off. Must get it. Potato I have. Creaky wardrobe. No use disturbing her. She turned over sleepily that time. He pulled the halldoor to after him very quietly, more, till the footleaf dropped gently over the threshold, a limp lid. Looked shut. All right till I come back anyhow.

He crossed to the bright side, avoiding the loose cellarflap of number seventyfive. The sun was nearing the steeple of George's church. Be a warm day I fancy. Specially in these black clothes feel it more. Black conducts, reflects (refracts is it?), the heat. But I couldn't go in that light suit. Make a picnic of it. His eyelids sank quietly often as he walked in happy warmth. Boland's breadvan delivering with trays our daily but she prefers yesterday's loaves turnovers crisp crowns hot. Makes you feel young. Somewhere in the east: early morning: set off at dawn, travel round in front of the sun, steal a day's march on him. Keep it up for ever never grow a day older technically. Walk along a strand, strange land, come to a city gate, sentry there, old ranker too, old Tweedy's big moustaches leaning on a long kind of a spear. Wander through awned streets. Turbaned faces going by. Dark caves of carpet shops, big man, Turko the terrible, seated crosslegged smoking a coiled pipe. Cries of sellers in the streets. Drink water scented with fennel, sherbet. Wander along all day. Might meet a robber or two. Well, meet him. Getting on to sundown. The shadows of the mosques along the pillars: priest with a scroll rolled up. A shiver of the trees, signal, the evening wind. I pass on. Fading gold sky. A mother watches from her doorway. She calls her children home in their dark language. High wall: beyond strings twanged. Night sky moon, violet, colour of Molly's new garters. Strings. Listen. A girl playing one of these instruments what do you call them: dulcimers. I pass.

Probably not a bit like it really. Kind of stuff you read: in the track of the sun. Sunburst on the titlepage. He smiled, pleasing himself. What Arthur Griffith said about the head-piece over the *Freeman* leader: a homerule sun rising up in the northwest from the laneway behind the bank of Ireland. He prolonged his pleased smile. Ikey touch that: homerule sun rising up in the northwest.

He approached Larry O'Rourke's. From the cellar grating floated up the flabby gush of porter. Through the open doorway the bar squirted out whiffs of ginger, teadust, biscuitmush. Good house, however: just the end of the city traffic. For instance M'Auley's down there: n. g. as position. Of course if they ran a tramline along the North Circular from the cattle market to the quays value would go up like a shot.

Bald head over the blind. Cute old codger. No use canvassing him for an ad. Still he knows his own business best. There he is, sure enough, my bold Larry, leaning against the sugarbin in his shirtsleeves watching the aproned curate swab up with mop and bucket. Simon Dedalus takes him off to a tee with his eyes screwed up. Do you know what I'm going to tell you? What's that, Mr O'Rourke? Do you know what? The Russians, they'd only be an eight o'clock breakfast for the Japanese.

Stop and say a word: about the funeral perhaps. Sad thing about poor Dignam, Mr O'Rourke.

Turning into Dorset street he said freshly in greeting through the doorway:

— Good day, Mr O'Rourke.

— Good day to you.

– Lovely weather, sir.

– 'Tis all that.

JAMES JOYCE, *Ulysses* (1914–21).

A FORCE IN THE HOUSE
(1927)

THE house was left; the house was deserted. It was left like a shell on a sandhill to fill with dry salt grains now that life had left it. The long night seemed to have set in; the trifling airs, nibbling, the clammy breaths, fumbling, seemed to have triumphed. The saucepan had rusted and the mat decayed. Toads had nosed their way in. Idly, aimlessly, the swaying shawl swung to and fro. A thistle thrust itself between the tiles in the larder. The swallows nested in the drawing-room; the floor was strewn with straw; the plaster fell in shovelfuls; rafters were laid bare; rats carried off this and that to gnaw behind the wainscots. Tortoise-shell butterflies burst from the chrysalis and pattered their life out on the window-pane. Poppies sowed themselves among the dahlias; the lawn waved with long grass; giant artichokes towered among roses; a fringed carnation flowered among the cabbages; while the gentle tapping of a weed at the window had become, on winters' nights, a drumming from sturdy trees and thorned briars which made the whole room green in summer.

What power could now prevent the fertility, the insensibility of nature? Mrs McNab's dream of a lady, of a child, of a plate of milk soup? It had wavered over the walls like a spot of sunlight and vanished. She had locked the door; she had gone. It was beyond the strength of one woman, she said. They never sent. They never wrote. There were things up there rotting in the drawers – it was a shame to leave them so, she said. The place was gone to rack and ruin. Only the Lighthouse beam entered the rooms for a moment, sent its sudden stare over bed and wall in the darkness of winter, looked with equanimity at the thistle and the swallow, the rat and the straw. Nothing now withstood them; nothing said no to them. Let the wind blow; let the poppy seed itself and the carnation mate with the cabbage. Let the swallow build in the drawing-room, and the thistle thrust aside the tiles, and the butterfly sun itself on the faded chintz of the armchairs. Let the broken glass and the china lie out on the lawn and be tangled over with grass and wild berries.

For now had come that moment, that hesitation when dawn trembles and night pauses, when if a feather alight in the scale it will be weighed down. One feather, and the house, sinking, falling, would have turned and pitched downwards to the depths of darkness. In the ruined room, picnickers would have lit their kettles; lovers sought shelter there, lying on the bare boards; and the shepherd stored his dinner on the bricks, and the tramp slept with his coat round him to ward off the cold. Then the roof would have fallen; briars and hemlocks would have blotted out path, step, and window; would have grown, unequally but lustily over the mound, until some trespasser, losing his way, could have told only by a red-hot poker among the nettles, or a scrap of china in the hemlock, that here once some one had lived; there had been a house.

If the feather had fallen, if it had tipped the scale downwards, the whole house would have plunged to the depths to lie upon the sands of oblivion. But there was a force working; something not highly conscious; something that leered, something that lurched; something not inspired to go about its work with dignified ritual or solemn chanting. Mrs McNab groaned; Mrs Bast creaked. They were old; they were stiff; their legs ached. They came with their brooms and pails at last; they got to work. All of a sudden, would Mrs McNab see that the house was ready, one of the young ladies wrote: would she get this done; would she get that done; all in a hurry. They might be coming for the summer; had left everything to the last; expected to find things as they had left them. Slowly and painfully, with broom and pail, mopping, scouring, Mrs McNab, Mrs Bast stayed the corruption and the rot; rescued from the pool of Time that was fast closing over them now a basin, now a cupboard; fetched up from oblivion all the Waverley novels and a tea-set one morning; in the afternoon restored to sun and air a brass fender and a set of steel fire-irons. George, Mrs Bast's son, caught the rats, and cut the grass. They had the builders. Attended with the creaking of hinges and the screeching of bolts, the slamming and banging of damp-swollen woodwork, some rusty laborious birth seemed to be taking place, as the women, stooping, rising, groaning, singing, slapped and slammed, upstairs now, now down in the cellars. Oh, they said, the work!

VIRGINIA WOOLF, *To the Lighthouse* (1927).

TO THE SEA
(1939)

AND can it be it's nnow fforvell? Illas! I wisht I had better glances to peer to you through this baylight's growing. But you're changing, acoolsha, you're changing from me, I can feel. Or is it me is? I'm getting mixed. Brightening up and tightening down. Yes, you're changing, sonhusband, and you're turning, I can feel you, for a daughterwife from the hills again. Imlamaya. And she is coming. Swimming in my hindmoist. Diveltaking on me tail. Just a whisk brisk sly spry spink spank sprint of a thing theresomere, saultering. Saltarella come to her own. I pity your oldself I was used to. Now a younger's there. Try not to part! Be happy, dear ones! May I be wrong! For she'll be sweet for you as I was sweet when I came down out of me mother. My great blue bedroom, the air so quiet, scarce a cloud. In peace and silence. I could have stayed up there for always only. It's something fails us. First we feel. Then we fall. And let her rain now if she likes. Gently or strongly as she likes. Anyway let her rain for my time is come. I done me best when I was let. Thinking always if I go all goes. A hundred cares, a tithe of troubles and is there one who understands me? One in a thousand of years of the nights? All me life I have been lived among them but now they are becoming lothed to me. And I am lothing their little warm tricks. And lothing their mean cosy turns. And all the greedy gushes out through their small souls. And all the lazy leaks down over their brash bodies. How small it's all! And me letting on to meself always. And lilting on all the time. I thought you were all glittering with the noblest of carriage. You're only a bumpkin. I thought you the great in all things, in guilt and in glory. You're but a puny. Home! My people were not their sort out beyond there so far as I can. For all the bold and bad and bleary they are blamed, the seahags. No! Nor for all our wild dances in all their wild din. I can seen meself among them, allaniuvia pulchrabelled. How she was handsome, the wild Amazia, when she would seize to my other breast! And what is she weird, haughty Niluna, that she will snatch from my ownest hair! For 'tis they are the stormies. Ho hang! Hang ho! And the clash of our cries till we spring to be free. Auravoles, they says, never heed of your name! But I'm loothing them that's here and all I lothe. Loonely in me loneness. For all their faults. I am passing out. O bitter ending! I'll slip away before they're up. They'll never see. Nor know. Nor miss me. And it's old and old it's sad and old it's sad and weary I go back to you, my cold father, my cold mad father, my cold mad feary father, till the near sight of the mere size of him, the moyles and moyles of it moananoaning, makes me seasilt saltsick and I rush, my only, into your arms. I see them rising! Save me from those therrble prongs! Two more. Onetwo moremens more. So. Avelaval. My leaves have drifted from me. All.

But one clings still. I'll bear it on me. To remind me of. Lff! So soft this morning, ours. Yes. Carry me along, taddy, like you done through the toy fair! If I seen him bearing down on me now under white-spread wings like he'd come from Arkangels, I sink I'd die down over his feet, humbly dumbly, only to washup. Yes, tid. There's where. First. We pass through grass behush the bush to. Whish! A gull. Gulls. Far calls. Coming, far! End here. Us then, Finn, again! Take. Bussoftlhee, mememormee! Till thousandsthee. Lps. The keys to. Given! A way a lone a last a loved a long the

JAMES JOYCE, *Finnegans Wake* (1939).

CHARACTERISTICS
(1928)

HE stretches out his hand and picks up the paper. He reads:

Chest measurement.

Waist ditto.

Neck ditto.

Biceps ditto.

With the fumbling circumspection of the bedridden, the shoulders huddled, his right hand travels over his body. It squeezes the twin-pudding of the biceps. With the help of the other hand it constricts the waist-line while, extensors at full stretch, he flattens himself along the ground. Making a callipers of his index and thumb, he fixes them upon his neck, the thumb standing unsteadily upon the sterno-mastoid surface, while the point of the index seeks, underneath, the antipode required for the diameter. He removes this claw carefully, then holds it up before his face, a battered semicircle, disposing it in profile, the horny flukes stuck aslant in the red flesh, each podgy dactyl crowding out its neighbour. It remains there, the object of moody inspection. Gracefully relaxing, the index cranes out, a duck's neck emulating the lines of the swan, the remaining fingers drooping behind it. He stares at it, with little movement on either side, the face and hand suspended in front of each other, the arm a crazy bridge for them.

With pathetic aspiration, the index yearns forward again, then tries a graceful droop. The hand is turned over on its back, its mounts bulging with fatality, the scored and padded underside stiff with fat, above swollen annulate wrists.

'Look at that fist! No, I ask you!'

Pulley flashes an eye over the pendant pincer, as it is revolving back till it hangs with its fat legs dangling again.

'Yes the hands put on weight here. The feet too.'

He points this remark by advancing his own miniature ones, extending them side by side, a neat demure brace, tip-toeing alternately very slightly, in dainty rhythm.

'What does?'

The pulsing of a heavy musical instrument reaches them from the rear, a monotonous flat throb.

'What's your waist?' asks Satters.

' My—? Oh, I'm rather slightly built of course. I should say— I don't know. That's of no consequence, he's only teasing you.'

'Who?' Satters is examining the paper. 'I say. How can you measure the size of an eye. *Eyes. Size. Colour.* I haven't so much as seen my beastly eyes since I've been here.'

'That means *large* or *small*.'

'What are mine?' gruffly.

'Oh *large*. Very big. Lovely big ones! And *blue*.'

Without turning his head, Satters listens greedily.

'Grey?'

'No *blue*. True-blue!'

Satters' discouragement passes: sounds of suppressed good-humour are heard from him. He rolls and stretches full of lush self-feeling.

'I say look here. I'm not sure this was meant for my young eyes. Is it my mind that's not nice, or isn't that? Well!'

Pullman has an indulgent smile. He leans over, and Satters'
finger picks out for him the questionable words.

'What's that mean? Is that—'

'Yes.' Pulley snaps in to cut a long (and toothsome) story
short, beaming faintly with lazy indulgence; the babe has
found something to keep it quiet!

A silence sets in; Pullman conveys his attention to a remote
spot in the riverine middle-distance. There a naval engagement appears to be in progress. A half-dozen large fly-boats
are grappled in mid-stream, and the violent swarming of their
crews, which is just visible, pouring from one hull, swart and
almost flush with the tide, to the other, suggests some description of insect-conflict.

So Pulley mounts guard, alertly abstracted, satisfied that his
buxom charge is busy with his game of marbles provided by
the joking Bailiff for such occasions. All correct! a perfunctory
dart of the eye establishes that: the obscene facetiousness of the
form provided for this nursery constantly operates. Pulley
returns to the naval battle: he observes dark specks tumbling
from the extremity of the largest of the vessels. Evidently the
defeated faction being driven overboard: the peons often
fight: he sighs: it is no doubt one of their only recreations!
Other boats are now approaching the scene of the disturbance,
coming out from the celestial shore. His dutiful eye slews for
an instant back to his charge. Nothing unusual; but as it is
about to flit off again to the distant encounter it is checked. A
look of conventional anxiety clouds it as it hovers before
returning. *What is this?* the eyebrow curls in a fine voluble
question-mark. Impressive danger-signals have made their
appearance, but they are trite, he does not trouble to check
them. Still they are in for more trouble it is plain.

A stealthy convulsion, which had escaped his notice the first
time, is in progress. The symptoms prevail on his attention a
little, the inexorable professional eye lights up at contact with
a problem.

Satters still sprawls upon his back ripped open down the front to the waist, a hairy rift. The crumpled entrance-form is held stiffly before his nose as though every part of his face were shortsightedly participating in the Bailiff's expansive whim, the paper rattling where it touches some portion nearer than another. Teeth bared, belly shaking, he shivers and jumps in chilly silence, with catching of the breath and fierce hissing sighs. The tears roll down his cheek, ploughing their way through the moist nap of sweat that has collected.

Pulley, the polite faintly-ironical professional question-mark, sits on sentry-go. The face is concealed from him by the parchment form, which knocks incessantly against it with an inanimate rat-tat. This has the appearance of a crushed mask, but without eyeholes, lips, hair, or any furnishings, about to be fitted on, blank but plastic. Pulley peers idly at the dancing parchment; its palsied rat-tat proceeds. The headless figure beneath vibrates in secret enjoyment, so it seems, of a tip-top joke, which it is essential should be kept to itself. It hides its face: it dies of laughing!

Sometimes the monotonous seizure seems hastening to a climax. But it sinks again into its jog-trot of chattering syncopation. Pulley has an uneasy movement, a change of leg, a suppressed sigh. Dismal and vigilant, he gazes sideways at Satters. He has lost interest. The usual typhonic symptoms continue. The front of the thickset trunk is flung up and down in abrupt jumps, eructating with the fierce clockwork spasms of a dog with chorea. Pulley looks away. The disciplinary barges have reached the spot: they bump. There is a fresh excited swarming. A new battle begins. Many black specks catapult out to left and right, vanishing as they meet the glassy river. It is the exodus of the victors probably, before the onset of the city-police.

WYNDHAM LEWIS, *The Childermass* (1928).

AFTER CLARITY
(1952)

AND once, captain, on a showery night's fall in the thunder-nones of hot July, m' apricots big in the convent apron and the pretty gilly-flower to pink the white of his mason's paper hat; the Hammerer's summer-flashers from time to time and far off over the Arx of Julius, and nearer by and now and again brighted up old imaged Lud, as some tell is 'balmed 'Wallon, high-horsed above Martin *miles*, what the drovers pray to, full of our London ales and their 'Gomery fables.

Inclined against these shadowy courses, close-in, under the lower string-course, next the dark hunch of the gate. From the dripping impost the gusted drops moisted the ransom'd flesh of both of us – from the *right* side of the gate, cap-tin. The runnels brimmed so, was a marvel if the blesséd guardian head, cisted under, that keeps Lud's town, weren't down stream with dogs and garbage an' such poor Tibs as had come to the ninth death b' water.

In this wild eve's thunder-rain, at the batement of it, the night-shades now much more come on: when's the cool, even, after-light. When lime-dressed walls, petals on stalks, a kerchief, a shift's hem or such like, and the Eve's white of us ... *and* cap-tin, the bleached hemp of a fore-brace, the white of the wake beyond the dead-water, or the fresh paint-work, for'ard, eh? captain, looms up curiously exact and clear, more real by half than in the busy light as noses everywhere at stare-faced noon – more real ... but more of Faëry by a long chalk.

An' in this transfiguring after-clarity he seemed to call me his ... Fl - ora ... *Flora Dea* he says ... whether to me or into the darks of the old ragstone courses?

... how are you for conundrums, captain?

And again, once in especial,

at a swelt'rin' close August day's close, three sultry eves after
they sing *Gaudeamus* – on m' own name-day captain, the day
the British Elen found the Wood – Ceres big moon half ris
beyond her own Cornhill, behind de Arcubus as chimes *I do
not know*, at the same 'buttment of the guard-house wall, the
day-guard dismissed, the sergeant and his crawlers do the
small beer play at dice, within; the new-posted first night-
relief already a-nodding over his sloped stock – already a-bed
with the Queen o' Cockayne – or, champion in the stour he'd
fled ...

thank God

we've got the lightermen, captain!

Between the heats and the cool, at day's ebb and night-flow,
the lode already over the fen of Islington, pressed we was to
the same cranny of the wall to right of the same 'brassure of
the same right gate-jamb – so Janus save me, but bodies will.
The whitest of the Wanderers, what was Julius Caesar's
mother, white over toward Bride's Well, and this her fish
day – and again he says it, but this time it's *Bona Dea* he cries
... Hills o' the Mother he says, an' y'r lavender, the purple, he
says, an' then he says, but more slow:

Roma aurea Roma

Roma ... amor, amor ... Roma. Roma, wot's in the
feminine gender, he says.

DAVID JONES, *The Anathemata* (1952).

HERE AND NOW, BOYS
(1962)

THIS tree, for example, under which (for no known reason)
he found himself lying, this column of grey bark with the
groining, high up, of sun-speckled branches, this ought by
rights to be a beech tree. But in that case – and Will admired
himself for being so lucidly logical – in that case the leaves had

no right to be so obviously evergreen. And why would a beech tree send its roots elbowing up like this above the surface of the ground? And those preposterous wooden buttresses, on which the pseudo-beech supported itself – where did *those* fit into the picture? Will remembered suddenly his favourite worst line of poetry. 'Who prop, thou ask'st, in these bad days my mind?' Answer: congealed ectoplasm, Early Dali. Which definitely ruled out the Chilterns. So did the butterflies swooping out there in the thick buttery sunshine. Why were they so large, so improbably cerulean or velvet-black, so extravagantly eyed and freckled? Purple staring out of chestnut, silver powdered over emerald, over topaz, over sapphire.

'Attention.'

'Who's there?' Will Farnaby called in what he intended to be a loud and formidable tone; but all that came out of his mouth was a thin, quavering croak.

There was a long and, it seemed, profoundly menacing silence. From the hollow between two of the tree's wooden buttresses an enormous black centipede emerged for a moment into view, then hurried away on its regiment of crimson legs and vanished into another cleft in the lichen-covered ectoplasm.

'Who's there?' he croaked again.

There was a rustling in the bushes on his left and suddenly, like a cuckoo from a nursery clock, out popped a large black bird, the size of a jackdaw – only, needless to say, it wasn't a jackdaw. It clapped a pair of white-tipped wings and, darting across the intervening space, settled on the lowest branch of a small dead tree, not twenty feet from where Will was lying. Its beak, he noticed was orange, and it had a bald yellow patch under each eye, with canary-coloured wattles that covered the sides and back of its head with a thick wig of naked flesh. The bird cocked its head and looked at him first with the right eye, then with the left. After which it opened its orange bill, whistled ten or twelve notes of a little air in the pentatonic scale, made a noise like somebody having hiccups, and then, in a chanting phrase, *do do sol do*, said, 'Here and now, boys; here and now, boys.'

The words pressed a trigger, and all of a sudden he remembered everything. Here was Pala, the forbidden island, the place no journalist had ever visited. And now must be the morning after the afternoon when he'd been fool enough to go sailing, alone, outside the harbour of Rendang-Lobo. He remembered it all – the white sail curved by the wind into the likeness of a huge magnolia petal, the water sizzling at the prow, the sparkle of diamonds on every wave crest, the troughs of wrinkled jade. And eastwards, across the Strait, what clouds, what prodigies of sculptured whiteness above the volcanoes of Pala! Sitting there at the tiller, he had caught himself singing – caught himself, incredibly, in the act of feeling unequivocally happy.

'"Three, three for the rivals",' he had declaimed into the wind.

'"Two, two for the lily-white boys, clothèd all in green-oh; One is one and all alone . . .'"

Yes, all alone. All alone on the enormous jewel of the sea.

'"And ever more shall be so".'

After which, needless to say, the thing that all the cautious and experienced yachtsmen had warned him against happened. The black squall out of nowhere, the sudden, senseless frenzy of wind and rain and waves . . .

'Here and now, boys,' chanted the bird. 'Here and now, boys.'

The really extraordinary thing was that he should be here, he reflected, under the trees and not out there, at the bottom of the Pala Strait or, worse, smashed to pieces at the foot of the cliffs. For even after he had managed, by sheer miracle, to take his sinking boat through the breakers and run her aground on the only sandy beach in all those miles of Pala's rock-bound coast – even then it wasn't over. The cliffs towered above him; but at the head of the cove there was a kind of headlong ravine where a little stream came down in a succession of filmy waterfalls, and there were trees and bushes growing between the walls of grey limestone. Six or seven hundred feet of rock climbing – in tennis shoes, and all the footholds slippery with water. And then, dear God! those snakes. The black one looped over the branch by which he was pulling himself up. And five minutes later, the huge green one coiled there on the ledge, just where he was preparing to step. Terror had been succeeded by a terror infinitely worse. The sight of the snake had made him start, made him violently withdraw his foot, and that sudden unconsidered movement had made him lose his balance. For a long sickening second, in the dreadful knowledge that this was the end, he had swayed on the brink, then fallen. Death, death, death. And then, with the noise of splintering wood in his ears he had found himself clinging to the branches of a small tree, his face scratched, his right knee bruised and bleeding, but alive. Painfully he had resumed his climbing. His knee hurt him excruciatingly; but he climbed on. There was no alternative. And then the light had begun to fail. In the end he was climbing almost in darkness, climbing by faith, climbing by sheer despair.

'Here and now, boys,' shouted the bird.

But Will Farnaby was neither here nor now. He was there on the rock face, he was then at the dreadful moment of falling. The dry leaves rustled beneath him; he was trembling. Violently, uncontrollably, he was trembling from head to foot.

ALDOUS HUXLEY, *Island* (1962).

TAKE OFF THAT BEARD
(1930)

IN the study Father Rothschild and Mr Outrage were plotting with enthusiasm. Lord Metroland was smoking a cigar and wondering how soon he could get away. He wanted to hear Mrs Ape and to have another look at those Angels. There was one with red hair. . . . Besides, all this statesmanship and foreign policy had always bored him. In his years in the Commons he had always liked a good scrap, and often thought a little wistfully of those orgies of competitive dissimulation in which he had risen to eminence. Even now, when some straightforward, easily intelligible subject was under discussion, such as poor people's wages or public art, he enjoyed from time to time making a sonorous speech to the Upper House. But this sort of thing was not at all in his line.

Suddenly Father Rothschild turned out the light.

'There's someone coming down the passage,' he said. 'Quick, get behind the curtains.'

'Really, Rothschild . . .' said Mr Outrage.

'I say . . .' said Lord Metroland.

'*Quick*,' said Father Rothschild.

The three statesmen hid themselves. Lord Metroland, still smoking, his head thrown back and his cigar erect. They heard the door open. The light was turned on. A match was struck. Then came the slight tinkle of the telephone as someone lifted the receiver.

'Central ten thousand,' said a slightly muffled voice.

'*Now*,' said Father Rothschild, and stepped through the curtain.

The bearded stranger who had excited his suspicions was standing at the table smoking one of Lord Metroland's cigars and holding the telephone.

'Oh, hullo,' he said, 'I didn't know you were here. Just

thought I'd use the telephone. So sorry. Won't disturb you. Jolly party, isn't it? Good-bye.'

'Stay exactly where you are,' said Father Rothschild, 'and take off that beard.'

'Damned if I do,' said the stranger crossly. 'It's no use talking to me as though I were one of your choir boys . . . you old *bully*.'

'Take off that beard,' said Father Rothschild.

'Take off that beard,' said Lord Metroland and the Prime Minister, emerging suddenly from behind the curtain.

This concurrence of Church and State, coming so unexpectedly after an evening of prolonged embarrassment, was too much for Simon.

'Oh, all right,' he said, 'if you *will* make such a *thing* about it . . . it hurts too frightfully, if you knew . . . it ought to be soaked in hot water . . . ooh . . . ow.'

He gave some tugs at the black curls, and bit by bit they came away.

'*There*,' he said. 'Now I should go and make Lady Throbbing take off her wig. . . . I should have a really jolly evening while you're about it, if I were you.'

'I seem to have over-estimated the gravity of the situation,' said Father Rothschild.

'Who is it, after all this?' said Mr Outrage. 'Where are those detectives? What does it all mean?'

'That,' said Father Rothschild bitterly, 'is Mr *Chatterbox*.'

'Never heard of him. I don't believe there is such a person. . . . *Chatterbox*, indeed . . . you make us hide behind a curtain and then you tell us that some young man in a false beard is called Chatterbox. Really, Rothschild . . .'

'Lord Balcairn,' said Lord Metroland, 'will you kindly leave my house immediately?'

'*Is* this young man called Chatterbox or is he not? . . . Upon my soul, I believe you're all crazy.'

'Oh yes, I'm going,' said Simon. 'You didn't think I was

going to go back to the party like this, did you? – or did you?'
Indeed, he looked very odd with little patches of black hair
still adhering to parts of his chin and cheeks.

'Lord Monomark is here this evening. I shall certainly inform him of your behaviour . . .'

'He writes for the papers,' Father Rothschild tried to explain to the Prime Minister.

'Well, damn it, so do I, but I don't wear a false beard and
call myself Chatterbox. . . . I simply do not understand what
has happened. . . . Where are those detectives? . . . Will no
one explain? . . . *You treat me like a child,*' he said. It was all
like one of those Cabinet meetings, when they all talked about
something he didn't understand and paid no attention to
him.

Father Rothschild led him away, and attempted with
almost humiliating patience and tact to make clear to him
some of the complexities of modern journalism.

'I don't believe a word of it,' the Prime Minister kept saying. 'It's all humbug. You're keeping something back. . . .
Chatterbox, indeed.'

Simon Balcairn was given his hat and coat and shown to the
door. The crowd round the awning had dispersed. It was still
raining. He walked back to his little flat in Bourdon Street.
The rain washed a few of the remaining locks from his face;
it dripped down his collar.

They were washing a car outside his front door; he crept
between it and his dustbin, fitted his latchkey in the lock and
went upstairs. His flat was like *Chez Espinosa* – all oilcloth and
Lalique glass; there were some enterprising photographs by
David Lennox, a gramophone (on the instalment system) and
numberless cards of invitation on the mantelpiece. His bath
towel was where he had left it on his bed.

Simon went to the ice box in the kitchen and chipped off
some ice. Then he made himself a cocktail. Then he went to
the telephone.

'Central ten thousand . . .' he said. '. . . Give me Mrs Brace. Hullo, this is Balcairn.'

'Well . . . gotcher story?'

'Oh yes, I've got my story, only this isn't gossip, it's news – front page. You'll have to fill up the Chatterbox page on Espinosa's.'

'Hell!'

'Wait till you see the story. . . . Hullo, give me news, will you. . . . This is Balcairn. Put on one of the boys to take this down, will you? . . . ready? All right.'

At his glass-topped table, sipping his cocktail, Simon Balcairn dictated his last story.

'*Scenes of wild religious enthusiasm, comma, reminiscent of a negro camp-meeting in Southern America, comma, broke out in the heart of Mayfair yesterday evening at the party given for the famous American Revivalist Mrs Ape by the Viscountess Metroland, formerly the Hon. Mrs Beste-Chetwynd, at her historic mansion, Postmaster House, stop. The magnificent ballroom can never have enshrined a more brilliant assembly . . .*'

It was his swan-song. Lie after monstrous lie bubbled up in his brain.

'*. . . The Hon. Agatha Runcible joined Mrs Ape among the orchids and led the singing, tears coursing down her face . . .*'

Excitement spread at the *Excess* office. The machines were stopped. The night staff of reporters, slightly tipsy, as always at that hour, stood over the stenographer as he typed. The compositors snatched the sheets of copy as they came. The sub-editors began ruthlessly cutting and scrapping; they suppressed important political announcements, garbled the evidence at a murder trial, reduced the dramatic criticism to one caustic paragraph, to make room for Simon's story.

It came through 'hot and strong, as nice as mother makes it', as one of them remarked.

'Little Lord Fauntleroy's on a good thing at last,' said another.

'What-ho,' said a third appreciatively.

'. . . barely had *Lady Everyman finished before the Countess of Throbbing rose to confess her sins, and in a voice broken with emotion disclosed the hitherto unverified details of the parentage of the present Earl . . .*'

'Tell Mr Edwardes to look up photographs of all three of 'em,' said the assistant news editor.

'. . . *The Marquess of Vanburgh, shaken by sobs of contrition. . . . Mrs Panrast, singing feverishly. . . . Lady Anchorage with downcast eyes . . .*'

'. . . *The Archbishop of Canterbury, who up to now had remained unmoved by the general emotion, then testified that at Eton in the 'eighties he and Sir James Brown . . .*'

'. . . *the Duchess of Stayle next threw down her emerald and diamond tiara, crying "a Guilt Offering", an example which was quickly followed by the Countess of Circumference and Lady Brown, until a veritable rain of precious stones fell on to the parquet flooring, heirlooms of priceless value rolling among Tecla pearls and Chanel diamonds. A blank cheque fluttered from the hands of the Maharajah of Pukkapore . . .*'

It made over two columns, and when Simon finally rang off, after receiving the congratulations of his colleagues, he was for the first time in his journalistic experience perfectly happy about his work. He finished the watery dregs of the cocktail shaker and went into the kitchen. He shut the door and the window and opened the door of the gas oven. Inside it was very black and dirty and smelled of meat. He spread a sheet of newspaper on the lowest tray and lay down, resting his head on it. Then he noticed that by some mischance he had chosen Vanburgh's gossip-page in the *Morning Despatch*. He put in another sheet. (There were crumbs on the floor.) Then he turned on the gas. It came surprisingly with a loud roar; the wind of it stirred his hair and the remaining particles of his beard. At first he held his breath. Then he thought that was silly and gave a sniff. The sniff made him cough, and coughing made him breathe, and breathing made him feel very ill; but soon he fell into a coma and presently died.

So the last Earl of Balcairn went, as they say, to his fathers (who had fallen in many lands and for many causes, as the eccentricities of British Foreign Policy and their own wandering natures had directed them; at Acre and Agincourt and Killiecrankie, in Egypt and America. One had been picked white by fishes as the tides rolled him among the tree-tops of a submarine forest; some had grown black and unfit for consideration under tropical suns; while many of them lay in marble tombs of extravagant design).

EVELYN WAUGH, *Vile Bodies* (1930).

PURPOSE OF WALK
(1939)

THREE nights later at about eight o'clock I was alone in Nassau Street, a district frequented by the prostitute class, when I perceived a ramrod in a cloth cap on the watch at the corner of Kildare Street. As I passed I saw that the man was Kelly. Large spits were about him on the path and carriageway. I poked him in a manner offensive to propriety and greeted his turned face with a facetious ejaculation:

How is the boy! I said.

My hard man, he answered.

I took cigarettes from my pocket and lit one for each of us, frowning. With my face averted and a hardness in my voice, I put this question in a casual manner:

Anything doing?

O God no, he said. Not at all, man. Come away for a walk somewhere.

I agreed. Purporting to be an immoral character, I accompanied him on a long walk through the environs of Irishtown,

Sandymount and Sydney Parade, returning by Haddington Road and the banks of the canal.

Purpose of walk: Discovery and embracing of virgins.

We attained nothing on our walk that was relevant to the purpose thereof but we filled up the loneliness of our souls with the music of our two voices, dog-racing, betting and offences against chastity being the several subjects of our discourse. We walked many miles together on other nights on similar missions – following matrons, accosting strangers, representing to married ladies that we were their friends, and gratuitously molesting members of the public. One night we were followed in our turn by a member of the police force attired in civilian clothing. On the advice of Kelly we hid ourselves in the interior of a church until he had gone. I found that the walking was beneficial to my health.

The people who attended the College had banded themselves into many private associations, some purely cultural and some concerned with the arrangement and conduct of ball games. The cultural societies were diverse in their character and aims and measured their vitality by the number of hooligans and unprincipled persons they attracted to their deliberations. Some were devoted to English letters, some to Irish letters and some to the study and advancement of the French language. The most important was a body that met every Saturday night for the purpose of debate and disputation; its meetings, however, were availed of by many hundreds of students for shouting, horseplay, singing and the use of words, actions and gestures contrary to the usages of Christians. The society met in an old disused lecture theatre capable of accommodating the seats of about two hundred and fifty persons. Outside the theatre there was a spacious lobby or anteroom and it was here that the rough boys would gather and make their noises. One gas-jet was the means of affording light in the lobby and when a paroxysm of fighting and roaring would be at its height, the light would be extinguished as if by a supernatural or diabolic agency and the effect of the darkness in such circumstances afforded me many moments of physical and spiritual anxiety, for it seemed to me that the majority of the persons present were possessed by unclean spirits. The lighted rectangle of the doorway to the debate-hall was regarded by many persons not only as a receptacle for the foul and discordant speeches which they addressed to it, but also for many objects of a worthless nature – for example spent cigarette ends, old shoes, the hats of friends, parcels of damp horse dung, wads of soiled sacking and discarded articles of ladies' clothing not infrequently the worse for wear. Kelly on one occasion confined articles of his landlady's small-clothes in a neatly done parcel of brown paper and sent it through a friend to the visiting chairman, who opened it *coram populo* (in the presence of the assembly), and examined the articles fastidiously as if searching among them for an explanatory note, being unable to appraise their character instantaneously for two reasons, his failing sight and his station as a bachelor.

Result of overt act mentioned: Uproar and disorder.

FLANN O'BRIEN, *At Swim-Two-Birds* (1939).

LIBERTY HALL
(1944)

JUST then the Beeders came in, Sir William and Lady. Big man with a bald head and monkey fur on the back of his hands. Voice like a Liverpool dray on a rumbling bridge. Charming manners. Little bow. Beaming smile. Lady tall, slender, Spanish eyes, brown skin, thin nose. Greco hands. Collector's piece. I must have those hands, I thought, arms probably too skinny but the head and torso are one piece. I should need them together.

Lady Beeder was even more charming than her husband. 'I'm so delighted, Mr Gulley Jimson – I know you hardly ever pay visits. I did not dare to ask you – but I hoped,' and she asked me to tea. People like that can afford it. Nothing to them to send their cushions to the cleaners.

What I like about the rich is the freedom and the friendliness. Christian atmosphere. Liberty Hall. Everything shared because there is too much. All forgiveness because it's no trouble. Drop their Dresden cups on the fireplace and they smile. They are anxious only that you should not be embarrassed, and spoil the party. That's their aim. Comfort and joy. Peace on earth. Goodwill all round.

When I first met Hickson, I could have kissed his beautiful boots, I loved them for themselves, works of art, and he was so full of goodwill that it came off him like the smell of his soap, linen, hair cream, tooth wash, shaving lotion, eyewash and digestive mixture. Like the glow of a firefly. Calling for something. Until he got burnt up, poor chap. A flash in the dark. For, of course, the rich do find it hard to get through the needle's eye, out of heaven. And to spend all your life in paradise is a bit flat. Millionaires deserve not only our love but our pity. It is a Christian act to be nice to them.

When Lady Beeder asked me if my tea was all right, I said, 'Yes, your ladyship. Everything is all right. I am enjoying myself so much that you will have to throw me downstairs to get rid of me. I think you and Sir William are two of the nicest people I've ever met. You have lovely manners and lovely things, a lovely home, and very good tea. I suppose this tea costs four and sixpence a pound, it is worth it. Genius is priceless.'

The Professor kept coughing and making faces at me, but I wasn't afraid of embarrassing nice people. I knew they would be used to unfortunate remarks. Rich people are like royalty. They can't afford to be touchy. Richesse oblige. And, in fact, they kept on putting me at my ease; and paying me compliments all the time. And when I told them how I had been turned out of my studio by the Cokers, they said they hoped that I would come and stay over the week-end, to keep the Professor company while they were away.

'I'm sorry we can't offer you a bed beyond Monday, but we have only two bedrooms.'

'I could sleep on the sofa,' I said.

'Oh, Mr Jimson, but we couldn't allow you to be so uncomfortable.'

'Then why shouldn't Sir William sleep with the Professor and I'll sleep with her ladyship. You can count me as a lady – at sixty-seven.'

Alabaster turned green and coughed as if he was going into consumption. But I knew I couldn't shock cultured people like the Beeders. They get past being shocked before they are out of school, just as they get over religion and other unexpected feelings.

'A very good idea,' said Sir William, laughing. 'I am greatly complimented,' said the lady, 'but I'm afraid I should keep you awake. I'm such a bad sleeper.'

'Perhaps,' said Sir William, getting up, 'Mr Jimson would like to see some of your work, my dear.'

'Oh no, Bill, please.'

'But, Flora, that last thing of yours was really remarkable – I'm not suggesting that it was up to professional standards. But as a quick impression –'

'Oh no,' said her ladyship, 'Mr Jimson would laugh at my poor efforts.'

But of course they both wanted me to see her work and say that it was wonderful. And why not? They were so kind, so good.

'Why,' I said, 'amateurs do much the most interesting work.'

The Professor began to hop about like a dry pea on the stove. He coughed and made faces at me, meaning 'Be careful, be tactful, remember these people are used to luxury of all kinds.'

But I laughed and said. 'Don't you worry, Professor, I'm not pulling her ladyship's leg. I wouldn't do such a thing. I have too much respect for that charming limb.'

Sir William got out an easel and a big portfolio, in red morocco with a monogram in gold. And he took out a big double mount, of the best Bristol board, cut by a real expert, with a dear little picture in the middle. Sky with clouds, grass with trees, water with reflection, cows with horns, cottage with smoke and passing labourer with fork, blue shirt, old hat.

'Lovely,' I said, puffing my cigar. 'Only wants a title – what will you call it? Supper time. You can see that chap is hungry.'

'I think the sky is not too bad,' said she. 'I just laid it down and left it.'

'That's the way,' I said, 'Keep it fresh. Get the best colours and let 'em do the rest. Charming.'

'I'm so glad you like it,' said she. And she was so nice that I thought I should tell her something. 'Of course,' I said, 'the sky is just a leetle bit chancy, looks a bit accidental, like when the cat spills its breakfast.'

'I *think* I see,' said her ladyship, and Sir William said, 'Of course, Mr Jimson, you do get skies like that in Dorset. It's really a typical Dorset sky.'

I saw the Professor winking at me so hard that his face was like a concertina with a hole in it. But I didn't care. For I knew that I could say what I liked to real amateurs and they wouldn't care a damn. They'd only think, 'These artists are a lot of jealous stick-in-the-muds. They can't admire any art but their own. Which is simply dry made-up stuff, without any truth or real feeling for Nature.'

'Yes,' I said, 'that is a typical sky. Just an accident. That's what I mean. What you've got there is just a bit of nothing at all – nicely splashed on to the best Whatman with an expensive camel-hair –'

'I *think* I see what you mean,' said her ladyship. 'Yes, I *do* see – it's most interesting.'

And she said something to Sir William with her left eyelash, which caused him to shut his mouth and remove the picture so suddenly that it was like the movies. And to pop on the next. A nice little thing of clouds with sky, willows with grass, river with wet water, barge with mast and two ropes, horse with tail, man with back.

'Now that's lovely,' I said. 'Perfect. After de Windt. Look at the wiggle of the mast in the water. What technique.'

'My wife has made a special study of watercolour technique,' said Sir William. 'A very difficult medium.'

'Terrible,' I said. 'But her ladyship has mastered it. She's only got to forget it.'

'I *think* I see what Mr Jimson means,' says she. 'Yes, cleverness is a danger . . .'

And she looked at me so sweetly that I could have hugged her. A perfect lady. Full of forbearance towards this nasty dirty old man with his ignorant prejudices.

'That's it,' I said. 'It's the jaws of death. Look at me. One of the cleverest painters who ever lived. Nobody ever had anything like my dexterity, except Rubens on a good day. I could show you an eye – a woman's eye, from my brush, that beats anything I've ever seen by Rubens. A little miracle of brush work. And if I hadn't been lucky I might have spent the rest of my life doing conjuring tricks to please the millionaires, and the professors. But I escaped. God knows how. I fell off the tram. I lost my ticket and my virtue. Why, your ladyship, a lot of my recent stuff is not much better, technically, than any young lady can do after six lessons at a good school. Heavy-handed, stupid-looking daubery. Only difference is that it's about something – it's an experience, and all this amateur stuff is like farting Annie Laurie through a keyhole. It may be clever but is it worth the trouble? What I say is, why not do some real work, your ladyship? Use your loaf, I mean your brain. Do some thinking. Sit down and ask yourself what's it all about.'

And both of them, looking at me with such Christian benevolence that I felt ready to tell them almost the truth, went off together.

'But, Mr Jimson, don't you think – of course, I'm not a professional – that the intellectual approach to art is the great danger.'

'Destructive of true artistic feeling,' Sir William rumbled. 'Don't you think, Mr Jimson, that the greatness of the French impressionists like Manet and Monet was perhaps founded on their rejection of the classical rules?'

'Oh Lord,' I said. 'Listen to them. Oh God, these poor dears – and didn't Manet and Monet talk about their theories of art until the sky rained pink tears and the grass turned purple – didn't Pissarro chop the trees into little bits of glass? And Seurat put his poor old mother through the sausage machine and roll her into linoleum. What do you think Cézanne was playing at, noughts and crosses, like a Royal Academy portrait merchant, fourteen noble pans in exchange for a K.B.E.? Jee-sus,' I said; for they were so nice and polite, the lambs, that they didn't care a damn what I said. It passed right over them like the brass of a Salvation band hitting the dome of St Paul's. They were so rich and Christian that they forgave everybody before he spoke and everything before it happened, so long as it didn't happen to them. 'Jee-minny Christy,' I said. 'What you think I been doing all my life – playing tiddly winks with little Willie's first colour-box? Why friends,' I appealed to their better halves, 'what do you see before you, a lunatic with lice in his shirt and bats in his clock' (this was for her ladyship on the maternal side), 'a poodle-faking crook that's spent fifty years getting nothing for nothing and a kick up below for interest on the investment' (this was for Sir William on the side of business common sense), 'or somebody that knows something about his job.'

Her ladyship and Sir William both smiled and laid their hands on my arm.

'Dear Mr Jimson,' said she, 'don't think I don't agree with every word. I can't say how grateful I am –'

'A great privilege,' Sir William rumbled, 'and believe me, we know how to appreciate it. Yes, most valuable and illuminating.'

'But dear me,' said her ladyship, 'it's nearly half-past eight.'

'Good God,' I said, 'I haven't got in the way of your dinner.'

'Not at all,' said Sir William. 'We dine at any time.'

'Perhaps Mr Jimson will stay to dinner,' said she.

And I stayed to dinner. I knew it would be good. The rich, God bless them, are supporters of all the arts, bootmaking, dressmaking, cookery, bridge, passing the time of day. We had seven courses and six bottles. But Sir William, poor chap, was a teetotaller and his wife drank only hock for the figure. A half bottle for half a figure. So the Professor and I shared the rest. He had a glass of claret and a suck of port, I had wine.

JOYCE CARY, *The Horse's Mouth* (1944).

THE PROPHET AND THE LOCALS
(1952)

THOUGH Bernard was instinctively distrusted by the local gentry, as, with the disappearance of the last few estates, the mixed collection of commuting civil servants, barristers, and stockbrokers, and a smaller intermingling of local farmers felt themselves to be, they yet enjoyed the presence of a public figure among them. If only he had lived up to his position, had specialized in good food, a good cellar, and a 'philosophy of life' that took you above everyday things, they would not have minded his talking over their heads, would even have welcomed the reassertion of their prejudices in terms that were a bit out of their depth. They would have liked affirmation of their private conviction that the grievances and grudges they felt against a changing social order should be considered the reawakening of spiritual values. As for the faint rumblings of sexual unorthodoxy, many of them would have been glad to evidence breadth of mind, so long as the testimony was not asked too publicly. 'Spenlow was telling me the courts are choc-a-bloc with these cases every day, wasting the time of the police. If it wasn't for this damned Nonconformist government the law would have been changed long ago,' they would have said; or their wives, 'Darling, don't be so egotistical, just because you like one thing. . . . It's pathetic, really, more than anything else.' If only he wouldn't pour out all this undergraduate rubbish, would be a little more responsible, in fact. Nevertheless, almost all of them remembered occasions when they had 'got on so well' with him, when it had been 'amazing what an intelligent interest he took' or 'how amusingly he could sum the others up'.

It was a young farmer, one of those especially convinced of an understanding with Bernard, who now brought public attention to the unfortunate topic of Vardon Hall. 'Congratulations, sir,' he said. 'When do you hold the Victory celebrations?' Bernard registered the penalties one incurred for showing off one's powers with the shy. He remembered that the 'sir' had seemed to him a pathetic imitation of public-school behaviour, gleaned from out-of-date novels. He also remembered flattering the young man by entwining his stories of rags at the local agricultural college with his own Cambridge reminiscences. A charming, if rather pathetic, snob, he had thought him. Now, he just seemed a snob. As for the boyishness, Bernard now could see only an oaf. As always, however, his conscience turned in reverse. His own snobbery seemed far more disgusting. He sat down by the young man's side in expiation.

'Oh,' Bernard smiled, 'it's a victory of the mind, you know;

they're only celebrated by clean living and high thinking, unfortunately.' He was gratified by the farmer's smile to note how exactly he had remembered the level of humour to which the young man could aspire. He evidently believed that this was in a range beyond the reach of the rest of the company, though Bernard could have told him that he was wrong. But then the more intelligent men present probably had less charm. In any case if they both got pleasure out of the fake. ... Warming up to the encounter, he pushed Vardon Hall and all that concerned himself aside with grinning modesty. 'What about the Morris Eight?' he asked. 'Do you still feel doubtful?'

'Oh yes,' said the boy. 'It's definitely no use buying a new car unless you can go into the fifteen-hundred class. If I was going for anything, I'd go for an old Rolls. In any case, *our* old bus will get by with a new engine . . .'

But the diversion was not to succeed. The topic of Vardon Hall was too close to the hearts of everyone. It was the latest symbol of the war they were waging against a changing world. The war that, like the Cold War, was so frightening because so unfamiliar, so bound up with the ordinary process of living. One day the earth would tremble underneath your feet and nothing happened, the next day would seem so calm and yet the social seismograph registered an earthquake.

ANGUS WILSON, *Hemlock and After* (1952).

INCIDENT IN VIETNAM
(1955)

THE weeks moved on, but somehow I hadn't yet found myself a new flat. It wasn't that I hadn't time. The annual crisis of the war had passed again: the hot wet *crachin* had settled on the north: the French were out of Hoa Binh, the rice-campaign was over in Tonkin and the opium-campaign in Laos. Dominguez could cover easily all that was needed in the south. At last I did drag myself to see one apartment in a so-called modern building (Paris Exhibition 1934?) up at the other end of the rue Catinat beyond the Continental Hotel. It was the Saigon *pied-à-terre* of a rubber planter who was going home. He wanted to sell it lock, stock, and barrel. I have always wondered what the barrels contain: as for the stock, there were a large number of engravings from the Paris Salon between 1880 and 1900. Their highest common factor was a big-bosomed woman with an extraordinary hair-do and gauzy draperies which somehow always exposed the great cleft buttocks and hid the field of battle. In the bathroom the planter had been rather more daring with his reproductions of Rops.

'You like art?' I asked and he smirked back at me like a fellow conspirator. He was fat with a little black moustache and insufficient hair.

'My best pictures are in Paris,' he said.

There was an extraordinary tall ash-tray in the living-room made like a naked woman with a bowl in her hair, and there were china ornaments of naked girls embracing tigers, and one very odd one of a girl stripped to the waist riding a bicycle. In the bedroom facing his enormous bed was a great glazed oil painting of two girls sleeping together. I asked him the price of his apartment without his collection, but he would not agree to separate the two.

'You are not a collector?' he asked.

'Well, no.'

'I have some books also,' he said, 'which I would throw in, though I intended to take these back to France.' He unlocked a glass-fronted book-case and showed me his library – there were expensive illustrated editions of *Aphrodite* and *Nana*, there was *La Garçonne*, and even several Paul de Kocks. I was tempted to ask him whether he would sell himself with his collection: he went with them: he was period too. He said, 'If you live alone in the tropics a collection is company.'

I thought of Phuong just because of her complete absence. So it always is: when you escape to a desert the silence shouts in your ear.

'I don't think my paper would allow me to buy an art-collection.'

He said, 'It would not, of course, appear on the receipt.'

I was glad Pyle had not seen him: the man might have lent his own features to Pyle's imaginary 'old colonialist', who was repulsive enough without him. When I came out it was nearly half past eleven and I went down as far as the Pavillon for a glass of iced beer. The Pavillon was a coffee centre for European and American women and I was confident that I would not see Phuong there. Indeed I knew exactly where she would be at this time of day – she was not a girl to break her habits, and so, coming from the planter's apartment, I had crossed the road to avoid the milk-bar where at this time of day she had her chocolate malt. Two young American girls sat at the next table, neat and clean in the heat, scooping up ice-cream. They each had a bag slung on the left shoulder and the bags were identical, with brass eagle badges. Their legs were identical too, long and slender, and their noses, just a shade tilted, and they were eating their ice-cream with concentration as though they were making an experiment in the college laboratory. I wondered whether they were Pyle's colleagues: they were charming, and I wanted to send them home, too. They finished their ices and one looked at her watch. 'We'd better be going,' she said, 'to be on the safe side.' I wondered idly what appointment they had.

'Warren said we mustn't stay later than eleven-twenty-five.'

'It's past that now.'

'It would be exciting to stay. I don't know what it's all about, do you?'

'Not exactly, but Warren said better not.'

'Do you think it's a demonstration?'

'I've seen so many demonstrations,' the other said wearily, like a tourist glutted with churches. She rose and laid on their table the money for the ices. Before going she looked around the café, and the mirrors caught her profile at every freckled angle. There was only myself left and a dowdy middle-aged Frenchwoman who was carefully and uselessly making up her face. Those two hardly needed make-up, the quick dash of a lipstick, a comb through the hair. For a moment her glance had rested on me – it was not like a woman's glance, but a man's, very straightforward, speculating on some course of action. Then she turned quickly to her companion. 'We'd better be off.' I watched them idly as they went out side by side into the sun-splintered street. It was impossible to conceive either of them a prey to untidy passion: they did not belong to rumpled sheets and the sweat of sex. Did they take deodorants to bed with them? I found myself for a moment envying them their sterilized world, so different from this world that I inhabited – which suddenly inexplicably broke in pieces. Two of the mirrors on the wall flew at me and collapsed half-way. The dowdy Frenchwoman was on her knees in a wreckage of chairs and tables. Her compact lay open and unhurt in my lap and oddly enough I sat exactly where I had sat before, although my table had joined the wreckage around the Frenchwoman. A curious garden-sound filled the café: the regular drip of a fountain, and looking at the bar I saw rows of smashed bottles which let out their contents in a multi-coloured stream – the red of porto, the orange of cointreau, the green of chartreuse, the cloudy yellow of pastis, across the floor of the café. The Frenchwoman sat up and calmly looked around for her compact. I gave it her and she thanked me formally, sitting on the floor. I realized that I didn't hear her very well. The explosion had been so close that my ear-drums had still to recover from the pressure.

I thought rather petulantly, 'Another joke with plastics: what does Mr Heng expect me to write now?' but when I got into the Place Garnier, I realized by the heavy clouds of smoke that this was no joke. The smoke came from the cars burning in the car-park in front of the national theatre, bits of cars were scattered over the square, and a man without his legs lay twitching at the edge of the ornamental gardens. People were crowding in from the rue Catinat, from the Boulevard Bonnard. The sirens of police-cars, the bells of the ambulances and fire-engines came at one remove to my shocked ear-drums. For one moment I had forgotten that Phuong must have been in the milk-bar on the other side of the square. The smoke lay between. I couldn't see through.

I stepped out into the square and a policeman stopped me. They had formed a cordon round the edge to prevent the crowd increasing, and already the stretchers were beginning to emerge. I implored the policeman in front of me, 'Let me across. I have a friend . . .'

'Stand back.' he said. 'Everyone here has friends.'

He stood on one side to let a priest through, and I tried to follow the priest, but he pulled me back. I said, 'I am the Press,' and searched in vain for the wallet in which I had my card, but I couldn't find it: had I come out that day without it? I said, 'At least tell me what happened to the milk-bar': the smoke was clearing and I tried to see, but the crowd between was too great. He said something I didn't catch.

'What did you say?'

He repeated, 'I don't know. Stand back. You are blocking the stretchers.'

Could I have dropped my wallet in the Pavillon? I turned to go back and there was Pyle. He exclaimed, 'Thomas.'

'Pyle,' I said, 'for Christ's sake, where's your Legation pass? We've got to get across. Phuong's in the milk-bar.'

'No, no,' he said.

'Pyle, she is. She always goes there. At eleven-thirty. We've got to find her.'

'She isn't there, Thomas.'

'How do you know? Where's your card?'

'I warned her not to go.'

I turned back to the policeman, meaning to throw him to one side and make a run for it across the square: he might shoot: I didn't care – and then the word 'warn' reached my consciousness. I took Pyle by the arm. 'Warn?' I said. 'What do you mean "warn"?'

'I told her to keep away this morning.'

The pieces fell together in my mind. 'And Warren?' I said. 'Who's Warren? He warned those girls too.'

'I don't understand.'

'There mustn't be any American casualties, must there?' An ambulance forced its way up the rue Catinat into the square, and the policeman who stopped me moved to one side to let it through. The policeman beside him was engaged in an argument. I pushed Pyle forward and ahead of me into the square before we could be stopped.

We were among a congregation of mourners. The police could prevent others entering the square; they were powerless to clear the square of the survivors and the first-comers. The doctors were too busy to attend to the dead, and so the dead were left to their owners, for one can own the dead as one owns a chair. A woman sat on the ground with what was left of her baby in her lap; with a kind of modesty she had covered it with her straw peasant hat. She was still and silent, and what struck me most in the square was the silence. It was like a church I had once visited during Mass – the only sounds came from those who served, except where here and there the Europeans wept and implored and fell silent again as though shamed by the modesty, patience and propriety of the East. The legless torso at the edge of the garden still twitched, like a chicken which has lost its head. From the man's shirt, he had probably been a trishaw-driver.

Pyle said, 'It's awful.' He looked at the wet on his shoes and said in a thick voice, 'What's that?'

'Blood,' I said. 'Haven't you ever seen it before?'

He said, 'I must get them cleaned before I see the Minister.' I don't think he knew what he was saying. He was seeing a real war for the first time: he had punted down into Phat Diem in a kind of schoolboy dream, and anyway in his eyes soldiers didn't count.

'You see what a drum of Diolacton can do,' I said, 'in the wrong hands.' I forced him, with my hand on his shoulder, to look around. I said, 'This is the hour when the place is always full of women and children – it's the shopping hour. Why choose that of all hours?'

He said weakly. 'There was to have been a parade.'

'And you hoped to catch a few colonels. But the parade was cancelled yesterday, Pyle.'

'I didn't know.'

'Didn't know!' I pushed him into a patch of blood where a stretcher had lain. 'You ought to be better informed.'

'I was out of town,' he said, looking down at his shoes. 'They should have called it off.'

'And missed the fun?' I asked him. 'Do you expect General Thé to lose his demonstration? This is better than a parade. Women and children are news, and soldiers aren't, in a war. This will hit the world's Press. You've put General Thé on the map all right, Pyle. You've got the Third Force and National Democracy all over your right shoe. Go home to Phuong and tell her about your heroic dead – there are a few dozen less of her country people to worry about.'

A small fat priest scampered by, carrying something on a dish under a napkin. Pyle had been silent a long while, and I had nothing more to say. Indeed I had said too much. He looked white and beaten and ready to faint, and I thought, 'What's the good? he'll always be innocent, you can't blame the innocent, they are always guiltless. All you can do is control them or eliminate them. Innocence is a kind of insanity.'

He said, 'Thé wouldn't have done this. I'm sure he wouldn't. Somebody deceived him. The Communists . . .'

He was impregnably armoured by his good intentions and his ignorance. I left him standing in the square and went on up the rue Catinat to where the hideous pink Cathedral blocked the way. Already people were flocking in: it must have been a comfort to them to be able to pray for the dead to the dead.

Unlike them, I had reason for thankfulness, for wasn't Phuong alive? Hadn't Phuong been 'warned'? But what I remembered was the torso in the square, the baby on its mother's lap. They had not been warned: they had not been sufficiently important. And if the parade had taken place would they not have been there just the same, out of curiosity, to see the soldiers, and hear the speakers, and throw the flowers? A two-hundred-pound bomb does not discriminate. How many dead colonels justify a child's or a trishaw driver's death when you are building a national democratic front? I stopped a motor-trishaw and told the driver to take me to the Quai Mytho.

GRAHAM GREENE, *The Quiet American* (1955).

ON THE TIP
(1961)

EIGHT-WHEELED lorries came by the motorworks and followed each other towards the high flat tongue of land that had been raised by months of tipping and was slowly covering a nondescript area of reedgrass and water. From nearly every precipice men walked to where they hoped the loads would be dumped. Empty sacks flapped over their shoulders, and they called to each other, waving sticks and rakes. Brian, having already used his judgement, was scraping into a heap of swarf and scrap steel picked clean days ago, but which still gave off a pleasant smell of aluminium shavings and carbolic, oil and the brass dust of big machines his father had sometimes worked. He kept one eye on the rapid movements of his flimsy rake, and the other on a small pile of wood covered with a sack nearby. Bert had promised to be at the tips later, and Brian hoped he'd come soon to get something from the four lorries – and the convoy of high-sided horsecarts trailing at walking pace behind.

'Where's it comin' from, mate?' Brian asked. Steelpins were popped out and the back ascended slowly. Half a dozen men, waiting for the avalanche of promise, watched the heavy handle being worked by a driver who rarely spoke to the scrapers, as if he were ashamed of being set within the luxurious world of hard labour. Even uncommitting banter was rare, and the scrapers looked on, waiting, never offering to help so as to get the stuff rolling sooner to their feet. 'Prospect Street, young 'un,' the driver answered.

Them old houses. A few bug-eaten laths. Wallpaper, dust and brick were already streaming down the bank, filling up oil-stained swamp-pools and crushing rusty tins at the bottom. A piece of wall made a splash like a bomb, and that was that. The back was wound up, and the lorry driven off. Brian rubbed pieces of cold water from his ear. Men were scraping systematically at the rammel, though expecting little from those poverty-stricken, condemned, fallen-down rabbit-holes on Prospect Street. Yet you never knew: such exercise in hope may gain a few brass curtain rings, a yard of decayed copper-wire (from which the flex could be burned over the flames) or perhaps a piece of lead piping if it was a lucky day. A man whistled as he worked: speculation ran too high for speech.

Brian, having netted a few spars of wood, rubbed grit from his knees and stood up, gripped by a black, end-of-the-world hopelessness: Please, God, send a good tip, he said to himself. If you do I'll say Our Father. 'What's up, kid?' Agger called from the top of the bank.

'I'm fed up,' Brian said gloomily.

Men looked around, grinning or laughing. 'Are yer 'ungry?' Brian said no, scraped a few half-bricks to reveal a fair-sized noggin of wood. 'Sure? There's some bread and am in my coat pocket if y'are,' Agger said.

'No thanks. I've got some snap as well.'

'What yer fed up for then?' He couldn't answer. Like the old man often said: Think yourself lucky you've got a crust o' bread in your fist. Then you can tek that sour look off your clock. But Brian couldn't. 'What does your dad do?' Agger wanted to know.

'He's out o' work' – already forgetting despair.

Agger laughed. 'He's got a lot o' cumpny.' Agger came on the tips every morning – in time for the first loads at nine – pushing an old carriage-pram, an antique enormous model that may once have housed some spoonfed Victorian baby and been pushed by a well-trimmed maid. There was no rubber on the wheels; all paint had long since blistered from its sides, and a makeshift piece of piping served for a handle. Another valued possession of Agger's was a real rake unearthed from a load of brick and tile tippings, an ornate brass-handled tool of the scraper's trade with which he always expected to pull up some treasure, good reaching under the muck for good, but which he used with relish whether it made him rich or not. Other scrapers envied it: Brian once heard one say: 'Lend's your rake five minutes, Agger. I'll just get some wood for the fire.' The men around stopped talking, and Agger stayed mute: just looked at the man – a faint touch of contempt at such ignorance of the rules of life – though the blank look was forced on to his face mainly because the request was unexpected, and unanswerable if he was to maintain his sharp gipsy-like dignity. The man got up and walked away, beyond the fire's warmth. 'The daft fucker,' Agger said loudly. 'What does he tek me for? He wants chasing off the bleddy premises.'

Agger often referred to the tips as 'the premises' – a high-flown name as if 'premises' was the one word and only loot he had carried off under his coat from some short term of employment – at being ordered off them himself by a despairing gaffer. 'Premises' to Agger was synonymous with some remote platform of life where order might have been created from the confusion within himself, if only he could be respected as king for some qualities he hadn't got – but wanted because he knew them to exist.

Winter and summer he wore a black overcoat that reached to his ankles and flapped around his sapling body. On the morning when his weekly gatherings had been sold to the scrapshop for a few shillings, each deep pocket of his coat held a quart bottle of tea, panniers that steadied the folds of an otherwise voluminous garment. Each morning he coaxed a fire from the abundant surface of the tip, stoked it to a beacon with old oil cloth, tar-paper and arms of brackenish wood that had laid between the floors and walls of back-to-back houses during generations both of people and bugs.

On fine days, Brian noticed, some scrapers worked little, stood talking by the fire, and only ran madly with coats waving when a lorry came; others scraped industriously every minute of the day whether there was a fresh tip or not, working solidified rubble on the off-chance of finding something that might have been missed. Brian belonged to the latter sort, searching the most unpromising loads because hope was a low-burning intoxication that never left him.

While the damp-wind – seemingly foiled by jersey and coat – concentrated on Brian's face, he forgot it was also reaching into his body. He whistled a tune through a mixture of brick, wood-chippings and scraps of slate, feeling snatched only when the division between an unreal cotton-wool dreamland and the scratches on his numbed fingers broke down and flooded him with a larger sensation: 'snatched' – eyes and face muscles showing what the innermost body felt even though he hadn't been aware of it, perished through and through, so that a blazing fire would only bring smarting eyes and a skin thicker though not warmer.

Agger worked nearby, cleverly wrapped up and more impervious to cold because he had been on the tips longer than anyone else – straight from Flanders at twenty, he said. The useless slaughter of employable sinews had crushed his faith in guidance from men 'above' him, so that he preferred the tips even when there had been a choice. Sometimes he'd gaze into the quiet glass-like water of the nearby canal and sing to himself – a gay up-and-down tune without words – punctuating his neanderthal quatrains with a handful of stones by aiming one with some viciousness into the water, watching the rings of its impact collide and disappear at the bank before breaking out again into another verse that came from some unexplored part of him. Born of a breaking-point, his loneliness was a brain-flash at the boundary of his earthly stress. Still young-looking, though lacking the jauntiness of youth, perhaps out of weakness he had seen the end too near the beginning, had grafted his body and soul into a long life on the tips even before his youth was finished. The impasse he lived in had compensations however, was the sort that made friends easily and even gave him a certain power over them.

Brian broke wood into small pieces and filled his sack, stuffing each bundle far down. 'How are yer going to carry it?' Agger asked.

'On my back.'

'It'll be too 'eavy.'

'I'll drag it a bit then.' After a pause for scraping, Agger wondered: 'Do you sell it?'

'Sometimes.'

'How much do you want for that lot?' Brian reckoned up: we've got plenty at home. I wain't mek much if I traipse it from door to door. 'A tanner.'

'I'll buy it,' Agger said. 'I know somebody as wants a bit o' wood. I'll gi' yer the sack back tomorrow.' Brian took the sixpence just as 'Tip,' someone screamed towards a corporation sewer-tank veering for the far side of the plateau. Agger ran quickly and Brian followed, more for sport since his only sackbag rested by Agger's pram.

He scrambled down the precipice to watch the back open above like a round oven door, a foul liquid stink pouring out. Then the body uptilted and a mass of black grate-and-sewer rubbish eased slowly towards the bank, coming out like an enormous sausage, quicker by the second, until it dropped all in a rush and splayed over the grass at the bottom. 'Watch your boots,' Agger shouted as he began scraping through it. 'This stuff'll burn 'em off.' He turned to Brian: 'Don't come near this 'eap, nipper. You'll get fever and die if you do.'

Brian stood back as half a lavatory bowl cartwheeled down from a lorry-load of house-rammel. 'Tek a piss in that, Agger,' the bowler shouted. It settled among petrol drums and Brian amused himself by throwing housebricks at it until both sides caved in. One of the men uncovered a length of army webbing: 'Here's some o' your equipment from France, Agger' – throwing it like a snake at his feet.

Agger held it on the end of an inferior rake. 'It ain't mine, mate. I chucked all my equipment in the water on my way back' – put his foot on it and continued scraping. The stench made Brian heave: he ran up the bank holding his nose, and stopped to breathe from fifty yards off.

At twelve they straggled to the fire for a warm. All swore it looked like rain, some loading their sacks to go home, though Agger and most of the others stayed through the afternoon. Brian took out his bread, and Agger passed him a swig of cold tea. Jack Bird lay back to read a piece of newspaper: 'Now's your chance, Agger,' he said, lighting a lunchtime Woodbine. 'What about joinin' up for this war in Abyssinia?'

Agger reclined on a heap of shavings. 'You on'y join up

when they stop the dole and chuck us off these bleeding premises – when there's nowt left to do but clamb.'

'They'll never stop the dole,' Jack Bird said. 'It's more than they dare do.'

'It wouldn't bother me, mate,' Agger rejoined, 'because there'll allus be "tips", just like there'll allus be an England. You can bet on that.'

ALAN SILLITOE, *Key to the Door* (1961).

SECOND FRONT
(1966)

To Paul's surprise he now saw infantrymen in the next plot to the tanks, dug into new slit trenches. He hadn't noticed them arrive. Each trench was an oblong pit just large enough for a man to crouch in. Under their hessian-beribboned hats the infantrymen were active over their heaps of earth in the morning freshness, cleaning rifles and rummaging in their packs of food and clothing. They worked among their heaps of gravelly spoil like a race of primitives, Stone Age dwellers. The whole orchard was crowded with these infantry. These would go forward soon, to make the front line and to win territory with their vulnerable bodies. Looking at them reflectively the tank men felt the luxury of their two inches of steel and weighed it against the tank men's special peril – the bulk of his machine at a distance and his special claim for attention from enemy anti-tank gunners and rocket teams. The sense of security of the tank men had evaporated on Queen Beach, where they had seen the first broken monsters. Even so, they were glad they were not infantry, having to dig themselves into the ground at every step, using their own muscles. The narrow slit trenches in the dark earth looked like graves.

When the infantry left the security of their trenches there was nothing but cloth between them and the knife-edge fragments that whipped out in fans from exploding missiles.

Paul studied their faces under their yellow and green head-gear, indistinct in the undergrowth in their drab costume. Even living, they resembled disturbingly the heavy sack-like corpses of the beach dunes. The wood, and the laager of tanks swarmed now with the drab shapeless animals that men are in war, shaving in cold water, digging, chewing, carrying arms, fumbling with grubby khaki towels or relieving themselves into the hedges and undergrowth. It was the moment before the cohesion of battle plans, when order would be restored. They bustled at toilet and packing, while the officers were in their order groups. Soon the crackling voices on the radios, crayonings on maps, orders spoken with quiet determination, would bring an aspect of system to these swarming night-stale herds.

The birds whistled loudly now, blackbirds and thrushes, as they do in English fields in summer. Larks were soaring in their striving way. A breeze of morning ran along in the poplars and elms and in the tall wheat, still green, as the sun threw a happy glory over the Norman countryside. Paul suddenly noticed a strange white and black shape on the ground behind the trees in the far distance – then another, then another. Aeroplanes? Then he saw that they were smashed fusilages – of the grounded gliders which had dived overhead last evening into enemy territory and now lay like huge broken magpies along the Orne, gaunt and queer. Intermittently the quick growl of fast Spandau machine-guns played away to the west: fighting which had never ceased to the flank had gone on all night and doubled its fury now in the growing light. Brens replied with their slow pulse: POCKPOCKPOCKPOCK. More intense became the noise of falling shells, like banging doors, slam after slam. Was it a counter attack? Already, after one night, these noises seemed accepted, familiar. Yet there would be new voices. There were other noises, new sounds, that Paul did not know.

He heard one now, as he watched the infantry. It was a soft *siffle*, high in the air, like a distant lark, or a small penny whistle, faint and elf-like, falling. But then, with a spiral pulsing flutter, it grew to a hissing whirr. Behind it he heard the soft sharp thuds, of the weapon, and was striving to remember where he had heard the noise before. Mortars! That was it! But hardly had the thought come before the first bombs were among them. He had never expected the violence to be so terrible. The mortar bombs landed with ferocious blasts, followed by a whine of fragments which cut into the trees, driving deep white scars into their trunks and filling the air with torn shreds of tree foliage whirled about in clouds of blue-black smoke. The concussion made his head ache and ring, but the sequence of bombs came on and on relentlessly, whistling and whispering down with their horrible fluttering shiver in the ears.

Men dived, the infantry into the earth, the tank men under their tanks or down the hatches, ripping their clothes as they became hooked on projections in the panic. Without ceremony or dignity the shapeless bodies flew and crowded into holes between tanks and earth, or lay trying to tear themselves into the ground.

The mortar bombardment lasted perhaps three minutes. But to Paul it seemed hours, as he simply lay with his face in the grass, a little way from his tank, pinned down. The wood heaved like a creature that bulged and rocked, as the mortar bombs exploded blackly in the trees. Paul watched at first transfixed in terror, but then pressed his head down into the grass as a bomb fell his side of the orchard, and fragments whirred over his head to clatter against the side of his tank. Dirt and fumes flew over him, the noise became a ringing pain in his head. The oatmeal taste became bitter with the taste of fear and death in his mouth. He clung with his nails to small pieces of earth, and twisted grass bents, tugging at them in expectation of losing a leg or half his body to one of the siffling streams of bombs. He prayed for it to cease: he willed himself away: he swore never to be caught out of a closed tank again: he lost every conviction, political, moral, human he would have capitulated to any enemy, believed in any God he had been required to believe in – if only the reward were to be relieved from the terror of the falling spate of mortar bombs.

But then, suddenly, came a second wind of morale: the body, too much tortured by what it heard and felt, ceased any longer to react. He was beyond fear, beyond demoralization; his feelings had gone totally shocked and dead. He had withdrawn any tendency towards deep feelings from his regimental companions, long ago, before the invasion. Men exert a general comradeship in war, but deeper personal affections are largely closed off, like bulkheads sealed. They cannot be afforded.

But now Paul Grimmer cut off his feelings for himself: he no longer loved himself. He allowed his self to become expendable. He hated the Army for bringing him into this hell. He lost all trust in the regiment, in comradeship, in action against the enemy. He was utterly divided and alienated, bent only on survival. Now, he had discovered how to react to mortaring, by dividing himself from himself. He almost felt he was looking down on himself lying on the earth, while his intellect exercised fantastic tricks of detachment, seeking to survive. His mind felt it could survive, even if his body was hit.

DAVID HOLBROOK, *Flesh Wounds* (1966).

BEING A WRITER
(1960)

HOME! I thought. And the full extent of my good luck suddenly became clear to me. After all the years of shiftless, half-alive unproductive existence, I was all ready to be enshrined as a G.O.M. I could see myself sitting for half an hour each morning inside one of those lattice windows, doodling exquisite sentences, hesitating over the *mot juste* up to the very second before opening time. The suitcases had been getting rather heavy, in spite of my improved condition, but suddenly they seemed no heavier than balloons. I was along that path in a trice, and actually had to hold back for Daphne so that we could go up the garden path together. I couldn't wait to embrace my fortunate destiny. Thomas Rogers, the gnarled old sage of rural England. Famous author mistaken for sexton.

So we settled down. From that mention of the village pub you'll gather that I soon established a framework of regular habits, such as middle-aged man must have. And, in fact, the material circumstances of life arranged themselves very well. Daphne and I had the biggest bedroom, and her father was very good about contracting himself into one-third of the house when he'd been used to having all of it. And there we were, all snug and shipshape, with Daphne getting the three meals on the table every day and curling up beside me at night for eight hours' good country slumber.

It was all so perfect that I began to worry. Before the first fortnight was over I was mentally rooting round for snags like a hedgehog grubbing for beetles. Notice the country imagery. Oh, I was the boy for that. There was going to be the scent of new-mown hay about every page I wrote from then on.

And still those snags didn't show up. Daphne went on being

placid and not expecting too much, and I went on being affectionate to her and finding it easier all the time. And Alex kept himself pretty much out of the way. That was the old man's name, Alex. I had to call him by it, of course, and I noticed that Daphne's habit of calling him 'Daddy' didn't last after the first two or three days. She seemed to find it easier if she called him Alex, too; in fact I overheard her asking him if he minded. He grunted something, with his usual conservation of energy over anything that didn't catch his interest, and the deal was on. I wasn't too keen on it myself – it always sounds odd to me when children call their fathers by their Christian names, as if they were just people and not their progenitors – but it wasn't any business of mine. So there we were: Daphne, Tom and Alex. Two men of fifty and one woman of twenty-five. In a cottage, in summer. With no work to do, no landlord, and no worries.

The stage was all set for the next act in the drama of my soul. And clearly, that was going to consist mainly of writing words on sheets of paper. All I had to do, to settle myself into my new life as a G.O.M., was to produce some of my 'later work'. It needn't be much; a few pages at a time. If the stuff was a bit slow in coming out, all the better. I could sell a couple of thousand words now and then as 'Work in Progress', and keep everybody's breath good and bated.

I saw it all so plainly. And yet the perfection of the conditions inhibited me from starting. I couldn't all at once get used to not having any little obstacles or discouragements to push against. At least, that was the reason I gave to myself. On several successive mornings, as soon as the breakfast had been cleared away, I sat down at the table just inside one of those charming lattice windows. In front of me I had arranged a neat pile of virgin paper, and three writing implements: my fountain-pen, an ordinary wooden pen with a steel nib, and a soft pencil. For that (as several magazine articles had disclosed, twenty and thirty years before, to a palpitating public) was my habit. After a couple of pages with one implement, I'd begin to feel the sharpness and alertness fading away. I'd lose the sense of holding a pen with a feel of its own, and just begin to write mechanically, inertly, like a clerk. Then it would be time to take up the other pen, or the pencil. My manuscripts all had passages of soft pencil interspersed among the ink. The dealer who had bought them from me, after I had started going downhill and wanted to earn a few pounds any easy way, had treated the pencil passages with fixative. Heigh-ho.

There was the paper, there were the two pens and the pencil. And I'd look at them for a quarter of an hour and then go outside and walk round the fields in the steamy heat, trying to get ideas. No matter how early I was outside, it was always steamy and hot. The air felt used-up. But at least I had the sense not to make that into an excuse. In fact, I rather like conditions of that sort. I'm not one of your types who need to be braced up. On the contrary, what I need is to be relaxed; put into a muggy state where I'm not tying myself up in knots. Then it flows out. That's how I always found it so easy to talk well in the Black Lion, when I'd got a cargo of drink weighing me comfortably down to the Plimsoll line.

So I sat there for half a dozen mornings together. Looking at the paper and pens and the pencil. Then getting up and walking about outside. It didn't take much of that before it was opening-time. A drink would do me good, I'd think, and off I'd go and get into conversation with the idlers in the village tap-room. Not that I could do a Black Lion act in there, of course. They didn't know me from Beelzebub, let alone Adam. I was just the newcomer who'd married the old chap's daughter from the cottage. Some pretty sly grins I used to get, at first. But that wore off; after all, I'd behaved in a pretty natural way, and they understood my motives. It was what any of them would have done, given half a chance. I soon became accepted and taken for granted. Settling down, I thought to myself rather uneasily; settling down. I'll soon have the inspiration flowing.

But it didn't, and that's all there was to it. Nothing came. The hot steamy weather went on, and the regular meals and eight hours' sleep went on, and I went on. Went on going down to the pub and having a quiet pint or two, wandering about the fields and lanes, chatting with Daphne and Alex.

Alex. He didn't seem to be getting on any better than I was. Instead of working away regularly at one or other of these hobbies he was supposed to be going to take up, he seemed unable to settle to anything. Tropical fish, photography, stamps, beer mats, matchbox lids, model railways, book-binding – there it all was, waiting for him, the whole wonderful world of damn foolish hobbies. And yet he couldn't make up his mind.

Still, I couldn't worry about him. I had my own all-important problem, and it mounted every day. In the end I just gave up all attempt to write anything, and turned my full attention on to myself in an effort to find out what was wrong. Had something died? Was I just someone who used to be a writer? We're supposed to change completely every seven years; it was more than twice that since I had last written a word. For a moment, thinking along these lines, I felt close to panic. But then I calmed down. After all, commonsense reassured me, I *knew* I wasn't a completely different man from the author of *Plain Crackers* and *The Fighting Spaniel*. I was that man, a little older, a little more frayed, but newly determined to get a grip on himself.

Well, what was it, then? I was leaning over a gate, staring across a field of oats, when I got what I thought was the answer. I was too important and too dead. If I'd been an unknown author, eager to attract attention and prove him-self, my mind would have lost its inhibitions and the ideas would have come. Or if, on the other hand, I'd kept going instead of having those two decades of silence, I'd have had a public accustomed to keeping their eyes on me and expecting a book every so often; and that, too, would have been comforting. But I was in the worst position imaginable. A couple of books that had entered the modern Pantheon; then nothing. A living ghost. An extinct volcano, with not a whisper of smoke out of its crater; not even a tourist attraction, and certainly no threat to the neighbouring villages. Just a name, marked on the map and reasonably certain of being marked on every successive map, because it had once been impressive.

I leaned on the gate. *Something* has to get me going, I thought. Some kind of shove. But I couldn't think what. Of course, what I really needed was a spot of critical attention. A really good article written about my work, ending with a question mark. What, if anything, can we expect from a writer with this kind of past achievement to his credit? Etc., etc. And, of course, I knew I had damn all chance of any such thing. The criticism had been done, and I was quietly embalmed. The kind of mention I was getting in surveys of modern literature was just the sort of thing that survey-writers copy out from their card-indexes. *Plain Crackers* occupied about the same place in the contemporary literary consciousness as, say, Thomson's *Seasons*.

If only I knew any critics to speak to. But I'd never come across any: not real ones, anyway. The Black Lion mob included plenty of hacks who wrote reviews; but it was no good appealing to them. They were satellites, owing light and motion to larger bodies. If a big critic had turned his attention to me, they'd have followed suit. But I couldn't expect them to try to show any initiative. The moon doesn't warm the earth.

I wandered back to the cottage, very depressed. I knew I had only myself to depend on; and that after all the trouble I'd taken to get all my problems solved. The cottage, the wife, the regular meals, all would be wasted unless I could lift this load that was pinning me down.

That evening – that very evening, so help me God – another blow fell. Old Alex seemed more restless than ever, and I began to wonder if he was going to start making some kind of trouble, such as asking me for a share of the housekeeping expenses or something. But to do him justice, it wasn't anything like that. It wouldn't have been so bad, if it had been.

He fidgeted about during supper, and kept glancing at me with those little shoe-button eyes. I nearly asked him for God's sake to come out with it, whatever 'it' might be, but I stuck to my lifelong resolution, 'Never speak first.' So, after a due amount of humming and hawing, he opened up.

'You know, Tom,' he said, as we sat in our armchairs and Daphne got on with the washing-up in the kitchen. 'I just don't seem to have found the kind of outlet for my energies that I was looking for.'

'Why not play the gilt-edged?' I suggested. I haven't an earthly idea what playing the gilt-edged is, but it sounds as if it would need a lot of energy.

He took no notice, in that frightening way of his. Just went ahead with his own train of thought.

'I get catalogues, and one thing and another,' he said, 'but none of the stuff really attracts me. And I tell you what, Tom. My thoughts keep coming back to one thing.'

I sat still as a mouse.

'Writing,' he said.

I knew it, I thought. Sooner or later they all think they can write.

'A couple of years ago, when I first came here, I used to amuse myself in the evenings, writing a bit,' he went on. 'I wrote a story. But I never published it.'

I nearly laughed when I heard that. It was just the way people used to go on in the Black Lion. I wrote a story but I never published it. Not, I couldn't get it published. They never said that. I write, but I don't publish. Big of him. He doesn't want to discourage everyone else. Make them die of envy. They'd take one look at his stuff, swell up and die.

'You wrote a story,' I said resignedly. 'And your thoughts keep coming back to writing another.'

'That's right,' he said.

'Well, write it, then,' I said.

He looked at me uneasily. 'I don't really want to,' he said. And it sounded quite sincere, damn it. He genuinely didn't seem to want to.

'What are you trying to tell me, Alex?' I said, leaning forward.

' I'm not sure,' he said helplessly. 'It's just that I can't settle to anything. And I keep thinking about writing. Only I don't want to write. I don't see any point in going on writing without publishing, and I don't know, I shrink from that. It's like entering a new life, to be a published author, with people reading your books and talking about you to each other. It's too big a change for a man of my age.'

JOHN WAIN, *Nuncle* (1960).

ON THE BUS

(1957)

THERE seemed so many things to be happy about. She could not have named them, but as the large Corporation bus came up she felt that even the cold was delightful. Miss Brooks would see it in terms of the deadening snow that was littered everywhere, but to Katherine the frost made everything stand alone and sparkle. Even getting on the bus gave a momentary flicker of pleasure, as if she were entering on a fresh stage of some more important journey. She rubbed a space clear on the window as they moved off, watching the shops of City Road go past. City Road was several miles long. In the middle of it were twin scars where tramlines had been taken up. In some of the little shop-windows candle-ends were burning to melt the frost from the glass. They were all very much alike, selling tobacco and newspapers, or bread and canned food, or greengroceries. But they made a living from people dwelling in the many poor streets around them, who went no further for their shopping. As it was Saturday, there were plenty of them about: women of the district carrying baskets from one shop to another, leaning on the counters for five minutes' dark, allusive conversation, waiting patiently outside butchers' and fish-shops. Here and there old men, muffled up to their scrawny necks, leaned against walls filling their pipes with stenching tobacco cut and sold in sticky segments. Files of papers hung outside the newsagents. Yes, she thought, imagining the wedding rings and the scale-pans gritty from weighing vegetables, they'd certainly wonder how she got here. This kind of scene – though it reminded her of them – would mean nothing to the Fennels at all. They only noticed things that artists had been bringing under their noses for centuries, such as sunsets and landscapes. Or was that unjust? It was all very well saying the Fennels would notice this or that, but her memories of them were not at all clear. When she stayed with them, she had not been half observant enough, thinking no doubt that she would never see them again, so that all that remained was a mingled flavour of where they had lived and how they had treated her, and the kind of things they had said. Could she remember what they had looked like? She remembered Robin's face clearly, and Mr Fennel's to a lesser extent: Mrs Fennel had grown confused with one of the mistresses at school. And Jane she could not remember at all. That was odd. Katherine reckoned on having a good memory for faces.

The truth of the matter was, she could not now keep them out of her mind, and they were constantly linking up with whatever she thought or did. She looked from the unevenly-travelling bus, and saw a cheap dress shop, where a bareankled girl was arranging a copy of a stylish model; then a linen-draper's, with an old ceremonial frontage; a milk-bar, permanently blacked-out, with the door ajar and no-one on the tall stools; a pawn-shop window crowded with old coins, shirts, a theodolite, bed-pans and a harp; a public-house door with a bright brass rail, just opening; a sudden gap of high, papered walls and a heap of bricks, furred with frost, where a house had been destroyed. There was nothing in all this to remind her of them, yet it did.

The bus stopped, restarted, took on more passengers. The buildings outside grew taller and impressive. The streets were wider; they at last came to the end of City Road and circled slowly along one-way streets in the centre of the city. Many people hurried by, with a flickering of white collars and newspapers. They passed the cathedral yard, glimpsed the long, soot-encrusted glass roof of a railway station, halted at a set of lights by a doorway bearing a dozen professional brass plates. Here and there girls dressed in overcoats sat huddled in cigarette-kiosks, reading, and down a side-street a man was selling baked potatoes from an ancient roaster.

She had left Miss Green to herself: they were sharing a double-seat downstairs. Miss Green was nearest the gangway, and the bus had become so crowded that a shopping basket swayed above her head, from which hung the end of a leek. At every movement of the owner it tapped Miss Green's hair. But she had looked mutely in front of her and said nothing.

Now she leaned against Katherine.

Katherine accordingly gave her more room. But Miss Green said:

'I don't feel well. I'm sorry. I must get out.'

Katherine glanced at her. She looked ghastly.

'All right.'

She signalled to the conductress, and got Miss Green to the platform at the back of the bus. At the next stop it swerved alongside the pavement and put them down. Miss Green went and sat on a low wall from which the railings had been removed, her head low. Katherine stood by her.

'Do you feel faint or sick?' she asked helplessly.

'Sick,' said Miss Green after a while. She tilted back her head as if the cold air were wet muslin laid across her forehead.

They had not reached Bank Street, but it would have been the next stop. This was a large square, the formal centre of the city, two sides of which were taken up by the Town Hall and Municipal Departments, under which the bus had dropped them. In the middle of the square was a small green, with flowerbeds and seats; over the branches of the leafless trees on the third side was the high-pillared façade of the Central City Library, and on the last side were low reticent shop windows, tailors and jewellers. The green was covered with snow.

PHILIP LARKIN, *A Girl in Winter* (1947).

AFTER THE FOOTBALL
(1960)

HE must have mentioned this episode to Judith – I'm not so sure he didn't stop in the Booth doorway and watch me – for it was one of the first things she mentioned when I went up to the Mayor's Parlour, as they now called their house.

'Do you see her much?' she said, half-concerned.

'I don't see her at all,' I told her, and she didn't mention her again.

They had Shirley out on a rug on the back lawn and we spent the Sunday afternoon playing with her. 'Come on you little bastard,' Maurice would say and the kid'd giggle like hell. 'Yes – *you* I mean. You funny little bastard you,' and he tickled his stubby finger into her belly.

'He's always calling her that,' Judith complained to me.

'Well, she nearly was,' Maurice said seriously. He rolled over and over with her, holding her like a precious ball.

'He ought to be in a circus with her,' Judith said. 'Come on, Tarzan, you and me'll go in the house and get some beer.'

When we were alone she said, 'Do you think Morry likes being married? You know – right at bottom. Do you think he's got over it?'

I didn't think she'd have asked me if she wasn't sure herself. 'It's the only way he'd ever have got married. He's the luckiest man to have tumbled with you.'

'But I think he's beginning to find it a bit of a strain. It's only natural for a man like him to be laying a different woman each night.'

'You're soft with him, Judy. You have to treat Maurice hard – to get anywhere.' I was irritated by her for flaunting Maurice like this – showing off her security. She was a different woman from the one I'd known in the shop doorway. Marriage had 'made her'.

'*You*'ve found that?' she said. She opened the fridge door and pulled out the beer. She watched me open it, and we both poured it into glasses. 'What's he like now, with other women?'

'They call him daddy.'

'Do they? Really?' She laughed.

'Don't let him know,' I told her, since it wasn't true. But Maurice was behaving well, and I didn't have the heart to make Judith disbelieve it. We went back with the beer. His small stocky body crouched over the kid.

Later on that evening Maurice and me went for a walk up the lane to Caulsby Castle. He ticked off each house as we passed them, knocking the occupants down into County Hall, Ed Philips-secret-athlete, and teacher types. He liked to keep them that way, then he could make out he was different. We were both laughing when we vaulted the stile, and fell in the long grass in a funny, private hysteria. How long we sat laughing I don't know. We rolled about like a couple of tramps, pushing each other or just pulling faces to start off another peal of screaming. When a couple passed us on their evening stroll, Maurice had only to point to them and say, 'Teachers' and the screams started all over again. We staggered around, pulling each other up, pushing each other down, holding together to keep upright, fighting, and making noises, until, as suddenly as it had begun, it stopped, and we sat crosslegged, exhausted, the laughter dying down in shallow simpers.

We climbed the mound of the castle with our arms wrapped round each other. It was warm. From the top of the hill the valley and city were being swallowed in a low mist, reddened by the dead sun as it dropped in the valley top. Red hot penny in the slot.

'What had you thought of doing after you've finished laking football,' Maurice said, sobered and looking at the sun as if it was a person. 'Still carry on at Weaver's? Open a pub?'

'I hadn't thought. It's a bit early yet.'

'I'd been thinking on starting a business.'

The big red disc seemed to be the right place for him to look. 'When?'

'As soon as I've got enough capital. How d'you feel about joining me?'

He dug at the ground with the toe of his shoe. It was stone dust from the keep. He could never stay still.

'Whose idea is it?'

'The old man's – you know, father-in-law. He's even prepared to come in with us. He thinks I should make a start now, so I can build up something well before I'm due to finish.'

'What sort of business had you got in mind?'

'Locational transport – conveyors, maybe working up to coal screening plant, and that kind of thing.'

I laughed, and he added, 'Parkes has a lot of experience with that sort of thing. He says it's not half as difficult as it sounds. It's something he's always wanted to do himself.'

'He might be right so long as you've a fortune to start off with.'

'You don't need that much, Arthur. Not to begin with. All we need to start with is a good-sized prefabricated building, a bit of transport, and maybe two or three men. It'd be all assembly work at first – contracting, for tenders.'

'But you'd still need *some* money.'

'I've some – you've some. Parkes has a drop.' He looked at me suggestively, but I couldn't see what he was getting at in those dark eyes.

'What about the other thirty or forty thousand?'

'Don't be shy, Art. You've got a bit stacked away – I'm not that badly off. Parkes – he's got a pile, I'm almost sure. While we're still playing we've got a chance to start something like this. Don't you agree? We could live off football to begin with. We wouldn't have to worry about making a living. And that's a big start. Otherwise – it's going to be a pub or oblivion. Look at the way Frank's having to hang on. He daren't stop playing – he's got used to the money, and he finds he won't be able to manage without.'

'If you'd said a sports shop I'd have been ready to believe you.'

'That's no good. A shop's no good. The country's overflowing with bloody shopkeepers. We want something big, where it's either bust or zoom.'

'Supposing I said all right. You still haven't said where all the money comes from. All we could buy is the desk for the office.'

'Aw now don't be *that* thick, Art.' He looked at me with assumed disappointment.

A long shadow, from the remnant of the castle, curved over the hill we were on. In the air around us a few swallows darted and swayed, and below, in the dark green pool of the small moat, pebbles splashed where a couple of kids were playing.

'You mean Slomer, I bet,' I said.

'He's the money, Art.'

His look of shared confidence only increased and his feet fidgeted in the dust. 'What's the matter? He'd raise a loan. I know for a fact he would. He's done it for all sorts of different people afore.'

'I've sold myself enough, Maurice. Five hundred quid I got. That's all the share I need. He'd want all of you. Don't you know what Slomer's like? You want to ask Ed Philips. Slomer'd want the lot.'

'He'd want to make interest. That's what he's like. He'd want a good investment, and we could give him it. That's the great thing with Slomer. It doesn't matter who you are so long as you work his way. And his way's to make a profit.'

'He's a sick man. He's not like other men. You should see the way he behaves – the way he acts and talks to people.'

'It's his money we want. Not his photograph . . . Come on, Arthur. I bet you could carry a lot of sway with him. He's a big man. He's the one big string you can pull. I know. And it can take us right out of the ditch.'

I didn't argue with him. We went back, our arms still wrapped round each other, talking about last Saturday's match and the way Mellor played.

He was quiet the rest of the evening, and Judith said to me suspiciously, 'Just what have you been telling him, Tarzan, about me?'

DAVID STOREY, *This Sporting Life* (1960).

Argument

◄—►►

ENGLISH COMMUNISM
(1896)

WHILE I think that the hope of the new-birth of society is certainly growing, and that speedily, I must confess myself puzzled about the means toward that end which are mostly looked after now; and I am doubtful if some of the measures which are pressed, mostly, I think, with all honesty of purpose, and often with much ability, would, if gained, bring us any further on the direct road to a really new-born society, the only society which can be a new birth, a society of practical equality. Not to make any mystery about it, I mean that the great mass of what most non-socialists at least consider at present to be socialism, seems to me nothing more than a *machinery* of socialism, which I think it probable that socialism *must* use in its militant condition; and which I think it *may* use for some time after it is practically established; but does not seem to me to be of its essence. Doubtless there is good in the schemes for substituting business-like administration in the interests of the public for the old Whig muddle of *laissez faire* backed up by coercion and smoothed by abundant corruption, which, worked all of it in the interest of successful business men, was once thought such a wonderful invention, and which certainly was the very cement of society as it has existed since the death of feudalism. The London County Council, for instance, is not merely a more useful body for the administration of public business than the Metropolitan Board of Works was: it is instinct with a different spirit; and even its general *intention* to be of use to the citizens and to heed their wishes, has in it a promise of better days, and has already done something to

461

raise the dignity of life in London amongst a certain part of the population, and down to certain classes. Again, who can quarrel with the attempts to relieve the sordidness of civilized town life by the public acquirement of parks and other open spaces, planting of trees, establishment of free libraries and the like? It is sensible and right for the public to push for the attainment of such gains; but we all know very well that their advantages are very unequally distributed, that they are gains rather for certain portions of the middle-classes than for working people. Nay, this socialist machinery may be used much further: it may gain higher wages and shorter working hours for the working men themselves: industries may be worked by municipalities for the benefit both of producers and consumers. Working-people's houses may be improved, and their management taken out of the hands of commercial speculators. More time might be insisted on for the education of children; and so on, and so on. In all this I freely admit a great gain, and am glad to see schemes tried which would lead to it. But great as the gain would be, the ultimate good of it, the amount of progressive force that might be in such things would, I think, depend on *how* such reforms were done; in what spirit; or rather what else was being done, while these were going on, which would make people long for equality of condition; which would give them faith in the possibility and workableness of socialism; which would give them courage to strive for it and labour for it; and which would do this for a vast number of people, so that the due impetus might be gained for the sweeping away of all privilege. For we must not lose sight of the very obvious fact that these improvements in the life of the larger public can only be carried out at the expense of some portion of the freedom and fortunes of the proprietary classes. They are, when genuine, one and all attacks I say on the 'liberty and property' of the non-working or useless classes, as some of those classes see clearly enough. And I admit that if the sum of them should become vast and deep reaching enough to give to the useful or working classes intelligence enough to conceive of a life of equality and co-operation; courage enough to accept it and to bring the necessary skill to bear on working it; and power enough to force its acceptance on the stupid and the interested, the war of classes would speedily end in the victory of the useful class, which would then become the new Society of Equality.

Intelligence enough to conceive, courage enough to will, power enough to compel. If our ideas of a new Society are anything more than a dream, these three qualities must animate the due effective majority of the working-people; and then, I say, the thing will be done.

Intelligence, courage, power *enough*. Now that *enough* means a very great thing. The effective majority of the working people must I should think be something as great in numbers as an actual mechanical majority; because the non-working classes (with, mind you, their sworn slaves and parasites, men who can't live without them) are even numerically very strong, and are stronger still in holding in their hand the nine points of the law, possession to wit; and as soon as these begin to think there is any serious danger to their privilege – i.e., their livelihood – they will be pretty much unanimous in defending it, and using all the power which they possess in doing so. The necessary majority therefore of intelligence, courage, and power is such a big thing to bring about, that it will take a long time to do so; and those who are working for this end must clearly not throw away time and strength by making more mistakes than they can possibly help in their efforts for the conversion of the working people to an ardent desire for a society of equality. The question then, it seems to me, about all those partial gains above mentioned, is not so much as to what advantage they may be to the public at large in the passing moment, or even to the working people, but rather what effect they will have towards converting the workers to an understanding of, and ardent desire for Socialism; true and complete Socialism I mean, what I should call Communism. For though making a great many poor people, or even a few, somewhat more comfortable than they are now, somewhat less miserable, let us say, is not in itself a light good; yet it would be a heavy evil, if it did anything towards dulling the efforts of the whole class of workers towards the winning of a real society of equals. And here again come in those doubts and the puzzlement I began by talking about. For I want to know and to ask you to consider, how far the betterment of the working people might go and yet stop at last without having made any progress on the *direct* road to Communism. Whether in short the tremendous organization of civilized commercial society is not playing the cat and mouse game with us socialists. Whether the Society of Inequality might not accept the quasi-socialist machinery above mentioned, and work it for the purpose of upholding that society in a somewhat shorn condition, maybe, but a safe one. That seems to me possible, and means the other side of the view: instead of the useless classes being swept away by the useful, the useless classes gaining some of the usefulness of the workers, and *so* safeguarding their privilege. The workers better treated, better organized, helping to govern themselves, but with no more pretence to equality with the rich, nor any more hope for it than they have now. But if this be possible, it will only be so on the grounds that the working people have ceased to desire real socialism and are contented with some outside show of it joined to an increase in prosperity enough to satisfy the cravings of men who do not know what the pleasures of life might be if they treated their own capacities and the resources of nature reasonably with the intention and expectation of being happy. Of course also it could not be possible if there be, as we may well hope, an actual necessity for new development of society from out of our present conditions: but granting this necessity, the change may and will be exceedingly slow in coming if the working people do not show their sense of the necessity by being overtaken by a longing for the change and by expressing that longing. And moreover it will not only be slow in coming but also in that case it can only come through a period of great suffering and misery, by the ruin of our present civilization: and surely reasonable men must hope that if the Socialism be necessary its advent shall both be speedy and shall be marked by the minimum of suffering and by ruin not quite complete. Therefore, I say, what we have to hope for is that the inevitable advance of the society of equality will speedily make itself felt by the consciousness of its necessity being impressed upon the working people, and that they will consciously and not blindly strive for its realization. That in fact is what we mean by the education into Socialism of the working classes. And I believe that if this is impossible at present, if the working people refuse to take any interest in Socialism, if they practically reject it, we must accept that as a sign that the necessity for an essential change in society is so far distant, that we need scarcely trouble ourselves about it. This is the test; and for this reason it is so deadly serious for us to find out whether those democratic tendencies and the schemes of new administration they give birth to are really of use in educating the people into *direct* Socialism. If they are not, they are of use for nothing else; and we had best try if we can't make terms with intelligent Tories and benevolent Whigs, and beg them to unite their intelligence and benevolence, and govern us as kindly and wisely as they can, and to rob us in moderation only. But if they are of use, then in spite of their sordid and repellent details, and all the sickness of hope deferred that the use of such instruments assuredly brings us, let us use them as far as they will go, and refuse to be disappointed if they will not go very far: which means if they will not in a decade turn into a united host of heroes and sages a huge mass of men living under a system of society so intricate as to look on the surface like a mere chance-hap muddle of many millions of necessitous people, oppressed indeed, and sorely, not by obvious individual violence and ill-will, but by an economic system so far reaching, so deeply seated, that it may well seem like the operation of a natural law to men so uneducated that they have not even escaped the reflexion of the so-called education of their masters, but in addition to their other mishaps are saddled also with the superstitions and hypocrisies of the upper classes, with scarce a whit of the characteristic traditions of their own class to help them: an intellectual slavery which is a necessary accompaniment of their material slavery. That as a mass is what revolutionists have got to deal with: such a mass indeed I think could and would be vivified by some spark of enthusiasm, some sudden hopeful impulse towards aggression, if the necessity for sudden change were close at hand. But is it? There are doubtless not a few in this room, myself perhaps amongst them (I say *perhaps* for one's old self is apt to grow dim to one) – some of us I say once believed in the inevitableness of a sudden and speedy change. That was no wonder with the new enlightenment of socialism gilding the dullness of civilization for us. But if we must now take soberer views of our hopes, do not reproach us with that. Remember how hard other tyrannies have died, though to the economical oppression of them was added obvious violent individual oppression, which as I have said is lacking to the heavy tyranny of our times; and can we hope that it will be speedier in its ending than they? I say that the time is not now for the sudden kindling of the impulse of direct aggression amongst the mass of the workmen. But what then! are we to give up all hope of educating them into Socialism? Surely not. Let us use all means possible for drawing them into socialism, so that they may at last find themselves in such a position that they understand themselves to be face to face with false society, themselves the only possible elements of true society.

WILLIAM MORRIS, *Fabian Tract 113* (1903), *Collected Works*, vol. 23.

FALSE CATEGORIES
(1908–14)

I THINK that history is necessary in order to *emancipate* the individual from the influence of certain *pseudo-categories*. We are all of us under the influence of a number of abstract ideas, of which we are as a matter of fact unconscious. We do not see them, but see other things *through* them. In order that the kind of discussion about 'satisfaction' which I want may be carried on, it is first of all necessary to rob certain ideas of their status of categories. This is a difficult operation. Fortunately, however, all such 'attitudes' and ideologies have a gradual growth. The rare type of historical intelligence which investigates their origins can help us considerably. Just as a knowledge of the colours extended and separated in the spectrum enables us to distinguish the feebler colours confused together in shadows, so a knowledge of these ideas, as it were *objectified*, and *extended* in history enables us to perceive them hidden in our own minds. Once they have been brought to the surface of the mind, they lose their *inevitable* character. They are no longer categories. We have lost our *naïveté*. Provided that we have a great enough length of history at our disposal, we then always vaccinate ourselves against the possibility of harbouring false categories. For in a couple of thousand years the confused human mind works itself out clearly into all the separate attitudes it is possible for it to assume. Humanity ought therefore always to carry with it a library of a thousand years as a balancing pole.

The application of the historical method to the present subject is this: It is possible by examining the history of the Renaissance, to destroy in the mind of the humanist, the conviction that his own attitude is the *inevitable* attitude of the emancipated and instructed man.

We may not be able to convince him that the religious

attitude is the right one, but we can at least destroy the *naïveté* of his canons of *satisfaction*.

T. E. HULME, 'Humanism' in *Speculations* (1924).

HUMANISM AND RELIGION
(1908–14)

IT is these categories, these abstract conceptions, which all the individuals of a period have in common, which really serve best to characterise the period. For most of the characteristics of such a period, not only in thought, but in ethics, and through ethics in economics, really depend on these central abstract attitudes. But while people will readily acknowledge that this is true of the Greeks, or of Brazilian Indians, they have considerable difficulty in realising that it is also true of the modern humanist period from the Renaissance to now. The way in which we instinctively judge things we take to be the inevitable way of judging things. The pseudo-categories of the humanist attitude are thought to be on the same footing as the objective categories of space and time. It is thought to be impossible for an emancipated man to think sincerely in the categories of the religious attitude.

The reason for this is to be found in the fact already noticed that we are, as a rule, unconscious of the very abstract conceptions which underlie our more concrete opinions. What Ferrier says of real categories, 'Categories may be operative when their existence is not consciously recognised. First principles of every kind have their influence, and, indeed, operate largely and profoundly long before they come to the surface of human thought, and are articulately expounded,' is true also of these pseudo-categories. We are only conscious of A, B . . . and very seldom of (h). We do not see that, but other things *through it*; and, consequently, take what we see for facts, and not for what they are – opinions based on a particular abstract valuation. This is certainly true of the *progressive* ideology founded on the conception of man as fundamentally good.

It is this unconsciousness of these central abstract conceptions, leading us to suppose that the judgments of value founded on them are *natural* and *inevitable*, which makes it so difficult for anyone in the humanist tradition to look at the religious attitude as anything but a sentimental survival.

But I want to emphasise as clearly as I can, that I attach very little value indeed to the *sentiments* attaching to the religious attitude. I hold, quite coldly and intellectually as it were, that the way of thinking about the world and man, the conception of sin, and the categories which ultimately make up the religious attitude, are the *true* categories and the *right* way of thinking.

I might incidentally note here, that the way in which I have explained the action of the central abstract attitudes and ways of thinking, and the use of the word *pseudo*-categories, might suggest that I hold relativist views about their validity. But I don't. I hold the religious conception of ultimate values to be right, the humanist wrong. From the nature of things, these categories are not inevitable, like the categories of time and space, but are *equally objective*. In speaking of religion, it is to this level of abstraction that I wish to refer. I have none of the feelings of *nostalgia*, the reverence for tradition, the desire to recapture the sentiment of Fra Angelico, which seems to animate most modern defenders of religion. All that seems to me to be bosh. What is important is what nobody seems to realize – the dogmas like that of Original Sin, which are the closest expression of the categories of the religious attitude. That man is in no sense perfect, but a wretched creature, who can yet apprehend perfection. It is not, then, that I put up with the dogma for the sake of the sentiment, but that I may possibly swallow the sentiment for the sake of the dogma. Very few since the Renaissance have really understood the dogma, certainly very few inside the Churches of recent years. If they appear occasionally even fanatical about the very word of the dogma, that is only a secondary result of belief really grounded on sentiment. Certainly no humanist could understand the dogma. They all chatter about matters which are in comparison with this, quite secondary notions – God, Freedom, and Immortality.

The important thing is that this attitude is not merely a *contrasted* attitude, which I am interested in, as it were, for purpose of *symmetry* in historical exposition, but a real attitude, perfectly possible for us today. To see this is a kind of conversion. It radically alters our physical perception; so that the world takes on an entirely different aspect.

T. E. HULME, 'Humanism' in *Speculations* (1924).

AN IDEA OF TRADITION
(1917)

IN English writing we seldom speak of tradition, though we occasionally apply its name in deploring its absence. We cannot refer to 'the tradition' or to 'a tradition'; at most, we employ the adjective in saying that the poetry of So-and-so is 'traditional' or even 'too traditional'. Seldom, perhaps, does the word appear except in a phrase of censure. If otherwise, it is vaguely approbative, with the implication, as to the work approved, of some pleasing archaeological reconstruction. You can hardly make the word agreeable to English ears without this comfortable reference to the reassuring science of archaeology.

Certainly the word is not likely to appear in our appreciations of living or dead writers. Every nation, every race, has not only its own creative, but its own critical turn of mind; and is even more oblivious of the shortcomings and limitations of its critical habits than of those of its creative genius. We know, or think we know, from the enormous mass of critical writing that has appeared in the French language the critical method or habit of the French; we only conclude (we are such unconscious people) that the French are 'more critical' than we, and sometimes even plume ourselves a little with the fact, as if the French were the less spontaneous. Perhaps they are; but we might remind ourselves that criticism is as inevitable as breathing, and that we should be none the worse for articulating what passes in our minds when we read a book and feel an emotion about it, for critizing our own minds in their work of criticism. One of the facts that might come to light in this process is our tendency to insist, when we praise a poet, upon those aspects of his work in which he least resembles anyone else. In these aspects or parts of his work we pretend to find what is individual, what is the peculiar essence of the man. We dwell with satisfaction upon the poet's difference from his predecessors, especially his immediate predecessors; we endeavour to find something that can be isolated in order to be enjoyed. Whereas if we approach a poet without this prejudice we shall often find that not only the best, but the most individual parts of his work may be those in which the dead poets, his ancestors, assert their immortality most vigorously. And I do not mean the impressionable period of adolescence, but the period of full maturity.

Yet if the only form of tradition, of handing down, consisted in following the ways of the immediate generation before us in a blind or timid adherence to its successes, 'tradition' should positively be discouraged. We have seen many such simple currents soon lost in the sand; and novelty is better than repetition. Tradition is a matter of much wider significance. It cannot be inherited, and if you want it you must obtain it by great labour. It involves, in the first place, the historical sense, which we may call nearly indispensable to anyone who would continue to be a poet beyond his twenty-fifth year; and the historical sense involves a perception, not only of the pastness of the past, but of its presence; the historical sense compels a man to write not merely with his own generation in his bones, but with a feeling that the whole of the literature of Europe from Homer and within it the whole of the literature of his own country has a simultaneous existence and composes a simultaneous order. This historical sense, which is a sense of the timeless as well as of the temporal and of the timeless and of the temporal together, is what makes a writer traditional. And it is at the same time what makes a writer most acutely conscious of his place in time, of his own contemporaneity.

No poet, no artist of any art, has his complete meaning alone. His significance, his appreciation is the appreciation of his relation to the dead poets and artists. You cannot value him alone; you must set him, for contrast and comparison, among the dead. I mean this as a principle of aesthetic, not merely historical, criticism. The necessity that he shall conform, that he shall cohere, is not onesided; what happens when a new work of art is created is something that happens simultaneously to all the works of art which preceded it. The existing monuments form an ideal order among themselves, which is modified by the introduction of the new (the really new) work of art among them. The existing order is complete before the new work arrives; for order to persist after the supervention of novelty, the *whole* existing order must be, if ever so slightly, altered; and so the relations, proportions, values of each work of art toward the whole are readjusted; and this is conformity between the old and the new. Whoever has approved this idea of order, of the form of European, of English literature will not find it preposterous that the past should be altered by the present as much as the present is directed by the past. And the poet who is aware of this will be aware of great difficulties and responsibilities.

In a peculiar sense he will be aware also that he must inevitably be judged by the standards of the past. I say judged, not amputated, by them; not judged to be as good as, or worse or better than, the dead; and certainly not judged by the canons of dead critics. It is a judgment, a comparison, in which two things are measured by each other. To conform merely would be for the new work not really to conform at all; it would not be new, and would therefore not be a work of art. And we do not quite say that the new is more valuable because it fits in; but its fitting in is a test of its value – a test, it is true, which can only be slowly and cautiously applied, for we are none of us infallible judges of conformity. We say: it appears to conform, and is perhaps individual, or it appears individual, and may conform; but we are hardly likely to find that it is one and not the other.

To proceed to a more intelligible exposition of the relation of the poet to the past: he can neither take the past as a lump, an indiscriminate bolus, nor can he form himself wholly on one or two private admirations, nor can he form himself wholly upon one preferred period. The first course is inadmissible, the second is an important experience of youth, and the third is a pleasant and highly desirable supplement. The poet must be very conscious of the main current, which does not at all flow invariably through the most distinguished reputations. He must be quite aware of the obvious fact that art never improves, but that the material of art is never quite the same. He must be aware that the mind of Europe – the mind of his own country – a mind which he learns in time to be much more important than his own private mind – is a mind which changes, and that this change is a development which abandons nothing *en route*, which does not superannuate either Shakespeare, or Homer, or the rock drawing of the Magdalenian draughtsmen. That this development refinement perhaps, complication certainly, is not, from the point of view of the artist, any improvement. Perhaps not even an improvement from the point of view of the psychologist or not to the extent which we imagine; perhaps only in the end based upon a complication in economics and machinery. But the difference between the present and the past is that the conscious present is an awareness of the past in a way and to an extent which the past's awareness of itself cannot show.

Someone said: 'The dead writers are remote from us because we *know* so much more than they did.' Precisely, and they are that which we know.

I am alive to a usual objection to what is clearly part of my programme for the *métier* of poetry. The objection is that the doctrine requires a ridiculous amount of erudition (pedantry), a claim which can be rejected by appeal to the lives of poets in any pantheon. It will even be affirmed that much learning deadens or perverts poetic sensibility. While, however, we persist in believing that a poet ought to know as much as will not encroach upon his necessary receptivity and necessary laziness, it is not desirable to confine knowledge to whatever can be put into a useful shape for examinations, drawing-rooms, or the still more pretentious modes of publicity. Some can absorb knowledge, the more tardy must sweat for it. Shakespeare acquired more essential history from Plutarch than most men could from the whole British Museum. What is to be insisted upon is that the poet must develop or procure the consciousness of the past and that he should continue to develop this consciousness throughout his career.

What happens is a continual surrender of himself as he is at the moment to something which is more valuable. The progress of an artist is a continual self-sacrifice, a continual extinction of personality.

T. S. ELIOT, 'Tradition and the Individual Talent' (1917), in *Selected Essays*.

EQUALITY AND INEQUALITY
(1931)

WHEN the contrast between the circumstances of different social strata is so profound as today, the argument – if it deserves to be called an argument – which suggests that the incomes they receive bear a close relation to their personal qualities is obviously illusory. In reality, as has often been pointed out, explanations which are relevant as a clue to differences between the incomes of individuals in the same group lose much of their validity when applied, as they often are, to interpret differences between those of individuals in different groups. It would be as reasonable to hold that the final position of competitors in a race were an accurate indication of their physical endowments, if, while some entered fit and carefully trained, others were half-starved, were exhausted by want of sleep, and were handicapped by the starters. If the weights are unequal, it is not less important, but more important, that the scales should be true. The condition of differences of individual quality finding their appropriate expression is the application of a high degree of social art. It is such a measure of communism as is needed to ensure that inequalities of personal capacity are neither concealed nor exaggerated by inequalities which have their source in social arrangements.

So, while the successful professional or business man may be justified in assuming that, if he has outdistanced his rivals, one important cause is his own 'application, industry, and honesty', and the other admirable qualities rightly prized by Lord Inchcape, that gratifying conclusion is only half the truth. His talents must be somewhat extraordinary, or his experience of life unusually limited, if he has not on occasion asked himself what his position would have been if his father had been an unemployed miner or a casual labourer; if he had belonged to one of the 9,397 families in Bermondsey – over 30 per cent of the total number – living in 1927 at the rate of two or more persons to a room, or had been brought up in one of the one-apartment houses in the central division of Glasgow, 41 per cent of which contained in 1926 three or more persons per room; if he had been one of the million-odd children in the elementary schools of England and Wales who are suffering at any given moment from physical defects; and if, having been pitched into full-time industry at the age of fourteen, he had been dismissed at the age of sixteen or eighteen to make room for a cheaper competitor from the elementary school. He may quite rightly be convinced that he gets only what he is worth, and that the forces of the market would pull him up sharply if he stood out for more. What he is worth depends, however, not only upon his own powers, but upon the opportunities which his neighbours have had of developing their powers. Behind the forces of the market stand forces of another kind, which determine that the members of some social groups shall be in a position to render services which are highly remunerated because they are scarce, and to add to their incomes by the acquisition of property, whilst those belonging to others shall supply services which are cheap because they are over-supplied, but which form, nevertheless, their sole means of livelihood.

Such forces are partly, no doubt, beyond human control; but they are partly the result of institutions and policy. There is, for example, the unequal pressure of mere material surroundings, of housing, sanitation, and liability to disease, which decides that social groups shall differ in their ability to make the best use of their natural endowments. There is inequality of educational opportunity, which has as its effect that, while a favoured minority can cultivate their powers till manhood, the great majority of children, being compelled to compete for employment in their early adolescence, must enter occupations in which, because they are overcrowded, the remuneration is low, and later, because their remuneration has been low, must complete the vicious circle by sending their children into over-crowded occupations. There is the nepotism which allots jobs in the family business to sons and relations, and the favouritism which fills them with youths belonging to the same social class as its owners. There is inequality of access to financial information, which yields fortunes of surprising dimensions, if occasionally, also, of dubious repute, to the few who possess it. There is the influence of the institution of inheritance in heightening the effects of all other inequalities, by determining the vantage-ground upon which different groups and individuals shall stand, the range of opportunities which shall be open to them, and the degree of economic stress which they shall undergo.

The wage-earner who reflects on the distribution of wealth is apt, as is natural, to look first at the large dividends or watered capital of the firm by which he is employed. The economist looks at the large blocks of property which are owned by individuals and transmitted to their descendants, and which yield large incomes whether profits per cent are high or low. He insists, with Professor Cannan, that 'the inequality in the amounts of property which individuals have received by way of bequest and inheritance is by far the most potent cause of inequality in the actual distribution of property'; and points out, with Mr Henderson, that the evil is progressive, since it causes 'an initial inequality ... to perpetuate itself throughout subsequent generations in a cumulative degree'; and urges, with Mr Simon, that 'inheritance is responsible, not only for the most excessive, but for the most unjust and indefensible, inequalities.' Such statements are confirmed by the valuable researches of Mr Wedgwood, who has made the economic effects of inheritance, almost for the first time, the subject of inductive investigation. The conclusion which he draws from the examination of a sample of large estates at Somerset House is perturbing. It is that, 'on the whole, the largest fortunes belong to those with the richest parents. . . . In the great majority of cases the large fortunes of one generation belong to the children of those who possessed the large fortunes of the previous generation . . . . There is in our society an hereditary inequality of economic status which has survived the dissolution of the cruder forms of feudalism.'

The advantages and disabilities which these phenomena create are properly described as social, since they are the result of social institutions, and can by the action of society be maintained or corrected. Experience shows that, when combined, as is normally the case, with extreme disparities of economic power between those who own and direct, and those who execute and are directed, but rarely own, they clog the mechanism of society and corrode its spirit. Except in so far as they are modified, as they partially have been, by deliberate intervention, they produce results surprisingly similar to those foretold by the genius of Marx. They divide what might have been a community into contending classes, of which one is engaged in a struggle to share in advantages which it does not yet enjoy and to limit the exercise of economic authority, while the other is occupied in a nervous effort to defend its position against encroachments.

It is the habit of favoured classes in all ages and all nations to treat such odious truths as the Greeks treated the Furies. They hope to avert the consequences of social divisions by describing them by some other titles than the names of ill-omen that properly belong to them. But the Furies are Furies because, having listened to polite euphemisms for two thousand years, they have acquired the unpopular habit of considering, not words, but facts, and they are not, unfortunately, so easily placated. As the history of the last half-century shows, the resentment which finds its expression in economic tension is not local and evanescent, but widespread and permanent. As a social movement, it is an attempt to abolish the element of privilege in social arrangements, not by imposing an arbitrary uniformity on varying capacities, but by making the material conditions of culture and civilization available to all, instead of to a minority. As an industrial movement, it is an attempt to check the tendency of economic power to slip into economic tyranny, not by destroying authority, but by substituting a system of industrial government based on consent, and conducted in accordance with a settled constitution, for its control by the will of property-owners and their agents.

R. H. TAWNEY, *Equality* (1931).

MODERN INTELLECTUALS
(1935)

SO far we have been considering modern cynicism in a rationalistic manner, as something that has intellectual causes. Belief, however, as modern psychologists are never weary of telling us, is seldom determined by rational motives, and the same is true of disbelief, though sceptics often overlook this fact. The causes of any widespread scepticism are likely to be sociological rather than intellectual. The main cause always is comfort without power. The holders of power are not cynical, since they are able to enforce their ideals. Victims of oppression are not cynical, since they are filled with hate, and hate, like any other strong passion, brings with it a train of attendant beliefs. Until the advent of education, democracy, and mass production, intellectuals had everywhere a considerable influence upon the march of affairs, which was by no means diminished if their heads were cut off. The modern intellectual finds himself in a quite different situation. It is by no means difficult for him to obtain a fat job and a good income provided he is willing to sell his services to the stupid rich either as propagandist or as Court jester. The effect of mass production and elementary education is that stupidity is more firmly entrenched than at any other time since the rise of civilization. When the Czarist Government killed Lenin's brother, it did not turn Lenin into a cynic, since hatred inspired a lifelong activity in which he was finally successful. But in the more solid countries of the West there is seldom such potent cause for hatred, or such opportunity of spectacular revenge. The work of the intellectuals is ordered and paid for by Governments or rich men, whose aims probably seem absurd, if not pernicious, to the intellectuals concerned. But a dash of cynicism enables them to adjust their consciences to the situation. There are, it is true, some activities in which wholly admirable work is desired by the powers that be; the chief of these is science, and the next is public architecture in America. But if a man's education has been literary, as is still too often the case, he finds himself at the age of twenty-two with a considerable skill that he cannot exercise in any manner that appears important to himself. Men of science are not cynical even in the West, because they can exercise their best brains with the full approval of the community; but in this they are exceptionally fortunate among modern intellectuals.

If this diagnosis is right, modern cynicism cannot be cured merely by preaching, or by putting better ideals before the young than those that their pastors and masters fish out from the rusty armoury of outworn superstitions. The cure will only come when intellectuals can find a career that embodies their creative impulses. I do not see any prescription except the old one advocated by Disraeli: 'Educate our masters.' But it will have to be a more real education than is commonly given at the present day to either proletarians or plutocrats, and it will have to be an education taking some account of real cultural values and not only of the utilitarian desire to produce so many goods that nobody has time to enjoy them. A man is not allowed to practise medicine unless he knows something of the human body, but a financier is allowed to operate freely without any knowledge at all of the multifarious effects of his activities, with the sole exception of the effect upon his bank account. How pleasant a world would be in which no man was allowed to operate on the Stock Exchange unless he could pass an examination in economics and Greek poetry, and in which politicians were obliged to have a competent knowledge of history and modern novels! Imagine a magnate confronted with the question: 'If you were to make a corner in wheat, what effect would this have upon German poetry?' Causation in the modern world is more complex and remote in its ramifications than it ever was before, owing to the increase of large organizations; but those who control these organizations are ignorant men who do not know the hundredth part of the consequences of their actions. Rabelais published his book anonymously for fear of losing his University post. A modern Rabelais would never write the book, because he would be aware that his anonymity would be penetrated by the perfected methods of publicity. The rulers of the world have always been stupid, but have not in the past been so powerful as they are now. It is therefore more important than it used to be to find some way of securing that they shall be intelligent. Is this problem insoluble? I do not think so, but I should be the last to maintain that it is easy.

BERTRAND RUSSELL, 'On Youthful Cynicism', in *In Praise of Idleness* (1935).

WE NEED ONE ANOTHER
(1930)

WE lack peace because we are not whole. And we are not whole because we have known only a tithe of the vital relationships we might have had. We live in an age which believes in stripping away the relationships. Strip them away, like an onion, till you come to pure, or blank nothingness. Emptiness.

That is where most men have come now: to a knowledge of their own complete emptiness. They wanted so badly to be 'themselves' that they became nothing at all: or next to nothing.

It is not much fun, being next to nothing. And life ought to be fun, the greatest fun. Not merely 'having a good time', in order to 'get away from yourself'. But real fun in being yourself. Now there are two great relationships possible to human beings: the relationship of man to woman, and the relationship of man to man. As regards both, we are in a hopeless mess.

But the relationship of man to woman is the central fact in actual human life. Next comes the relationship of man to man. And, a long way after, all the other relationships, fatherhood, motherhood, sister, brother, friend.

A young man said to me the other day, rather sneeringly, 'I'm afraid I can't believe in the regeneration of England by sex.' I said to him: 'I'm sure you can't.' He was trying to inform me that he was above such trash as sex, and such commonplaces as women. He was the usual vitally below par, hollow, and egoistic young man, infinitely wrapped up in himself, like a sort of mummy that will crumble if unwrapped.

And what is sex, after all, but the symbol of the relation of man to woman, woman to man? And the relation of man to woman is wide as all life. It consists in infinite different flows between the two beings, different, even apparently contrary. Chastity is part of the flow between man and woman, as to physical passion. And beyond these, an infinite range of subtle communication which we know nothing about. I should say that the relation between any two decently married people changes profoundly every few years, often without their knowing anything about it; though every change causes pain, even if it brings a certain joy. The long course of marriage is a long event of perpetual change, in which a man and a woman mutually build up their souls and make themselves whole. It is like rivers flowing on, through new country, always unknown.

But we are so foolish, and fixed by our limited ideas. A man says: 'I don't love my wife any more, I no longer want to sleep with her.' But why should he always want to sleep with her? How does he know what other subtle and vital interchange is going on between him and her, making them both whole, in this period when he doesn't want to sleep with her? And she, instead of jibbing and saying that all is over and she must find another man and get a divorce – why doesn't she pause, and listen for a new rhythm in her soul, and look for the new movement in the man? With every change, a new being emerges, a new rhythm establishes itself; we renew our life as we grow older, and there is real peace. Why, oh, why do we want one another to be always the same, fixed, like a menu-card that is never changed?

If only we had more sense. But we are held by a few fixed ideas, like sex, money, what a person 'ought' to be, and so forth, and we miss the whole of life. Sex is a changing thing, now alive, now quiescent, now fiery, now apparently quite gone, quite gone. But the ordinary man and woman haven't the gumption to take it in all its changes. They demand crass, crude sex-desire, they demand it always, and when it isn't forthcoming, then – smash-bash! smash up the whole show. Divorce! Divorce!

I am so tired of being told that I want mankind to go back to the condition of savages. As if modern city people weren't about the crudest, rawest, most crassly savage monkeys that ever existed, when it comes to the relation of man and woman. All I see in our vaunted civilization is men and women smashing each other emotionally and psychically to bits, and all I ask is that they should pause and consider.

For sex, to men, means the whole of the relationship between man and woman. Now this relationship is far greater than we know. We only know a few crude forms – mistress, wife, mother, sweetheart. The woman is like an idol, or a marionette, always forced to play one role or another: sweetheart, mistress, wife, mother. If only we could break up this fixity, and realize the unseizable quality of real woman: that a woman is a flow, a river of life, quite different from a man's river of life: and that each river must flow in its own way, though without breaking its bounds: and that the relation of man to woman is the flowing of two rivers side by side, sometimes even mingling, then separating again, and travelling on. The relationship is a life-long change and a life-long travelling. And that is sex. At periods, sex-desire itself departs completely. Yet the great flow of the relationship goes on all the same, undying, and this is the flow of living sex, the relation between man and woman, that lasts a lifetime, and of which sex-desire is only one vivid, most vivid, manifestation.

D. H. LAWRENCE, 'We Need One Another' (1930), in *Phoenix* (1936).

AN IDEA OF THE WRITER
(1948)

ALL those whose success in life depends neither upon a job which satisfies some specific and unchanging social need, like a farmer's, nor, like a surgeon's, upon some craft which he can be taught by others and improve by practice, but upon 'inspiration', the lucky hazard of ideas, live by their wits, a phrase which carries a slightly pejorative meaning. Every 'original' genius, be he an artist or a scientist, has something a bit shady about him, like a gambler or a medium.

Literary gatherings, cocktail parties and the like, are a social nightmare because writers have no 'shop' to talk. Lawyers and doctors can entertain each other with stories about interesting cases, about experiences, that is to say, related to their professional interests but yet impersonal and outside themselves.

Writers have no impersonal professional interests. The literary equivalent of talking shop would be writers reciting their own work at each other, an unpopular procedure for which only very young writers have the nerve.

No poet or novelist wishes he were the only one who ever lived, but most of them wish they were the only one alive, and quite a number fondly believe their wish has been granted.

In theory, the author of a good book should remain anonymous, for it is to his work, not to himself, that admiration is due. In practice, this seems to be impossible. However, the praise and public attention that writers sometimes receive does not seem to be as fatal to them as one might expect. Just as a good man forgets his deed the moment he has done it, a genuine writer forgets a work as soon as he has completed it and starts to think about the next one; if he thinks about his past work at all, he is more likely to remember its faults than its virtues. Fame often makes a writer vain, but seldom makes him proud.

Writers can be guilty of every kind of human conceit but one, the conceit of the social worker: 'We are all here on earth to help others; what on earth the others are here for, I don't know.'

When a successful author analyzes the reasons for his success, he generally underestimates the talent he was born with, and overestimates his skill in employing it.

Every writer would rather be rich than poor, but no genuine writer cares about popularity as such. He needs approval of his work by others in order to be reassured that the vision of life he believes he has had is a true vision and not a self-delusion, but he can only be reassured by those whose judgment he respects. It would only be necessary for a writer to secure universal popularity if imagination and intelligence were equally distributed among all men.

When some obvious booby tells me he has liked a poem of mine, I feel as if I had picked his pocket.

Writers, poets especially, have an odd relation to the public because their medium, language, is not, like the paint of the painter or the notes of the composer, reserved for their use but is the common property of the linguistic group to which they belong. Lots of people are willing to admit that they don't understand painting or music, but very few indeed who have been to school and learned to read advertisements will admit that they don't understand English. As Karl Kraus said: 'The public doesn't understand German, and in Journalese I can't tell them so.'

How happy the lot of the mathematician! He is judged solely by his peers, and the standard is so high that no colleague or rival can ever win a reputation he does not deserve. No cashier writes a letter to the press complaining about the incomprehensibility of Modern Mathematics and comparing it unfavorably with the good old days when mathematicians were content to paper irregularly shaped rooms and fill bathtubs without closing the waste pipe.

To say that a work is inspired means that, in the judgment of its author or his readers, it is better than they could reasonably hope it would be, and nothing else.

All works of art are commissioned in the sense that no artist can create one by a simple act of will but must wait until what he believes to be a good idea for a work 'comes' to him. Among those works which are failures because their initial conceptions were false or inadequate, the number of self-commissioned works may well be greater than the number commissioned by patrons.

The degree of excitement which a writer feels during the process of composition is as much an indication of the value of the final result as the excitement felt by a worshiper is an indication of the value of his devotions, that is to say, very little indication.

The Oracle claimed to make prophecies and give good advice about the future; it never pretended to be giving poetry readings.

W. H. AUDEN, 'Writing', in *The Dyer's Hand* (1948).

MEASURING VALUES
(1951)

I WANT now to say something about the Richards Theory of Value, expounded in *The Principles of Literary Criticism* and *Science and Poetry*. It has the great merit of getting away from the mere assertion that previously existing theories are Emotive, but I think it raises new puzzles about whether it is Emotive in its turn. A brief quotation from the *Principles* will, I take it, be sufficient to recall what the theory is about (an 'appetency' is a positive impulse):

Anything is valuable which will satisfy an appetency without involving the frustration of some equal or more important appetency. ... The importance of an impulse [is] the extent of the disturbance of other impulses in the individual's activities which the thwarting of the impulse involves. ... Thus morals become purely prudential.

I understand that we have about a million impulses a minute, so the calculation involved might be pretty heavy. But some estimate of the result is certainly envisaged:

The purpose of the theory is just to enable us to compare different experiences with respect to their value; and their value, I suggest, is a quantitative matter.

There is also an 'experimental test' of the truth of the theory, in that all men 'when they can choose' choose to satisfy more appetencies rather than less. It seems clear that they might always do it and yet sometimes be ill-advised; however, after saying that all men agree Professor Richards can reasonably take for granted that he agrees too. No doubt the choice must have an emotive basis, but this would equally be true of the choice to believe an absolutist ethic.

I do feel that something like this is probably true, but one must not take it to say very much. As regards the previous question, whether our moral sentiments correspond to something in the nature of the universe, I do not see that the Richards theory does anything to alter the state of doubt. It has the merit of making our judgments tolerably independent of theories about the universe, but one can still argue that, since the universe is such as to be able to produce us, it cannot be wholly alien to us. One can also still believe (to use a phrase of Professor J. B. S. Haldane's) that it is not only queerer than we know but queerer than we can know. Mr T. S. Eliot, indeed, said that the Richards theory was 'probably quite true', but that he could believe a religious theory of value as well. The idea of measuring value has been objected to as such, but it is at least a traditional one, since the Christian God is to give us all marks on Judgment Day. No doubt there would be a free-will problem, in a practical form, if the scientists claimed to have worked out the calculation, but it would always be possible to claim that they had done it wrong. It may be that the human mind can recognise actually incommensurable values, and that the chief human value is to stand up between them; but I do not see how we could know that they were incommensurable till the calculation had been attempted.

There is a separate group of objections about the technique proposed. You may doubt whether one impulse has a value at all, any more than an atom has a temperature; but an extrapolation of this kind might still be a quite harmless fiction, as the basis for a method of calculating. Value seems to come into the sphere of fact of its own accord, rather like imaginary numbers into the solution of real equations; but for rigorous logic you have then to go back and alter the definitions of the numbers in the equations – they were always complex numbers but with null imaginary parts. An inherent capacity for taking part in valuable situations can, I suppose, be imputed even to an electron. It is much more difficult, I think, to see why impulses should all have equal values, positive or negative; this is not a peculiarity of the Richards theory, but a view which Bertrand Russell has also maintained. It seems to me an unconscious bit of politics; democracy is invoked. But the point about democracy is not that people all really have equally good judgement; no sane man believes this; the claim is that the government or the constitution has no right to presume that some group of citizens has better judgement than the rest. People with better judgement must try to convince their neighbours, and not over-rule them. Now it may be said that a Theory of Value has itself a sort of political claim; if it were seriously applied, it would be applied in politics as well as elsewhere; and it would be no use telling people that some impulses were better than others, even if they actually are. It is not enough that there is justice; there must be 'evident justice'; and the only way to convince people (to disprove an idea that 'push-pin is better than poetry' or what not) is to insist that you are starting fair. No doubt the falsity of the pretence that all *men* are equal entails a certain risk, and the same for *impulses*, but there is less risk in it than in any attempt to prejudge their different values, because this is certain to be an 'interested' one. On this view, it might be a duty to act in all public affairs as though the Theory of Value was true, even though everyone believed, correctly, that it was false. I remember long ago attending a lecture by Bertrand Russell at Cambridge, a dramatic affair, with the experts watching him keenly as some new paradox was expounded, and his own eyes shifting alertly and guardedly from one man whose theoretical toes were being trodden on to another whose turn was now coming. He brought out a coin, and the business about 'me seeing my penny' was gone through with some new twist; for quite a time, the eyes of everyone seemed to be shifting one way or another and back to this object. Then somebody at the back of the room began to laugh, and it turned out that what he had got was half-a-crown. I thought it a very neat symbol of the Whig aristocrat and his democratic views; the actual value of his coin was a thing he would not have considered it polite to notice. Now on this view of the Theory of Value it is very definitely a 'pseudo-statement', a fiction adopted for good mental effects; but the question whether the effects are really 'good', in some other sense of the term than that defined by the Theory of Value (that is whether the risk has been overcome), is sure to be a real one.

In any case, it is clear that a theory of value must itself be valued. I do not think there is any fallacy in calling this secondary process an emotive one; what you do is to see whether your feelings can be made to accept the valuations given by the theory. When Professor Richards begins his sentence 'Anything is valuable which . . .' the word may be supposed to be primarily emotive 'Try to obtain anything which . . .' and secondarily redefinition 'I will in future mean by "valuable" anything which . . .'. Hence, when we have made the redefinition and given the word its new sense, it is no longer 'merely emotive' (though still emotive) and can be used to make true or false assertions. This, I think, is clearly what was intended; it would follow for instance from the footnote I have quoted from *The Meaning of Meaning*. Thus the moral or aesthetic judgements of a person who agrees with Professor Richards may all be regarded as factual, and I don't see why this should not be true if they are written in verse. It will be agreed that this is a tempting offer. But even though the word itself is not Emotive it seems likely that the whole passage in which the word occurs will be predominantly concerned to affect the reader's attitudes, and will therefore be Emotive by the other criterion. Thus, even if you agree that all impulses have equal value, it remains, I think, a question of great subtlety whether a statement of the Theory of Value is a 'pseudo-statement' or not. One does not get clear from *Science and Poetry* what sort of pseudo-statements can still be valuable when they are recognised as such, and yet some of them must be of this sort because they are to save us from the collapse of the Magical View of Nature. I take it that the idea of God cannot healthily be used as a fiction on the mere ground that it does you good; certainly an atheist can entertain it in his reading to good effect, but only because he is imagining some person who does believe in God, not because he is pretending that he himself does. And at the other extreme there seem to be fictions which are automatic. All the arts depend on empathy, something like 'attributing feelings or impulses to objects of sense and then sympathising with them'. But this is instinctive; it may have caused the Magical View of Nature, but would not collapse with it, and does not need to be viewed as a statement at all, whether pseudo or not. The difficulty is to see what beliefs form the class in between these two, for which the idea of a pseudo-statement is required; you must be able to use them as statements for emotional effect without feeling that you are cheating yourself. To be sure, there are a great variety of verbal fictions, perhaps 'the spirit of the age' will do as an example, which one should be able to use without fuss but with awareness that they may need analysing on occasion; Vaihinger's *Philosophy of As If* presented a very mixed bag of these entities, as well as I remember, without constructing much of a philosophy of them. On the whole they seem of the nature of shorthand rather than of edification; they are easily regarded as metaphors. Or it might be said that the good pseudo-statements are cases where you are expected to show tact in not pressing your deductions from the statement in unreasonable directions; this would be unfair because the man could have stopped you if he had put in enough qualifications. But what the term is aiming at must be something more serious. And, of course, I don't deny, at the other extreme, that a good deal of firm ignoring of the facts around one may be positively heroic, or agreeably spirited; there is the same general notion as the pseudo-statement theory when E. M. Forster writes (in *What I Believe*) 'The people I respect must behave as if they were immortal and as if society were eternal.' But surely this kind of thing is a matter of temperament or tradition, not of doctrine; if it is taken quite seriously it becomes insane or factitious, and in either case disagreeable. I am looking for the pseudo-statements which are to be the basis for the arts of the future, which can be a reliable support for valuable attitudes. It seems a plausible view that the Theory of Value itself is the only important candidate.

WILLIAM EMPSON, *The Structure of Complex Words* (1951).

'MIND' AND 'MATTER'

(1951)

LET us begin by considering the use of the words 'mind' and 'matter'. Evidently people think that they mean something when they use these words, and they do not think that they are in the habit of using them for the same events. Going no deeper than the verbal level, if the distinction between the words 'mind' and 'matter' means anything we should try to understand what it means, and if it does not mean anything we should be clear about that also.

Philosophers and other thinking people who have assumed that there is some distinction between mind and matter have been chiefly concerned with two different questions: (1) What is the relationship between those events we call mental and the collection of matter which we call our brains? and (2) Are the things which we perceive with our senses wholly material or, as some have thought, wholly mental, or partly one and partly the other? As we shall see, these questions are intimately related to one another.

People sometimes put it in this way: 'Is matter *really* mental?' or 'Is the mind *really* a manifestation of the matter of which the brain is composed?' Evidently there is something which they mean by matter which, at first sight at any rate, is different from mind, and conversely – whatever these two terms may turn out to represent when we get to know more about them.

Let us, without attempting to define matter, look at some instances of the use of the term. If we ask someone to give us some examples of matter he might say that it consists of solids, liquids and gases, or that it exists in the form of tables and chairs, muscles and bones, nerves and brains. If we then say: 'What do you mean by the mind, or what would you regard as mental?' he might find it more difficult to reply. Thought would certainly seem to be mental, for thinking is perhaps the most characteristic function of the mind, as we use the term. Feeling and willing? Yes, those would probably also be regarded as mental. But what about sensation? Is there something mental about colours, touches and sounds? Here we should begin to get into a difficulty; in fact, we should find ourselves at once involved in the ancient controversy between the idealist and the realist. On the one hand, if we regard sensations as a state of consciousness and assume that the mind is somehow involved in consciousness, we can make out a case for treating them as mental; but on the other hand, the colour of the table certainly seems to be in some way part of the table, though the sound of a bell is not in quite the same way part of the bell and a touch on my hand appears to come into yet another category, because it is not exactly part of the object touching me nor can it be described as part of my hand.

Instead of talking about isolated sensations let us think of a solid object which I hold in my hand. I perceive that object through touches and pressures, and feelings of heat or cold, together with information derived from the posture of my fingers and the extent to which they are separated by the object from the palm of my hand. Are all these sensations mental or are they part of the object? If I feel that a stone in my hand is cold I do so only because it causes a fall of temperature in my skin which makes my fingers colder than they were and excites certain nerve-endings. Yet I usually speak of the stone and not of my hand as being cold, though I can remember a small child putting his hand in the river and saying, 'I am going to feel my hand in the water.'

Let us leave this question on one side for the moment and turn now to what we call the world of matter. How do we know about the tables and chairs, about other people's bodies and brains and, for that matter, about our own bodies and brains? Let us see what happens when somebody else, whom we will call the observer, sees a colour or hears a sound.

The physical stimulus, as we call it, excites the appropriate receptor organ, in this case the eye or ear, and this in turn starts an electrical impulse in the corresponding nerve running to the brain. These nerve-impulses differ somewhat in minor details, including the rate at which they are conducted towards the central nervous system, but they are substantially alike, and no neurophysiologist believes that differences in the nature of the impulses conducted by the ingoing nerves correspond to differences in the kind of sensation which they lead us to experience. Thus merely from recording the electrical disturbances which accompany the passage of a nerve-impulse and observing their characteristics it is impossible to say whether the sensation with which they are concerned is one of sight, hearing, sound, taste or touch, and, indeed, it is not until such nerve-impulses reach what may be called their end-stations in the brain that we experience a sensation at all. It would seem, therefore, that what determines our awareness of a sensation, and also its nature, is the arrival of a nerve-impulse, or more probably a series of nerve-impulses, at the appropriate end-station in the brain.

We have other evidence in support of this view, for clinical neurology teaches us that we can experience a sensation without any sensory organs being excited, and without any impulse travelling up an ingoing nerve. All that is necessary is that the appropriate area of brain should be excited in some other way. Thus we know that if one of the end-stations of the brain normally concerned with sensation is stimulated by the electrical discharge which underlies an epileptic fit, or by the disturbance which constitutes an attack of migraine, the patient will experience a sensation corresponding in quality to the area of brain excited, and we know further that a very wide range of sensations, including sight, smell, sound, taste, touch and others, can all be reproduced by exciting the appropriate area of the cortex, some of them even by the surgeon using an electrical stimulus on the conscious patient. It is true that the sensations produced in this way are usually of a somewhat crude kind, but then the stimulus is of a crude kind, and, when once the principle has been accepted that the application to the brain of a stimulus which is capable of evoking a response will produce a sensation, there is no reason to doubt that if we were able to deliver a more refined and complicated stimulus, complicated in its organization both in space and time, we could reproduce more complex kinds of sensation.

What follows from this? We have seen that a physical stimulus excites a sensory receiving-organ, and this a nerve-impulse, which is in no way like the original physical stimulus and that this in turn sets going a disturbance in the end-station in the brain which is probably in certain respects unlike the nerve-impulse, and certainly is quite unlike the original physical stimulus, and it is upon this disturbance in the brain that sensation depends. Hence the brain state which constitutes the physical basis of a sensation is always quite unlike the physical stimulus which impinges upon the body and which has been in one way or another directly set in motion by the external object which we experience. Thus the relationship between the brain state which underlies the sensation and the physical object of which that sensation makes us aware is merely that the brain state is the last of a series of events caused by the physical stimulus. Whatever the relationship between the brain state underlying a sensation and the corresponding awareness of the sensation in consciousness it would seem to follow that the sensation must be quite unlike the physical stimulus originating in the outside world and exciting the sense-organs.

It follows also that the experience of a given sensation must always be later in time than the physical event which initiates it. Indeed, it must be later in time than the excitation of the receptors on the surface of the body by that physical event, since the nerve-impulse takes time to travel from the surface of the body to the brain. How much later in time it is than the physical event will depend obviously upon the distance of the object concerned from the body and the rate of propagation of the physical stimulus through the intervening medium. The speed of light is so great that only a fraction of a second intervenes between the time when a light wave is reflected from any object on the earth and the time when it strikes the eye of the observer. This interval is so short that for all practical purposes it can be neglected, and we normally pay no attention to it. We behave as though we see something happening at the very moment at which it happens. We cannot do this, however, in the sphere of astronomy where years may pass between the moment at which a light wave leaves a star and that at which the eye perceives it. If it takes several years for the light from a star at which I am now looking to reach my eye, the star can no longer be in the position at which I see it, and, indeed, if it had ceased to exist in the interval between the present moment and that at which the light wave left it I should have no means of discovering the fact. Owing to the relatively slow speed of sound compared with that of light this anomaly may become obvious even on the surface of the earth when sound is concerned. The sound of a jet-plane comes from a different point in the sky from that at which we see the plane.

W. RUSSELL BRAIN, *Mind, Perception and Science* (1951).

BIOGRAPHICAL NOTES

ARNOLD, MATTHEW (1822–88): poet and critic; son of Thomas Arnold of Rugby; Inspector of Schools, 1851–83; *The Strayed Reveller* (1849), *Empedocles on Etna* (1852), *Poems* (1853), *Poems, 2nd Series* (1855), *New Poems* (1867), *Culture and Anarchy* (1869), *Literature and Dogma* (1873), *Essays in Criticism* (1865 and 1888). *p. 297*

AUDEN, WYSTAN HUGH (born 1907): poet; *The Orators* (1932), *Dance of Death* (1933), *Ascent of F6* (with Christopher Isherwood, 1936), *The Age of Anxiety* (1947), *Nones* (1951), *Homage to Clio* (1960). *p. 484*

AUSTEN, JANE (1775–1817): novelist; *Sense and Sensibility* (1811), *Pride and Prejudice* (1813), *Mansfield Park* (1814), *Emma* (1816), *Persuasion* (1818), *Northanger Abbey* (written 1798, published 1818). *pp. 109, 114*

BAGEHOT, WALTER (1826–77): critic; editor of *The Economist* from 1860; literary essays in 1850s; *The English Constitution* (1867), *Physics and Politics* (1872). *p. 294*

BAMFORD, SAMUEL (1788–1872): Lancashire handloom weaver and radical; *Passages in The Life of a Radical* (two volumes, 1844). *p. 85*

BENNETT, ENOCH ARNOLD (1867–1931): novelist; *The Old Wives' Tale* (1908), *Clayhanger* (1910), *Hilda Lessways* (1911), *Riceyman Steps* (1923). *p. 376*

BEWICK, THOMAS (1753–1828): engraver; born in Northumberland and worked mainly in Newcastle; *General History of Quadrupeds* (1790), *History of British Birds* (1797 and 1804); wrote account of his life for his children, published as *Memoir of Thomas Bewick, by Himself* (1862). *p. 59*

BRAIN, WALTER RUSSELL (1895–1967): neurologist; President of the Royal College of Physicians, 1950–57. *Mind, Perception and Science* (1951); *The Nature of Experience* (1959). *p. 492*

BRONTË, CHARLOTTE (1816–55): novelist; *Jane Eyre* (1847), *Shirley* (1849), *Villette* (1853); first novel, *The Professor*, published posthumously (1857). *p. 215*

BRONTË, EMILY (1818–48): poet and novelist; *Wuthering Heights* (1847). *p. 212*

BIOGRAPHICAL NOTES

BUCKLE, HENRY THOMAS (1821–62): historian; *The History of Civilisation in England* (two volumes, 1857 and 1861). *p. 290*

BURKE, EDMUND (1729–97): political writer; *Thoughts on the Causes of the Present Discontents* (1770), *Reflections on the Revolution in France* (1790), *Letter to a Noble Lord* (1796). Member of Parliament 1774–94. *pp. 122, 123*

BUTLER, SAMUEL (1825–1902): satirist and critic; *Erewhon* (1872), *The Fair Haven* (1873), *Life and Habit* (1878), *Erewhon Revisited* (1901), *The Way of All Flesh* (published posthumously, 1903). *p. 263*

CARLYLE, THOMAS (1795–1881): critic and historian; *Sartor Resartus* (1838), *The French Revolution* (1837), *Chartism* (1839), *On Heroes, Hero-Worship and the Heroic in History* (1841), *Past and Present* (1843), *Latter Day Pamphlets* (1850), *Frederick the Great* (1858–65). *p.283*

CARROLL, LEWIS, pen-name of DODGSON, CHARLES LUTRIDGE (1832–98): mathematician; in addition to mathematical works, 1860–93, *Alice's Adventures in Wonderland* (1865), *Through the Looking-Glass* (1872), *The Hunting of the Snark* (1876). *p. 245*

CARY, ARTHUR JOYCE LUNEL (1888–1957): novelist; *Aissa Saved* (1932), *The African Witch* (1936), *Mister Johnson* (1939), *The Horse's Mouth* (1944), *A Fearful Joy* (1949), *Prisoner of Grace* (1952), *Not Honour More* (1955). *p. 422*

COBBETT, WILLIAM (1762–1835): political writer; *Political Register*, from 1802, *Rural Rides* (1820–30), *Advice to Young Men* (1829). *pp. 68, 129, 147*

COLERIDGE, SAMUEL TAYLOR (1772–1834): poet and critic; *Poems on Various Subjects* (1796), *Lyrical Ballads*, with William Wordsworth (1798), *Christabel* and *Kubla Khan* (1816), *Biographia Literaria* (1817), *Aids to Reflection* (1825), *The Constitution of Church and State* (1830). Edited and published *The Friend* (1808–10). *p. 130*

CONRAD, JOSEPH, pen-name of KORZENIOWSKI, JOZEF TEODOR KONRAD (1857–1924): novelist; *Almayer's Folly* (1895), *Lord Jim* (1900), *Nostromo* (1904), *The Secret Agent* (1907), *Under Western Eyes* (1911). Born in the Ukraine, of Polish parents, Conrad became a British sailor and in 1886 received his master mariner's ticket and naturalization. He left the sea in 1893. *p. 370*

CONSTABLE, JOHN (1776–1837): painter; exhibited from 1802; 'the father of modern landscape painting'. *pp. 90, 268*

BIOGRAPHICAL NOTES

DARWIN, CHARLES ROBERT (1809–82): scientist; *Journal of Researches* (1839), *Origin of Species* (1859), *The Descent of Man* (1871). *pp. 158, 176*

DE QUINCEY, THOMAS (1785–1859): essayist; *Confessions of an English Opium-Eater* (1821), *Suspiria de Profundis* (1845), *Vision of Sudden Death* (1849). *p. 74*

DICKENS, CHARLES (1812–70): novelist; *Pickwick Papers* (1837–9), *Nicholas Nickleby* (1839), *Martin Chuzzlewit* (1843), *Dombey and Son* (1848), *David Copperfield* (1850), *Bleak House* (1853), *Hard Times* (1854), *Little Dorrit* (1857), *Great Expectations* (1861), *Our Mutual Friend* (1865). *pp. 196, 200, 202*

DISRAELI, BENJAMIN (1804–81): novelist and politician; *Vivian Grey* (1827), *Alroy* (1833), *Coningsby* (1844), *Sybil* (1845), *Tancred* (1847), *Lothair* (1870), *Endymion* (1880). Member of Parliament from 1837, and Prime Minister 1868, and 1874–80. *p. 193*

DRY, THOMAS (1888–1916): watchmaker; killed in action, France, August 1916, after service in Gallipoli with 23rd Battalion, Australian Imperial Force. *p. 325*

EDGEWORTH, MARIA (1767–1849): novelist; *Castle Rackrent* (1800), *Leonora* (1806), *Tales of Fashionable Life* (1809 and 1812), *Helen* (1834). *p. 101*

ELIOT, GEORGE, pen-name of EVANS, MARY ANN (1819–80): novelist; *Scenes from Clerical Life* (1857), *Adam Bede* (1859), *The Mill on the Floss* (1860), *Silas Marner* (1861), *Felix Holt* (1866), *Middlemarch* (1872), *Daniel Deronda* (1876). *pp. 218, 221, 281*

ELIOT, THOMAS STEARNS (1888–1965): poet and critic; *Prufrock and Other Observations* (1917), *The Sacred Wood* (1920), *The Waste Land* (1922), *Homage to John Dryden* (1924), *Ash Wednesday* (1930), *Murder in the Cathedral* (1935), *Idea of a Christian Society* (1939), *Four Quartets* (1943), *Notes towards the Definition of Culture* (1948), *The Cocktail Party* (1949), *The Elder Statesman* (1958). *p. 470*

EMPSON, WILLIAM (born 1906): poet and critic; *Seven Types of Ambiguity* (1930), *Some Versions of Pastoral* (1935), *The Structure of Complex Words* (1951), *Milton's God* (1961), *Collected Poems* (1955). *p. 487*

FARADAY, MICHAEL (1791–1867): Scientist; active research from 1812, first published paper 1816; discovered electromagnetic rotation, 1821; demonstrated electromagnetic induction, 1831; basic laws of electrolysis. *p. 64*

FORSTER, EDWARD MORGAN (born 1879): novelist; *Where Angels Fear to Tread* (1905), *The Longest Journey* (1907), *A Room with a View* (1908), *Howards End* (1910), *Passage to India* (1924). *p. 379*

FOX, HAROLD MUNRO (1889–1967): scientist; *The Nature of Animal Colours* (with G. Vevers, 1960); papers on physiology. *p. 338*

GALT, JOHN (1779–1839): novelist; *Ayrshire Legatees* (1820), *Annals of the Parish* (1821), *Sir Andrew Wylie* (1822), *The Entail* (1824), *Autobiography* (1834). *p. 105*

GASKELL, ELIZABETH CLEGHORN (1810–65): novelist; *Mary Barton* (1848), *Ruth* (1853), *Cranford* (1853), *North and South* (1855), *Sylvia's Lovers* (1863), *Wives and Daughters* (1865). *p. 186*

GIBBON, LEWIS GRASSIC, pen-name of MITCHELL, JAMES LESLIE (1901–35): novelist; *Sunset Song* (1932), *Cloud Howe* (1933), *Grey Granite* (1934). *p. 396*

GISSING, GEORGE (1857–1903): novelist; *Demos* (1886), *The Nether World* (1889), *New Grub Street* (1891), *Born in Exile* (1892), *In the Year of Jubilee* (1894). *p. 259*

GREENE, HENRY GRAHAM (born 1904): novelist; *Brighton Rock* (1938), *The Power and the Glory* (1940), *The Heart of the Matter* (1948), *The End of the Affair* (1951), *The Quiet American* (1955), *A Burnt-out Case* (1961). *p. 440*

GODWIN, WILLIAM (1756–1836): philosophical writer and novelist; *Political Justice* (1793), *Caleb Williams* (1794), *St Leon* (1799), *Essay on Sepulchres* (1808), *Mandeville* (1817), *Cloudesley* (1830). *p. 92*

HARDY, THOMAS (1840–1928): novelist and poet; *Desperate Remedies* (1871), *Under the Greenwood Tree* (1872), *Far from the Madding Crowd* (1874), *Return of the Native* (1878), *The Mayor of Casterbridge* (1886), *The Woodlanders* (1887), *Tess of the D'Urbervilles* (1891), *Jude the Obscure* (1895). *pp. 255, 257*

HAZLITT, WILLIAM (1778–1830): essayist; *Principles of Human Action* (1805), *The Round Table* (1817), *The English Poets* (1818), *English Comic Writers* (1819), *The Spirit of the Age* (1825). *pp. 145, 157*

HOGGART, RICHARD (born 1918): critic; *Auden* (1951), *The Uses of Literacy* (1957). *p. 343*

HOLBROOK, DAVID (born 1923): poet and critic; *English for Maturity* (1961), *The Quest for Love* (1964), *Flesh Wounds* (1966), *Object Relations* (1967). *p. 443*

HOLLOWAY, JOHN (born 1920): poet and critic; *The Victorian Sage* (1953), *The Charted Mirror* (1960), *The Landfallers* (1962). *p. 350*

HULME, THOMAS ERNEST (1883–1917): poet and critic; early poems published in 1912; his philosophical writings edited, after his death in action, in *Speculations* (1924) and *Notes on Language and Style* (1929). *p. 467, 468*

HUNT, JAMES HENRY LEIGH (1784–1859): essayist; edited *The Examiner, The Indicator* and *The Companion*; *Story of Rimini* (1816), *Imagination and Fancy* (1844), *Autobiography* (1850, rev. 1859). *p. 65*

HUXLEY, ALDOUS LEONARD (1894–1963): novelist; *Crome Yellow* (1921), *Point Counter Point* (1928), *Brave New World* (1932), *Ape and Essence* (1948), *Island* (1962). *p. 411*

HUXLEY, THOMAS HENRY (1825–95): scientist; *Man's Place in Nature* (1863), *Elementary Physiology* (1866), *Scientific Memoirs* (edited 1898–1903), *Collected Essays* (edited 1898). *p. 300*

JAMES, HENRY (1843–1916): novelist; born New York, settled London 1876; *Roderick Hudson* (1875), *The Europeans* (1878), *Portrait of a Lady* (1881), *What Maisie Knew* (1897), *The Awkward Age* (1899), *The Ambassadors* (1903), *The Golden Bowl* (1904). *p. 363*

JEFFERIES, JOHN RICHARD (1848–87): essayist and novelist; *Hodge and his Masters* (1880), *Bevis* (1882), *Story of My Heart* (1883), *The Open Air* (1885), *Amaryllis at the Fair* (1887). *p. 173*

JONES, DAVID (born 1895): painter; *In Parenthesis* (1937), *The Anathemata* (1952), *The Wall* (1955). *p. 410*

JONES, ALFRED ERNEST (d. 1958): psychiatrist; *Social Aspects of Psychoanalysis* (1924), *Sigmund Freud, Life and Work* (3 vols., 1953–7). *p. 354*

JOYCE, JAMES AUGUSTINE ALOYSIUS (1882–1941): novelist; *Dubliners* (1914), *Portrait of the Artist as a Young Man* (1916), *Ulysses* (1922), *Finnegans Wake* (1939). *pp. 397, 404*

KEATS, JOHN (1795–1821): poet; *Poems* (1817), *Endymion* (1818), *Lamia and Other Poems* (1820), *Letters*, edited 1848 and 1900. *p. 70*

KILVERT, ROBERT FRANCIS (1840–79): diarist; as clergyman in Radnorshire and Herefordshire kept diary 1870–79. This was discovered in 1937 and published in edited form 1938–40. *p. 179*

KINGSLEY, CHARLES (1819–75): novelist; *Yeast* (1848), *Alton Locke* (1850), *Hypatia* (1853), *Westward Ho* (1855), *Hereward the Wake* (1866). *p. 161*

LAMB, CHARLES (1775–1834): Essayist; *Works of Charles Lamb* (1818), *Essays of Elia* (1823), *Last Essays of Elia* (1833). pp. *137, 139*

LARKIN, PHILIP (born 1922): poet and novelist; *The North Ship* (1945), *Jill* (1946), *A Girl in Winter* (1947), *The Less Deceived* (1955). p. *453*

LAWRENCE, DAVID HERBERT (1885–1930): novelist and poet; *The White Peacock* (1911), *Sons and Lovers* (1913), *The Rainbow* (1915), *Women in Love* (1920), *Lady Chatterley's Lover* (1928); uncollected work in *Phoenix* (1935). pp. *387, 481*

LEWIS, PERCY WYNDHAM (1882–1957): novelist; *Tarr* (1918), *Time and Western Man* (1927), *The Childermass* (1928), *Men Without Art* (1934), *The Human Age* (1955). p. *406*

MACAULAY, THOMAS BABINGTON (1800–59): historian; *Essays* (1843), *History of England* (1848 and 1855). p. *269*

MAYHEW, HENRY (1812–87): journalist; *London Labour and the London Poor* (1851, 1856; final form 1864). p. *166*

MEREDITH, GEORGE (1828–1909): novelist; *The Ordeal of Richard Feverel* (1859), *Beauchamp's Career* (1875–6), *The Egoist* (1879), *Diana of the Crossways* (1885). p. *232*

MILL, JOHN STUART (1806–73): philosopher; *Logic* (1843), *Political Economy* (1848), *On Liberty* (1859), *Utilitarianism* (1863), his *Autobiography* published posthumously, 1873. p. *277*

MORRIS, WILLIAM (1834–96): poet; *The Earthly Paradise* (1868–70), *Dream of John Ball* (1888), *News from Nowhere* (1891). His socialist essays and lectures belong to the last ten or twelve years of his life. p. *461*

NASMYTH, JAMES (1808–90): engineer; invented steam hammer in 1839; made many improvements in machine tools and hydraulic machinery; his autobiography edited by Samuel Smiles in 1883. p. *153*

NEWMAN, JOHN HENRY (1801–90): theologian; *University Sermons* (1843), *Idea of a University* (1852), *Apologia pro Vita Sua* (1864), *Grammar of Assent* (1870). p. *273*

O'BRIEN, FLANN, pen-name of NOLAN, BRIAN (1911–66): novelist; *At Swim-Two-Birds* (1939), *The Hard Life* (1961), *The Dalkey Archive* (1964). p. *420*

ORWELL, GEORGE, pen-name of BLAIR, ERIC HUGH (1903–50): novelist; *Down and Out in Paris and London* (1933), *Keep the Aspi-*

distra Flying (1936), *The Road to Wigan Pier* (1937), *Coming Up for Air* (1939), *Animal Farm* (1945), *Nineteen Eighty-Four* (1949). *p. 332*

OWEN, ROBERT (1771–1858): political writer; *A New View of Society* (1813), *Observations on the Effect of the Manufacturing System* (1815), *Life of Robert Owen, written by himself* (1857). Report to the County of Lanark (1821). *p. 141*

PAINE, THOMAS (1737–1809): political writer; *Common Sense* (1776), *Rights of Man* (1791), *The Age of Reason* (1794–5 and 1807). *p. 126*

PATER, WALTER HORATIO (1839–1904): critic; *Studies in the History of the Renaissance* (1873), *Marius the Epicurean* (1885), *Appreciations* (1889), *Greek Studies* (1894). *p. 309*

PEACOCK, THOMAS LOVE (1785–1866): novelist; *Headlong Hall* (1816), *Nightmare Abbey* (1818), *Crotchet Castle* (1831), *Gryll Grange* (1860). *p. 118*

PRIESTLEY, JOSEPH (1733–1804): scientist; *History and Present State of Electricity* (1767), *Disquisition relating to Matter and Spirit* (1777), *Corruptions of Christianity* (1782), *Memoirs* (1795). *p. 61*

RUSKIN, JOHN (1819–1900): critic and essayist; *Modern Painters* (1843–60), *Seven Lamps of Architecture* (1849), *The Stones of Venice* (1851–3), *Political Economy of Art* (1857), *Unto This Last* (1862), *Time and Tide* (1867), *Fors Clavigora* (1871–87). *pp. 181, 287*

RUSSELL, BERTRAND ARTHUR WILLIAM (born 1872): philosopher; *The Principles of Mathematics* (1903), *Philosophical Essays* (1910), *The Analysis of Mind* (1921), *Education and the Social Order* (1932), *History of Western Philosophy* (1945), *Unpopular Essays* (1950). *p. 479*

RUTHERFORD, MARK, pen-name of WHITE, WILLIAM HALE (1831–1913): novelist; *Autobiography of Mark Rutherford* (1881), *The Revolution in Tanner's Lane* (1887), *Miriam's Schooling* (1890). *p. 251*

SCOTT, WALTER (1771–1832): novelist; *Waverley* (1814), *The Antiquary* (1816), *Rob Roy* (1817), *The Heart of Midlothian* (1818), *Kenilworth* (1821), *Quentin Durward* (1823), *The Fair Maid of Perth* (1828). *p. 96*

SHAW, GEORGE BERNARD (1856–1950): dramatist; *Plays Pleasant and Unpleasant* (1898), *Three Plays for Puritans* (1900), *Man and Superman* (1903), *Back to Methuselah* (1921), *Saint Joan* (1923). *p. 321*

SHELLEY, PERCY BYSSHE (1792–1822): poet; *Queen Mab* (1813), *Alastor* (1816), *Revolt of Islam* (1817), *The Cenci* (1819), *Prometheus Unbound* (1820), *Adonais* (1821), *Defence of Poetry* – uncompleted at his death. *p. 135*

SILLITOE, ALAN (born 1928): novelist; *Saturday Night and Sunday Morning* (1958), *The Loneliness of the Long Distance Runner* (1959), *Key to the Door* (1961). *p. 437*

SOMERVILLE, ALEXANDER (1811–?1865): political writer; flogged, with a hundred lashes, in 1832, on a charge arising from political activity as a soldier; *Autobiography of a Working Man* (1848), *The Whistler at the Plough* (1852). *p. 155*

SOUTHEY, ROBERT (1774–1843): poet and essayist; *Thalaba* (1801), *A Vision of Judgment* (1821), *Sir Thomas More, or Colloquies on the Progress and Prospects of Society* (1829), *The Doctor* (1834–7). *p. 148*

STEPHEN, LESLIE (1832–1904): critic; *Free Thinking and Plain Speaking* (1873), *History of English Thought in the Eighteenth Century* (1876–81), *An Agnostic's Apology* (1893), *The English Utilitarians* (1900). *p. 305*

STOREY, DAVID MALCOLM (born 1933): novelist; *This Sporting Life* (1960), *Flight into Camden* (1960), *Radcliffe* (1963). *p. 456*

TAWNEY, RICHARD HENRY (1880–1962): historian; *The Acquisitive Society* (1921), *Religion and the Rise of Capitalism* (1926), *Equality* (revised, 1931). *p. 475*

THACKERAY, WILLIAM MAKEPEACE (1811–63): novelist; *Vanity Fair* (1847–8), *Henry Esmond* (1852), *The Newcomes* (1853). *p. 204*

TROLLOPE, ANTHONY (1815–82): novelist; *Barchester Towers* (1857), *Doctor Thorne* (1858), *Orley Farm* (1862), *Phineas Finn* (1869), *The Way We Live Now* (1875). *p. 237*

TYAS, JOHN WILLIAM (*fl.* 1819): reporter; joined *The Times* 1817; imprisoned at Peterloo; subsequently parliamentary reporter with a long record on the newspaper. *p. 77*

WAIN, JOHN BARRINGTON (born 1925): novelist; *Hurry on Down* (1953), *Living in the Present* (1955), *A Travelling Woman* (1959). *p. 447*

WAUGH, EVELYN ARTHUR ST JOHN (1903–66): novelist; *Decline and Fall* (1928), *Vile Bodies* (1930), *Scoop* (1938), *Put Out More Flags* (1942), *Brideshead Revisited* (1945), *Officers and Gentlemen* (1955), *Unconditional Surrender* (1961). *p. 415*

BIOGRAPHICAL NOTES

WEBB, BEATRICE (1858–1943): historian; with Sidney Webb, *Trade Unionism* (1894 and 1920), *English Local Government* (1906–29), *English Poor Law Policy* (1910); *My Apprenticeship* (1926), *Our Partnership* (published posthumously, 1948). *p. 317*

WELLS, HERBERT GEORGE (1866–1946): novelist; *The Time Machine* (1895), *Kipps* (1905), *Tono Bungay* (1909), *History of Mr Polly* (1910), *Shape of Things to Come* (1933). *p. 358*

WILSON, ANGUS (born 1913): novelist; *The Wrong Set* (1949), *Hemlock and After* (1952), *Anglo-Saxon Attitudes* (1956), *The Old Men at the Zoo* (1961). *p. 428*

WOOLF, LEONARD SIDNEY (born 1880): political writer; *After the Deluge* (2 vols., 1931 and 1939), *Sowing* (1960), *Growing* (1961), *Beginning Again* (1964), *Downhill All the Way* (1967). *p. 323*

WOOLF, ADELINE VIRGINIA (1882–1941): novelist; *The Voyage Out* (1915), *Jacob's Room* (1922), *Mrs Dalloway* (1925), *To the Lighthouse* (1927), *Between the Acts* (1941). *p. 402*

WORDSWORTH, WILLIAM (1770–1850): poet; *The Evening Walk* and *Descriptive Sketches* (1793), *Lyrical Ballads* (with S. T. Coleridge, 1798), *Poems in Two Volumes* (1807), *The Excursion* (1814), *The Prelude* (published posthumously, 1850). *p. 133*

MORE ABOUT PENGUINS

Penguinews, which appears every month, contains details of all the new books issued by Penguins as they are published. From time to time it is supplemented by *Penguins in Print*, which is a complete list of all available books published by Penguins. (There are well over three thousand of these.)

A specimen copy of *Penguinews* will be sent to you free on request, and you can become a subscriber for the price of the postage. For a year's issues (including the complete lists) please send 30p if you live in the United Kingdom, or 60p if you live elsewhere. Just write to Dept EP, Penguin Books Ltd, Harmondsworth, Middlesex, enclosing a cheque or postal order, and your name will be added to the mailing list.

Some other books published by Penguins are described on the following pages.

Note: *Penguinews* and *Penguins in Print* are not available in the U.S.A. or Canada

THE PENGUIN BOOK OF
ENGLISH SHORT STORIES

EDITED BY CHRISTOPHER DOLLEY

Some of the stories in this collection – such as Wells's 'The Country of the Blind' and Joyce's 'The Dead' – are classics; others – like Dickens's 'The Signalman' and Lawrence's 'Fanny and Annie' – are less well known. But all of them – whether funny, tragic, wry or fantastic – show their authors at their concise best. Which makes this representative collection, at the very least, ferociously entertaining.

LITERACY AND DEVELOPMENT
IN THE WEST

CARLO M. CIPOLLA

Mass literacy is scarcely a century old. How did this skill, which had always been a bulwark of civilized values, become also an important agent of social progress?

Professor Cipolla approaches this question with the quantitative method which he used in his earlier Pelican, *The Economic History of World Population*. He ranges from medieval monastic communities, where literacy was the sacred monopoly of small elites, through the bustle of nascent capitalism and the polemics and printing presses of the Reformation, to that great watershed in popular education, the Industrial Revolution.

This book is an object-lesson in the craft of the historian. From European recruitment papers, statistics, marriage registers and legal documents the author has isolated and reconstructed a crucial but neglected process of historical change – the transformation of a world bound by custom, ceremony and spectacle into a sophisticated technical civilization under the rule – and sometimes the tyranny – of the printed word.

OUR LANGUAGE

SIMEON POTTER

Can we ever know too much about the words we use every day of our lives? It is the purpose of this book to present a clear and up-to-date picture of the English language as it is spoken and written in all its amazing variety and complexity. Professor Potter believes that more people today are interested in speech than ever before and that a new spirit of linguistic enterprise and adventure is astir. Can we make the English language of tomorrow yet more effective as a means of communication?

'The author is brilliantly successful in his effort to instruct by delighting. He has only 200 pages at his disposal, yet he contrives not only to give a history of English, but also to talk at his ease on rhyming-slang, names, spelling reform, American English, and much else. The book is admirably clear in its main outlines, but its interest for the common reader derives from the wealth of examples at every point: the chapter on names is particularly well done. Altogether a fascinating book' – *Higher Education Journal*

THE PELICAN GUIDE
TO ENGLISH LITERATURE

EDITED BY BORIS FORD

What this work sets out to offer is a guide to the history and traditions of English Literature, a contour-map of the literary scene. It attempts, that is, to draw up an ordered account of literature that is concerned, first and foremost, with value for the present, and this as a direct encouragement to people to read for themselves.

Each volume sets out to present the reader with four kinds of related material:

   (i) An account of the social context of literature in each period.

  (ii) A literary survey of the period.

 (iii) Detailed studies of some of the chief writers and works in the period.

 (iv) An appendix of essential facts for reference purposes.

The *Guide* consists of seven volumes, as follows:

1. THE AGE OF CHAUCER

2. THE AGE OF SHAKESPEARE

3. FROM DONNE TO MARVELL

4. FROM DRYDEN TO JOHNSON

5. FROM BLAKE TO BYRON

6. FROM DICKENS TO HARDY

7. THE MODERN AGE